CAMBRIDGE STUDIES IN
CHINESE HISTORY, LITERATURE AND INSTITUTIONS

General Editors
PATRICK HANAN AND DENIS TWITCHETT

Hsün Yüeh (A.D. 148–209)

Hsün Yüeh (A.D. 148–209)

The Life and Reflections of an
Early Medieval Confucian

by

CHI-YUN CHEN

Associate Professor of History
University of California, Santa Barbara

CAMBRIDGE UNIVERSITY PRESS

CAMBRIDGE
LONDON . NEW YORK . MELBOURNE

Published by the Syndics of the Cambridge University Press
The Pitt Building, Trumpington Street, Cambridge CB2 1RP
Bentley House, 200 Euston Road, London NW1 2DB
32 East 57th Street, New York, NY 10022, USA
296 Beaconsfield Parade, Middle Park, Melbourne 3206, Australia

Library of Congress Catalogue Card Number: 74–79135

ISBN: 0 521 20394 5

First published 1975

Printed in Great Britain
at the University Printing House, Cambridge
Euan Phillips, University Printer

To
CH'IEN MU
and
YANG LIEN-SHENG

'What I have recounted here may be examined against real facts and verified; they rightly constitute counsels of lasting value which may be applied in myriad situations without becoming unreasonably inflexible.'

(Han-chi, hsü)

'One must comprehend the law of nature and examine the nature of men; peruse the canonical Classics and cross-examine them against the records of past and present events; take heed of the different conditions of men and penetrate into their subtlest details; avoid the extreme and grasp the mean; take reference from the Five Elements in their mutations; and place all these in different combinations and sequences; then one may dimly envisage an approximation of the ultimate truth.'

(Han-chi, Lun)

'Words should be simple and straight; but why were the words of our Sage so subtle and intriguing? The answer is: Truth itself is subtle and intriguing; to communicate the truth, the Sage could not but use subtle and intriguing words.'

(Shen-chien)

'Symbols cannot perfectly represent the quintessence of things; words cannot fully convey the intent of what one wishes to say. Therefore, the Six Classics, though extant, are but the dregs left behind by the Sage.'

(Hsün Ts'an)

Contents

Preface

In publishing this book, I wish to express my gratitude to Professor Ch'ien Mu (founder of the New Asia College and the New Asia Research Institute, Hongkong) and Professor Lien-sheng Yang (the Harvard–Yenching Professor of Chinese History, Harvard University). Professor Ch'ien introduced me to the study of China's history some eighteen years ago; Professor Yang guided me through my doctoral programme at Harvard and has given me constant advice and assistance since. To both of them, this book is dedicated.

This book is based partly on my doctoral work at Harvard. I am grateful both to the Harvard–Yenching Institute and to the Harvard Graduate School of Arts and Sciences for their Fellowships and travel grants in support of my study and research. I wish to express my thanks to Professor Robert Hightower who read and criticized my draft dissertation and to Dr Glen Baxter for his good counsel and help. I am also much indebted to my friend Professor Edward Dreyer (now at the University of Miami) who read the entire draft of my dissertation and helped me in many ways to improve the English style.

A great part of my original dissertation was written while teaching at the University of Malaya. I am thankful for the assistance of my former colleagues there and for the liberality of the University in granting me study leave. I am particularly grateful to Professor Wolfgang Franke of the University of Hamburg who was visiting professor in the University of Malaya during my stay there and who introduced me to German scholarship related to my field. Many studies and publications by Japanese scholars mentioned in the book were consulted during my stay at the Institute of Humanistic Studies of the Kyoto University. I wish to thank Professors Yoshikawa Kojiro, Miyazaki Ichisada, and especially Hiraoka Takeo for their hospitality and valuable assistance.

The revision of my original dissertation into the present book was completed at Santa Barbara, California. I am greatly indebted to the University of California at Santa Barbara for Faculty Research Grants

ix

in 1968/70 and a Faculty Fellowship in the summer of 1969 which enabled me to broaden the scope of my study and to rewrite my dissertation into its present form. And I am most grateful for the support and encouragement which I have received from my colleagues in the Department of History at Santa Barbara, especially Professor Immanuel C. Y. Hsü. I wish to thank Mrs Ronald Hathaway for her comments and criticism on my English style.

Finally I am grateful for the advice and scholarly criticism from Professor Denis Twitchett, Editor of the series of Cambridge Studies in Chinese History, Literature and Institutions, who spent many hours reading and editing the typescript. I am truly thankful for the valuable assistance which I received in many ways from Dr Michael Loewe, reader for the Press, Mr Colin Jones, Editor of the Press in New York, and Mr Michael Black, Publisher and Editorial Director of the Press in England. But for their efforts, I cannot imagine when and how this book may be published.

It is impossible to acknowledge all the help which I received from my family, my friends, and the academic world at large. They form the holistic world order in which I find my being.

Of course, the responsibility for whatever shortcomings and mistakes remain rests solely on myself.

Santa Barbara, California

C. Y. C.

The Hsün Family Tree

(Important members of the extended Hsün family of Ying-ch'uan in eight generations)

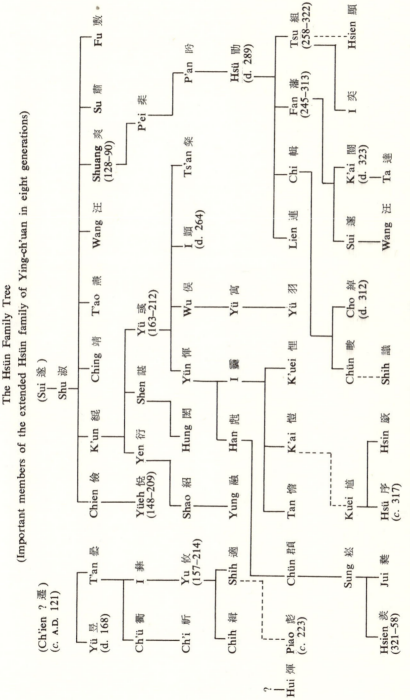

Note. The above Hsün family tree is based on Wang Tsao's 'Shih-shuo hsü-lu', in *Shih-shuo hsin-yü*, with cross-references from the dynastic histories. *Cf.* also Yano (1960), 14–18; Yoshinami (1956), 69.

1
Introduction: The Confucian élite
in an era of transition

Hsün Yüeh (A.D. 148–209), whose life and thought are the main concern of the present study, lived in a time of great political upheavals and profound social change. The imperial rule of the Later Han had been in decline since the beginning of the second century. Its authority had suffered still further reverses in 166–84 when the palace eunuchs who had gained control of the court began to persecute their political opponents with ever increasing severity and aroused strong protests and resistance among the ruling classes. In 184 the authority of the court was dealt a fatal blow by the Yellow Turban rebellion. Although the rebellion was suppressed by the combined efforts of various loyalist groups the Han dynasty never recovered its former strength. In the ensuing years the power of the state fell into the hands of new leaders who had built up strong personal followings during these times of trouble: the frontier generals, the great civil officials with either factional or regional support, and those local magnates who now emerged to positions of influence on the national scene. The Later Han came to a virtual end as a dynasty in 189 when some of these new leaders sent their forces to attack the palace, massacred the eunuchs, and drove the emperor to flight. In 190 the imperial capital at Loyang was sacked and destroyed by the soldiers of the frontier general Tung Cho. The last Han ruler remained the captive for many years of Tung and his lieutenants.[1]

After some years of civil disturbance and near anarchy, in 196 a group of militarist leaders who declared themselves loyal to the Han régime restored the outward form and appearance of a court administration. The group was led by Ts'ao Ts'ao (155–220), a strong man who was destined to shape China's dynastic history in the following decades. Hsün Yüeh, who had up to this time been an obscure provincial figure, was invited to take a leading place at that titular court. He was at the time forty-eight years old. From then until his death thirteen years later, he was engaged on an arduous programme of scholarly work. Two important examples of his writings survive, the *Han-chi* (Chronicles of

1

Han) and the *Shen-chien* (Extended Reflections). These two works represent Hsün Yüeh's effort to review the history of the Han dynasty and to reflect on the wider issues of his time; both works were completed in the crucial period of political upheaval and ideological controversy that accompanied the fall of the Han empire.[2]

During the subsequent Age of Disunity and in early T'ang times Hsün Yüeh enjoyed a great reputation as a model Confucian, as an outstanding political thinker, and as an exemplary historian. With the rise of Neo-Confucianism in Sung times, Hsün Yüeh's fame underwent an eclipse. But his influence is still evident in the works of some Sung scholars, most notably in the *Tzu-chih t'ung-chien* by Ssu-ma Kuang (1019–86), perhaps the greatest Chinese history of all time. Today, Hsün Yüeh is mainly known in China as a pioneer among dynastic chroniclers, and the full significance of his thought has yet to be given adequate recognition.[3]

The present volume attempts to study in detail Hsün Yüeh's life and works. In addition to the analysis of his surviving works, the *Han-chi* and the *Shen-chien*, attention will be paid to those historical events that formed an important influence on him and upon the development of his thought, as well as to the influence which he exerted on the leading men of his own day and upon the events of subsequent ages. In this way it is hoped that we will attain a fuller and deeper appreciation both of the intrinsic value of Yüeh's thought and scholarship and of his individual contribution to China's historiography.

Like the other Confucians of his time, Hsün Yüeh and his writings have never been subjected to intensive study, although they have been known to Chinese scholars and not infrequently cited in modern Sinological works.[4] But in spite of this scholarly neglect, the *Han-chi* became so familiar to Chinese scholars that certain assumptions about it have come to be taken for granted. For instance, it has been repeatedly stated that Hsün Yüeh was given a subsidy by the imperial Han court and commissioned to compile a simpler and condensed version of the *Han-shu* (History of the Former Han Dynasty) of Pan Ku (died A.D. 92), and that the resulting work, the *Han-chi*, was a 'subsidized dynastic chronicle' written by a professed loyalist. The only value of this work to the modern scholar has been considered to be that it preserves an early (third century) and hence less corrupt version of the *Han-shu* which may be used for the purpose of textual collation.[5] This has done grave injustice to Hsün Yüeh's complex thought and his sophisticated scholarship. For one thing, a careful scrutiny of the external and internal evidence concerning the *Han-chi* will show that the 'court subsidy' was negligible. The record reveals only the extreme poverty of the Han titular régime and the hardships under which Hsün Yüeh produced his historical masterpiece. The present version of the *Han-chi* presents a host of textual problems of its own and its present version is even more corrupt than is the present text of the *Han-shu*.[6] In a similar way, Hsün Yüeh's second major work, the *Shen-chien*, has been assumed to be a Han Confucian loyalist's discourse on politics, preserved in its entirety to the present day. This again is only a half-truth in so far as it relates either to Hsün Yüeh's presumed loyal disposition or to the contents and the textual problems of the *Shen-chien*.[7]

The prime difficulty of a detailed study of Hsün Yüeh lies in the extreme paucity of information. The 'Biography of Hsün Yüeh' in the *Hou-Han shu* (History of the Later Han Dynasty) provides only an elliptical résumé of the subject's official and literary career in fewer than three hundred characters, consisting mostly of an enumeration of Hsün Yüeh's offices and the titles of his writings. This résumé serves as an introductory note to the lengthy excerpts quoted from the *Shen-chien* and the *Han-chi*, which constitute the bulk of the biography.[8] Even the statement in this biography about the circumstances in which Hsün Yüeh produced his two major works appears to be somewhat misleading.[9] For a more complete and accurate picture one has to grope one's way through the labyrinth of the traditional Chinese historiography of the late Han period.[10]

Scattered in other sections of the *Hou-Han shu*, there are some detailed descriptions of the important events that occurred during the latter part of the Later Han rule, such as the movement of protest (*ch'ing-i*) led by the dissident literati; the imperial persecution of the dissident partisans (*tang-ku*); a series of purges, *coups d'état* and rebellions, including the Yellow Turban uprising in A.D. 184; the destruction of the imperial capital by Tung Cho in 190; the restoration of the Han court at Hsü in 196; and the beginning of the 'Pure Conversation' (*ch'ing-t'an*) movements among the élite circles at Hsü. All these incidents, which involved many of the senior notables at the last Han court, formed the background of Hsün Yüeh's life and thought. The 'Biography of Hsün Yüeh' in the *Hou-Han shu*, elliptic as it is, does provide some clues to Hsün Yüeh's part in these episodes or his reaction to them, and this is amply borne out by a more detailed study of the *Han-chi* and the *Shen-chien* as they have come down to us.

Direct and corroborative evidence as set forth in the following chapters shows that Hsün Yüeh's life passed through at least four phases. The first phase fell under the period of eunuch power and of the intense imperial persecution of the dissident élite (*tang-ku*) which ended in A.D. 184 with the outbreak of the Yellow Turban rebellion. During this period, the court was dominated by the palace eunuchs; many friends and older relatives of Hsün Yüeh became leaders of the protest (ch'ing-i) movement and were persecuted. Yüeh himself was compelled to live in provincial ' seclusion ', where he observed with righteous indignation the ever increasing abuse of imperial power by the Later Han ruler and his agents. The second phase began with the Yellow Turban rebellion in 184 and ended with the ' restoration ' of the Han court at Hsü in 196. During these years of civil turmoil Yüeh's native place, the Ying-ch'uan Commandery in present day Honan Province, was repeatedly racked by warfare and he not only watched the fabric of the empire crumbling into pieces and the decline of civil order but also witnessed the unruly and unbridled conduct of those frontier generals, regional warlords and local magnates who usurped the authority of the state. It is during this period that Hsün Yüeh and many of his friends and relations turned from being harsh critics of the Han imperial rule to being its ardent supporters, as the source of civil authority and good order in society.

The third phase of Hsün Yüeh's life began with his official appointment at the newly restored Han court at Hsü. Hsü had formerly been a district town in Ying-ch'uan, Yüeh's native commandery, and many of the notables of that area who were now loyalists to the Han thus formed a court élite circle under the new régime. The *Han-chi*, compiled by Hsün Yüeh in 198–200, gives testimony both to this élite's bitter memories of the past and of their protest movement (ch'ing-i) and also to their pious hope for a real Han restoration under the Chien-an reign (196–220). The last phase of Yüeh's life began shortly after his completion of the *Han-chi*. Ts'ao Ts'ao, the strong man behind the Chien-an reign, achieved a series of victories in the battlefield against his rivals during the years 200–5 and his attitude toward the Han court became steadily less friendly. The hope for a genuine restoration was shattered and many in the élite circles at Hsü faced persecution by Ts'ao. The *ch'ing-i* movement which had begun in the form of ' honest criticism ' and overt political protest was now turned into the evasive direction of ' pure discourse ', later known as *ch'ing-t'an*.[11] The *Shen-chien*, submitted to the Han throne by Hsün Yüeh in 205, was the earliest and most complete record of the last phases of *ch'ing-i* and of the initial *ch'ing-t'an* discourses. In fact, the first two chapters of the *Shen-chien*, on politics and on current issues respectively, may be taken as the last exposition of his political ideals as expressed in *ch'ing-i* terms, while the remaining three chapters, containing many dialogues on letters and scholarship and on the mystery of human nature and the supernatural, represent his new efforts in the direction of *ch'ing-t'an*. Politically and intellectually Hsün Yüeh thus emerges as a representative figure of the cultural élite of his time.

There are other factors which enhance Hsün Yüeh's prominence among the court élite of the Chien-an period. The Hsün family's background is highly involved. Historically, the rise to prominence of the Hsün family of Ying-ch'uan coincided almost exactly with the decline of the Later Han régime and the emergence of the early medieval Chinese élite in the latter half of the second century and the early part of the third century. Members of Yüeh's family were involved in almost all the major developments of their time, figuring prominently in the political, intellectual and military affairs both in the capital and in the provinces, and actively participating in events closely related to the fall of the Later Han and the rise of its successor régimes. Yüeh was thus living not only among men of ideas but was also constantly in the company of men of action. By temperament he was closer to the intellectuals but through his family he also had close connections with the real centre of political power, i.e. the rule by the strong men, the military and the politically active which in the Chien-an era meant essentially Ts'ao Ts'ao and his group.

This situation gave Hsün Yüeh, the historian and thinker, certain advantages and disadvantages. It provided him with an insight into both the realm of ideas and the realm of reality. It made him feel both the weight of tradition and the pressure of change. It enabled him to understand the complexity of events and issues, contemporary or historical. But it also strained his capacity to compromise and to synthesize. Here lies a clue to the many contradictions and inconsistencies in Hsün Yüeh's work, contradictions which range from the substance of his discourse on history, social customs, and classical scholarship, to the basic modes of his thinking and the very style of his writing – contradictions which exemplify the dilemma in which the majority of the leading men of China during the third and fourth centuries found themselves.

Post-Han China was torn by an unresolved tension between the centrifugal and the centripetal forces in society and political institutions. While conditions in the Age of Disunity (the four centuries after the fall of the Later Han) accelerated the development toward decentralization and favoured the growth of regionalism, clan solidarity, and landed aristocracy (all these features characterizing a peculiar type of medieval Chinese 'feudalism'), this development was constantly restrained by institutional inertia and the tradition of state centralism and bureaucratic rule.[12] The social and political order which emerged was neither genuine feudalism nor strong bureaucratic rule but a structure dominated by an élite which combined both feudalistic and bureaucratic attributes.[13]

Although many of the political leaders in the immediate post-Han period were those 'strong men' whose initial power was locally or regionally based and whose maximum sphere of dominance was determined by the regional sub-divisions of the realm, they failed to develop a viable local government system even within their limited local arenas. Despite the obliteration of a strong imperial power centre, these new leaders remained deeply immersed in the traditions of bureaucratic government and continued to think politically in terms of imperial rule. The ideologies and activities of these leaders were characterized by their continual attempts at imperial restoration. These attempts went through two phases. The first phase was characterized by efforts to restore the fallen Han dynasty; these were begun during the years 196–220 by the élite at Hsü and continued during the years 221–63 by the Shu-Han state in Szechuan. The second phase was characterized by the efforts under the Ts'ao–Wei dynasty, 221–65, and the Chin dynasty, 265–316, to maintain the imperial order despite the change of dynasties. The régime that these leaders restored was the ghost rather than the reality of empire. Although the Chin dynasty ruled over a re-unified China from 280 to about 300, the facade of unity which it restored rested on an extremely tenuous basis and very soon the empire succumbed to further outbreaks of civil strife and the inroads of barbarian invaders. Nevertheless the legacy of imperial rule and bureaucratic government persisted.[14]

On the ideological level, a stalemate may be found in the rivalry of Confucianism, Legalism, and Taoism during the movements of the *ch'ing-i* and the *ch'ing-t'an*. Legalism, which had triumphed with the rise of the Ch'in imperial order in the third century B.C., was the advocate of despotic power; Taoism, which had defied such order or power, was the advocate of the freedom of the élite. Confucianism with its emphasis on harmony and the Golden Mean was an advocate of compromise and synthesis of extremes. During the long centuries of Han rule, Confucianism had become the imperial orthodoxy submerging both Legalism and Taoism while absorbing many of their elements into its own grand synthesis. The spirit of all-inclusiveness inherent in this new type of Confucianism was weakened as the Han dynastic rule continued and its institutions became more and more inflexible. During the *ch'ing-i* movement toward the end of the Later Han, voices advocating drastic political measures by 'the strong men' and attitudes of militant defiance or non-conformity frequently appeared even among the Confucian circles. Elements from the Legalist and the Taoist extremes began to overshadow the Confucian precept of harmony and the mean.

Historians generally agree that the *ch'ing-i* movement was inspired by Confucian moralism and that the *ch'ing-t'an* movement which appeared in post-Han times was strongly influenced by Taoist anarchism and libertinism. With the decline of the centralized empire, political and ideological control was relaxed. The cultural élite enjoyed greater freedom of thought than hitherto. Many non-Confucian schools of ancient thought were revived and came to the fore. Literature, liberated from the constraint of orthodox didacticism, flourished greatly and grew more various. A strong reaction set in against the decaying socio-political order in general and against the Confucian ritual and formalism in particular, a reaction which found its expression not only in the thought and words but also in the very style of life of the élite in the *ch'ing-t'an* circles. This new freedom, enthusiastically publicized by its Taoist advocates, and no less fiercely denounced by their critics, has attracted much attention from historians, both at the time and since.[15]

The severe condemnation of Taoist and *ch'ing-t'an* libertinism by its contemporary critics whose censorious attitudes have since become an important strand in the Chinese moral interpretation of history indicates the relative strength of Legalism and Confucianism. The Legalist, who advocated the quick resolution of problems by 'the sword of the strong man', was the least tolerant. With the breakdown of rationalized and legitimized government power and the rejection of the Confucian moral and political synthesis, there disappeared the cohesive element that had formerly existed between various potentially conflicting sectors in the state and society, particularly that between the politically powerful and the intellectually and socially prominent sectors within the ruling class. The leaders in the immediate post-Han era split into mutually hostile camps both in their ideological controversies and in their factional strife. Those among the intellectual and social élite who adopted the non-conformist, individualistic Taoist attitude were confronted on the other side by those who supported the Legalist belief in the draconian exercise of authority and power, and by a militarist leader who had acquired such power in a time of civil turmoil and was prepared to use the sword against his opponents. In these circumstances, Taoist defiance rapidly turned into that escapism, eccentric libertinism and extremes of individualism which give its special flavour to the history of the *ch'ing-t'an* movement.[16]

The dramatic encounters between the Taoists and their Legalist persecutors somehow obscured the role of the Confucians. The significance of Confucianism at this time lay in the honoured tradition and in their advocacy of moderation and conciliation in a period characterized by the violent extremes represented by Taoism and Legalism. Among the leaders of this time there were many who refrained from extremes. Most of these men supported authority and criticized Taoism; they were often confused with the Legalists who did the same thing, and this has seriously obscured the important post-Han Confucian currents of thought. Among the critics of Taoism there were few who advocated the use of coercive power against dissent; others, the majority, gave counsel against the extremes and advocated moral constraints. They remained firmly in the Confucian centre and should be properly recognized as such.

However, the ideological Confucian centre was continuously shrinking. The Confucians, being most of them at the centre of power and responsibility, could not isolate themselves from the outside world or from the extremes of Taoism and Legalism. This, perhaps more than anything else, accounts for the confusion and obscurity which characterizes the Confucianism of the post-Han centuries.[17] Even in the works of well-known Confucians, such as Hsün Yüeh, we may find many non-Confucian elements which give a new slant to their Confucian protestations. Compromise or imperfect synthesis, which had been an essential feature of Han Confucianism, continued to characterize the majority of post-Han Confucians. The capacity to compromise and to synthesize which epitomized the Confucian tradition in the heyday of imperial expansion thus left a strong legacy in the period of imperial decline, political fragmentation, and ideological diversification. But Confucianism was no longer able to impose this compromise from a position of impregnable political strength.

The weakened but still pervasive influence of Confucianism in the Age of Disunity may be seen in the kind of protest made by two men of such different backgrounds and political inclinations as the Legalist ruler Ts'ao P'i (Emperor Wen of Wei, reigned 220–6) [18] and the Taoist poet Juan Chi (210–63, one of the Seven Worthies of the Bamboo Grove prominent in *ch'ing-t'an* circles).[19] In exultant spirit, Ts'ao P'i stated in his 'Exemplary Essay on Literature' (*Tien-lun Lun-wen*) that 'literature is the greatest enterprise of the state and the immortal glory [of mankind]'.[20] In more reflective mood, Juan Chi wrote the following lines in one of his poems entitled 'Speaking My Mind' (*Yung-huai shih*):

> When I was thirteen or fourteen, I delighted
>   in the study of History and the Odes. . . .
> I climbed up mountains to greet what I so piously expected.
> All I saw were tombs and mounds on the hills.
>
> I occupied myself with the study of great books
> And now I laugh at my folly.[21]

Critics have generally considered the statement by Ts'ao P'i to be a declaration of the independence of *belles-lettres* from the constraint of Confucian didacticism, and the poem by Yüan Chi to be a denunciation of the Confucian canonical works. Nonetheless, in both these un-Confucian statements one may find some Confucian influences in the educational background and the ideological perspective of their authors. To Ts'ao P'i, literature remained a socially useful subject and an important concern of the state – a specifically Confucian postulate. In the case of Yüan Chi, the Confucian ' great books ' not only constituted the very educational background which distinguished him as one of the cultural élite but also posed as the only ideological alternative to total disillusionment and nihilism.[22] The failure of the disenchanted élite in their non-Confucian pursuits shows the durability of the old tradition. Confucianism thus maintained its residual constraint over the Taoist and the Legalist extremes, and provided a tenuous cohesion to a divided China.[23]

When all these factors are considered, one should be surprised not at the ambivalence and inconsistency in Hsün Yüeh's life and thought but rather at the inner coherence which Yüeh achieved with effort in the face of tremendous difficulties. In the study of the *Han-chi*, one will find the effort made by Hsün Yüeh to transcend the contradiction between his critical attitude to decadent institutions and his loyalty toward the Han, to compromise between the pro-Han and the pro-Ts'ao pressures of his time, to mitigate the extremity of militarist centralism and anarchistic localism, and to stand firm for moderation, flexibility, and inner rectitude. In analyzing the *Shen-chien*, one will find the effort made by Hsün Yüeh to transcend his own mental perspective as a historian so as to penetrate into the ' darkness ' of reality, to accommodate and criticize both Taoism and Legalism so as to preserve the true Confucian spirit of all-inclusiveness and yet adhere to a Golden Mean.[24] The success or failure of Hsün Yüeh in this effort, his merits and short-comings, in a sense evinces the strength and the weakness of the Chinese cultural heritage which persisted into the Age of Disunity.

2

Imperial decline and the new élite

THE LITERATI IN A CONSERVATIVE RÉGIME

Hsün Yüeh was born in A.D. 148 (the second year of the *Chien-ho* era) during the reign of the Emperor Huan which lasted from A.D. 147 to 167. By that time the decline of the Later Han dynasty had already gone a long way.[1] Emperor Huan, the tenth ruler of the Later Han, had come to the throne under very special circumstances. His two predecessors had been child figureheads who had survived only for a short while on the throne: Emperor Ch'ung came to the throne in A.D. 144 at the age of two, and died five months later; Emperor Chih came to the throne in A.D. 145 at the age of eight and died a year and a half later.[2] In the subsequent selection of a successor to the throne from members of the ruling house of Liu, the court, under the control of the eunuchs and the family of the Empress dowager (by birth a member of the Liang family), rejected an older and more competent candidate, the Prince of Ch'ing-ho, and chose the Marquis of Li-wu who became the Emperor Huan.[3] To ensure the continuing good will of the Liang family, the emperor in A.D. 147 married a younger sister of Liang Chi, the Grand General and Regent of State. For the subsequent twelve years, Liang Chi usurped almost all powers of the court, ignoring the emperor as well as the eunuchs.[4] In A.D. 159, the emperor finally conspired with the eunuchs to depose Liang Chi by a *coup d'état*; and this started the long period in which the eunuchs dominated the court.[5] This in turn intensified the struggle between the eunuchs and their opponents in the imperial bureaucracy, a struggle which lasted for many years and led to a series of persecutions, agitations and intrigues, and eventually brought about the downfall of the dynasty.

The struggle between the eunuchs and their opponents was the main political factor leading to the downfall of the Later Han; but there were other deepset forces which had long been eroding the foundation of the empire.[6] Some of these forces originated in the deep-rooted and intransigent regionalism which had long beset the ancient Chinese imperial order.[7] Even in the heyday of Han rule, the subcurrent of parti-

10

cularist local traditions and regional interests had persisted beneath the formidable facade of imperial unity erected and maintained by the Han rulers and their bureaucracy. Waves of strong reaction, coming mainly from the local magnates and the large and powerful clans with special landed interests in the provinces had obstructed the many reform attempts made by the rulers of the Former Han dynasty (202 B.C.–A.D. 5).[8] These same forces had exploded into open rebellion when Wang Mang (reigned A.D. 8–23) usurped the throne of the last ruler of the Former Han and initiated a drastic political and economic reform.[9]

In the endemic civil turmoils following the fall of Wang Mang, the Han house had been restored in A.D. 25 by Liu Hsiu (reigned A.D. 25–57), a member of a remote branch of the Former Han ruling house. Liu Hsiu became Emperor Kuang-wu of the Later Han dynasty and he succeeded in reunifying China largely through his skilful manipulation of the various groups of regional warlords and local magnates that had emerged in the time of civil warfare.[10] Under the pressure of resurgent regionalism, the Later Han court adopted an attitude of compromise and retrenchment. The court's modest attempt at registering the local population and the landholdings in A.D. 39 provoked widespread unrest in the provinces, and the attempt had to be abandoned. Thenceforward, the court cautiously avoided any drastic measures which might upset the local equilibrium.[11]

To entrench the rule of the dynasty, however, the early emperors of the Later Han, Kuang-Wu, Ming-ti (reigned A.D. 58–75), and Chang-ti (reigned A.D. 76–88), made continuous efforts of reform in other directions. Central to these efforts was the reorganization of the imperial court. To prevent the future usurpation of dynastic power from within the central administration, the authority of the bureaucracy and of the literati of the 'outer court' was drastically reduced. The offices of Chancellor (Ch'eng-hsiang) and Imperial Secretary (Yü-shih ta-fu) became sinecures and were replaced by a Triumvirate of Ducal Ministers (Ssu-t'u, Ssu-ma, and Ssu-k'ung, collectively knowns as the San-kung), whose responsibility was 'to sit and deliberate on the Way' (tso-erh lun-tao). The important administrative functions of the former offices of the Chancellor and the Imperial Secretary were assumed by those lesser officials who served as Masters-of-writing (Shang-shu) or Attendants (Huang-men shih-lang) at the court. These Masters-of-writing and Court Attendants eventually became constituent members of the State Secretariat (later the Imperial Cabinet) and the Grand Council at the imperial court in post-Han times.[12]

The 'inner court' which rendered personal service to the emperor was also reorganized. In Former Han times, the 'inner court' had comprised many counsellors and secretaries selected from among the literati to serve the emperor in the palace and to counsel him on important affairs of state. Toward the end of the Former Han however this inner court had come under the domination of those relatives by marriage of the ruling house who served as Regents of State (*Fu-cheng*) 'controlling the inner court' (*Lu shang-shu shih*). It was from this 'inner court' that the usurper and reformer Wang Mang rose to the throne.[13] In Later Han times, the 'inner court' staffed by officials was replaced by an elaborate eunuch service bureau in the palace, from which non-eunuchs were excluded. Even relatives by marriage of the ruling house who were currently serving as Regents of State were permitted only occasional entrance to the emperor's palace apartments. And only a limited number of Masters-of-writing and Court Attendants served in the vestibule of the palace to help draft and transmit the decrees of the emperor and the palace bureau. A sharp division thus evolved between the palace (as the emperor's residence) and the formal court (the central administrative organ) and between the eunuch and the non-eunuch elements in government.[14]

This reorganization of the central government, designed to give the dynastic ruler a firm control over the centres of power, soon produced many adverse effects. It alienated the Han emperor and his palace establishment from the outside world, and led to antagonism between the emperor and his relatives by marriage (the Regents of State), between the palace eunuch establishment and the court officials, and among various factions in the imperial bureaucracy. The intrigues through which Emperor Huan and the eunuchs maintained their domination over the court was only one element in the antagonism which as a whole fragmented the Later Han régime.[15]

Although the Later Han emperors or their deputies thus exercised despotic control over the central administration, their authority in the provinces was quite limited.[16] This situation was vividly described in a popular saying of the time: 'Orders from the regional and local governments [*Chou* and *Chün*] came like thunderbolts; Imperial Decrees (from the Capital) were received merely to decorate the wall.'[17] While the chief officials in the regional and local government, such as the Imperial Commissioner of the Province (*Chou, Tz'u-shih*), the Grand Administrator of the Commandery (*Chün, T'ai-shou*), and the Magistrate of the District (*Hsien, Ling* or *Chang*), were appointed by the imperial court, the real administration at these levels was carried out by administrative assistants and functionaries (*Ts'ung-shih, Yuan, Shih*, etc.) recruited on the spot by the chief official.[18] These assistants and functionaries had a double status: on the one hand, they constituted a local sub-bureaucracy as an extension of the imperial rule; on the other hand, they were members of the local communities and came to be representatives of local interest and influence.[19]

Since the chief official in the regional or local government was usually not a native of the area under his jurisdiction, the effectiveness of his administration largely depended on his personal will power, moral integrity, experience, and prestige; on strong support afforded by the central authority; and on the co-operation which he received from the local sub-bureaucracy and the community at large.[20] As the internal struggle at the imperial court undermined the central authority and adversely affected the merits and morale of these chief officials in the provinces, the centrifugal tendency toward regional and local interests became progressively more noticeable. In the administrative process, the local staff who became more and more affected by local or clan influences were at least in a position to mitigate or obstruct any measure imposed by the central government which threatened their position. Some chief officials, unable to stand out against such local influence on their staff, came themselves under its sway.[21] The efforts made by the Later Han rulers to fend off the pressures of regionalism and localism thus gradually produced the opposite effect.

Caught in this conflict between centralism and localism were the literati, who found themselves the immediate victims of Later Han conservatism. The literati, also known as the scholar-officials, were an ambivalent social group in ancient China. On the one hand, they were for the most part either holders of government offices or candidates for such offices, and thus subject to the political favour and control of the court; on the other hand, they were the most cultivated element in society and the state; the élite who articulated the traditional and the rational values of the social and political order of their times. This double status put the literati in a position of conflict between their political, their social and their cultural attachments, as well as between their high ideals and their institutionalized interests.[22]

Historically, the literati had been the foremost champions of the ideal of a 'Grand Unity' (ta-i-t'ung) embodied in an imperial universal political ordering of 'all-under-heaven' (t'ien-hsia). Within this order, every one would have his rightful position and play his proper role in accordance with cosmologico-moral precepts culminating in the emperor possessing Mandate of Heaven (T'ien-ming) to rule.[23] But the literati were also among the first to become aware of the imperfection of that same awesome imperial authority and particularly its abuse by the dynastic rulers. The rise and the disastrous downfall of the first unified Chinese empire of Ch'in in the third century B.C. had been a historical lesson bitterly learned by the literati.[24] During the Former Han dynasty, most of the idealists among the literati had been engaged in continual struggle against the wayward dynastic rulers above and the recalcitrant local forces below. Although the influence of the idealistic literati diminished with the rise of dynastic despotism and local resistance, they preserved their status and prestige as the principal office-holders in the empire; through their manipulative interpretation of the time-honoured Confucian classics, they still posed as the rightful moral censors of society and state. And Confucianism, as it was interpreted by the ambivalent Han literati, became an increasingly ambivalent ideology.[25]

As Han rule continued, Confucianism came to permeate not only the literate bureaucracy but also society at large. The process was, however, two-way. Since it offered office, power, and prestige, Confucian education and the civil service system recruited an ever-widening group of entrants from society at large. And through nominal conversion to Confucianism, many other social groups (particularly the economically privileged) gradually penetrated the Confucian hierarchy and the literate bureaucracy. The social background and status of the literati were therefore continuously changing in Han times. What was originally a group of learned, progressive-spirited individuals eventually became a hereditary privileged élite in post-Han China.[26] Although the Han literati produced a number of idealists who voiced their criticisms of society and the state and initiated repeated reform programmes in the spirit of early Confucianism, their efforts towards a high ideal lost momentum.[27] The progressive spirit of Han Confucianism somehow expired together with the régime of the usurper–reformer Wang Mang in the early years of the first century A.D.

In view of the ambivalent social background and the changing ideology of the Han literati, it is almost meaningless to argue whether Wang Mang was a true Confucian, whether his reform was in accord with the genuine Confucian ideal, or whether his régime had the support of the Confucian élite. For under the Han Confucian banner there were different types of literati; there were the career bureaucrats, the mere office-seekers, the newly-converted gentry, the devoted scholars, and the visionary idealists, almost all of whom professed to be Confucians. The only common background which characterized them as literati was the literary education which they had received. This education was based on the study of a body of heterogeneous writings handed down by early Confucian masters. In the Former Han dynasty these writings came to be canonized as the Confucian orthodox scriptures (*ching*, the canonical classics), from which different types of literati drew widely varied doctrinal inferences to suit their own interests or their own versions of Confucianism.[28]

From the historical records, we find that the Han literati's attitudes towards Wang Mang's régime were just as varied. While there were some Confucians (particularly among the new converts from the local magnates and gentry) who condemned Wang Mang and rejoiced at his downfall, there were also many famous Confucian scholar-officials who had served under Wang Mang and remained loyal to him to the bitter end. In addition there were those who had not actively supported Wang Mang but were nonetheless disillusioned at his downfall.[29]

In Later Han times, the conditions of these different types of literati, their attitudes toward the restored Liu ruling house, and the treatment which they received from the court also varied. The Later Han court's policy of compromise toward the local big clans and landed magnates (many of whom were the new Confucian converts) has been mentioned before. Besides this, the Emperor Kuang-wu and his successors seem to have made it a point in their conservative reform to mollify those other types of literati whose loyalty to the restored dynasty was doubtful.

For those who still aspired to an official career, the Later Han court revived and expanded the Confucian education and the civil service system (which had been instituted under the Former Han) to facilitate their entrance into official life. But the constructive Confucian spirit permeating these systems in Former Han times gradually disappeared during the Later Han. Although the Imperial Academy (*T'ai-hsüeh*) at the Later Han capital continued to grow in size and came to consist of a student body of some 30,000 men in the latter part of the first century A.D., its programme of instruction steadily deteriorated. Most of the official erudites (*Po-shih*) in the Imperial Academy eventually ceased to teach, and in the second century many of their students were drawn into political activism.[30]

The Modern Text School (*Chin-wen*) of Han Confucianism, which had been a prime moving force behind the progress toward Confucianizing the state and society in Former Han times, lost both its political and intellectual vigour in the Later Han. It became the mere official orthodoxy – a stepping stone for the career bureaucrats or opportunist office-seekers who wished to enter official life.[31] The Confucian interpretation of the Mandate of Heaven, which had been an essential political postulate of the Modern Text School orthodoxy in the Former Han dynasty, was now clouded by a new thesis espoused by the Later Han court, a new thesis which emphasized portents rather than the Confucian classics as the direct revelation of divine intelligence.[32]

According to orthodox Confucian theory, the political power of a ruling dynasty found its justification in a cosmic-moral order, in which every human being would have his rightful place, the good man would be properly rewarded and the bad duly punished, and above all the worthiest would receive the mandate to rule over all-under-heaven. This postulate not only justified the founding of a new dynasty, i.e. the Han, by the worthiest upon the receipt of the Mandate of Heaven, it also justified and indeed necessitated a periodical change of dynasty with the change of such a Mandate (*ke-ming*, political revolution). The Confucians, through their interpretation of the will of heaven, thus arrogated to themselves the power to provide a moral sanction for the political order.[33]

Moral virtue, however, was something difficult to assess, particularly when it concerned the worthiness of a sovereign power or the qualification of a dynastic ruler. Portents, construed as indications of the judgment of the supernatural, had therefore been used by many Confucians in Former Han times to supplement their interpretation of a cosmic-moral order culminating in the Mandate of Heaven.[34] But it was during Later Han times that portents superseded the Confucian canons proper as the basic element in a new concept of the dynastic Mandate, a concept espoused by the court. According to this new concept, the Han dynasty had been restored after Wang Mang's downfall not only because the moral virtue of the Liu house excelled that of Wang Mang (a postulate which was difficult to prove), but also because this was the will of a mystic divinity.[35] To support the latter view, the court needed only to manipulate omen-interpretation to its advantage. The apocryphal books *ch'an* and *wei*, assumed to have come from sources of divine intelligence, now superseded the Confucian canons as the court's sacred writ. And the house of Liu, through its manipulation of the apocryphal *ch'an* and *wei*, now assumed a position of sanctity which was beyond mundane reproof, thus neutralizing the traditional Confucian sanction on their authority. Under these circumstances, the orthodox Modern Text School of Confucianism continually degenerated until it eventually perished together with the Later Han régime in the third century.[36]

While the office-seekers as well as some well-intentioned literati under the Later Han rule spent their time in the study of orthodoxy and omen-interpretation, other devoted Confucian scholars (including some masters of the Modern Text School) began to turn their attention elsewhere. To satisfy their intellectual needs, these scholars developed an interest in the unofficial school claimed to have preserved the Ancient Text version of the Confucian classics, which the official erudites in the Imperial Academy denounced as a forgery. These Ancient Texts were used by scholars to collate the orthodox Modern Text School version of the Confucian classics. This branch of Confucian learning, with its implicitly apolitical and emphatically antiquarian interest in textual criticism and scholastic synthesis, eventually replaced the official Modern Text School orthodoxy in post-Han times and became the principal Confucian school till the rise of neo-Confucianism in the eleventh century.[37]

Towards this group of devoted scholars, the attitudes of the Later Han rulers varied between tolerance and occasional patronage. Several Later Han emperors tried to include the Ancient Text School in the expanded Imperial Academy, but their efforts were abortive because of the strong opposition of the official erudites. These emperors continued to promote and encourage study of the Ancient Text School traditions, while the court upheld the Modern Text School as the official orthodoxy in the Imperial Academy.[38]

A critical reappraisal of the entire Confucian tradition was made during the middle of the first century by Wang Ch'ung (A.D. 27–91), whose remarks on the disparity between the moral attainment and the social status or political fortune of men threw the Confucian synthesis of the cosmic-moral and the socio-political orders into further disarray.[39] In the middle of the second century, the long discredited Legalist doctrines found a powerful new spokesman in Ts'ui Shih (ca. 110–70), who revealed the darker side of Han society and advocated a more realistic approach to current social and political problems.[40] These radical thinkers, however, were the lone critics in their times. It was only after the downfall of the Later Han in the third century that their opinions came to be better appreciated.[41]

The authority of Han official orthodoxy was corroded by still another type of disillusioned literati who had lost interest in an official career and were not satisfied with mere academic studies. They turned their attention inward and found a more satisfactory moral order within the individual self and its concentric world; the family, the clan, and the local community. This change of attitude was said to have been favoured by the Emperor Kuang-wu after his restoration of the Han dynasty. The historical records show that many literati, on grounds of moral integrity, refused to serve in the new court, and that the Emperor Kuang-wu, honouring their integrity, not only granted them their wishes but also treated them with exceptionally high esteem.[42] A new trend developed toward a personalist view of individual morality. A new

standard for the evaluation of men based on individual virtue and
personal cultivation rather than upon official attainment, literary com-
petence, or doctrinaire scholarship soon emerged and drew on the
occult authority of physiognomy and other evidence of mystic intelligence.[43] The new criteria of leadership based on personal charisma
received an enthusiastic response from the new Confucian converts in
the provinces, where the influences of the literati and the local gentry
converged.[44]

All these developments signified grave troubles for Han rule. As
mentioned before, the literati had been articulate advocates and ardent
supporters of the unitary imperial order. It was in the imperial order
that the literati found the embodiment of their ideal of a Grand Unity,
as well as the institution which best served their own interests. Although
in Later Han times the social composition of the literati had become
more varied and their interest in bureaucratic administration somewhat
declined, as a special group of notables sharing a common Confucian
educational background the literati still constituted a relatively coherent
force in the unitary empire. Either as actual office-holders (ranging
from the high literati at the court to the lesser ones in the local sub-
bureaucracy) or as the educated élite in society at large, they were in a
position to affect the precarious equilibrium between centralism and
localism in the continuing power struggle.

The conservative policies of the Later Han rulers were in the long run
self-defeating. The concessions made by the court to the landed interest
of the local magnates seriously undermined the position and the morale
of the literati in the imperial bureaucracy. The reform of the central
government excluded the high literati from the centre of power, and led
to fierce struggles between the literati and the other elements of the court.
The Later Han rulers' well-intended but short-sighted treatment of the
various types of literati further weakened the authority of the Confucian
orthodoxy and the strength of the Confucian élite as a coherent group.
All this happened in a time when the antagonism between centralism
and localism was at a high point, and the dynasty needed the strong
support of Confucianism and the literati.

As it happened, the old Confucian emphasis on public order, government service and civic virtue was gradually replaced by a new emphasis
on private relationships, personal interests or obligations, and individual
or familial morality. Confucianism, which had previously given an
ideology and rationale to the centralizing forces in the state, now tended
to strengthen the centrifugal tendencies in society. And the literati,
heretofore the arch-pillars in the Han imperial structure, began in

increasing numbers to condemn imperial despotism and to protest against the corrupt court.[45]

As early as the second half of the first century A.D., a number of the indignant literati had already begun to make remonstrances against the court which was then controlled by a series of high-handed empresses dowager. These empresses and their relatives, with the occasional support of the palace eunuchs, dominated the court in the name of the titular boy emperors.[46] Within this small coterie of despots the power struggle ran its own course. Under the title of a boy emperor, relatives of the ruling empress dowager tended to usurp almost all the power of the state and ignore the boy emperor, his eunuch attendants and the officials of the bureaucracy alike. When the boy emperor came of age inside the palace, he could muster only the support of the equally disgruntled eunuchs to regain control of the court through a *coup d'état*. This was the way in which a succession of Later Han emperors came to power in A.D. 92, 121, 125 and 159.[47] During the intervening long reigns of Emperor An (A.D. 107–25), Emperor Shun (126–44), and Emperor Huan (147–67) – and all of them gained control of the court in this way – the eunuchs eventually out-manoeuvred the relatives by marriage of the ruling house and extended their political domination from the inner palace to the bureaucracy of the outer court.[48] Meanwhile, the consort families of the ruling house were gradually driven into alliance with the literati.[49] And the dissident literati began to focus their criticism on the palace eunuchs who now represented a greater menace to their ideal and office. Thus by the middle of the second century the power struggle at the court had divided the ruling class into two principal parties: the eunuchs supported by the Han ruler, and the anti-eunuch league formed by the dissident literati and the court aristocrats. Because of the divergent social origins of the literati, their movement against the eunuchs soon ramified into other sectors of the society (particularly the local gentry). The most tumultuous years of Later Han history ensued.[50]

PERSECUTION, AGITATION, AND THE HSÜN FAMILY OF YING-CH'UAN

Until the reign of the Emperor Huan, the struggle between the eunuchs and their opponents was carried on mainly at the imperial court, although this inevitably produced some repercussions in the provinces where the followers of different factions contended for local power.[51] In A.D. 166 when Hsün Yüeh was eighteen years old, the palace eunuchs, outraged by their opponents' criticism, inflicted the first poli-

tical persecution on the anti-eunuch league. The persecution is historically known as the *tang-ku* (*tang*, partisans; *ku*, house-arrest and other
repressive measures).[52]

A number of the dissident literati at the court were dismissed from
office and imprisoned; others were sent back to the cities and towns
where they had come from, probably to house-arrest. There were still
others who voluntarily resigned their posts and went to the provinces.
Many of these dissident literati continued to criticize the eunuch-domi-
nated court. Once back home, they renewed their relationship with
the more militant local leaders. The struggle rapidly spread through
into the provinces, where the original political protest by the literati
(*ch'ing-i*) both reinforced and confused other issues through the factionalism of the local power-holders. This turned many of the Han
provinces into hotbeds of agitation.[53]

The exact origin of these factional disputes, which were known as
tang-lun in Later Han times, is not clear. (*Tang-lun* probably originally
referred to a type of local public opinion but might also be used as
the shortened term for *tang-jen chih-lun*, strife among local factional
groups.) The historians clearly record that these factions were linked
to both the protest movement led by the literati (*ch'ing-i*) and the persecution directed by the eunuchs against the dissident partisans (*tang-
ku*).[54] This shows the close connection between the empire-wide movement emanating from the high literati in the capital and the local
struggles involving the lesser notables in the province, though the details
of this connection cannot be ascertained. On the one hand, the empire-
wide movement might represent a convergence of scattered local
developments; on the other hand, the local or regional disturbances
might have been an extension or ramification of the factional struggles
from the imperial capital.[55]

The character *tang*, as used in the terms *tang-lun* and *tang-ku*, presents a philological ambiguity. The word has an archaic meaning of a
geographic locality, as in the term *hsiang-tang* (a local community).
But it also has the derived meaning of a faction, or a political party
(especially in modern usage). Since Confucius himself was said to have
disfavoured factionalism or partisanship in a gentleman's conduct, the
term *tang* in its second meaning acquired a strong pejorative connotation in traditional usage, but it remained a commendatory term in its
first meaning.[56] This ambiguous usage of the term *tang* in Later Han
times gives us a clue to the interpretation of the political movement
and persecution involving the dissident partisans (*tang*) at that time.
To the dissident literati, their own movement of protest seemed a perfectly respectable one, even though it had been complicated by partisan-

ship and local interests. But to their opponents (the eunuch clique), the movement probably stood for evil factionalism and regionalism, utterly detrimental to good social order and to the interests of the imperial court.[57]

According to the dynastic history *Hou-Han shu*, the early manifestations of partisan factionalism in the provinces had taken the form of inspired conflicts of pseudo-public opinion concerning the reputation of local personalities, and often degenerated into mere character assassination. Two early examples of such partisan propagandism are recorded in the *Hou-Han shu*. The first case concerns Emperor Huan's former tutor Chou Fu, a native of the Kan-ling district (in what is now Shantung province). Chou Fu was appointed to the powerful post of Master-of-writing at the court soon after Emperor Huan came to the throne in A.D. 147. Fang Chih, who served at the same time as Governor of the Metropolitan Commandery of Ho-nan (*Ho-nan yün*), also came from the same native district and enjoyed much higher prestige. Their fellow countrymen in Kan-ling compared the character of these two officials in the following doggerel couplets:

> An exemplar for all-under-heaven: Fang Po-wu
> [the style of Fang Chih];
> An ex-tutor who received his official seal
> as a result of favouritism: Chou Chung-chin
> [the style of Chou Fu].

The supporters and clients of these two officials thus ridiculed one another in partisan squabbles which split the people of Kan-ling into two factions (*tang*) and gave rise to early partisan propagandism (*tang-i*).[58] This episode seems to indicate that, although the targets of the polemics held posts at the imperial court, partisan activities on their behalf took place from an early stage in the provinces. It also shows that, even at this early stage, partisan propaganda had already turned into censure of the despotic power of the Han ruler. Imperial favouritism continued to be a prime target of criticism by the literati in their *ch'ing-i* movement.[59]

The second case of local partisan propaganda noted by the historian occurred slightly later in the reign of the same Emperor Huan. It concerns two court-appointed administrators in provincial offices. One named Tsung Chih, who served as the Grand Administrator of the Ju-nan Commandery (in the upper Huai river valley), had delegated most of his administrative authority to one of his locally recruited assistants named Fan P'ang. Another of the Nan-yang Commandery (northwest of the Ju-nan Commandery), did the same to his assistant, Ch'en Chih. Their critics thereupon contrived the following doggerel:

> The Grand Administrator of Ju-nan is Fan
>   Meng-po [i.e. the style of Fan P'ang, the assistant];
> Tsung Chih [the court-appointed Administrator] only
>   signs the documents.
> The Grand Administrator of Nang-yang is Ch'en
>   Kung-hsiao [style of Ch'en Chih, the assistant];
> Ch'eng Chin [the court-appointed Administrator] only
>   sits and whistles.[60]

Both Fan P'ang (Fan Meng-po) and Ch'en Chih (Ch'en Kung-hsiao), were from the lower ranks of the literati who served in the regional government sub-bureaucracy. But they were active in the *ch'ing-i* movement and later became targets of the eunuch-directed *tang-ku* repression.[61] This indicates that in the later years of Emperor Huan's reign the protest movement led by the high literati had tended to merge with local factional struggles (*tang-lun* or *tang-i*), and that the anti-eunuch league had already found strong support among the lesser literati in regional government and the sub-bureaucracy.[62]

This type of partisan propaganda appeared to play a highly effective role in Later Han politics. The *Hou-Han shu* notes that it was soon adopted by many notables in the imperial capital for the purposes of their own power struggles. The literati, who found their regular channels of remonstration (criticism of affairs of state presented in memorials to the throne) repeatedly blocked by the palace eunuchs, turned more and more to the irregular medium of partisan propaganda to express their grievances.[63] By vigorously exploiting these media, the anti-eunuch league soon broke through the established bureaucratic channels of remonstration and developed a socio-political movement of protest – a movement that involved many of the discontented aristocrats, the disillusioned literati, the student activists from the Imperial Academy, and other nondescript adventurers from the provinces, including several members of Hsün Yüeh's family. Their propaganda, initially directed against the corrupt eunuchs, soon developed into an agitation which toward the end of the second century involved the whole imperial structure of the Later Han.[64]

The departure of the many dissident bureaucrats from the court, and the extension of the literati's *ch'ing-i* agitation into the provinces, both occasioned by the first *tang-ku* persecution in A.D. 166, thus marked a turning point in Later Han politics. During the preceding centuries of imperial rule and Confucian consolidation, many elements of the local élite had been attracted to (and absorbed by) the imperial-Confucian hierarchy. Through this process, the local leadership had been able to find representation in the high literati circles and the imperial bureaucracy. Many of the literati-bureaucrats who had sprung from the local élite probably still preserved their connections there and even occasionally served as spokesmen for the local interest, but they had nonetheless become a distinctive status group in the central power hierarchy, standing for a universalistic value system and sustaining a façade of political unity – a hierarchy which served as a buffer between the imperial authority and the regional or local leadership.[65]

Political reverses, however, now compelled many of these high literati-bureaucrats to retreat to the provinces and to seek shelter and support from the local leadership.[66] There ensued an active give-and-take between these two groups. The literati approached the provincial notables with the appeal to a higher goal in life and politics. The local people appeared favourably impressed. And many of them, particularly the younger generation of the local élite, began to support the empire-wide protest movement with their local resources. They not only provided shelter for the political refugees but also participated in their political agitation, strengthening it with their material means and manpower, their local prestige and influence, and above all, adding their own element of militancy and belligerence.[67] It is largely out of this alliance between the dissident literati-bureaucrats in exile from the court and the local élite that a new generation of leaders later emerged upon the historical scene in early medieval China.[68] In this context, we now turn to examine the activities of the members of the notable Hsün clan of the Ying-ch'uan area during the last years of the Later Han rule.

Of those provincial areas which now became the foci of the political agitations of the literati, the Ying-ch'uan Commandery deserves special attention because of its direct connection with the events leading to the downfall of the Later Han and the rise of its successor régime in the third century. The Ying-ch'uan Commandery, in the upper Huai river valley some 500 *li* (approximately 114 miles) southeast of the imperial capital Loyang, had been a troublesome area throughout the Han. In Former Han times, the area was noted for its unruly local magnates and powerful clans and was considered extremely difficult to control by the imperial government.[69] In Later Han times, the commandery gained greatly in political importance, probably because of its proximity to Loyang, the Later Han imperial capital, and to Nan-yang Commandery (bordering Ying-ch'uan in the southwest) from which the Later Han royal house had originated.[70]

In the second century A.D., the Ying-ch'uan Commandery became a stronghold of the anti-eunuch partisans. The *Hou-Han shu* records that when the dissident scholar Tu Mi resigned his office at the capital and returned to Ying-ch'uan he ' made frequent visits to the commandery administrators and the district magistrates in that area '. Once Tu Mi was reprimanded by a chief official in the area for his interference with local affairs, and he retorted by saying that everything he did sprang from high moral causes.[71] Meanwhile, another dissident scholar-official, Li Ying, also returned to Ying-ch'uan, where he concentrated on teaching and gathered around him more than one thousand disciples.[72] Both Tu Mi and Li Ying were well-known leaders of the anti-eunuch league. Teaching and social contacts thus became the early means through which the exiled high literati approached their provincial partisans. It is during this period that some members of Hsün Yüeh's family who lived in Ying-ch'uan were approached in similar ways by the anti-eunuch partisans, perhaps for the first time.

The original status of the Hsün family is difficult to ascertain. It was said that they descended from Hsün K'uang, a great Confucian master of the third century B.C.[73] The validity of this claim cannot be checked, for the dynastic histories make no mention of any person in the family between the generation of Hsün K'uang and Hsün Shu (A.D. ?100– ?167), Yüeh's grandfather, who claimed to be K'uang's descendant in the eleventh generation (here treated as the founder of the Hsün family in Ying-ch'uan). In other words, the Hsün family in Ying-ch'uan had not produced a single member worthy of mention in the dynastic history during the previous ten generations, or some three hundred and fifty years. All we know in that period is that Hsün Shu's father was named Sui,[74] and that there was a court minister in Emperor An's service named Hsün Ch'ien who was described as a man upright in character but having no taste for Confucian classical learning.[75] We do not however know Ch'ien's native place and therefore cannot ascertain whether he was related to the Hsün family in Ying-ch'uan.

In spite of the obscurity of its early history, the Hsün family had become both wealthy and influential in Ying-ch'uan during Hsün Shu's life-time; the family residence was known as *Hsi-hao* (lit. Western Magnate); Shu's eight sons were collectively known as the 'Eight Dragons'.[76] The Hsün clan as a whole grew to considerable size and by the end of the second century was capable of organizing itself for armed self-defence in times of civil turmoil.[77] All these factors suggest that the family ranked highly among the local élite of Ying-ch'uan who were rallying to the campaign against the eunuchs waged by the literati during the *tang-ku* persecutions.

According to the *Hou-Han shu*, Hsün Shu had twice served as a district Magistrate and each time voluntarily resigned his post ' so as to cultivate his mind and care for his material interest at home '. His wealth rapidly multiplied, and he generously distributed it to help his needy relatives and ' friends '. He was highly praised as a good judge of character, which probably implies that he had a certain influence over the selection and promotion of civil service members in the local area. We are also told that Hsün Shu was a man 'lofty in character', 'learned but having no taste for the orthodox classical learning', and that 'he was often criticized by the mundane Confucianists'.[78] It appeared that, until Hsün Shu's generation, the Hsün notables of Ying-ch'uan were only modestly imbued with Confucianism, as befitted their ambiguous status as the local élite.[79]

A person like Hsün Shu, if he had the ill luck to live under some of the Former Han rulers such as the Emperor Wu two centuries earlier, might well have been the target of contempt and persecution by the literati-bureaucrats.[80] But the tide had changed. Imperial control over the provinces had since become lax, and an official career or scholastic accomplishments commanded less prestige. A provincial notable like Hsün Shu now found his material comforts and local influence more attractive than a career of service in imperial officialdom. However, the Hsün family was soon to change its attitude.

Some time between A.D. 152 and 166, when the literati's ch'ing-i protest movement was gathering momentum, the Hsün family came into close contact with Ch'en Shih (104–87), a retired district magistrate also living in Ying-ch'uan. An anecdote relates that the Hsün house was frequently visited by the Ch'en who, being very poor, arrived at the Hsün household en masse: 'Yüan-fang [the elder son of Ch'en Shih] drove the carriage; Chi-fang [the third son] walked in the rear carrying his father's staff; Chang-wen [a grandson], who was still a child, sat inside the carriage.' Similarly, the host also presented all his male offspring: 'The third son [of Hsün Shu] answered the door; the sixth son served the drink; the other sons prepared the feast [all of them Hsün Yüeh's uncles]; the infant grandson, Yü [Hsün Yüeh's cousin], sat on his grandfather's lap.' The meeting of these two families was said to have produced such a frightening omen that the Imperial Grand Astronomer (T'ai-shih) submitted a warning report of astrological changes to the throne.[81]

The event, however, had another interesting facet. That the Ch'en were a small and impecunious household while the Hsün were a large and wealthy family was carefully noted in the Hou-Han shu.[82] Ch'en Shih had had a long service career in the imperial bureaucracy. Having begun as a minor sub-bureaucratic functionary, he was selected to attend the Imperial Academy; after his graduation there, he served consecutively in a number of government bureaux where he came into contact with different sectors of the top hierarchy of officialdom, including the leading eunuch Hou Lan and the Ducal Minister (Ssu-

k'ung) Huang Ch'iung.[83] Hsün Shu, on the other hand, had somewhat reluctantly served two terms as district magistrate; his interests and connections had been locally oriented.[84] These two families thus represented two important groups in Han China – the bureaucrats and the local élite whose coming together was occasioned by the *tang-ku* persecution of A.D. 166 [85]

Hsün Shu, who had retired long before A.D. 166, was not personally involved in the first *tang-ku* episode. On the other hand, Ch'en Shih, a career bureaucrat, had suffered under the persecution and had been released from prison only shortly before he met with the Hsün.[86] It is probable, therefore, that he initiated the meeting in order to discourse on his grievances. The militant self-righteousness of the notable members of the Hsün clan suited the mood of the dissident. A certain economic interest may also be inferred from the fact that the Ch'en were poor and the Hsün rich and generous. On the other hand, the influence of the Ch'en on the Hsün may be noted in that, though the Hsün household was not lacking in domestic help, they nonetheless presented all their male sons to perform the offices of hospitality during the gathering; an action calculated either to please – or to emulate – their respected guests.

In another anecdote, this time relating Hsün's visit to Ch'en Shih, the latter also had his sons prepare the meal. The food was, however, not ready in time. The third son of Ch'en Shih, replying to his father's inquiry, said that he had overheard a conversation between his father and Hsün Shu which he considered too good to be missed; and so he stayed to listen and forgot about the food. Ch'en Shih then asked his son whether he understood the conversation. When the son answered that he did, Ch'en Shih made him explain it to Hsün Shu's sons.[87] This anecdote seems to imply that the Hsün's were on the receiving end of the discourse. The content of the conversation was not recorded. It may have been something in the *ch'ing-i* category, which was much in vogue among the dissident partisans at that time.

A sudden turn in the political fortune of the Hsün family came when Hsün Yüeh was twenty years of age. Some time between A.D. 166 and 167, the first *tang-ku* persecution for a moment subsided and the Emperor Huan, arch-patron of the eunuchs, died. A new Regent of State was appointed to assist the succeeding boy-Emperor Ling (aged 12 by Chinese reckoning) who reigned from A.D. 168 to 189. Many of the previously dissident bureaucrats immediately rallied to the new Regent and were returned to government posts. They brought with them their large coteries of militant partisans recently recruited in the provinces, including at least three of the Hsün notables from Ying-ch'uan.[88]

Hsün Shuang (128–90), the sixth son of Hsün Shu, was recommended to the throne in A.D. 166 as a candidate for office in recognition of his 'Distinguished Filial Piety' (*Chih-hsiao*). He was granted a court audience and appointed a Gentleman-in-attendance (*Lang-chung*). On this occasion, he submitted a severely critical statement on the affairs of state, particularly concerning the corruption of the palace establishment. He then abandoned his office in A.D. 167, probably returning to his home province to observe mourning for his father's death.[89] In the meantime or slightly later, Hsün Shuang's two cousins, Hsün Yü (died c. 168) and Hsün T'an, also entered government service. One of them was appointed to be the Chancellor of P'ei (in the lower middle Huai river valley); the other to be the Grand Administrator of Kuang-yang (near present-day Peking). The *Hou-Han shu* mentions that the two Hsün brothers were extremely self-righteous; they determined to rid the area under their jurisdiction of the eunuch cliques; whenever an adherent of the eunuch clique committed an offence in the P'ei and the Kuang-yang Commanderies, the Hsün would execute the culprit without mercy.[90]

The hostile attitude of the partisans of the literati toward the eunuchs soon brought a new violence to the old strife. Some of these militant partisans, like the two Hsün brothers, were probably recruited by the dissident literati directly from the local magnates; others perhaps came from those literati who had accustomed themselves to a life of violent action by their contact with the belligerent local magnates. In both cases, these partisans of the dissident literati, now having strong local support, began to resort to physical violence against the eunuch clique whose power was centrally oriented and was thus relatively weak at the local level.[91]

This led to a drastic reaction from the eunuchs. In a *coup d'état* in A.D. 168, the eunuchs killed the new Regent of State, Tou Wu, and the Ducal Minister, Ch'en Fan (both of them leaders of the anti-eunuch league), and imprisoned many partisans of the league. More than a hundred of the imprisoned partisans, including at least one of the Hsün brothers, subsequently died in prison. The persecution, known as the second *tang-ku*, was soon extended to the provincial and local governments, where six or seven hundred anti-eunuch partisans suffered varying degrees of punishment, ranging from death to house-arrest.[92] In A.D. 172, more than one thousand students in the Imperial Academy were arrested by the court on account of their anti-eunuch demonstrations.[93] In A.D. 176, the eunuchs issued an additional blacklist for the persecution of the partisans' disciples, former subordinates, and relatives.[94]

All the members of the extended Hsün family in Ying-ch'uan, except Hsün Shu and his eldest son Hsün Chien (both of whom had died), were thus affected by the new persecution in one way or another.[95] The Hsün family's involvement in the second *tang-ku* persecution accounts for much of the obscurity of the early years of Hsün Yüeh's life. Yüeh's 'Biography' in the *Hou-Han shu* merely states that 'he lived in retirement and was hardly known to people outside the family circle'. This implied that Hsün Yüeh was then leading a secluded, 'semi-underground', existence which was typical of many other partisans of the dissident literati under the *tang-ku* persecution.[96]

Imperial persecution, however, tended to strengthen the solidarity and the prestige of the dissidents and their party in the provinces. Many fugitives from the persecution received shelter and hospitality from their provincial hosts, in spite of the heavy penalties meted out by the eunuch-controlled court. Some of these fugitives used the opportunity to extend their contacts with the local élite, in whom their dissident political message found an ever more enthusiastic audience.[97] The anti-eunuch alliance occasionally developed into secret organizations. One of the fugitives, Ho Yung (died 190), a former student leader in the Imperial Academy, made extensive connections with the local élite and organized a secret mission to provide relief to those who suffered under the imperial persecutions. Among his partners in this secret mission were three other notables: Yüan Shao (died A.D. 202), a junior member of a high aristocratic family, Ts'ao Ts'ao, the son of a court official, and Hsün Yü (163–212), a paternal nephew of Hsün Shuang and a cousin of Hsün Yüeh.[98]

The second *tang-ku* persecution lasted for sixteen years, from A.D. 168 to 184. During this period, Hsün Shuang, who also suffered under the persecution, lived 'underground', first in an unknown coastal area and subsequently in the Han river valley (the valley extends from the southern part of the present Shansi province to the northern part of the Hupei province; the exact location of Hsün Shuang's hiding place cannot be ascertained). There he produced a complete set of Commentaries on the Confucian Canons and became a great Confucian master of his time. Among his works were the *Li-chuan* (Commentary on the Book of Rites), *I-chuan* (Commentary on the Book of Changes), *Shih-chuan* (Commentary on the Book of Odes), *Shang-shu cheng-ching* (Correct Readings of the Book of Historical Documents), *Ch'un-ch'iu t'iao-li* (Exposition of the Principles of the Spring-and-Autumn Annals), *Han-yü* (Remarks on Han Affairs), *Kung-yang wen* (Problems of the

Kuang-yang School of Confucianism), *Pien-ch'an* (Criticism on Prognostic Writings), and *Hsin-shu* (New Analects or Discourses).[99]

All these works by Hsün Shuang are now lost. But from a great number of quotations of his Commentary on the Book of Changes found in the works of later scholars, we can see that Hsün Shuang had interpreted the Canons in a drastically unorthodox manner, making extensive use of both the Confucian and non-Confucian traditions to convey a strongly anti-dynastic teaching. He praised the virtue of filial piety and family solidarity and denigrated the authority of the imperial rule, fervently denouncing the corrupt court and vindicating militant dissension. His message seems to be that a strong-willed and self-righteous social group (the *yuan-shih* or the lower and middle élite), when misplaced or maltreated, should keep on agitating and, when this fails to change the course of events, should challenge the unjust rule in open rebellion, even if this means the destruction of the established dynasty. This ominous message became a grim reality in the downfall of the Han dynasty barely two decades later.[100]

We do not know how much influence Hsün Shuang's teaching had on the actual political events of its time. Hsün Yüeh later testified that Hsün Shuang's works, particularly his unorthodox *I-chuan*, were well received by the élite, and that ' in the areas of the greater provinces of Yen and Yü [roughly the middle Yellow River and upper Huai river valleys], everyone who studied the *I* [Book of Changes] followed Hsün Shuang's teaching '.[101] Meanwhile some of the junior members of his family were assuming an important role in other anti-eunuch activities. The exact part played by Hsün Yüeh's cousin, Hsün Yü, in the secret mission organized by Ho Yung is not recorded. A reasonable conjecture is that he supported the impecunious Ho Yung with the Hsün family's resources and local influence. Both Hsün Yü and his grandfather Hsün Shu were noted for their generosity in helping their ' friends '. And, when Ho Yung died in A.D. 190, Hsün Yü had him buried in the Hsün household's graveyard, an act that seemed to imply Ho's status of dependence on the Hsün.[102]

Financial support for similar causes, meanwhile, was given by other wealthy partisans of the literati. For example, the *Hou-Han shu* recorded that Cheng T'ai, the son of a famous Later Han Confucianist and himself a big landlord, had sensed the coming of political troubles and associated himself with a number of militant local leaders. He almost exhausted the income from an estate of some 40,000 *mou* (about 1,300 acres) of land to support their political activities.[103]

During the time of the second *tang-ku* persecution, the anti-eunuch partisans thus evolved an ideological position, and some measure of organization. Their alliance expanded to include a wide cross-section of aristocrats, bureaucrats, literati and local magnates, and they possessed intimate knowledge of the political machinery of both the higher and the lower levels. The movement of protest gradually developed an anti-dynastic undertone as the struggle against the eunuchs became more violent and an increasing number of the bellicose local magnates were drawn into the movement.[104]

In this connection, it may be observed that the sacrosanct status of the Han dynasty was perhaps never called into doubt in the minds of the dissident high literati, in spite of the belligerent activities of the lower echelons of the anti-eunuch league. To the high-ranking literati and bureaucrats, the *ch'ing-i* movement was still a righteous loyal protest. They were against the palace eunuchs who usurped and abused the imperial authority, and not against the imperial authority or the principle of dynastic rule itself. Even for some of those high literati who ventured a severe criticism of the imperial court or the emperor's person, a distinction may still be made between the emperor as an individual human being and the imperial rule as a sacred institution. The difference between the eunuch and the court controlled by the eunuch, or between the emperor as a corrupted individual and the imperial rule as a sanctified tradition, however, became less distinct to the lesser élite who participated in the agitation. As the struggle ramified into the lower hierarchy of the élite and as more and more bellicose local magnates were drawn into the movement, the demand for violent action began to obliterate the subtle differences between the dissident's anti-eunuch and anti-Han objectives, as Hsün Shuang's *I-chuan* teaching showed.[105]

CONFUCIANS, TAOISTS, AND THE YELLOW TURBANS

From A.D. 168 to 184, when the eunuchs and their political opponents were engaged in fierce power struggles at the capital, outbreaks of violence under the guise of government persecution and repression, assassinations, blood feuds, and banditry increased rapidly in the provinces.[106] This general deterioration of law and order culminated in A.D. 184 when the Han rule was eventually wrecked by an empire-wide insurrection, an insurrection known as the Yellow Turban rebellion because of the coloured turban worn by the insurgents.[107]

The prevalent view of the Yellow Turban rebellion is that it originated from a popular religious movement, the *T'ai-p'ing tao*, which linked a corrupted Taoist doctrine with certain alien inspirations (particularly from the newly-imported Buddhism); that it drew its strength from the peasant masses who were suffering extreme economic deprivation and were attracted to the popular religion of their time for spiritual consolation, material relief, and the anticipation of an Era of Great Peace (*T'ai-p'ing*); and that it developed at a time when administration was in decline and the ruling class was undermined by partisan struggles, leaving the way open for a mass movement to culminate in a widespread uprising.[108]

The ideal of 'Great Peace' or *t'ai-p'ing*, embraced by the insurrectionists in A.D. 184, was not a simple popular material concept, but originated from some highly respectable sources. It had been fostered and championed by various groups of the literati around the third century B.C. in close connection with their own rise to power under the establishment of a universal imperial order.[109] The slogan *t'ai-p'ing* and its variants, such as the 'Grand Unity' (*ta-i-t'ung* or *ta-t'ung*), 'Peace for All under Heaven' (*p'ing t'ien-hsia* or *t'ien-hsia p'ing*), or 'Perfect Equilibrium and Harmony' (*chung-ho*), had been formulated in numerous classical works with diverse philosophical or political inclinations.[110] Under the Han rule, the 'Era of Great Peace' (*T'ai-p'ing shih*) was envisaged, particularly by scholars of the Modern Text *Kung-yang* School of the Confucian orthodoxy as the highest stage of political and cultural attainment on earth.[111]

The colour adopted by the Yellow Turbans was similarly derived from an honoured tradition.[112] According to the Chinese cosmic view of history first expounded by the School of *Yin-yang* cosmology and later incorporated into the *Kung-yang* and other traditions of Han Confucianism, the rise and fall of dynasties followed certain preordained patterns. These patterns corresponded to the cosmic order of the Five Elements as they succeeded one another: Wood, Fire, Earth, Metal and Water. Each element corresponded to a specific colour.[113] According to this theory, the Han dynastic rule corresponded to the virtue (*te*) of the element Fire, represented by the colour Red.[114] Since Fire generated the element Earth, the dynasty would be replaced by a dynasty corresponding to the virtue of Earth, represented by the colour Yellow. This theory of cosmic and dynastic change had been adopted by many ambitious political leaders of Han times including the usurper Wang Mang prior to the founding of the Later Han dynasty. These leaders, in their bid for the throne, all proclaimed themselves blessed by the element Earth represented by the colour Yellow.[115] It was probably to counter this claim made by his various rivals that the Emperor Kuang-wu, restorer of the Han dynasty, had to prove that the reign of Fire still continued. To do this, he had to rely heavily on the divine inspiration of the apocryphal books of *ch'an* and *wei* to re-affirm the sacrosanctity of the restored Han dynasty, so giving rise to a more mystical interpretation of the Mandate of Heaven.[116]

It is not clear when and how these items which permeated the political thought of early Han times filtered down from the literati to the lower sectors of society. The leaders of the *T'ai-p'ing tao* and the Yellow Turbans may have received some inspiration from the anti-eunuch and anti-dynastic teaching of the dissident literati, or they may equally well have evolved a similar doctrine sanctioned by traditions within their own Taoist hierarchy.[117]

Taoism as an ancient school of thought was noted for its individualist, and sometimes even anarchist, inclinations. In those centuries of radical socio-political changes leading to the rise of the bureaucratic unified empire of Ch'in (221–207 B.C.), the Taoists had been noted for their defiance of the new order. In this sense, Taoism has often been identified as a source of revolutionary inspiration.[118] However, the Taoist political ideology, particularly its precept of non-action and non-intervention (*wu-wei*), seemed to be implicitly conservative rather than an inspiration to rebellion.[119] The Taoist hierarchy and its ideology had by this time undergone a complicated process of change both as a school of thought and as a popular religion. Taoist opposition to the new imperial bureaucracy had probably inspired both the conservatives and the revolutionary radicals whose joint efforts succeeded in overthrowing the Ch'in régime in 206 B.C.[120] For a short while during the early years of the Former Han dynasty, Taoism had won special favour at the court as a guiding principle of state and the Taoist idea of non-action became widely accepted. Non-action, as practised by the early Han rulers, resulted in a policy of non-interference which benefited the empire in the period of post-revolution recuperation.[121] It also helped to pacify the resurgent regional political forces by granting them greater freedom in local administration, thus contributing to the development of regionalism and landlordism in Han times.[122] But when non-action was preached to the masses, it became advocacy of passive acceptance of, or abject subservience to, the established order. The conservative orientation of early Han Taoism is thus quite obvious.

On the other hand, the Confucian ideal of the Mandate of Heaven and of 'rule by the virtuous', which had been advocated by the literati as a sanction for dynastic rule, could also be used to justify revolution against a dynasty which abused or misused its power.[123] In fact, although the Confucian literati had been in favour of a universal political order, many of them had also turned against the despotic Ch'in régime as a result of the downright abuse of the imperial authority by the Ch'in rulers.[124] And a group of Confucianists led by one of Confucius' descendants had been among the first to join the anti-Ch'in insurrection and die for its cause in 209–208 B.C.[125] It is therefore difficult to say that in ancient China the Taoists alone subscribed to principles which provided justification for rebellion.

The contrast between the Confucian and the Taoist ideologies in early Han times may be seen in a debate on political revolution between the Confucian Master Yüan-ku and the Taoist Master Huang which was held in the presence of the Former Han Emperor Ching-ti (reigned 156–141 B.C.). In this debate, the Taoist held that revolution against an established dynasty was unjustifiable, saying: ' The cap, though worn, must be put on the head; the shoes, though new, must be put under the feet – those in high station should remain high, while those in low station should remain low.' The Confucian, on the other hand, reiterated the theory of the Mandate of Heaven and its justification of dynastic revolution. The Emperor, probably embarrassed by the turn the arguments had taken, then discontinued the debate.[126]

The prominent position held by the Taoists in early Han times was soon yielded to the Confucians when the Han court revived and greatly expanded the imperial bureaucracy in the latter half of the second century B.C.[127] During the ensuing centuries, many Taoist adherents were probably converted to Confucianism through the established educational and civil service systems of the state, while at the same time many Taoist ideas were also absorbed into the highly syncretic Han Confucianism.[128] Other more faithful Taoists, however, retreated into the provinces where they were remote from the court's attention but might still enjoy popular support among the local leadership.[129]

During the Later Han dynasty, with the resurgence of regionalism, accompanied by a new emphasis on individual morality or charisma as the basis of personal leadership and a more mystical interpretation of the Mandate of Heaven for dynastic rule, Taoism regained much of its lost ground. As a tradition in classical thought and as a popular religion, it was widely supported in all levels of society, ranging from the court to the masses, and had a significant impact on many developments of Later Han times, including the Yellow Turban rebellion.[130]

Amidst the fervent agitations of the anti-eunuch élite during the latter part of the second century, it became increasingly difficult to distinguish a dissident Confucian from a defiant Taoist, just as it was difficult to distinguish between the literati and the gentry among the persecuted élite. The case of Luan Pa is a good example of the difficulty of distinguishing Taoist from Confucian in Later Han times. According to the Hou-Han shu, Luan Pa was a man upright in character and learned in the Confucian classics. He had once served as the Grand Administrator of the Kuei-yang Commandery (in the present-day Kwangsi province), when he introduced many Confucian educational and civil service institutions into that remote region of the empire. Later he was transferred to be the Grand Administrator of the Yü-chang Commandery (in the present-day Kiangsi province), where the native people had been very superstitious. In this situation Luan Pa relied on his knowledge of Taoist charms and used Taoist magic to combat popular witchcraft in that commandery. Luan Pa eventually became a staunch supporter of the anti-eunuch partisans and was forced by the eunuchs to commit suicide some time after the *coup d'état* of A.D. 168.[131]

As the anti-eunuch struggle ramified, many of the persecuted partisans who lived like fugitives in the provincial areas were known to their contemporaries as ' knights-errant ' (*yu-hsia*) – like the group of free-booters who in Former Han times had been closely connected with certain eccentric Taoists.[132] Many outspoken Taoists in Later Han times also joined in the Confucian chorus of remonstrance against the eunuchs through their memorials and petitions to the throne. In these memorials and petitions, the Taoists drew on exactly the same traditions of the *yin-yang* cosmology that had been cited by Hsün Yüeh's uncle, the Confucianist Hsün Shuang, in his earlier memorials to the throne.[133] Furthermore, many Confucian ideals, concepts and terms may also be found in the still extant (though somewhat corrupt) version of the Taoist tract *T'ai-p'ing ching* (The Canon of Great Peace), from which the name of the *T'ai-p'ing tao* probably derived.[134]

Sometime before A.D. 166, when the Yellow Turban leader Chang Chüeh (died 184) was about to inaugurate the religious movement which culminated in the popular insurrection eighteen years later, a man named Hsiang K'ai had presented to the court a Taoist religious tract entitled ' Yü Chi's Holy Writ ' (*Yü Chi Shen-shu*). Although the dynastic history of the period does not record the contents of this Taoist tract, it considers it to be identical with the *T'ai-p'ing ch'ing-ling shu*, a Taoist work generally considered to be an earlier version of the *T'ai-p'ing ching* which inspired Chang Chüeh's movement.[135] Some scholars have even suggested that Hsiang K'ai was, in fact, the author of the *T'ai-p'ing ching* or at least had refurbished a popular religious tract and ascribed it to the legendary Taoist Yü Chi to give it religious authority.[136] Since both the Taoist religion and the *T'ai-p'ing tao* movement had become clandestine in Later Han times, it is difficult to pinpoint their inter-relationship, or their connections with the Confucianist and Taoist elements in high literati circles.[137]

According to the dynastic history, Hsiang K'ai was ' an authority on many ancient traditions and well versed in *Yin-yang* cosmology '. In his memorials to the throne, Hsiang K'ai quite openly sympathized with the dissident partisans and made forthright denunciations of the eunuch establishment in the palace. He drew his references from a number of heterogeneous traditions, ranging from Confucianism, Taoism and *Yin-yang* cosmology to some very early Chinese Buddhist tracts. Hsiang K'ai was subsequently prosecuted by the court for being a heretic, but his punishment was mitigated by the emperor who considered his opinions to be adequately supported by respectable traditions. In A.D. 168, when the anti-eunuch partisans temporarily regained their court positions under the new regent Tou Wu, Hsiang K'ai was recommended to the throne as a candidate for office by an acknowledged leader of the partisans. He declined the favour and instead preferred to stay in his native place where he was considered an outstanding leader. In A.D. 188, he was again recommended to the court, this time together with the two greatest Confucian celebrities of the day, Cheng Hsüan (A.D. 127–200) and Hsün Shuang. But he again declined the favour.[138]

The case of Hsiang K'ai has, however, another important facet. The Biography of Hsiang K'ai in the *Hou-Han shu* failed to mention that some time in A.D. 185, Hsiang K'ai and Ch'en I (a dissident partisan) gathered a band of their militant clients in a conspiracy with the Imperial Commissioner of the Ch'i province (in the present-day Shantung and part of the Hopei province) to stage an uprising against the court, and disguised their actions as a military operation against a branch of the surviving Yellow Turbans.[139] While Hsiang K'ai was a local Taoist leader who had spoken out against the eunuchs, Ch'en I was a distin-guished member of the literati whose father Ch'en Fan (the most pro-minent Confucian leader in the anti-eunuch league) had been killed by the eunuchs in the *coup d'état* of A.D. 168.[140] The co-operation of Hsiang K'ai, Ch'en I, and the Imperial Commissioner of the Ch'i province in an uprising against the court indicates the complex composition of an expanding alliance which was not only anti-eunuch but also anti-Han. In this rebellion Confucianism became no less dangerous as a source of inspiration than Taoism.

The historical record shows that, before the Yellow Turban uprising in A.D. 184, the *T'ai-p'ing tao* movement had gathered strong popular support and developed a complex mass organization. Its leader Chang Chüeh was said to have received the allegiance of several hundred thou-sand followers from eight of the thirteen provinces (*chou*) in the Han empire. It was further mentioned that Chang Chüeh ' had organized his mass followers into thirty sections, each under the control of an Adept [*fang*] who in turn commanded the sub-section leaders [*ch'ü-shuai*]; the

Grand Adepts each controlled over ten thousand adherents and the Lesser Adepts controlled from six to eight thousand men '. [141]

The *Hou-Han shu* records that Chang Chüeh ' had so misleadingly dazzled the people that the masses of the whole realm went over to his side carrying their treasures with them '.[142] This statement is substantiated by the writing of a later Taoist who mentioned that ' Chang Chüeh had deceived the hundred surnames and made a great profit, accumulating cash and fine cloth piled up like mountains '.[143] From these accounts, it seems clear that this subversive movement had attracted not only poor peasants but also many wealthy notables in the provinces. Furthermore, this subversive movement seems to have received the general acquiescence of the local officials and élite, for we are told that: ' [Though Chang Chüeh's movement was quite well known to some regional officials, these officials of] the provinces and the commanderies avoided and shunned the subject; they did not want to hear about it. They merely talked to each other about it but did not make any official report on it [144]; and that ' Chang Chüeh and his disciples took the wrong way, but they were called the great worthies ',[145] presumably by the local élite, with whom the popular movement had close contacts.

Early in the year A.D. 184, the secret of Chang Chüeh's impending uprising was disclosed to the court by an informer T'ang Chou, who had formerly been a disciple of Chang Chüeh. It was alleged that Chang Chüeh's Grand Adept, Ma Yüan-i,

had enlisted tens of thousands of men from the provinces of Ching and Yang [in the Yangtze river valley], intending to assemble at Yeh, east of the imperial capital of Loyang, for an uprising; and Ma Yüan-i, in his frequent trips to the capital, had secured the co-operation of the eunuchs Feng Shü, Hsü Feng and others to stage an uprising on the fifth day of the third lunar month [4 April] of the same year both inside and outside the capital.

Using this information, the imperial court made an intensive search for Chang Chüeh's followers ' in the palace, among the guards, and among the people '. Ma Yüan-i was then caught and executed. Chang Chüeh escaped, and hurriedly began the Yellow Turban uprising in the second lunar month of that year (29 February–29 March 184).[146] All this happened when Hsün Yüeh was aged thirty-six (thirty-seven by Chinese reckoning).

The crisis occasioned by the Yellow Turban uprising was immediately used by the dissident élite as a pretext to denounce the eunuchs and to exert pressure on the throne. The *Hou-Han shu* preserves several memorials, submitted to the throne by the literati in office on this occasion, which contain severe criticism of the eunuchs and implicit sympathy for the rebels. The argument in these memorials often went like this: in order to be rid of the outside evil of the rebellion, the court must first rid itself of the inner evil fostered by the eunuchs; and to prevent the persecuted partisans from co-operating with the rebels, the *tang-ku* repression must be brought to an end. Some even argued that if these conditions were met by the court, the rebellion would disappear by itself.[147]

The eunuchs, with the support of the Han emperor, were for a while successful in fending off such political pressures. Several critics who denounced the eunuchs or sympathized with the rebels were accused and executed by the court for complicity with the Yellow Turbans.[148] A series of accusations and counter-accusations thus evolved between the eunuchs and their opponents at the court, which greatly confounded the issue. The historical records of the Yellow Turbans' connection with either the eunuchs or the anti-eunuch partisans are, as a result, highly confused.[149] Some leaders in both the eunuch and the anti-eunuch factions probably knew about the religious movement and its popular strength and wanted their agents to manipulate it to their political advantage; in their struggles, the secret leaked out; accusations and counter-accusations from both sides ensued and the movement was forced into open rebellion.

The strength and the destructive power of the Yellow Turban rebellion were probably also exaggerated in the reports made to the throne by the provincial officials and the local élite.[150] From the fragmentary accounts preserved in the *Hou-Han shu*, it seems that the Yellow Turbans were especially hostile to those branches of the imperial family ruling the provincial principalities. At least five of these princely families were destroyed by the rebels: Liu Yün, Prince of Chi-an (in the present Shantung province), was killed; Liu Hsü, Prince of An-p'ing (in the present Hopei province), and Liu Chung, Prince of Kan-ling (also in Shantung), were captured, and Chung's heir-designate was killed; Liu I, Prince of Hsia-p'i (in the present Kiangsu province), and Liu Hao, Prince of Ch'ang-shan (in Hopei), both fled their territories.[151] On the other hand, some members of élite circles are said to have been quite well-treated by the Yellow Turbans. This, however, may also be part of the élite's propaganda and should be taken with caution.[152]

Under pressure both from inside and outside, and in the face of widespread rebellion, the Han court finally yielded to the dissident partisans and lifted the *tang-ku* persecution on the seventh day of the third lunar month of the same year (5 April 184).[153] Many dissident partisans were again re-appointed to government service.[154] The influence of these reconciled partisans, particularly the militant local notables in the anti-eunuch alliance, greatly strengthened the position of the imperial forces against the Yellow Turbans. The victory won by the Han loyal forces was quick and decisive. Within ten months, the main forces of the Yellow Turbans were routed.[155] But the winners were neither the eunuchs, nor the Han court.

Even some of the field commanders of the Han imperial army failed to enjoy the spoils of their victories. The first general commissioned by the court to fight against the Yellow Turbans was Lu Chih, a famous Confucian scholar who had earlier petitioned the throne against the tang-ku persecutions. After some initial victories, he was disgraced by the eunuchs and relieved of his command. Later, he became a militant partisan of the anti-eunuch league.[156] The decisive battles against the rebels were won by three other Han generals, Huang-fu Sung, Chu Chün, and Wang Yün, two of whom were also subsequently discredited by the eunuchs.[157]

These early victories were won by the loyal forces in Ying-ch'uan (the native place of the prominent Hsün family) and its neighbouring areas, all of which had been provincial strongholds of the anti-eunuch partisans. This shows the influence of the reconciled partisans over the outcome of the struggle between the court and the rebels. The backgrounds and the tactics of the three Han commanders fighting in the Ying-ch'uan area thus deserve special attention. Huang-fu Sung was a Confucianist, who had urged the throne to withdraw the tang-ku persecution when he first received his commission to campaign against the rebels; he was said to have subsequently recruited a number of the 'élite militia' (ching-yung) into his forces. Chu Chün had been noted for his 'uprightness and generosity in his native place'; his force consisted of many 'household soldiers' (chia-ping), who were probably armed retainers of the local magnates.[158] The third general, Wang Yün, who was appointed to be the Imperial Commissioner of the Yü province with jurisdiction over the Ying-ch'uan Commandery, was an avowed enemy of the eunuchs. After petitioning the throne against the tang-ku measures, he proceeded to invite Hsün Yüeh's uncle Hsün Shuang, one of the persecuted partisans, to serve on his staff. Together with the two other generals, Wang Yün inflicted a serious defeat on the Yellow Turbans and accepted the surrender of several hundred thousand rebels in Ying-ch'uan.[159]

During his campaign in Ying-ch'uan, Wang Yün allegedly captured from the rebels some letters which had been exchanged between the Yellow Turbans and the palace eunuchs. It was this discovery which led to the execution of the eunuchs Feng Hsü and Hsü Feng who had originally been accused by the informer T'ang Chou. Chang Jang and other high-ranking eunuchs were also implicated, but they were pardoned by the emperor. This piece of evidence against the eunuchs, like many other accusations and counter-accusations, came from questionable sources, if one takes into account the outright anti-eunuch background of Wang Yün and Hsün Shuang.[160]

After the Yellow Turban insurrection the Han court lost almost all its residual control over the provincial areas. In A.D. 188, the office of the Imperial Commissioner (*Tz'u-shih*) in the provinces was changed to that of Governor-general (*Chou-mu*), a permanent office which had greater administrative autonomy and effective power than its predecessor.[161] A considerable measure of authority was now delegated to the provinces. Meanwhile, the struggle at court between the eunuchs and their militant opponents continued. To remedy its own military weakness, the court created its own Palace Guard unit in the eighth lunar month (9 September–8 October) of A.D. 188. A eunuch was appointed Commander-in-chief of these units, with eight Lieutenants (*Hsiao-wei*) under him, each in control of one unit of Guards.[162]

The Han eunuchs, unlike those in the later T'ang dynasty, were completely inexperienced in military affairs. They miscalculated the newly-won strength of their opponents and made the mistake of discrediting and subsequently downgrading several prominent Han generals, including Lu Chih, Huang-fu Sung, and Wang Yün. For this or other reasons, they failed to secure the support of the rank-and-file of the Palace Guards. In spite of their eunuch Commander-in-chief the actual control of these Guards fell into the hands of the Lieutenants Yüan Shao and Ts'ao Ts'ao, two former leaders in the dissident partisans' secret mission, who recruited many of their militant followers to the Guard units.[163] The final stage of the struggle between the eunuchs and the anti-eunuch league was in sight.

3

The Han–Wei transition

CIVIL TURMOIL AND 'RESTORATION'

On 15 May A.D. 186, the Emperor Ling, the grand patron of the eunuchs, died. A new boy emperor came to the throne and a new regent, Ho Chin, was appointed.[1] The anti-eunuch partisans immediately rallied to the new regent and persuaded him to give his support to their imminent military action against the eunuchs. But Ho Chin, uncertain of the strength of the anti-eunuch league, delayed so that he could invite some of the frontier generals to help him in the plot despite the protest of the partisans, who advocated immediate action. During this period of suspense, the secret leaked out. The eunuchs staged a last *coup d'état* and murdered Ho Chin on 22 September 189.[2]

When the chief partisans Yüan Shao and his cousin Yüan Shu heard of this, they immediately led their supporters among the Palace Guards to attack the palace.

The palace gate was closed. Yüan Shu and others attacked it with their weapons, while the eunuchs under the Yellow Gate [at the vestibule of the palace where the Master-of-writing and the Court Attendants were situated] armed themselves to defend the corridor. At sunset, Yüan Shu set fire to the Green-frame Gate [the emperor's residence], compelling Chang Jang and other eunuchs to retreat. Jang and others then took as hostages the empress dowager, the boy emperor, his brother the Prince of Ch'en-lou and other officials inside the palace and fled to the Northern Palace [former residence of the early Later Han emperors] through a hidden passage.

The massacre then began:

Yüan Shu surrounded the Northern Palace and closed all the gates. He commanded his soldiers to arrest all the eunuchs. These were then summarily put to death, all of whom, young and old, totalled more than two thousand heads. There were some persons who bore no beards and were executed by mistake.

On 23 September 189, the eunuchs Chang Jang and others took the Emperor and the Prince of Ch'en-lou and went out on foot through the Northern Gate. They arrived at the town of Hsiao-chin [north of the imperial capital of Loyang] by night.

40

These fleeing eunuchs were finally caught by another group of their foes:

The Master-of-writing, Lu Chih [the downgraded general] and the Honan Provincial Administrative Assistant, Min Kung, arrived at the bank of the river, and met the Emperor's ' retinue ' by night. Min Kung severely cursed the eunuch Chang Jang and others. He then personally took his sword and killed several of them. Jang and the others were greatly frightened. They folded their hands, prostrated and knocked their heads on the ground before the Emperor to bid him farewell, saying: ' Your servants will die. Your Majesty please take care of yourself.' They then threw themselves into the river and died.

Kung helped the Emperor and the Prince of Ch'en-lou walk southward by night, groping their way in the glimmering light of the fireflies. After they had walked a few miles, they obtained a bare cart and together rode on it to Lo-hsien. The next day, the Emperor alone rode on a horse while the Prince of Ch'en-lou and Kung shared one horse between them to proceed southward from Lo-hsien. They were later joined by some of the high-ranking ministers.[3]

These records, though noticeably exaggerated and dramatized, serve as vivid illustrations both of the complete humiliation of the Han emperor and also of the belligerency of the new élite, which shadowed the more violent events to come.

After the *coup d'état*, the victorious partisans demanded full control of the central administration, placing themselves not only in charge of the outer court but also of those offices inside the palace traditionally held by the eunuchs.[4] Hsün Yü, a cousin of Hsün Yüeh and a leader in the former secret mission of partisans, was appointed Commandant of the Palace (*Shou-kung ling*).[5] The new élite had thus come to a turning-point in their political fortunes: they had now become the dominant faction in the Han court and were henceforth to identify their cause with the imperial rule which they had previously so ruthlessly under-mined.

The power of the new élite was soon cut short by another even more militant group, the veteran generals who had built up their personal armies during the campaigns against the Yellow Turbans and whose loyalty to the Han throne had been severely shaken by the humiliation endured by the emperor at the hands of the victorious anti-eunuch partisans.[6] The frontier general Tung Cho, who had been invited by Ho Chin to support the anti-eunuch operation, arrived belatedly at the scene of turmoil and installed himself as military dictator in the imperial capital. Soon after his entrance into Loyang, on 28 September of the same year he deposed the boy emperor and enthroned another child, the Prince of Ch'en-lou, who became Emperor Hsien, the last ruler of the Later Han.[7]

The new élite, however, were strong enough to defy Tung Cho. They repudiated Tung Cho's improper manipulation of the imperial power.[8] When Tung Cho threatened them with force, all four former leaders of the anti-eunuch partisans' secret organization went into action again: Yüan Shao left Loyang and went to the eastern provinces (Shan-tung), where he was soon in command of a formidable military alliance against Tung Cho.[9] Hsün Yü returned to Ying-ch'uan where he led his clansmen (who had organized themselves in self-defence units) to join forces with Yüan Shao.[10] Ts'ao Ts'ao also left the capital; he secretly went under a false name to the eastern provinces, where he organized a small army of his own.[11] Ho Yung (the former student leader) alone remained in the capital, where he planned a *coup d'état* against Tung Cho; when the plot failed, he committed suicide.[12]

Under pressure from the militant partisans, on 9 April A.D. 190, Tung Cho forced the Han court to move from Loyang to Ch'ang-an, the old capital of the Former Han dynasty. The devastation of Loyang occasioned by Tung Cho's abandoning the city is painted in sombre colours in the dynastic history:

In Loyang, there were by that time numerous mansions owned by dignitaries of the court and other relations of the ruling house. These mansions stood opposite one another, treasuring an abundance of gold, fine cloths and other valuables.

Tung Cho gave rein to his soldiers to pillage these mansions, carrying away women and girls and plundering money and goods, under the name of 'ransack investigations'.

He then transferred the Son-of-Heaven westward to Ch'ang-an. At the same time, he also removed all the people of Loyang, who numbered several million. On their way, these people were driven hard and run down by Tung Cho's footsoldiers and cavalry, while trampling upon one another. They also suffered starvation and plunder. Their corpses, lying upon one another, filled up the road.

When he abandoned Loyang, Tung Cho also burned all the imperial palaces, temples, official mansions, and civilian residences. Within two hundred *li* [about 45 English miles] of the capital, not a single human being or house survived.[13]

The great Han empire thus came to an end, though its ill-fated ruler, Emperor Hsien, continued to rule in name and led a humiliating existence until A.D. 220.

According to the historical records, the Emperor Hsien and his retinue of court dignitaries, having been forced by Tung Cho to evacuate Loyang and move to the west, arrived and set up court at the ruined city of Ch'ang-an on 27 April A.D. 190. Tung Cho himself remained in Loyang to deal with his military opponents in the eastern provinces. He joined the court at Ch'ang-an a year later and was finally assassinated by some of the court dignitaries on 22 May 193. These court dignitaries, however, failed to agree upon a policy to pacify the frontier soldiers who had been formerly under Tung Cho's command. These soldiers then mutinied and captured Ch'ang-an on 28 June. From A.D. 193 to 195, the roaming bands of soldiers under the command of Tung Cho's former lieutenants kept the emperor and his retinue captive and fought among themselves for the spoils. They continued to ravage the regions near Ch'ang-an for several years but eventually dwindled away.[14]

The suffering of the Emperor Hsien and his retinue of court dignitaries at the hands of marauding soldiers was vividly portrayed in the following record:

Li Chüeh, Kuo Ssu and Fan Ch'ou [all Tung Cho's former lieutenants] struggled among themselves for power. These generals became suspicious of one another. On 22 April A.D. 195, Chüeh dispatched his paternal nephew Ch'ien to lead several thousand soldiers and lay siege to the palace. On that day, the Son-of-Heaven [was forced to] move to Chüeh's camp.

Chüeh also moved the imperial treasury of gold and silk-cloth, the imperial carriages and other articles to his camp, and then set fire to the imperial palace and other court buildings, and destroyed all the civilian residences. . .

The emperor sent his court officials to reconcile Chüeh and Ssu. Ssu instead detained all these high-ranking officials as hostages. The unruly soldiers fought their battles in front of the emperor's person. . . . Chüeh again moved the emperor, this time to his north camp, and cut off his contact with the outside. The emperor's personal attendants were all starved by hunger. The emperor begged to have five piculs of rice to feed his attendants. Chüeh only gave him some stale ox-bones which stank and were inedible.[15]

The skirmishing between these former lieutenants of Tung Cho raged on inconclusively. The emperor and his court officials, however, finally succeeded in persuading their captors to let them return to Loyang. In the seventh lunar month (24 August–21 September) of A.D. 195, the emperor and his retinue left Li Chüeh's camp in the confusion of skirmishes among the warring generals and started their hazardous journey toward the east through the camps of the various feuding groups.[16]

Later, Li Chüeh and Kuo Ssu regretted that they had let the emperor go eastward. . . . They pursued the court retinue and caught up with them for battle on the eastern river bank in the Hung-nung Commandery [bordering the present Honan and Shensi provinces]. The casualties inflicted on the court officials and soldiers were inestimable. . . .

The emperor walked out from the camp and arrived at the river bank. He intended to go to the boat, but the bank was more than one hundred feet high. So he was lowered by a silken rope. The other people either crawled along the bank or threw themselves down from the height, killing or injuring themselves without being attended to.[17]

On 4 August 196, the emperor finally returned to the ruined city of Loyang. But the sufferings of the court did not end there. The various generals who had accompanied the emperor eastward or who had joined his retinue during the journey began to fight for power among themselves while the court and its civilian bureaucracy remained destitute. The extreme deprivation of the Han court at Loyang was recorded in the following passage:

By that time, the palaces and mansions in Loyang had all been destroyed by fire. The various officials had to cut down the wild thorns and live amongst the bare walls. The governors of the provinces and commanderies each had strong armies under their command and would not pay tribute. The court officials were starved and exhausted. The attendants in the State Secretariat [Shang-shu lang] and those still lower in rank had to go out and pick wild grains for food. Some of them starved to death among the bare walls or were killed by vagabond soldiers.[18]

While the Han emperor and his retinue of court dignitaries (many of whom were former leaders in the anti-eunuch alliance, including several members of Hsün Yüeh's family and probably Hsün Yüeh himself) were enduring such sufferings between Ch'ang-an and Loyang, other former leaders of the anti-eunuch and anti-Tung Cho alliance were busily fighting with one another for local dominance in the eastern provinces. The two major contenders were Yüan Shao and Ts'ao Ts'ao, the two surviving leaders of Ho Yung's secret organization. The military alliance under Yüan Shao's leadership in the eastern provinces had been torn apart by internal power struggle and mutual suspicion and had achieved very little in campaigns against Tung Cho's marauding soldiers during the years A.D. 190–6.[19] Meanwhile, the small band of soldiers under Ts'ao Ts'ao's command had developed into a strong army, and by A.D. 196 had become Yüan Shao's arch rival in the north China plain.[20] Hsün Yü (Hsün Yüeh's cousin and a third leader in Ho Yung's former organization) had first joined forces with Yüan Shao, but in A.D. 191 he had switched to Ts'ao Ts'ao's side.[21]

During his hazardous escape to the east, the Emperor Hsien had sent his messengers to seek assistance from both Yüan Shao and Ts'ao Ts'ao. Yüan Shao, who had tried unsuccessfully to enthrone a puppet emperor of his own in 191, considered the presence of the emperor in his domain undesirable and therefore ignored the plea.[22] On the other hand, Ts'ao Ts'ao promptly responded to the emperor's call by sending a small army to escort the imperial retinue to Loyang, and he himself personally went there for an audience of Emperor Hsien on 28 September A.D. 196.[23]

Ts'ao's action seems to have been based on farsighted planning and shrewd calculation of his own long-term political advantage,[24] although throughout his life, he himself insisted that he had made this decision from ' loyalty ' and on high moral grounds.[25]

On 7 October, Ts'ao Ts'ao successfully persuaded (or coerced) the Han court to move from Loyang to Hsü, formerly a district city in the all-important Ying-ch'uan Commandery which was now under Ts'ao Ts'ao's domination. The titular Han court thus settled at the new interim capital Hsü and adopted the new reign title: Chien-an (' Establishing Peace '). Ts'ao Ts'ao received a new title as the Grand General controlling the Imperial Secretariat (*Ta-chiang-chün, Lu Shang-shu-shih*).[26] Hsün Yü became Acting Prefect of the Imperial Secretariat (*Shou Shang-shu-ling*), while Hsün Yüeh and K'ung Jung, a famous Confucian, were appointed to posts on the personal staff of the Emperor Hsien.[27] A number of other high literati or court dignitaries also returned to their court positions at Hsü.[28] The fugitive wanderings of the Emperor Hsien and his retinue thus came to an end. Many of the court notables, Hsün Yüeh among them, now expected a genuine restoration of the glorious Han rule, like the restoration achieved by Emperor Kuang-wu in the second quarter of the first century A.D. [29] This expectation, however, brought them only disillusion.

The restoration of the titular Han court at Hsü in A.D. 196 was a turning point in the political fortunes of Ts'ao Ts'ao's régime. Before the restoration, Ts'ao Ts'ao was merely one of many irregular military adventurers in the north China plain. He had captured a few cities but could not hold them for long. His prestige was much lower than Yüan Shao's. Although Ts'ao Ts'ao's soldiers were better organized and more effectively commanded, their conduct on the battlefield was no better than that of any other marauding soldiers. The unruly conduct of his soldiers, together with Ts'ao Ts'ao's high-handed measures (which were probably adopted in an attempt to cope with the chaotic political and military situation) had alienated many of the local magnates inside his domain who repeatedly plotted against him. Only two years before the Chien-an ' restoration ', while Ts'ao Ts'ao was conducting a military operation in the eastern part of the Shantung province, a serious revolt was staged by the local magnates in the west of Shantung which would have destroyed Ts'ao Ts'ao's home base but for Hsün Yü, who helped bring the situation under control.[30]

The situation drastically changed after the Chien-an ' restoration '. The restored Han court enabled Ts'ao Ts'ao to clothe many of his military and civil policies with the authority of the decrees emanating from the titular Son-of-Heaven. It also provided Ts'ao Ts'ao with the time-honoured bureaucratic channels for recruiting many talented young men to his active service and for mitigating the enmity of the haughty dignitaries and the militant local magnates simply by appointing them to prestigious sinecures at the court.[31] With this new prestige and support, Ts'ao Ts'ao defeated his military rivals one by one in the north China plain. In the tenth year of Chien-an (A.D. 205), he eliminated his arch opponent, Yüan Shao, and extended his control over the four provinces, Chi, Ch'ing, Yü and Ping. He now controlled the northern half of China.[32]

The ' restored ' Han court in the Chien-an era was a three-fold régime. The Han emperor was the titular sovereign in the Palace Court which consisted of a few Attendants and a Custodian of Archives (*Mi-shu-chien*), an office which Hsün Yüeh occupied until his death in A.D. 208. The function of this court establishment was merely ritualistic. Ts'ao Ts'ao, holding an official appointment from the Han emperor, controlled a military high command comprising both military and civilian staff. These were in charge of all important decision-making and policy-execution in the vital spheres of military, financial, and local administration. A third establishment, the civilian bureaucracy, comprising the Ducal Ministers and other court dignitaries co-ordinated by the Imperial Secretariat (*Shang-shu*, formerly office of the Master-of-writings), took care of routine administration and mediated between the Palace Court and Ts'ao Ts'ao's *de facto* command.[33]

To support economically such an unwieldy establishment, the Chien-an régime made special efforts to control the economy of the region under their domination, particularly some essential agricultural products. Military-agricultural colonies (*t'un-t'ien*), which had been used by the Emperor Wu of the Former Han for the direct support of his frontier defence establishment, were revived to meet the emergency situation in the heart of north China. Fields abandoned by their owners during the civil turmoil were placed under government administration. Landless and vagabond people were recruited to cultivate and to settle on these lands. This measure was first tried in a limited area near the new capital at Hsü and later extended to other parts of Ts'ao's domain. Official supervisors with such military titles as *Tien-nung hsiao-wei*, Colonel-in-charge-of-agricultural-work, were sent under Ts'ao Ts'ao's orders to the various commanderies and districts to set up similar colonies.[34] A combined tax-rental levy was exacted from the cultivators of these farm colonies at the rate of 50 to 60 per cent of the crop, depending on whether the tenant farmers could provide their own draft animals.[35] In addition, soldiers not on active war service were also required to cultivate military colonies (*ping-t'un*). Irrigation systems were constructed by the government along the Ying river, which connected the vital Ying-ch'uan region with the fertile Huai river valley, and also along the Huai river in the southern area where Ts'ao's forces were confronted by the various regional military groups in the Yangtze valley.[36]

The success of these programmes provided a firm economic basis to the Ts'ao régime. It also lessened the difficulty of its position concerning tax relief for the élite. Since revenue from these farm colonies seems to have provided the main financial resources of the Ts'ao régime, the tax on the independent households (essentially the big or small landlords) remained relatively low throughout the period: a land tax based on about one thirtieth of the crop and a household tax of two *p'i* (about 60 English feet) of silk-cloth and two catties (488 grams) of silk floss per family. The low incidence of such taxes seems to have ensured the acquiescence in the Ts'ao régime of the lesser landowners.[37]

During the period of pacification and settlement following its final victory over Yüan Shao in 205, the Ts'ao régime lost much of its military vigour. Internally, the three-fold régime of the Chien-an reign gave rise to conflicting and overlapping centres of authority resulting in continuous political tension and strife. Externally, Ts'ao Ts'ao's attempt to reunify the whole of China was frustrated by a military alliance between a group of the southern élite headed by Sun Ch'üan in the lower Yangtze valley and the regional armies in the middle Yangtze valley under the command of Liu Piao and Liu Pei, both of whom were members of distant branches of the Han ruling family. In A.D. 208, Ts'ao Ts'ao personally led an expedition to the south, but his forces were routed. From then on, Ts'ao Ts'ao devoted his attentions to consolidating the north, though he never relinquished his ambition of re-unifying China. The military alliance in the south soon broke down. Sun Ch'üan continued to rule over the lower Yangtze region, while Liu Pei expanded westward and in A.D. 214 took over the Szechuan region from Liu Chang, yet another member of the Han ruling family. Liu Piao, the Governor-general of Ching-chou in the middle Yangtze, died in A.D. 208, and the area formerly under his control became a buffer zone between the three warring régimes of Ts'ao Ts'ao, Sun Ch'üan and Liu Pei, who had now effectively divided China among them.[38]

BUREAUCRACY, POLITICAL LOYALTY, AND THE NEW LEADERS

With the destruction of Loyang in A.D. 190, the Later Han empire crumbled. But the Chinese cultural tradition, its values and customs, its cultural heritage and, last but not least, its legacy of bureaucratic administration, persisted. The persistence of the Han imperial legacy may, first of all, be seen in the efforts at 'restoration' made by the various groups of self-designated 'loyalists' during the early years of the third century. These efforts showed that traditional bureaucratic administration, though long undermined by inanition and eroded by military force, was to the new élite the only acceptable way of government and provided the only alternative to anarchy in the Age of Disunity.[39]

The political leaders in the early years of the third century had originated from different sections of the old society: among them were court aristocrats, literati-bureaucrats, members of the local élite, frontier generals, and other nondescript adventurers of lowly origins. Most of them had joined in a loose alliance against the palace eunuchs during the last years of the Later Han. The conglomeration of these leaders (most notably the literati-bureaucrats and the local élite) into an anti-eunuch league during a political struggle which lasted for more than thirty years had somewhat obliterated the old distinctions of status among these leaders. The social chaos following the Han collapse had also obscured the original background of the new leading élite.[40]

In the crisis following the destruction of Loyang, these new leaders faced a crucial test of strength in their struggles for political survival and continued dominance. In this process, a tentative distinction may be drawn between two groups: those who maintained local support, and those who did not – i.e. those warlords who struggled for regional domination in the eastern provinces and those court dignitaries who had lived as virtual hostages in the hands of the various warring generals during the years A.D. 189–200 and later.

Other historical circumstances affected the membership of these two groups. For instance, a court official who happened to be stationed outside the troubled regions had a better chance to survive the initial turmoil and later, on his own personal initiative and with local support, to develop a regional base of his own. Of the eleven leaders in the eastern provinces who originally formed the military alliance which challenged Tung Cho in A.D. 190, nine were currently court-appointed officials serving in the provincial and commandery administration. The remaining two, Yüan Shu and Ts'ao Ts'ao, held the court titles of General of the Rear (*Hou chiang-chün*) and Gentleman Counsellor (*I-lang*) respectively.[41] Of these, Yüan Shu, Yüan Shao, and Ts'ao Ts'ao came from among the junior leaders of the anti-eunuch league; Yüan I was Shao's cousin; Han Fu had been a high-ranking court official; K'ung Ti, Liu Tai, and Ch'iao Mao came from among the most prominent literati; Chang Miao had been a local magnate and an acknowledged patron of the anti-eunuch league; Wang K'uang and Pao Hsin originated from the local magnates who had rendered service to Yüan Shao in the anti-eunuch movement.[42] On the other hand, those local magnates whose home-bases lay in the areas near the capital cities Loyang or Ch'ang-an found it difficult to survive the ravages of civil war. In spite of the popular support which they might have in their own locality, these local leaders sooner or later found themselves uprooted by the marauding soldiers and shared the same fate as the helpless courtiers in the entourage of the Han emperor.[43]

By a strange coincidence, members of the extended Hsün family in Ying-ch'uan were split between the two groups above-mentioned. In A.D. 190, Yüeh's uncle Hsün Shuang had responded to a summons to a court service at Loyang, bringing with him some members of his family (probably including Hsün Yüeh) into Tung Cho's domain.[44] Meanwhile, Yüeh's cousin Hsün Yü had left Loyang and returned to Ying-ch'uan to organize a campaign against Tung Cho. In Ying-ch'uan, Hsün Yü tried to persuade those local magnates who had set up a para-military defensive system there to leave the commandery and follow him to join forces with Yüan Shao in the eastern provinces. He pointed out that Ying-ch'uan was a region of such strategic importance that it would soon be engulfed in the civil war. Many of these local magnates were, however, too much attached to their home-bases to heed this advice. In A.D. 190–2, the whole of Ying-ch'uan Commandery was devastated by Tung Cho's soldiers. Hsün Yü alone succeeded in leading his clansmen to emigrate to the eastern provinces, thanks to the foresight and political instinct which the Hsün had acquired in their previous involvement in court politics.[45]

Political shrewdness or expertise acquired through bureaucratic experience seems to have been an important factor in the success or failure of the new leaders of this transition period. As early as A.D. 189, when Tung Cho became military dictator at Loyang, he soon fell under the strong influence of the intriguing literati-bureaucrats. These learned men persuaded Tung Cho to let Yüan Shao and his bellicose partisans loose in the eastern provinces. They also urged Tung Cho to recruit into court service many literati formerly in the anti-eunuch league.[46]

Hsün Shuang, who had hitherto refused several court appointments, accepted the invitation and, within three days of his arrival at Loyang in A.D. 190, was installed as a Ducal Minister (*Ssu-k'ung*).[47] Wang Yün, another former leader of the anti-eunuch league, was also promoted to be a Ducal Minister (*Ssu-t'u*) and served concurrently as the Acting Prefect of the Imperial Secretariat at the court under Tung Cho's military dictatorship.[48]

Wang Yün soon won the full confidence of Tung Cho. When Cho forced the Han court to move to Ch'ang-an, he entrusted Yün with the care of the titular imperial bureaucracy (a charge similar to that which was later entrusted to Hsün Yü by Ts'ao Ts'ao in the early Chien-an era). According to the *Hou-Han shu*, Wang Yün made a conscientious effort to preserve the tradition of imperial rule in these turbulent years. He carefully selected and brought with him a number of important state documents to Ch'ang-an; the mere possession of these gave the hostage court significant prestige. Wang Yün soon produced a set of ordinances for use at the new court. In A.D. 192, he even succeeded in conspiring with several of Tung Cho's lieutenants to stage a *coup d'état* and killed Tung Cho. Wang Yün himself was in turn killed by mutinous soldiers a few months later, but the court bureaucracy persisted.[49]

Although the court dignitaries in the Han emperor's retinue lacked the support of a regional base or a personal army, they nonetheless maintained with courage and determination a tenacious hold on their office. And they continued to exercise considerable influence, directly and indirectly, over the military who posed as their captors.[50] A clear indication of this was the reinstitution of the Imperial Academy together with the civil service examination in A.D. 193 in the midst of savage fighting among Tung Cho's several lieutenants.[51]

While the imperial court thus struggled to maintain its titular sacrosanctity and authority in the face of grave adversity, the regional leaders, who were possessors of the real power, were confronted with problems of conflicting loyalty arising from the absence of any effective bureaucratic guidance. Although the regional leaders in the eastern provinces were engaged in an outright struggle among themselves for territorial power they all nevertheless professed to be Han loyalists. This professed loyalty to the Han cause, however, varied from mere propagandist rhetoric to fundamental doctrinaire conviction.[52]

It may be noted that absolute loyalty to the dynasty had not been a strong tradition in Han times. During the early years of the Former Han rule, the notion seemed to have a wide currency among the élite that the Liu House had grasped its imperial mandate by chance and by worldly means. This is illustrated in the oft-quoted sayings that ' the Han dynasty was founded on horseback ',[53] and that ' it seized its fortune [*lu*, deer, alluding to political fortune of the dynasty] in a ruthless pursuit '. The latter allusion, known as *chu-lu* or ' chasing the deer ', was recorded in a conversation dated about 196 B.C., which reads: ' The Ch'in régime had lost its *lu* [deer – i.e. political fortune]. All-under-heaven chased after it. Those who rode high on horse-back grabbed it first [and became the emperor] '.[54]

Only after a long period of consolidation did the Han dynasty gradually come to ascribe its legitimacy to the Mandate of Heaven. But the notion of limited dynastic loyalty persisted, and was frequently reinforced by the Confucian notion of a right to revolution against a dynasty which had lost its moral justification to rule and the pseudo-scientific theory of dynastic change influenced by the cosmic elements. The latter theory had its exponents in both Taoist and Confucian circles during the first century B.C. For example, a memorial submitted to the throne by the Confucian minister Kai K'uan-jao in 60 B.C. reads: ' The changing of dynasties is like the change of the four seasons. Those who have accomplished their tasks should leave their posts. An unsuitable person should not occupy the throne.' [55] Toward the end of the Former Han rule, the theory of *chu-lu* or ' chasing the deer ' regained much currency among the élite.[56] It was partly to counter this dangerous notion that the conservative Later Han court had to subscribe to a more mystical interpretation of the Mandate of Heaven.[57]

The Later Han dynasty's command of the loyalty of the élite was further shaken during the third quarter of the second century, when the belligerent local élite took over the leadership of the anti-eunuch movement.[58] The tenuous loyalty of these so-called ' loyalists ' to the Han court may be seen in the advice given by Yen Chung to the Han general Huang-fu Sung during their campaign against the Yellow Turbans in A.D. 184. Yen Chung had come from the Han-yang Commandery (formerly the T'ien-shui Commandery in the upper Yellow River valley) where the Yen clan was known as one of the four most powerful big clans in Former Han times.[59] After Huang-fu Sung had defeated the Yellow Turbans, Yen Chung advised him to turn his army against the court, saying: ' The Way of Heaven shows no favouritism [to any particular dynasty, i.e. the Han]. The hundred surnames align themselves only with a competent [ruler]. . . How can you face northward to serve a mediocre Han ruler? ' Yen Chung further advised Sung to accomplish first a military conquest of the empire, and then ' Appeal to the Lord-on-High and show Him the Mandate of Heaven [by virtue] of the imperial unification . . . pushing the perishing Han throne off its shaken foundation.' [60] Although this advice was not accepted by Huang-fu Sung, it constituted the line of action subsequently followed by many of the so-called loyalists during the turmoils after the destruction of Loyang in A.D. 190.

Ostensibly, most of these loyalists were working toward the Han restoration. But many of their loyal pronouncements were no more than lip-service.[61] Even for those who had a real interest in seeing Han rule restored, there were still different visions of the intended restoration. In most of the high sounding loyalist rhetoric, the restoration was envisioned as merely the maintenance of the Han court as a symbol of imperial unity. The history of the Spring-and-Autumn period (c. 721–

482 B.C.) during which the Chou dynasty survived and maintained its sovereignty at Loyang while its vassal states were contending with one another for political hegemony was as frequently alluded to in these loyal utterances as the slogan of ' chasing the deer '.[62]

Despite its tenuity and insincerity, dynastic loyalty maintained its grip on the contending regional leaders in these years of turmoil. Its tremendous impact can be seen nowhere more clearly than in the disasters falling upon those who completely disregarded it, i.e. Yüan Shao and Yüan Shu. The military alliance in the eastern provinces was originally dominated by Yüan Shao and his half-brother Yüan Shu, who organized the alliance in opposition to Tung Cho's replacement of the young emperor by another candidate of his own choice.[63] Since Yüan Shao opposed the enthronement by Tung Cho of the new Emperor Hsien, he tried in A.D. 191 to enthrone a candidate of his own, Liu Yü (a member of the Liu House and a Ducal Minister, *Ssu-ma*, of the Han court). Liu Yü, however, dared not accept the throne. He thought it improper even to pose as acting emperor.[64] The issue thus dragged on.[65]

By late 195 and early 196, when the Emperor Hsien appealed to both Yüan Shao and Ts'ao Ts'ao for assistance, separate discussions of the appeal were held in both Yüan Shao's and Ts'ao Ts'ao's camps.[66] In Yüan Shao's camp, the decision was to ignore the emperor's appeal, whereas in Ts'ao Ts'ao's camp Hsün Yü's support of the loyalist cause won over the opposition and resulted in the ' restoration ' at Hsü.[67] Even Hsün Yü, however, was not a doctrinaire loyalist. In his arguments for supporting the Han court, the psychological appeal of loyalism, the prestige of the emperor, and the possibility of controlling the administration effectively, all of which would benefit the Ts'ao camp, were carefully considered.[68] The argument was repeated by Hsün Yü in A.D. 200 before the final battle was fought between Ts'ao Ts'ao and Yüan Shao.[69] Evidence of the reverses suffered by Yüan Shao in these episodes may be seen in his subsequent acceptance of an official appointment from the court through Ts'ao Ts'ao in A.D. 196 and the high-sounding admonition which he received from the Emperor Hsien through Ts'ao's manipulation.[70]

The presumptuous Yüan Shu was in an even worse situation. Shu had considered his position strong enough to bid for the throne himself. He sent a letter to a former associate, alluding to the idea of ' chasing the deer ', but received a rebuff.[71] Nonetheless, he declared himself emperor in A.D. 197 and received a still stronger rebuff from one of his former subordinates, Sun Ts'e (the regional leader in the Lower Yangtze river valley).[72] Yüan Shu's army soon suffered a series of defeats from A.D.

197 to 198. In desperation, he turned over the imperial title to Yüan Shao and died in frustration in A.D. 199.[73]

In his last letter to Yüan Shao, Yüan Shu wrote:

The Han dynasty has long since lost the realm. The Son-of-Heaven is controlled by his ministers. Political power lies in the private households. The influential magnates contend with one another and divide the domain among themselves. This does not differ from the situation in the last years of the Chou dynasty when the realm was divided into seven states. In the end, the strongest would conquer them all...

Now you control the territory of four provinces with a population of one million households. In terms of real strength, none is your equal. In terms of virtue, none is your superior. Although Ts'ao Ts'ao wishes to support the declining and minister to the weak [i.e. the Han imperial court], how can he extend a lineage which has already been terminated? [74]

While this letter clearly illustrates the recurrent political idea of 'chasing the deer', it also reveals some deepset habits of mind in the new élite. For a person like Yüan Shu, loyalty to the Han dynasty could be readily dismissed, as witnessed by the ruthless manner in which he had conducted the siege of the Han palace in A.D. 189, or by the arrogant way in which he later declared himself emperor despite considerable opposition. But even in the mind of such an iconoclast, the only possible solution to China's problems lay in a political re-unification to which the current stage of fragmentation was but a transition.

Although Yüan Shao did not accept the imperial title himself, he seemed implicitly to agree with Yüan Shu's idea of 'chasing the deer'.[75] Here, however, both of them seriously miscalculated the degree of loyalty to the Han dynasty which persisted, far more widespread than the support for the claims of the Yüan family. This miscalculation became obvious in the general opposition to both Yüan Shu and Yüan Shao in their later years when their influence sharply declined.[76]

In the historical allusion made by Yüan Shu in the letter quoted above, the fact is overlooked that, although the Chou dynasty had lost control over its vassals, it nonetheless had retained a great degree of its symbolic authority during the Spring-and-Autumn period. Similarly, loyal sentiment to the increasingly powerless Han court, though continuously diminishing, remained strong, certainly far stronger than that paid to the Yüan family. The élite's residual but persistent loyalty to the Han court was vividly illustrated by a posthumous letter written by Lu Chi, a member of the local élite of south China. Even after life-long service in a regional régime controlled by a former subordinate of Yüan Shu, Lu Chi still called himself a 'well-intentioned loyal subject of Han'.[77]

Both Yüan Shu and Yüan Shao made two serious mistakes over the issue of political loyalty: one concerns the very nature of limited or divided loyalty in ancient China; the other concerns the bureaucratic tradition with which the issue of political loyalty was inextricably intertwined. The first miscalculation subsequently cost the Yüan much of their prestige as well as their popular support; the second mistake accounted for many of the internal difficulties arising within the Yüan camps. These miscalculations weakened Yüan Shu's régime, prevented his consolidating his power, and helped Ts'ao Ts'ao to triumph in the struggles for power, and this produced an important impact on 'restoration' politics during the Chien-an reign.

As mentioned before, political loyalty to a dynasty had been neither absolute nor exclusive of other political or social obligations in Han or pre-Han China. Underlying it is an elusive concept of reciprocity (*pao*) as the basic principle of social relations, in which the relation between the ruler and the ruled is but one among other mutual relationships.[78] A clear statement of this principle of reciprocal relationship had been made by Confucius in his injunction that only a fit ruler deserves the proper loyalty of his subjects.[79] It is from this principle of reciprocity that a worldly notion of the Mandate of Heaven in terms of 'political debts' evolved.

According to this notion, a dynasty enjoys its power only by the good will and acceptance of the ruled. Such popular acceptance of the dynasty may be procured through the accumulated political merit and moral virtue of the dynastic rulers and of their pre-dynastic ancestors. The greater their cumulative contributions to the common good, the longer the dynasty will enjoy the Mandate of Heaven to rule. Conversely, the more evils that are accumulated by the rulers which thus counterbalance the accumulated merits of the dynasty, the shorter the dynastic rule will become. The Chou dynasty rose because of the cumulative merits of its ancestors and the glorious deeds of its founding rulers; the dynasty endured until its last ruler exhausted the stored-up grace of that dynasty.[80] Though the Han was a dynasty 'founded on horseback in pursuit of the deer' and thus was without impressive inherited grace, it sustained its rule through the cumulative merits of its early rulers who won the good will of their subjects, and the dynasty was therefore confirmed by the Mandate of Heaven. The accumulated merits of the early emperors of the Han dynasty, according to this theory, were largely nullified by the wicked rulers of the Later Han. Thus, the Mandate of Heaven would be withdrawn from the Liu and entrusted to another more meritorious house.[81] Even to a doctrinaire Confucian like Hsün Yüeh or his uncle Hsün Shuang, the Han dynasty seemed to have forfeited much of its loyal support from the élite on account of the waywardness of its recent rulers and their cruel persecution of the élite during the latter half of the second century.[82]

The same notion of cumulative merit and the same principle of reciprocity, when applied to other spheres of social and political relations, had strengthened the position and the solidarity of the dissident élite at the same time as it undermined the Han rule. The élite too had its loyal support based on achievements and accumulated merit, a formula which was extended in Later Han times to all kinds of social relationships, notably that of the master and disciple, of patron and client, and of superior and inferior. While the prestige and popular support of the élite increased due to its members' wholehearted devotion to a cause believed to be for the common good – i.e. the *ch'ing-i* as a righteous struggle against the wicked eunuchs – the solidarity of the dissident élite was similarly enhanced by mutual loyalty arising from their common suffering under the *tang-ku* persecutions.[83]

It was on this calculation of reciprocity and what was due to their own family's cumulative merit that Yüan Shu and Yüan Shao estimated the support due to their own régimes. Both Yüan Shu and Yüan Shao came from a family of the high élite and were themselves important leaders in the anti-eunuch alliance.[84] They had, as they themselves declared, their ' former disciples, clients, and subordinates spreading all over the empire '. It would therefore not have seemed too presumptuous for the Yüan to expect that they might receive the Mandate of Heaven to replace the Han.[85] However, the Yüan's understanding of the principle of reciprocity proved to be too simplistic. For it was precisely on these same principles of loyalty and reciprocity for past service that their opponents, many of them Yüan's former supporters, firmly rejected their pretensions. They pointed out that the Yüans for many generations had occupied a prominent position at the Han court and had on this account been able to spread their influence throughout the realm. It was therefore of first importance, in accordance with the principle of reciprocity, for the Yüan to repay their long-standing obligation to the Han with loyalty, not treason. The favours or obligations owed by others to the Yüan were thus largely outweighed by the Yüan's own disloyalty to the Han.[86]

In time of crisis, the estimation and enumeration of past merits, cumulative ' virtues ', and obligations seemed to play as crucial a part in the political lives of the new leaders as their intrigues and political manoeuvres. When competing claims were balanced in the light of this theory of obligation and of reciprocity, it appeared that none of these leaders in the immediate post-Han period had accumulated enough political credit or prestige to replace the Han as the rightful ruler of China.[87] This enumeration of the past merits and cumulative virtues of the Han imperial house as compared with those of their potential rivals was what Hsün Yüeh was supposed to perform when he was commissioned by the last Han emperor to compile and edit the *Han-chi* or Chronicles of Han, a task which Hsün Yüeh executed in the most exemplary manner in accordance with the formulae of reciprocity.[88]

Yüan Shao's open subversion of titular Han rule brought him not only the loss of prestige and fringe support, but also serious difficulties inside his own camp, particularly during his fierce struggle with Ts'ao Ts'ao in A.D. 195–202. Although Yüan Shao's army was numerically much stronger than Ts'ao Ts'ao's, the latter far excelled the former in military organization as well as in political and ideological policy – and this was largely the result of Ts'ao's ' restoration ' of the Han court at Hsü, an act which rallied an immediate and automatic response and widespread loyalty to Ts'ao's régime.[89] The relative weakness of the Yüan camp was clearly borne out in the following advice given to Ts'ao Ts'ao by Hsün Yü in A.D. 196 and 197: ' Yüan Shao controls his army through a loose command, with conflicting orders issuing from different quarters. Although he has many soldiers, he cannot use them effectively in fighting.'[90] The accuracy of this estimate was proved by the result of the subsequent battles between the two forces as well as by Ts'ao Ts'ao's own admission years later.[91] The disorganized manner in which Yüan Shao fought his losing battles against Ts'ao Ts'ao is well attested by the historical records. After the initial setbacks on the battlefield, the morale of Yüan Shao's soldiers quickly deteriorated. And Yüan Shao's lieutenants were more prone to fight for their own advantage than for Yüan's. After subverting political loyalty to the Han sovereign, Yüan Shao failed to substitute for it an obligatory loyalty to himself among his followers. The loyal dispositions of his lieutenants remained a matter of individual option based on the elusive principle of personal reciprocity and this failed to provide a reliable guideline for action in moments of extreme emergency.[92]

The complication arising from divided or conflicting loyalties in the Yüan camp may be seen in a case involving Yüan Shao and a subordinate named Tsang Hung. In A.D. 195, Ts'ao Ts'ao attacked a regional warlord named Chang Ch'ao. The latter sought help from a former subordinate, Tsang Hung, who had taken service under Yüan Shao. Tsang Hung asked Shao's permission to send a relief force to the aid of his former master, but Shao refused the request. After Ts'ao Ts'ao had defeated and killed Chang Ch'ao, Tsang Hung severed all his relations with Yüan Shao. In spite of Shao's repeated attempts to win Tsang Hung back to his party, the latter would not comply and chose rather to die by Shao's sword. In Tsang Hung's words, Yüan Shao himself had been disloyal to the Han dynasty and therefore could not constrain Hung by appealing to the highest cause of political loyalty; besides, Yüan Shao had also forced Tsang Hung to violate his personal loyalty to a former master by not permitting him to send a relief force; he could not therefore constrain Tsang Hung by appealing to the sense of personal obligation.[93]

Since Yüan Shao had commanded the largest army of clansmen and controlled a powerful alliance of the warlike regional leaders in this early transition period, he was often considered the prototype of the decentralized, clan-orientated, 'feudalistic', political forces which emerged in China during the Age of Disunity. His failure thus shows how difficult it was for these fragmented regional groups to develop a workable power structure to replace the imperial bureaucracy which they had subverted.[94]

Despite the desire of the prominent regional leaders to repudiate centralization and control from above, they often found it difficult to extricate themselves from issues involving the imperial court and were often compelled to do battle with other contenders in the struggle for imperial domination. The situation in Ch'ing-chou province (in the Shantung peninsula) serves as a good example. The province remained economically prosperous and militarily secure until A.D. 190. In that year, the Imperial Commissioner of this province was drawn into Yüan Shao's alliance. He joined with the other regional leaders, busily campaigning against Tung Cho, and seriously neglected his own local defence. The province was subsequently overrun and devastated by the surviving Yellow Turban rebels.[95]

During the years of protracted civil war, it became increasingly difficult for the regional leaders of moderate power or the local magnates of central China to survive in local isolation. Many of them perished. Others were absorbed into the principal warring groups.[96] For instance, K'ung Jung, a descendant of Confucius, built up a regional base centred on Pei-hai Commandery in the coastal area of Shantung. He had gathered considerable local support from the native officials and local élite and from certain groups of coastal aboriginal people and succeeded in holding that region until A.D. 196. But in that year he was compelled by military pressure to evacuate the territory and joined the Han court at Hsü.[97]

The local magnates who had a better chance to survive the civil war were those situated on the outer fringes of the empire. T'ien Ch'ou, for example, established a self-sufficient area under his own command in Yu-pei-p'ing Commandery near the northernmost frontier. But even so, he voluntarily joined Ts'ao Ts'ao's camp in A.D. 207.[98] After A.D. 208, when the whole of northern and central China had fallen under Ts'ao Ts'ao's control, the only effective resistance to Ts'ao came from the two independent régimes in the lower Yangtze valley and in Szechuan where the factors of distance, difficulty of terrain, cultural diversity, and strong regional solidarity of the native élite, combined with the emerging internal weaknesses of the Ts'ao régime in the north, worked together to frustrate Ts'ao Ts'ao's design for a complete imperial reunification.[99]

THE EARLY CHIEN-AN ERA, A.D. 196–210

The success of Ts'ao Ts'ao in consolidating and extending his domination over north China, in contrast to the failure of Yüan Shao and other regional leaders of the area in pursuing similar aims, was the most significant development in the years of transition from imperial unity to the Age of Disunity. However, even Ts'ao's relatively successful régime was also internally divided, although less so because of the cohering force given to it by its professed loyalty to the Han house. The leadership of Ts'ao's régime came from a broad range of backgrounds, from former Yellow Turban rebels to members of the great clans of the provinces. Although they were united in support of Ts'ao's struggle against external enemies, they varied widely in their commitment to his own personal leadership.[100]

In terms of their political loyalty, the ruling élite of the Chien-an era were divided into the pro-Han and the pro-Ts'ao factions, with other fringe groups forming a buffer between them.[101] In terms of ideology, the majority of this élite may be called Confucian in a loose sense, but there were numerous internal divisions within this loose conglomeration. The main dividing line seems to have been between those who were inclined towards institutional solutions and Legalism and could be called the Legalist-Confucians and those who were inclined toward Taoism and could be called the Taoist-Confucians. Many contemporaries were however ambivalent in their views and there were many other quite different tendencies too complicated to be sorted out.[102]

The nucleus of the Ts'ao leadership itself typified the ideological ambivalence prevalent in the early Chien-an era. Ostensibly, the Ts'ao leadership was working for the restoration of effective Han power, but in fact it was striving to establish and extend its own *de facto* rule. Ts'ao Ts'ao himself was a veteran general and politician. His practical experience on the battlefield and in government had given him skill in political intrigue and manipulative measures and swung his own personal inclination towards Legalism.[103] But under the influence of his chief counsellor, Hsün Yü, a genius in political and military strategy but also a devoted Confucian, Ts'ao Ts'ao moderated this inclination considerably, especially during the early years of the Chien-an reign.[104]

This ambivalence in Ts'ao Ts'ao's political and ideological tendencies was a major factor in the popular acceptance of his leadership in a time of conflicting interests and ideologies. To the majority of the élite, Ts'ao's leadership was a lesser evil than the other extremes, such as the revolutionary insurgents on the left or the unruly local magnates on the right.[105] This attitude towards Ts'ao's leadership is exemplified clearly by some remarks of Yüan Huan.

Yüan Huan was the son of a former Ducal Minister of the Han court. Anticipating the danger of civil disturbance in central China, he and his younger brother discussed the course most likely to ensure self-preservation. The younger brother proposed emigrating to a safe area on the outer frontiers. Huan disagreed and said:

The Han House is about to fall, and turmoil will shortly follow. If the whole realm falls into disorder, there is nowhere one may escape to. But if Heaven is to lose its Way, men must rely on their own moral to live. Only he who is strong in worldly affairs but nonetheless complies with the mores of propriety will be able to protect himself [and to provide shelter for others].

His younger brother, however, thought that in a time of crisis, each individual should follow his own disposition. He subsequently emigrated to the Chiao-chou province (the southwestern frontier region including a northern section of present Vietnam).[106] Huan chose to stay and eventually placed himself under the protection of Ts'ao Ts'ao, in whom he seemed to have found an embodiment of the ideal of ' a strong man with a strong sense of propriety'. The counsel which Huan offered to Ts'ao Ts'ao upon their first meeting projected the image which in theory and in fact they both shared: ' Weapons are dangerous instruments and should be used only as a last recourse. One must drum up the soldiers' morale by adhering to moral ideals [tao-te], and justify one's military actions on the principle of humanity and righteousness [jen-i].' According to the records, Ts'ao Ts'ao eagerly concurred with this image of a leader.[107]

The flexibility shown in Huan's advocacy of compromise between lofty moral ideals and the urgent needs of reality is further attested in the latter part of the same counsel, which reads:

Times have changed and so have the affairs of men. Different administrations need different policies – this should be carefully examined. Political systems and institutions have to be amended. They need not be the same in ancient and in modern times... Although one has to rely on military force to suppress disorder, one may supplement this with moral virtue [te]. This is truly the unchanging Way [tao] of all the Sage-rulers.[108]

This is exactly the precept which Hsün Yü frequently urged Ts'ao Ts'ao to comply with and which Hsün Yüeh himself resolutely expounded in his important writings, the *Han-chi* and the *Shen-chien*.[109]

Hsün Yüeh's family, which now lived under the patronage of the Ts'ao régime, epitomized the divided loyalties, the conflicting personal affiliations and the ambivalent ideological inclinations of the new élite. In the early years of the Chien-an era the Hsün family had members holding office in each of the overlapping and conflicting power structures of the Chien-an régime. Hsün Yüeh himself attended the Han emperor at the Palace Court; [110] his paternal cousin Hsün Yü served as the Acting Prefect of the Imperial Secretariat and was entrusted by Ts'ao Ts'ao with routine administration of the central government; [111] Hsün Yüeh's paternal nephew Hsün Yu served as Military Adviser (*Chün-shih*) in Ts'ao Ts'ao's high command and was the most trusted figure in Ts'ao's inner coterie.[112] These three members of the Hsün clan thus occupied important posts in three different key establishments of the composite Han–Ts'ao régime.

The three Hsün espoused different political causes and had different and ambivalent ideological leanings. Hsün Yüeh, often hailed as an exemplary Han loyalist, was essentially a Confucian with profound knowledge of Taoism and an occasional interest in Legalism.[113] Hsün Yu, who was denounced by later Confucians as a traitor to the Han cause, was a genius in political and military manoeuvres and was more inclined towards Taoism and Legalism.[114] Hsün Yü, whose role in the Han–Wei transition remains a matter of historical controversy, sometimes appeared to have strong Confucian convictions; but he was primarily an active political leader and an experienced bureaucrat who was often engaged in intrigues.[115] Their contributions to Ts'ao's leadership varied from that of providing ideological sanction to that of partisan support.

Ts'ao Ts'ao was a man of strong will engaged in a constant struggle for power. To such a man despotic domination was probably the means as well as the end in politics. In his early military operations, he had adopted some very high-handed measures in the conquered areas. These had aroused bitter resentment among the local élite, who posed a serious threat to Ts'ao's power [116] However, during the early period of the Chien-an era, *c.* A.D. 196–200, Ts'ao Ts'ao somewhat modified his attitude toward the élite, particularly after repeated warnings from Hsün Yü and other notables in the revived court bureaucracy.[117]

In the first year of Chien-an (A.D. 196) when the Han court had just been revived at Hsü, Ts'ao Ts'ao became jealous of the high prestige of the Ducal Minister (*Ssu-k'ung*) Yang Piao, head of the famous Yang clan which had produced many high-ranking officials in Later Han times. Ts'ao had Piao imprisoned on a contrived pretext. K'ung Jung, who had just deserted his regional base and had received an appointment at the Han court, went hurriedly to protest about this in person, addressing Ts'ao Ts'ao with a mixture of high moral precepts and bitter strictures. Ts'ao Ts'ao tolerated the outburst, but did nothing for Yang Piao. Later, Hsün Yü also interfered in favour of Yang Piao. The latter was there- fore released by Ts'ao Ts'ao, and a facade of unity was maintained between Ts'ao's coterie and the haughty court dignitaries.[118]

Underneath this personal conflict among the Chien-an élite, a deeper clash of political interests and ideologies went on. Within the Ts'ao coterie a group of Legalist-inclined bureaucrats had long advocated the institution of a more severe law code to cope with the disorderly political situation.[119] Among their proposals was the reinstitution of various kinds of punishments by mutilation which had been abolished as long ago as 167 B.C. by the Emperor Wen of the Former Han, an exemplary and benevolent ruler in the minds of many Han Confucians.[120] The proposal was strongly opposed by the Confucian dignitaries of the titular court bureaucracy, with K'ung Jung as their most outspoken leader.[121] Although Ts'ao Ts'ao himself was in favour of the proposal, he did not put it into practice because of the strong opposition from the Confucians.[122]

Ts'ao Ts'ao's attitude toward the court dignitaries hardened consider- ably after he had finally destroyed his chief rival Yüan Shao in A.D. 205. The tenacious Confucian tradition at the court represented by K'ung Jung, the arrogant descendant of Confucius, finally came into grave conflict with the Legalist realist policies favoured by Ts'ao Ts'ao. Some time before A.D. 208, Ts'ao Ts'ao wanted to prohibit the production and the use of liquor as a measure to maintain the supply of grain. K'ung Jung opposed the measure and exchanged a series of acrimonious letters with Ts'ao Ts'ao. He further suggested that, since the major part of China, with the exception of the Wu (lower Yangtze) and the Shu (Szechuan) regions, was now unified under the Han–Ts'ao régime, it was time for a full-scale reinstitution of civilian rule. That would have meant, implicitly, the end of Ts'ao Ts'ao's provisional authority as a military ruler and a genuine restoration of the Han dynastic rule. Ts'ao Ts'ao was enraged. He ordered K'ung Jung to be imprisoned and subsequently had his whole family summarily executed.[123]

K'ung Jung and Hsün Yüeh were intimate friends and colleagues. They were both well-known Confucians in the Chien-an era, and they both served as personal attendants to the Han emperor at the palace, where they gave daily discourses on current issues.[124] The execution of

K'ung Jung by Ts'ao Ts'ao, which occurred in the eighth lunar month (29 August–27 September) of A.D. 208, seems to have had a crushing effect on Hsün Yüeh, who died in the following year (A.D. 209) at the age of sixty-one (or sixty-two by Chinese reckoning).[125]

From A.D. 208 to 220, the Ts'ao régime enjoyed relative military security and economic stability but its internal political situation remained tense. The three-fold administrative system at Hsü, with its clustered dignitaries and overlapping sources of bureaucratic authority, continued to produce many conflicts of interest and intrigues. And Ts'ao Ts'ao, the *de facto* ruler, supported by the army and hardened by the lessons of civil warfare and intrigue, became a ruthless persecutor of his enemies—many of them his former colleagues in the anti-eunuch movement as well as in the restored Han imperial bureaucracy.[126]

Under these circumstances, the court dignitaries at Hsü, who had great prestige as men of learning and as leaders of society, and who were provided with sufficient material comforts from the incomes of their official emoluments or their lightly taxed estates, were feeling the mental strain caused by their powerless sinecure positions at court and their hazardous situation under the high-handed Ts'ao Ts'ao. These men were the last generation of the Han élite, and many of them had been leaders of the militant *ch'ing-i* protest movement. They now became the first elder generation of the new élite in the Age of Disunity. The changing conditions of their public situation as well as their private circumstances thus provided them much cause for reflection, probably not without some pricks of conscience.[127] They now retreated from their former political activism, either because of outside pressure or because of remorse at their own previous recklessness in politics. Gradually, the tradition of the militant political *ch'ing-i* protest was transformed into a convention of evasive *ch'ing-t'an* (pure or disinterested conversation), which was compounded of political nonchalance and introverted self-examination or criticism.[128]

High-handed as he was in political action, Ts'ao Ts'ao came neither from the ranks of marauding soldiers nor from the bloodthirsty frontier hordes. He was himself a seasoned product of the élite's idealistic political movement and of the civilian bureaucracy. Both Ts'ao Ts'ao and his son Ts'ao P'i (who later usurped the throne and terminated the puppet Han rule in A.D. 220) were themselves men of considerable learning and real poetic genius; they were quite tolerant of the élite's intellectual pursuits and ideological polemics so long as they did not pose a direct threat to their personal power. Under Ts'ao's leadership in the Chien-an transitional era new thought, new literature, and new moral precepts took their root and later flourished in the Cheng-shih era (A.D. 240–8) of the Wei dynasty.[129]

During the Chien-an era, the cause of Han restoration steadily declined. In the fifth year of Chien-an (A.D. 200), a secret plot against Ts'ao Ts'ao was uncovered which involved Tung Ch'eng, a brother-in-law of the Han emperor. Ts'ao Ts'ao had Tung Ch'eng and all Ch'eng's relatives (including his sister, a consort of the Emperor Hsien) put to death.[130] A similar fate befell the family of the Han empress (born a member of the Fu family) in A.D. 214 when her brother was implicated in another plot against Ts'ao Ts'ao. The whole Fu family, together with the empress and her two sons by the Han Emperor Hsien, were executed by Ts'ao.[131] The hope of a genuine restoration of Han rule had proved to be an illusion. In A.D. 208, Ts'ao Ts'ao abolished the office of Ducal Minister as the highest ranking post in the civil bureaucracy and revived the office of the Chief Minister (or Chancellor, Ch'eng-hsiang), an office which he himself then occupied. Thus, in name as well as in fact, Ts'ao had placed both the military high command and the titular imperial bureaucracy under his own firm control.[132]

In the same year A.D. 208, Ts'ao Ts'ao conquered the northern part of Ching-chou in the middle Yangtze and absorbed into the Chien-an régime another group of literati hitherto under the patronage of that southern régime.[133] The influx of this new group, which replaced some of the deceased or dying elders of the senior Chien-an élite (Hsün Yüeh, who died in A.D. 209, among them), not only added to the numerical strength of the cultivated élite in the Han–Ts'ao composite régime but also effected a change in direction in the ideological and intellectual trends of the late Chien-an era.[134]

The senior Chien-an élite, like Hsün Yüeh and some other members of his family, were men who had remained in northern China at the height of the political upheaval. Many of them had been active leaders in the ch'ing-i protest movement. They had either personally participated in or had closely watched the events that led to the Han downfall. During the early part of the Chien-an era, many of these men had become outspoken loyalists in the Han cause, while others had supported Ts'ao Ts'ao in his effort to establish a new political order. Although some of them later adopted an evasive, non-committal, or ambivalent political attitude under pressure and persecution from Ts'ao Ts'ao, their evasion or ambivalence was nevertheless the expression of serious efforts of reflection.

The literati from Ching-chou, however, were men of quite a different nature and environment. They were mostly men who had escaped from north China and migrated to the Yangtze river valley before or during the civil turmoil at the end of the second century.[135] The difference between these Ching-chou literati and the senior Chien-an élite may be seen in the different attitudes adopted by Yüan Huan and his younger brother Yüan Wei toward the problem of self-preservation in difficult times. Yüan Wei was a pure escapist whose impulse in a difficult time was to run away from trouble by emigrating to a safe place. Yüan Huan, however, had opted to stay on and face the trouble. In his own words, ' if Heaven is to lose its Way, men must rely on their own moral to live on '.[136] Yüan Huan's steadfastness was confirmed by the integrity which he showed in subsequent adversities.[137]

In contrast to men like Yüan Huan, the Ching-chou literati appeared to be of a much weaker calibre. After their escapist impulse had induced them to migrate to Ching-chou, they had had the good fortune to live under the patronage and protection of Liu Piao (the Governor-general of Ching-chou) for many years. But their contribution to that regional régime was almost negligible. Liu Piao's régime had been continuously weakened by extravagance and internal strife, which had reached a climax at the time of Ts'ao's conquest of the province.[138] The only achievement of this group of literati in Ching-chou lay in their literary and scholastic culture and refinement which accounted for their high prestige among men of letters.[139]

The position of the Ching-chou literati *vis-à-vis* the Ts'ao leadership also differed from that of the senior Chien-an élite. Many of the older Chien-an élite had been Ts'ao Ts'ao's comrades, first in their common struggle against the eunuchs and later in the effort to ' restore ' Han rule. Although their influence over the Han–Ts'ao régime had declined and many of them had since died at Ts'ao's hands, they were nonetheless held by Ts'ao in high regard.[140] The Ching-chou literati, on the other hand, were virtually Ts'ao's captives from his conquest of that region. Although owing to their literary and scholarly reputation, they were well-treated by their captor and were subsequently accepted into the Chien-an élite, they never achieved either the position or influence which had been held by K'ung Jung and Hsün Yüeh amongst the senior Chien-an élite. Neither were they as deeply committed to the cause of Han restoration as their predecessors. All they did was to follow the trend toward prevarication and political evasion set by the elderly élite in the middle Chien-an period.[141]

In this particular respect, the later Chien-an élite far out-distanced their predecessors. For many years, the elderly Chien-an élite had been searching for a remedy to the ills of their society and state, but their reflective efforts led simply to more personal dilemmas and a greater measure of ambivalence. The mood of the later Chien-an élite became even gloomier. Their political attitude was one of mere resignation. Worldly involvement, which to the senior Chien-an élite had become an unbearable burden, was to the later Chien-an élite an abhorrence. Still later (i.e. in the Cheng-shih era under the Wei rule) it became just something unfashionable. In the practice of the early Chien-an élite, the tradition of righteous *ch'ing-i* protest had already degenerated into ' disinterested discussion ' or *ch'ing-t'an*. In the later élite circles, it further degenerated from ' pure discourses ' into a convention of refined conversation.[142]

Meanwhile, Ts'ao Ts'ao and the inner circle of his supporters were relying more and more on their own power as a basis for a worldly régime. To counter the evasive and otherworldly attitude of those men of high prestige and Taoist leanings, the Ts'ao leadership became more determinately inclined toward Legalism. In A.D. 210, Ts'ao Ts'ao issued an order to seek out ' new men ' of unconventional calibre. He openly welcomed persons who did not necessarily possess either prestige or high social status, whose conduct or mores had been previously considered unacceptable by the old élite, but who nevertheless possessed practical worldly talents.[143] Ts'ao Ts'ao's Legalist inclination was thus clearly expressed. Co-operation between the Ts'ao leadership and the fringe élite circles, or the entente between the Taoist-inclined and the Legalist-inclined elements of the Han–Ts'ao régime, were no longer possible. The possibility of either co-operation or vigorous opposition between these two groups had come to an end in A.D. 210, one year after Hsün Yüeh's death.[144]

4

Hsün Yüeh: Family background, official career, and political attitudes

Very little is known of the early part of Hsün Yüeh's life before his appointment to the 'restored' Han court at Hsü in 196. The 'Biography of Hsün Yüeh' in the *Hou-Han shu* constitutes only a small part of the collective biographies of members of four outstanding families of Ying-ch'uan Commandery: the Hsün, the Han, the Chung, and the Ch'en, of which the accounts of the Hsün and the Ch'en make up the major portion. The first three sections of this chapter are devoted to notable members of the Hsün clan in three successive generations, represented respectively by Hsün Shu (Yüeh's grandfather), Hsün Shuang (Yüeh's uncle), and Hsün Yüeh himself. The sketch of Hsün Yüeh's own life in the 'Biography' is thus literally and historiographically submerged beneath the collective coverage of the extended Hsün family. Some supplementary information is to be found in the sections on the other notables of Ying-ch'uan, most significantly in the section on the Ch'en.[1]

The 'Biography of Hsün Yüeh' mentions that Yüeh died in the fourteenth year of the Chien-an reign (A.D. 209) at the age of sixty-two (by Chinese reckoning; that is, sixty-one by English reckoning).[2] Accordingly, the date of Yüeh's birth would fall in the second year of the Chien-ho reign of Emperor Huan, that is 148. At that time, the political power of the Liang family was supreme; the empress dowager (born a member of the Liang family) and the Regent of State, Liang Chi, dominated the court and overawed the emperor who was in fact put on the throne by the Liang. The influence of the palace eunuchs, though steadily rising, was temporarily over-shadowed. It was only eleven years later, in A.D. 159, that the emperor finally succeeded in conspiring with the eunuchs to exterminate the Liang family.[3]

From his birth till the end of Emperor Huan's reign in A.D. 167, Hsün Yüeh lived among the locally dominant and vastly ramified Hsün clan in Ying-ch'uan.[4] According to his 'Biography', he was the son of Hsün Chien who was himself the eldest son of Hsün Shu, ritual head of the whole extended Hsün clan in Ying-ch'uan.[5]

Hsün Chien died young, probably before Hsün Yüeh was twelve years of age. The 'Biography', immediately after mentioning Chien's death, states that: ' Yüeh, at the age of twelve, was able to make discourses on the *Ch'un-ch'iu* [the Confucian Spring-and-Autumn Annals].' The 'Biography' goes on: ' His [Yüeh's] family was poor and did not possess many books. But whenever he went to other people's houses and read some works, he could often memorize what he had read only once.' [6]

This statement presents some serious problems. First, it is said that Hsün Yüeh's family was poor, but in fact the extended Hsün family in Ying-ch'uan was rich and Hsün Shu, Yüeh's grandfather, was noted for his wealth, generosity, and influence in the locality.[7] Although Hsün Yüeh was orphaned at an early age, it would have been no problem for the family to provide for the comfort of an offspring in its chief line of descent. The statement calls attention not to any degree of real poverty but rather to Hsün Yüeh's modest station and relatively straitened circumstances amidst the otherwise excessively rich Hsün notables – one of those many contradictions that characterized Hsün Yüeh's life.

Secondly, it is said that Hsün Yüeh's family did not possess many books; this confirms a statement made earlier in Hsün Shu's biography which mentioned that ' Shu had no taste for the orthodox classical learning and was therefore looked down upon by many conventional Confucian scholars.' This unscholarly disposition of the Hsün elders contrasted sharply with the precocious inclination toward scholarship of two younger members of the family, Hsün Shuang and Hsün Yüeh – both of whom learned the Confucian classics at the age of twelve, according to their ' Biographies'.[8] Taken together, this evidence would seem to imply that the Hsün family had undergone a radical change in its social and intellectual orientation between the generation of Hsün Shu and that of Hsün Shuang – a relative decline in material fortune and an increased devotion to scholarship.

The *ch'ing-i* protest movement among the literati directed against the eunuchs intensified during the reign of Emperor Huan, and the Hsün family was engulfed in the movement some time after A.D. 166. Sometime between A.D. 152 and 166 the Hsün came into close contact with Ch'en Shih, already a central figure in the movement. When the Ch'en made their frequent visits to the Hsün household, Hsün Shu was in his fifties. Hsün Shuang in his twenties or thirties, and Hsün Yüeh himself was about four to eighteen years old.[9] At this point, the fortune and the status of the Hsün underwent a sudden change. The unscholarly Hsün Shu, hitherto despised by many Confucians, miraculously rose to be the mentor of the literati, and his eight sons were collectively called the ' Eight Dragons ' by the cultural élite.[10]

There is thus some reason to believe that the Ch'en may have exercised a considerable cultural influence over the Hsün at this juncture and Hsün Shuang, who appears to have been the only accomplished Confucian among the 'Eight Dragons', seems to have been the principal beneficiary. The statement in Hsün Yüeh's 'Biography' that he 'had to go to other people's houses to do his reading' thus seems to refer to the outside influence upon him from the literati circles; those 'other people' referred to would certainly have included the Ch'en, but Hsün Shuang, who was twenty years older than Hsün Yüeh, might also have been intended.

Since Hsün Shuang and Hsün Yüeh were the only accomplished Confucians in the Hsün family by the late second century to have left any formal scholarly works to posterity, the impact of the one on the other is easy to trace.[11] The passages in Hsün Yüeh's 'Biography' which describe his quietude, composure, refined manners, and intellectual disposition,[12] also suggest the overall guidance of the scholarly Hsün Shuang. This was in sharp contrast to the bold political adventures and intrigues of other members of the family, such as Hsün T'an's ruthless attack on the eunuch clique in Kuang-ling and Hsün Yü's co-operation with Ho Yung in the anti-eunuch partisans' underground missions.[13] From Yüeh's close relationship with Shuang, it seems possible that the orphaned Yüeh was raised under the latter's care after first his father and then Hsün Shu, head of the household, died.

The intellectual enlightenment of the Hsün resulted in the rapid rise of their prestige among the élite, thanks to the vigorous *ch'ing-i* propagandism of the anti-eunuch partisans, with whom the Hsün were now closely associated. This was indicated by the change of the name of the Hsün's local residence from *Hsi-hao* (lit. ' The Western Magnates ') to *Kao-yang* at the specific orders of the magistrate of that district. This magistrate considered that the virtue of the eight sons (the 'Eight Dragons') of Hsün Shu equalled the virtue of the eight sons of the legendary Emperor Kao-yang of remote antiquity, and so he ordered the name of the Hsün residence to be changed to *Kao-yang*.[14] This record, if it is reliable, shows extreme daring on the part of the district magistrate as well as the exceptionally high prestige of the Hsün in the locality – to compare the household of a commoner with that of a model sage emperor is a bold step.

There were other indications of the rapid rise of the prestige and social status of the Hsün. When Hsün Shu died, Li Ying, who served as Master-of-writing at the imperial court (the post had by this time become virtually that of a ranking minister in the court cabinet or Imperial Secretariat), specifically petitioned the court to allow him to observe mourning as if Hsün Shu had been his own teacher. Temples in memory of Shu were erected in several districts. A group of twenty-six literati were known to have written eulogies in his memory. One of Shu's eight sons later received two posthumous canonized styles, one from the magistrate of the Ying-yin district, the other from the Grand Administrator of the Ying-ch'uan Commandery. Shu's nephew was one of the 'Eight Elite' (pa-chün) leaders of the dissident partisans and had been given the propagandist label of 'the most generous friend in all-under-heaven'.[15]

The honours paid to Ch'en Shih were equally high. It was said that the Ducal Ministers at the court often publicly expressed their uneasiness because they had risen to such high offices while Ch'en Shih had not. There were several proposals to appoint Shih a Ducal Minister, but Shih repeatedly refused the honour. When Shih died in A.D. 187, the Regent of State sent a special messenger to attend the mourning service in which more than thirty thousand persons from all over the realm participated, some of them mourning as if for their own father.[16]

All this can only be understood in the context of the propagandist fever and partisan feeling which the ch'ing-i movement had aroused in élite circles. In a long discourse in the Han-chi Hsün Yüeh strongly censured these tendencies:

Those gentlemen violated the precept of proper conduct [li]. Those petty men transgressed the proscription of law. They speedily roamed about, overstepping their sphere of responsibilities and exceeding proper limits... They circumvented the respect due to their own father or elder brothers, transferring it to their guests and friends whom they treated with high honour. They thinned out the mutual obligations between blood relations and thickened the affection between friends and partisans. They neglected the rule of self-cultivation and curried favour with the multitude... In this manner, the current fashion was moulded and the correct Way was corrupted.[17]

This acrimonious comment on the type of political activity which many of the Hsün notables had followed, and on the kind of honour and eulogy which had been accorded Yüeh's own grandfather and uncles, seems to represent that effort of reflective self-criticism which characterizes Hsün Yüeh's thinking and writing in the subsequent Chien-an period.[18]

To return to the early part of Hsün Yüeh's life, a turning point was reached when Yüeh was twenty years old. The rapid intellectual and social elevation of the Hsün clan was shortly followed by disastrous events at the imperial court. The coup d'état in 168 took the lives of two top leaders of the anti-eunuch literati and led to the imprisonment and violent death of many of their partisans, including at least one of Hsün Yüeh's second cousins. The involvement of other members of the extended Hsün family in Ying-ch'uan may be inferred from the blacklist subsequently issued by the court in 176 for the persecution of the partisans" relatives.[19] Hsün Shuang's biography also mentions that he suffered under the *tang-ku* persecution for more than ten years.[20]

The involvement of Hsün Yüeh himself in this persecution is not explicitly mentioned, but it may be implied in a subsequent passage in Yüeh's ' Biography ', which reads: ' During the time of Emperor Ling [A.D. 168–89], when the palace eunuchs were in power, many of the literati retired to live in seclusion. Yüeh also lived in seclusion under the pretext of illness. His contemporaries hardly knew him. Only his paternal cousin Hsün Yü treated him with extraordinary esteem.' [21] It seems clear from this statement that Hsün Yüeh was affected by the persecution and also was forced to lead an ' underground ' existence like many other anti-eunuch partisans under the *tang-ku* measures. It is also probable that he lived with his uncle Hsün Shuang in the latter's hidden residence, known only to a few intimate relatives in the family including Hsün Yü, who remained active in the secret missions organized by the persecuted élite.

The imperial persecution produced an indelible impact on the youthful Hsün Yüeh. Many years later, when reflecting upon the awesomeness of the imperial rule, Hsün Yüeh characterized the dynastic rulers under six categories: the kingly ones, the orderly ones, the merely surviving ones, the grieving ones, the precarious ones, and the doomed ones. While he heartily exalted the kingly rulers, he unreservedly denounced the doomed ones, as witnessed in one of his discourses in the *Han-chi*:

He who confides himself to the crooked traducers, whom he employs in office, and banishes his loyal and virtuous [ministers from the court] . . . who, [in a fit of] anger, inflicts punishment much more severe than that which the law prescribes, who continues his misconduct and conceals his faults, blocks the way of the loyal and the virtuous, and executes those who give him honest admonition, may be called a doomed ruler . . . A doomed ruler is destined to perish.[22]

Hsün Yüeh tended to take an even gloomier view of dynastic rulers in his discussion of ' The Nine Conditions of the State ' in the *Shen-chien*. Here he characterized a ' well-ordered state ' as the only promising one out of a total of nine potential conditions of dynastic rule, and painted the rest of them in the darkest colours.[23]

In the light of the bitter struggles between the literati and the eunuchs and the *tang-ku* persecution directed by the latter, there is little doubt who had been the ' crooked traducers ' whom the doomed ruler had employed in office and what had been the ' punishments much more severe than that which the law prescribes ' inflicted upon the loyal and the virtuous.

In parallel with this definition of the ' six categories of Rulers ', Hsün Yüeh set out six categories of court ministers: the sage type, the virtuous type, the upright type, the ordinary type, the favouritist type and the deceitful type, and he concealed none of his aversion for those who enjoyed the illicit favour and intimacy of the ruler.[24] Hsün Yüeh's censure of those who had intimate access to a ruler was as overtly stated in another discourse in the *Han-chi*, which reads:

Oh, those favourites inside the palace, those intimate attendants, those wet-nurses, those drivers and bodyguards of the ruler have been causing trouble [to the state] ever since remote antiquity . . .

Their nature is not consonant with the Way; their intellect cannot com-prehend matters; in their service to the ruler, they follow only the dictates of their desires and seek only what is profitable; they assume the pose of agree-ment and respect in order to please the ruler's eye and ear; they pass off flattering appeasement as loyalty . . . furthermore, they have access [to the ruler] by personally attending at his left and right hand, and enjoy his intimacy morning and evening; they anticipate and attend to the ruler's wishes, and make use of the slightest opportunity to confuse the ruler's mind so as to gratify their own selfish desires; they never think of any farsighted plans and have no consideration of the important affairs of state.

Human nature is such that no one is without inadvertent moments: a ruler may, in a moment of negligence, fail to look into an affair and follow [the evil design of these people]; or he may know that they are wrong but is not able to make the decision to rid himself of them; or he may consider their lowly dealings too trifling and let them have their way; or his mind may be confused so that he completely trusts them; or his eyes may be dazzled so that he never has any suspicions of them. Such affairs all evolve from most trifling [beginnings] and develop into major [crises] with im-measurably subversive and utterly destructive effects [to the state], and doing the greatest harm to virtue.

Therefore, an enlightened ruler should trust only the high-ranking ministers and employ only the upright and the straight; he should never heed the request of those favourites inside the palace and those intimate attendants and flatterers.[25]

Hsün Yüeh's aversion to those who enjoyed the intimacy of a ruler again reflects his bitter experience under the repressive *tang-ku* measures directed by the eunuchs.

Although he wrote that 'an enlightened ruler should trust only the high-ranking ministers and employ only the upright and the straight', the chances of putting such a precept into practice in Han times were small. In another discourse in the *Han-chi*, Hsün Yüeh discusses the tragic fates of several meritorious scholars and officials during the enlightened reign of Emperor Wen (179–157 B.C.) of the Former Han dynasty, concluding his laments as follows:

To recognize a sage is difficult; to employ the proper man is not easy. This has been the difficulty for loyal ministers ever since ancient times. Even in an enlightened age (as that of Emperor Wen), they still had such [difficulties]. How much worse if they were living under unruly sovereigns or unenlightened rulers? ... This is why the loyal ministers wept blood and the virtuous scholars had their hearts broken.[26]

Under such circumstances, one may ask, how should a loyal and virtuous minister behave? The answer is given in yet another discourse in the *Han-chi*, which reads:

A person of exceptional intelligence will not be accepted by the world, a person of exceptional [excellence of] conduct will not be tolerated by his contemporaries. This is why such men in ancient times retired [from actually serving the state]. There are times when even though a man retires, he still cannot save himself; therefore they desert society and hide themselves in deep seclusion. Although heaven is high above, they dare not hold up their heads, and although earth is thick below, they dare not stamp their feet, lest they touch something dangerous.
The Ode reads:

> 'We say of heavens that they are high,
> But I dare not but stoop under them.
> We say of the earth that it is thick,
> But I dare not but walk daintily on it.
> Alas for the men of this time!
> Why are they such cobras and efts?'[27]

If basically a man dare not stand up in human society, how will he dare to stand up at the Imperial Court? If he cannot stand up alone against calamity, how will he dare to stand up against the age? If an innocent person can be falsely and slanderously accused, how will he dare to make [the slightest] offence [against those in power]? If even he who keeps his mouth shut can be defamed, who will dare to speak out?

Even if a man hides himself in deep seclusion, he will still be unable to save himself. That is why Ning-wu-tzu feigned stupidity and Chieh-yü acted the part of a madman; [28] these are [occasions of] extreme difficulty. If a man gives no thought to [feigning] stupidity and [acting] mad, he will not be able to keep himself safe in this world... That is why Ch'ü Yüan grudgingly drowned himself [29] and Pao Chiao resentfully exerted himself to death; [30] these are [occasions of] deepest sorrow.

These men feared that even after they had died, their bodies would not be buried deeply, far from the [evil] spirits; consequently, Hsü Yen tied a stone to [his body] and [jumped] into the sea; [31] Shen-tu Ti put himself into an earthen jar and [sank it] into the river; [32] these are occasions of utter bitterness. How mournful! Considering the spaciousness of the Universe, is it not heart-breaking to note that so minute an individual could not find a place to situate his body?

Therefore, the ancient people who feared troubles and wanted to evade them would use tricks to keep themselves safe, bending the straight to make it crooked, grinding the square to make it round, dirtying the cleanness of the white silk, and denying their own enlightened and upright conscience... To change life from death, safety from destruction – How difficult! [33]

In this discourse, the despair of the recluse is vividly conveyed – a despair which might have come from Hsün Yüeh's own personal experience as a youthful scholar living in seclusion for more than ten years under the imperial persecution.

In all of these discourses, Hsün Yüeh's attitude toward the literati is extremely sympathetic, while his attitude toward the imperial rulers tends to be very critical. In fact, his attitude toward the imperial rulers is so unfavourable that it seems inconsistent with Hsün Yüeh's posture as a loyalist at the Chien-an court. The contradiction becomes more remarkable when it is recalled that most of these discourses appeared in the *Han-chi*, an apologia produced under the aegis of the last Han ruler. There are, as will be discussed in a latter section, some ideological and historiographical reasons why Hsün Yüeh should have included these strictures on the Han rulers in the *Han-chi*, but these do not obscure the fact that Hsün Yüeh's view of the Han dynasty and its ruling house was highly complex.[34]

Since many of Hsün Yüeh's strictures on the Han throne were to some extent incongruous with his later position at the Han court, it is probable that many of them may have been conceived and written before his first appointment to the Han court at Hsü in A.D. 196–7. Hsün Yüeh's unfavourable comments on the Han court, his aversion to those having intimate access to the dynastic rulers, and his sympathy toward the wronged literati, were all highly representative of the attitudes of the *ch'ing-i* dissidents in the anti-eunuch protest movement which preceded the collapse of dynastic power and the Chien-an ' restoration '.

Hsün Shuang (whose unorthodox teachings largely reflected the view of the militant faction of the *ch'ing-i* protestors) had a very strong influence on the formative period of Hsün Yüeh's life.[35] In Yüeh's writings, the authority of Hsün Shuang is cited on many occasions.[36] In a discourse in the *Han-chi* on Confucian scholarship in Han times, Yüeh gave unreserved praise to Shuang's interpretation of the *Book of Changes*.[37] The ideas of change and permanence, revolution and restoration, and many dialectical concepts, which underlay Shuang's *I-ching* commentaries, also became the basic criteria in Yüeh's own reflections.[38]

Among Hsün Shuang's scholarly works was a *Han-yü* (Remarks on Han Affairs). According to Shuang's biography in the *Hou-Han shu*, the *Han-yü* was a book ' in which Hsün Shuang collected his accounts of the Han events, including both the praiseworthy and the blameworthy ones, so as to provide warning lessons to his time '.[39] Since Hsün Yüeh also expressly stated in the *Han-chi* that his discourses on Han events were intended to be a warning to his times,[40] it may be postulated that the motivation of both works was similar. It may be surmised that some of Hsün Yüeh's strictures on the Han court may have reflected a common attitude of the Hsün clan under the *tang-ku* persecutions. So Hsün

Yüeh's pronouncement that ' a doomed ruler is destined to perish ' may be a reiteration of Hsün Shuang's remark in his *I-ching* commentary that ' an unqualified [character] occupying the emperor's position will be destroyed and thrown away.' [41]

The author of the *Hou-Han shu*, by placing Hsün Yüeh's biography after that of Hsün Shuang and by using the following identical descriptions of Shuang and Yüeh, ' Shuang . . . at the age of twelve was able to discourse on the *Ch'un-ch'iu* ' and ' Yüeh . . . at the age of twelve was able to discourse on the *Ch'un-ch'iu* ', thus gives strong hints of the solidarity of the extended Hsün family and of the transmission of scholarship from one generation to the next in that family. In Yüeh's writings, the scholarly tradition of the Hsün found its ultimate fruition.

Hsün Yüeh's plight under the imperial persecution continued from 168, when he was twenty, until 184 when the Yellow Turban Rebellion compelled the Han court to abrogate the *tang-ku* measures. Hsün Yüeh was then thirty-six years of age. His ' Biography ' makes no mention of Hsün Yüeh's activities during the year of popular insurrection, although at this time Ying-ch'uan became a major field of battle. Since up to this point none of the Hsün had risen to high positions in the court service, Hsün Yüeh in all probability was still living among his clansmen in the Ying-ch'uan area. According to the record, Hsün Shuang was the first among the hitherto dissident Hsün to turn loyalist in the face of armed rebellion. He was specifically invited by Wang Yün, the newly appointed Imperial Commissioner of Yü Province, to serve on his staff in the campaign against the rebels, while other members of the Hsün clan were making preparations to protect themselves in the troubled area.[42]

After the Yellow Turban rebellion, the struggles between the eunuchs and the anti-eunuch alliance raged on at the court until the *coup d'état* on 22–3 September A.D. 189. This was then followed by Tung Cho's destruction of Loyang in April A.D. 190. The condition of Hsün Yüeh's life in these turbulent years again is not clear. In A.D. 189, his uncle Hsün Shuang, at the age of sixty-two, was abruptly appointed by Tung Cho to the post of Ducal Minister (*Ssu-k'ung*) at the Han court.[43] Meanwhile Yüeh's cousin Hsün Yü had left the capital for Ying-ch'uan, where he subsequently led his clansmen to join forces with Han Fu in the eastern provinces.[44] (Han Fu was then co-operating with Yüan Shao in the alliance against Tung Cho.) When Hsün Yü and his clansmen arrived in the Province of Chi, Han Fu had already been deposed by Yüan Shao.[45] In A.D. 191, Hsün Yü gave his support to another leader, Ts'ao Ts'ao.[46] Some of the Hsün clansmen went over with him to Ts'ao Ts'ao, while others remained in Yüan Shao's force.[47]

If Hsün Yüeh remained in his native commandery during the Tung

Cho crisis, he must have followed Hsün Yü to the eastern provinces and subsequently joined Ts'ao Ts'ao's force some time in A.D. 191, for it is stated in the dynastic history that the whole commandery of Ying-ch'uan was sacked by Tung Cho's marauding soldiers shortly after A.D. 192.[48] On the other hand, Yüeh might have left Ying-ch'uan and accompanied Hsün Shuang on his journey to Loyang in A.D. 189 and remained there. Hsün Shuang died in A.D. 190. Hsün Yu (A.D. 157–214, one of Yüeh's nephews) meanwhile was plotting against Tung Cho; when the plot was discovered, Tung Cho hurriedly removed the Han court together with the whole populace of Loyang to the old Former Han capital of Chang-an.[49] The miserable plight of the court retinue and the civilian masses in the hands of Tung Cho and his followers has already been described.[50] If Yüeh had accompanied Hsün Shuang to Loyang in A.D. 189, there would be little likelihood that he could have escaped the plight of the other residents of Loyang in those turbulent years. Thus, whether Yüeh stayed in Ying-ch'uan or accompanied Hsün Shuang to Loyang, he must have experienced a most difficult and hazardous change in his life during the tumultuous years A.D. 190–6, an experience which shaped his later intellectual life when he served at the ' restored ' Han court.

SERVICE AT THE 'RESTORED' HAN COURT, A.D. 196–209

The status and outlook of the Hsün family had changed considerably in the latter half of the second century. It had risen from being the family of a local notable to being one of the high élite. This change was consummated during the Tung Cho debâcle, when Hsün Shuang was promoted to the highest court rank of Ducal Minister, while the home base of the Hsün in Ying-ch'uan was utterly destroyed by marauding soldiers. The extended Hsün family was fragmented. One part (Hsün Shuang and Hsün Yu) fell under Tung Cho's control; another fragment (Hsün Yü and others) joined Yüan Shao's anti-Tung Cho alliance; those who remained in Ying-ch'uan perished in the subsequent civil warfare and anarchy. Those members in Yüan's alliance were further dispersed when Hsün Yü left the Yüan camp to join with Ts'ao Ts'ao; some members of the family followed Yü and some (Hsün Shen, Yü's brother, was one of them) chose to stay in the Yüan camp.[51] The latter group seems to have been decimated when Yüan's forces were finally routed by Ts'ao in 200–5, though we know that at least one of Hsün Shen's sons, Hung, was later active in minor élite circles during the Wei dynasty.[52] One thing which is quite clear is that at the beginning of the third century the Hsün were no longer provincial notables but had become simple court aristocrats; their prestige and influence were limited to the court bureaucracy, and they no longer had solid support from a local power base.[53]

The whereabouts of Hsün Yüeh during these turbulent years is not clear. The 'Biography of Hsün Yüeh' in the *Hou-Han shu*, after glossing over this part of Yüeh's life, goes on to state that 'Yüeh was first invited to government service at the office of the General Controlling the East [*Chen-tung chiang-chün*] Ts'ao Ts'ao.' [54] According to the *San-kuo chih* (History of the Three Kingdoms), Ts'ao received this title in the sixth lunar month (14 July–11 August) of 196, about five months after he had dispatched a small army to escort the emperor and the court retinue back to Loyang and one month before his personal audience there with the Han emperor. Ts'ao retained that title for three months and was promoted to the post of Grand General in the ninth month (10 October–8 November) of the same year, when the Han court was formally 'restored' at Hsü.[55]

If Hsün Yüeh had been in Hsün Shuang's company at Loyang in A.D. 189, he would have fallen into the hands of Tung Cho and subsequently accompanied the court retinue in their difficult journey to and from Ch'ang-an, thus coming into contact with the Ts'ao camp for the first time in the sixth lunar month of 196. On the other hand, if Hsün Yüeh had remained with his other family members in Ying-ch'uan, he would have been among those Hsün clansmen who followed Hsün Yü to join Yüan Shao and then subsequently switched to Ts'ao's camp in 191. In that case, Yüeh's first contact with Ts'ao Ts'ao could have come at any time during the five years before Ts'ao's ascendence to power.

The timing of Hsün Yüeh's first official appointment was important in determining his allegiance. As the record shows, even though he might have joined the Ts'ao camp some time before the Chien-an 'restoration', he did not receive any formal appointment from Ts'ao Ts'ao prior to Ts'ao's own submission to the court. In other words, Hsün Yüeh received his first appointment from Ts'ao Ts'ao only in the months after Ts'ao himself had formally declared his own loyalty to the Han court and had received his official title from the court in return. This meant that Hsün Yüeh received his official patronage only vicariously through Ts'ao Ts'ao and that he owed his ultimate allegiance to the Han sovereign, Emperor Hsien.[56]

According to the 'Biography', Hsün Yüeh was subsequently appointed to be a Gentleman-Attendant of the Yellow Gates (*Huang-men shih-lang*). He was later appointed Custodian of the Secret Archives (*Mi-shu chien*) and concurrently as Serving Within the Palace (*Chi-shih chung*) some time before 198, and was promoted to the rank of Palace Attendant (*Shih-chung*) some time before 200, still holding his office as Custodian of the Secret Archives.[57]

The posts of Gentlemen-Attendant, Serving Within The Palace, and

Palace Attendant all belonged to the category of ' palace service ' inside the emperor's personal residence, to be distinguished from the category of outer ' court office ' in the central administrative bureaucracy. Since these officials enjoyed special access to the emperor's person, they had developed considerable influence over the emperor in their advisory capacity, and in Former Han times had gradually formed a powerful ' inner court '. With the abolition of the ' inner court ' under the Later Han rule, the officials who held such titles were much reduced in numbers, their functions were generally taken over by the eunuchs, and their access to the emperor was blocked by the palace eunuchs.[58] After Yüan Shao's massacre of the palace eunuchs in A.D. 189, the ' palace service ' system was revived so as to induce members of the literati to render their personal service to the emperor in lieu of the eunuchs.[59] However, the dynasty was by then approaching an end. During the Chien-an era, the Han emperor was only a puppet and his attendants in the Palace Court could merely ' fold their hands and discourse on the Way '. The power of these attendants depended directly on the power of the reigning emperor.

A similar situation existed with respect to Hsün Yüeh's office as the Custodian of the Secret Archives. The origin of Secret Archives (*Mi-shu*) also dated back to Former Han times. In an effort to reverse the Ch'in dynasty's proscription against books, the Former Han emperors established an Imperial Treasury of Books (*Chung Mi-shu*). Important copies of ancient writings collected from the realm were deposited there, and renowned scholars were appointed to collate and edit these writings.[60] A formal office of the Custodian of the Secret Archives was said to have been created by the Emperor Huan of the Later Han in 159.[61] With the elimination of eunuch service at the palace and the transference of the office of Master-of-writing (*Shang-shu*) to the Imperial Secretariat, the Custodian of the Secret Archives inherited two kinds of secretarial function: clerical service inside the emperor's residence (formerly performed by the eunuch *Chung shang-shu*), and clerical service of the court (formerly performed by the Masters-of-writing, *Shang-shu*). Whenever there were governmental policies or measures needing sanction from the titular Son-of-Heaven, memorials on these matters were submitted to the Palace Court and the imperial sanction was given in formal decrees emanating from that office. In other words, they had all to go through Hsün Yüeh's hands.[62]

However, during the Chien-an era the pivot of real power was not in the hands of the emperor or in his court bureaucracy, but in the hands of Ts'ao Ts'ao and his personal associates. The official duties of Hsün Yüeh as the Custodian of the Secret Archives at the Palace Court were thus mainly confined to the ideological legitimation of the Han–Ts'ao régime and to maintaining the symbolic sacrosanctity of the titular court, in order to project the traditional image of the sovereign ruler as a Sage in the moral and intellectual realm.

Despite its lack of real power, the importance of the Palace Court in the early years of the Chien-an reign may be inferred from the presence at the court assembly of Hsün Yü, who in addition to being acting Prefect of the Imperial Secretariat, also held the title of Palace Attendant.[63] According to the *San-kuo chih* and the *Hou-Han shu*, Hsün Yü was widely acknowledged as leader of the civilian élite of the Chien-an régime and as the chief architect of the Han restoration at Hsü. Among his protégés were such prominent figures as Chung Yu (who later became the first Chancellor of the Wei Kingdom founded by Ts'ao Ts'ao's son), Ch'en Ch'ün (who became a Ducal Minister, *Ssu-k'ung*, of the Wei Kingdom and who later formulated the famous ' Nine-grade and Objective Evaluation of Personnel System ', *Chiu-p'in chung-cheng fa*), Tu Hsi (Ts'ao Ts'ao's Chief Military Counsellor), and Ssu-ma I (head of the Ssu-ma family which later ruled over a temporarily reunified China as the Chin Dynasty in 280).[64]

The ' Biography of Hsün Yüeh ' mentions that Yüeh, Hsün Yü, and the arrogant descendant of Confucius, K'ung Jung, ' all attended on the emperor at the Palace Court, where they gave their counsel and discourses day and night '.[65] Hsün Yü by that time was preoccupied with counselling Ts'ao Ts'ao on important military decisions and with setting up the government apparatus for the ' restored ' imperial court at Hsü.[66] Nonetheless, he too felt compelled to attend the Palace Court assemblies.

A private ' Biography of Hsün Yü ' (*Yü pieh-chuan*) mentions that ' From the time that Yü became the Prefect of the Imperial Secretariat, he often wrote memorials on state affairs. But before he died [in 212], he burned and destroyed all these memorials. Therefore, his marvellous counsels and secret proposals cannot now all be known.'[67] This indicates the essential difference between Hsün Yü and Hsün Yüeh in personal disposition and in official posture. Hsün Yü was a man of action. His principal concern was with current issues and with the formulation and execution of policy. Hsün Yüeh was basically a scholar. Although he was not unconcerned with current issues, both his disposition and his official responsibility inclined him to give ideological guidance to governmental policy and to deliberate upon the long-range effects of administrative measures – that is, literally, ' to sit and deliberate on the Way ' (*tso-erh lun-tao*).[68]

A Sung critic, Hu San-hsing (1230–1302), commenting on the three Hsün notables (Yüeh, Yü and Yu) of the Chien-an era, opined that while Hsün Yü and Hsün Yu were geniuses of intrigue, Hsün Yüeh was an honest but impractical scholar, which was why Ts'ao Ts'ao entrusted Yü and Yu with important administrative duties and left Hsün Yüeh to care for the emperor's affairs.[69] Hu San-hsing's judgement on the character of the three Hsüns is probably correct. But he left out of account the fact that Hsün Yü also attended the Han emperor at the palace, and he quite under-estimated the close relationship between Hsün Yü and Hsün Yüeh.

The 'Biography of Hsün Yüeh' specifically notes the exceptionally high regard which Hsün Yü had for Hsün Yüeh during the early and obscure period in their lives.[70] It was probably Hsün Yü who persuaded Hsün Yüeh (as well as other Hsün clansmen) to emigrate from Ying-ch'uan. It was also Hsün Yü, the right-hand man of Ts'ao Ts'ao, who probably recommended Hsün Yüeh first to Ts'ao's service and subsequently to court appointments. It seems clear that, because of the high esteem in which he held his cousin, Hsün Yü was instrumental in placing Yüeh in a position of great prestige and that in return Yüeh's ideas guided, to a certain extent, the political actions of Yü.

The 'Biography of Hsün Yüeh' mentions that the Han emperor was 'favourably inclined toward the canonical traditions'.[71] In 190–1, when the Han court was under Tung Cho's domination, Wang Yün, who had been put in charge of the court bureaucracy by Tung Cho, took special care to preserve the sacred archives of the court. As a special measure, the Confucian canon on filial piety, *Hsiao-ching*, was selected for specific honour.[72] In 193, when the Han emperor and his retinue were still in the hands of Tung Cho's feuding lieutenants, the court held a special state examination in which more than forty Confucian students passed, and received court appointments. And the Han emperor personally paid a state visit to the Imperial Academy. In 194, the emperor revived and himself performed the ritual of 'tilling the Sacred Field' (*Chi-t'ien*).[73] All these gestures were probably designed to bolster the dignity of the imperial court and to impress their military captors.[74]

In Hsün Yüeh's writings, a similar concern for the sacred image of the court was frequently expressed.[75] And in a counsel offered to Ts'ao Ts'ao, Hsün Yü said that 'moral education [*chiao-hua*], and military campaigns [*cheng-fa*] must be used together' and suggested that the régime should

gather together from all-under-heaven the great, talented and versatile Confucian scholars to study and discourse on the six Confucian classics, to edit and publish the historical records and commentaries, to preserve the ancient and modern scholastic traditions, to simplify those complicated and copious works, so as to single out the sacred truth and to exalt the study of ritual, and gradually to improve the reforming influence of education, so that kingliness and sageness may complement each other.[76]

Ts'ao Ts'ao, however, had no inclination towards such ideas. Politically and financially, his régime was not in a position to support any such grand design. Besides, although Ts'ao agreed with the idea of a leadership ' strong in earthly means but complying with the precept of propriety ', this was conceivably intended to refer to a much more lowly plan than that of ' kingliness and sageness ' as proposed by the Hsün. The image conceived by the Hsün properly belonged to the Han sovereign, as indeed it was intended to do during the Chien-an reign. Ts'ao had submitted to the mystique of Han rule mainly as a measure of expediency. He would not expand the mystique into an all-encompassing one, and certainly not in such a way as to encumber his own policy.[77]

The Hsün, on the other hand, had a vital interest in bolstering the sanctity of the throne on which the prestige and influence of the titular court and its bureaucrat-aristocrats depended. Further analysis shows that the Hsün were mainly responsible for gathering together the cultivated élite at Hsü. Many of the junior élite in the Chien-an period who later became the founders of the aristocratic establishment in medieval China were first recruited to the Han–Ts'ao régime by Hsün Yü. The list included Hsi Lü, Hua Hsin, Wang Lang, Hsün Yüeh, Hsün Yu, Tu Hsi, Hsin P'i, Chao Yen, Hsi Chih-ts'ai, Kuo Chia, Yen Hsiang, Wei K'ang, Chung Yu, Ch'en Ch'ün, and Ssu-ma I. Many in the list later rose to the rank of Chancellor, Ducal Minister, and Minister. The last of them, Ssu-ma I, eventually founded the family which usurped power from the Ts'ao–Wei ruler.[78]

Chung Yu, the Chancellor of the Ts'ao–Wei kingdom, was reported to have thought that ever since the death of Yen Hui, the most virtuous of the disciples of Confucius, only Hsün Yü had attained that level of perfect virtue. Once Yu was asked to compare himself with Yü, and he replied that all the officers of the Ts'ao régime were simply subordinates of Ts'ao, but Hsün Yü was partly Ts'ao's teacher and partly his friend – there could be no comparison at all.[79] Ssu-ma I, who received the posthumous title of Emperor Hsüan from the Chin dynasty, was also recorded to have said that while he had learned indirectly from the ancient classics about the worthies of remote antiquity he could personally give testimony to a unique worthy in the contemporary world, that is, ' the honourable lord Hsün ', Hsün Yü, who excelled all the other worthies that he knew of in the last hundred years or so.[80]

Ts'ao Ts'ao, a skilled politician, could not have failed to sense the menace to his power represented by the Hsün leadership. But he needed the prestige and the influence of the élite concentrated together in the civilian bureaucracy. His attitude was that of limited compromise. He tolerated the towering prestige of the élite to an extent, while he preserved tightly in his own hands the real power of government, control of the army and of the local power bases. Furthermore, he was able to counter Hsün Yü's influence by recruiting at least one of the Hsün notables, the very different Hsün Yu, to the hardcore of his own Ts'ao faction. The balance and the contrast between the influences of the two Hsün may be seen in a recorded saying of Ts'ao Ts'ao, that 'Hsün Yü promoted all the good unceasingly; Hsün Yu eliminated all the bad elements, also unceasingly.' [81]

With the influences and pursuits of the two Hsün thus counter-balancing one another in the sphere of real politics, the main task of bolstering the ritual dignity and the intellectual respectability of the Han court was therefore exerted through Hsün Yüeh's exiguous office. And Hsün Yüeh, in his role as Custodian of the Secret Archives at the Palace, seems to have carried out this task quite exemplarily, especially during the first five years of the Chien-an reign, 196–200. An important part of this task was the compilation of the *Han-chi*, finished in the fifth year of Chien-an. [82]

The basic plan for the *Han-chi* had probably been written by Hsün Yüeh before his appointment to the Chien-an court. And this outline probably contained a summary of the accounts and comments on Han events privately produced by Hsün Shuang, echoing his critical attitude toward the throne in the line of the *ch'ing-i* protest. [83] The finished compilation of *Han-chi* as it was commissioned by the Emperor Hsien, however, was to produce a formal apologia for the reigning imperial dynasty. This indicates that Hsün Yüeh's political posture underwent a profound change after he entered into service at the Han court. Like the majority of the Chien-an élite, Hsün Yüeh was a dissident-turned-loyalist, and the *Han-chi* shows considerable evidence of this. [84]

The political and intellectual ambiguity of Hsün Yüeh's major works, the *Han-chi* and the *Shen-chien*, will be analyzed in detail in the following chapters. Suffice it here to mention only the contradiction in Hsün Yüeh's attitude toward the literati and the other élite groups, as shown in the *Han-chi*. The present *Han-chi* contains several discourses expressing the author's severe condemnation of the unruly élite; this somewhat contradicts Hsün Yüeh's otherwise sympathetic attitude toward the literati.

Hsün Yüeh's criticism of the self-will of the élite was, first of all, conveyed in his comments on three types of 'disorderly' people (*yu*). These were: (1) *yu-hsia*, the disorderly stalwarts; (2) *yu-shui*, the intriguers; and (3) *yu-hsing*, the treacherous partisans. Hsün Yüeh denounced all of them as enemies of the moral order. According to Hsün Yüeh, *yu-hsia* were 'those who establish their strong and imposing positions so as to coerce and threaten others; those who linked together their private associations so as to build up their strength in the realm '. *Yu-shui* were ' those who rely on their persuasive language and devise intriguing plots, who traverse and gallop across the land, so as to manipulate the political situation of the time '. *Yu-hsing* were ' those who contrive the appearance of kind-heartedness [*jen*] so as to be popular in their time, and make partisans of their peers to produce vain prestige, so that they may enjoy power and profit in politics '.[85] In two other discourses in the *Han-chi*, Hsün Yüeh also criticized the big landlords and the regional warlords (*Chu-hou*, lit. feudal lords) as enemies of the imperial authority.[86]

Hsün Yüeh's criticism of the regional warlords can be understood in the context of the political situation of the Chien-an era. But his attack on three types of ' disorderly ' people poses an interesting question. The three *yu* denounced by Hsün Yüeh are historical groups closely related to the ' middle-class ' élite, i.e. the literati and the local magnates, from which many leaders of the anti-eunuch partisans in Later Han times had originated.[87] Not only do Hsün Yüeh's descriptions of the three *yu* tally with the activities of these leaders in their anti-eunuch (anti-dynasty) agitation; but many of these leaders were in fact referred to by their contemporaries as ' *yu-hsia* ' (disorderly stalwarts or knights-errant). These included at least two of the leaders, Yüan Shao and Ts'ao Ts'ao, of the partisans' secret mission in which Hsün Yü had been a member.[88] Moreover, the author of the *Hou-Han shu* in his Introduction to the ' Collective Biographies of the Persecuted Partisans ' (*Tang-ku lieh-chuan*) clearly traces the Later Han partisan activities to the tradition of *yu-hsia, yu-shui,* and *yu-hsing.*[89]

Hsün Yüeh's criticism of these groups and the activities of the three *yu* was therefore clearly inconsistent with the earlier political involvement of his own family in the anti-eunuch movements. It thus seems to represent Yüeh's sense of the obligations of his new position at the court, as well as his conscious effort at self-criticism. This impression is strengthened by a reservation which Hsün Yüeh makes in the last part of his attack on the three *yu*. He reasoned that: ' *Yu-hsia* had its origin in strong perseverance, in resisting prolonged pressures, in never forgetting the words of a promise, in accepting a dangerous mission in order to save the world in difficult times and to help one's peers.' And that: ' *Yu-shui* had its origin in carrying diplomatic missions to the far-away quarters and in not disgracing the command of one's lord ... thus deserving the people's admiration.' And that: ' *Yu-hsing* had its origin in moral virtue, in human-heartedness [*jen*] and in the sense of justice [*i*], in the sympathy for all and in the capacity to tolerate or to embrace the multitude ... so that all might advance to moral excellence in time and joyfully follow the Way.' Each of the tendencies could be a moral virtue, therefore, if it were done in accordance with the proper mean (*cheng*), but it would become a vice when carried to the extreme.[90]

Even in Hsün Yüeh's strictures on the three *yu* carried to excess, he censured only excessive contact and partisanship among non-family members. By implication, he still upheld the solidarity of the family, a basic postulate in Hsün Shuang's *I-ching* teaching.[91] The difference between Hsün Shuang's advocacy of family solidarity and Hsün Yüeh's ideal of family unity is that in Hsün Shuang's teaching, the interest of the family was seen as opposed to that of the state, whereas in Hsün Yüeh's ideal, the apparent opposition was resolved in the concept of a hierarchic and yet holistic world, encompassing heaven, earth and men. The changing political and ideological stance of the Hsün as dissidents-turned-loyalists turned a complete cycle in two generations – from Hsün Shuang's 'anti-Han' *I-ching* commentary to Hsün Yüeh's *Han-chi* apologia.

After finishing the *Han-chi*, Hsün Yüeh seems to have undergone another change in his thinking – a reorientation in the direction of *ch'ing-t'an* evasion and resignation. Some of his reflections in this direction were subsequently recorded in the *Shen-chien*, completed and submitted to the throne in the tenth year of Chien-an (A.D. 205). In this second work, Hsün Yüeh transcended his position as a court historian and developed a new role as an independent thinker.[92] This was, however, the last achievement of his life. He died four years later, and was the only one of the three prominent Palace Attendants of Emperor Hsien to die of a natural cause; the other two, K'ung Jung and Hsün Yü, met violent deaths in 208 and 212 respectively.[93]

5

Hsün Yüeh's works:
The *Han-chi* (Chronicles of Han)

In the *Han-chi hsü* or 'Foreword to the *Han-chi*',[1] the dates and the circumstances of the compiling of the *Han-chi* are mentioned as follows:

In the first year of Chien-an [196], our sovereign made a tour of inspection and arrived at Hsü-ch'ang, so as to control and protect the myriad states. Externally, he ordered the powerful minister [*k'ang-fu*] [2] to conduct punitive campaigns against those who did not submit themselves to the court. Internally, he put the seven governmental affairs in order and properly brightened the sacred reign. He comprehended and studied the canonical works, and perused other classical commentaries and traditions.

In the third year of the reign [198], he decreed that the Custodian of the Secret Archives Serving Within the Palace,[3] Hsün Yüeh, should copy and edit the *Han-shu* [History of the Former Han Dynasty] [4] and summarize its contents. He provided Yüeh with invaluable subsidy, with the *Shang-shu* [Master-of-writing or Imperial Secretariat] supplying papers and writing brushes and the *Hu-pen* [Guards As Rapid As A Tiger] supplying the copying scribes.

Yüeh thence summarized and pieced together the old documents [of the *Han-shu*], selecting sections from the Introductions, Tables, and Memoirs, and he put them together in the Chronicles of Emperors [*Ti-chi*], synchronizing and arranging the exemplary events in the [chronological order of] years and months...Together they made 30 *chüan* [chapters or sections], totalling several hundred thousand characters,[5] of the Chronicles of Emperors [*Ti-chi*]...

Then Yüeh was transferred to be a Palace Attendant. In the fifth year [A.D. 200] of the reign the work was completed.

This *Han-chi hsü* is placed under Hsün Yüeh's name in all existing editions of the *Han-chi*. Although some parts of the foreword, in content and in style, pose some questions concerning the validity of the ascription to him as author, in general his authorship of this document can be accepted. It seems to have been written either by Hsün Yüeh himself in his official capacity as Custodian of the Secret Archives at the Han court or by some of his assistants in that body.[6]

The official reason for compiling the *Han-chi*, as stated in the *Han-chi hsü*, had both an ostensible element and a covert intent. Ostensibly, the compilation was an effort to edit and condense the voluminous *Han-shu* so as to preserve its essence.[7] The *Han-chi hsü* further states that ' the Chronicles would be more concise and would make the [original] work easier to study. It would not undermine the original [*Han-*] *shu* but would be a convenience to [those who] use [it]. This is the professed intention of the present work [the *Han-chi*].' [8] This modest profession was probably made to forestall any uneasiness over the author's motives in the suspicious Ts'ao Ts'ao.

However, despite this apparent modesty of aim, the same *Han-chi hsü* in a later paragraph compares the *Han-chi* to the *Ch'un ch'iu* and other canonical classics of antiquity and declares that ' the import of all these works is the same – they are all renowned ordinances of antiquity . . . So is the import of the history and the chronicles of the Han.' It also declares that the *Han-chi* ' is the permanent teaching of the realm and the prime treasure of canonical writings '.[9]

Supporting these confident declarations there is a solemn enumeration of the intended contents of the *Han-chi* which, according to the *Han-chi hsü*, should consist of the following:

The meritorious deeds of our dynastic Founders and Ancestors; the accomplished rules of our past Emperors; the important ordinances and regulations of our Empire; disastrous and strange occurrences in Heaven and Earth; [accounts of] the meritorious ministers and renowned worthies; their marvellous counsels and good words; their extraordinary virtues and excellent conduct; all that which may set an exemplum or precedent in the ordinance.[10]

All these were obviously intended for the glorification of Han dynastic rule. Since political loyalty to the dynasty had never been absolute in Han or pre-Han China, in a time of political crisis it was imperative for the régime to present an account of its past merits and virtues so as to justify its right to continued rule. The *Han-chi* was thus an apologia for the Han court, as it was designed to enhance the sacrosanctity of the titular ruler and to secure the loyalty of his subjects in a difficult time.[11]

In addition, Hsün Yüeh felt that the Han dynastic history was quite as valuable as that to be found in the *Ch'un-ch'iu* and in the other canonical works relating to the various dynasties in antiquity, and for that reason deserved to take its place among the canonical classics. In making that claim, Hsün Yüeh elevated historical writing to the level of the canonical scriptures. At the same time, he degraded the sacred nature of the Canons by injecting an element of historicity into them. Though the Canons claimed to embody a transcendent truth about the Way, they were seen to be basically histories; their values were man-made and needed to be reiterated, to be confirmed by continued human endeavour.[12] Hence the *Han-chi hsü* stated:

The import of all these works [i.e. the canonical scriptures] is the same. . .
When it [the Way as embodied in these canonical and historical works] was
upheld [by men], it became the accomplished rule. But when it was
abandoned, it fell asunder on earth. When it was envisaged [by men], it
existed. But, when it was neglected, it perished. Therefore, the superior men
must prize it.[13]

So, despite the ostensible or official declaration of intent behind the
Han-chi (to make more concise the record of the Han presented by
the *Han-shu*), the real purpose behind this undertaking was to glorify the
restoration of the dynasty at Hsü and to support the titular sovereign's
claim that he ' was putting governmental affairs in order and properly
brightening the reign, primarily through his comprehension and study of
the canonical works and other classical traditions '.

Hsün Yüeh's feeling about the ' restoration' is apparent in the
panegyrics decorating the Foreword and the Preface of the *Han-chi*,[14]
in which the highly exalted image of the Han Court contrasts sharply
with the fugitive existence of the court and the parasitic nature of the
imperial retinue at the time when Hsün Yüeh was writing, as described
in a previous chapter. But Hsün Yüeh's vindication of the dynastic cause
goes much further than mere lip-service and ornamental cliches. It per-
meates the whole of the *Han-chi*. The following analysis of the organization of the *Han-chi* as we have it today may help to elucidate this point.

The *Han-chi* proper begins with an account of the birth of the Emperor Kao-tsu (reigned 206–195 B.C., founder of the Former Han
dynasty) [15] and concludes with an allusion to the restoration of the Han
by Liu Hsiu (the future Emperor Kuang-wu of the Later Han in A.D.
23).[16] In *chüan* 1, after the prefatory *hsü*, there is a long paragraph
(which appears to be a summary of *Han-shu* 21B : 27b and 25B : 23b)
exalting the ' dominant virtue' (*te*) of the Han dynasty according to the
theory of the Five Elements.[17] This is followed by a statement of the
genealogical claim of the ruling house of Liu to be descended from
the legendary Sage King Yao.[18]

The *Han-chi* proper consists of chronicles of the twelve rulers of the
Former Han divided into thirty *chüan*:

Chüan 1–4	Emperor Kao-tsu (reigned: 206–195 B.C.)
Chüan 5	Emperor Hui (194–188)
Chüan 6	Empress Kao (*née* Lü) (187–180)
Chüan 7–8	Emperor Wen (179–157)
Chüan 9	Emperor Ching (156–141)
Chüan 10–15	Emperor Wu (140–87)
Chüan 16	Emperor Chao (86–74) including the twenty-seven day rule of Prince Ch'ang-i in 74 B.C.)
Chüan 17–20	Emperor Hsüan (73–49)
Chüan 21–3	Emperor Yüan (48–33)
Chüan 24–7	Emperor Ch'eng (32–7 B.C.)

Chüan 28–9	Emperor Ai (6–1 B.C.)
Chüan 30	Emperor P'ing (A.D. 1–5, Wang Mang as regent; 6–8 Wang Mang as acting sovereign; 9–23 Wang Mang as Emperor)

Interspersed with the text of the Chronicles are many *lun* (discourses), in which Hsün Yüeh set down his personal comments on state affairs:

Emperors	Number of *lun*	Tabulation number
Kao-tsu	3	1–3
Hui	3	4–6
(Empress) Kao, *née* Lü	1	7
Wen	5	8–12
Ching	3	13–15
Wu	4	16–19
Chao	1	20
Hsüan	3	21–3
Yüan	4 (5) [a]	24–8
Ch'eng	5 (6)	29–34
Ai	4 (5)	35–9
P'ing	0	

[a] *Lun* 27 (*HC* 23.9b–10b) and *Lun* 28 (*HC* 23.10b–11) have been combined into one single discourse by mistake in all the present editions of the *HC*. For detailed discussion, see Ch'i-yün Ch'en, *Monumenta Serica* 27 (1968), 222–7. The same thing happened with the *lun* in the Chronicles of Emperors Ch'eng and Ai.

In the last *chüan*, after an account of the downfall of the ' New (*Hsin*) Dynasty ' and the tragic death of the ' usurper ' Wang Mang, there is a reference to the comment in Wang Mang's biography in the *Han-shu*, to the effect that Mang did not receive the Mandate of Heaven to rule but was destined to serve as a forerunner who cleared the way for a true sage-ruler (Emperor Kuang-wu of the Later Han) to emerge.[19] This comment is followed by an interesting dialogue between Pan Piao (father of Pan Ku and original author of the *Han-shu*) and the warlord Wei Hsiao. The passage reads:

After Wang Mang's downfall, the Empire fell into chaos. The major war-lords established their rule over provinces and commanderies; the minor ones took control of districts. Kung-sun Shu assumed the title of emperor at Shu [present-day Szechuan]. Wei Hsiao controlled Lung [roughly the present-day Shensi province], and he courted and rallied to his side many élite leaders; Pan Piao was there. . .

Hsiao asked Piao: ' In ancient times, when the Chou dynasty collapsed, the warring states contended with one another and the empire was parti-tioned for many generations before it was pacified again. Would that. . . happen again in the present time?. . .'

Piao's comment reads: ' The rise and fall of the Chou differed from that of the Han. In ancient times, Chou established the five noble ranks to allow the feudal lords to take part in administration.[20] Thus the root and trunk [of the state] were weakened while the branches and leaves became strong and powerful. . The Han followed the Ch'in system and administered the people through the commanderies and districts.[21] Thus no official family could hold power for more than a hundred years... Now the various strong men who control the provinces and commanderies all lack a family background comparable to the seven [pre-Ch'in] feudal houses... and people nowadays all sing their hymns in memory of Han. It is evident that they look up to the Liu [the house of the Han dynasty].'

Hsiao said: 'Your saying is sound so far as the contrast between the Chou and the Han is concerned. But it is quite irrelevant to observe that the ignorant people were used to the rule of the Liu and therefore to say that the Han will rise again. In former times, when the Ch'in lost its *lu* [deer, a homonym of *lu,* meaning official emolument or prerogative] the Liu family chased it and captured it.[22] In that time, did the people already know anything about the Han? '

Piao was impressed by this remark and was distressed by the incessant warfare and calamities of his time. He therefore wrote the *Wang-ming lun* [Discourse on the Mandate of an Emperor].[23]

Hsün Yüeh abstained from making any personal comment on the rule of Wang Mang in *chüan* 30. Instead, he chose to conclude this section by quoting in full the dialogue above from the *Han shu,* together with the text of the ' Discourse on the Mandate of an Emperor ', in which the virtues and the prognostic apparitions sanctifying the mandate of the Liu house were vividly painted. The Discourse ends with Pan Piao's counsel to potential leaders:

Should a strong man recognize this deepest [force], apprehend the danger and the warning...follow the wise path of [the Han loyalists] Ch'en Ying and Wang Ling, repress the improper ambition of Han Hsin and Ying Pu [the Han traitors], reject the misleading theory about ' chasing the *lu* [deer] ', realize that the conferment and the receipt of the sacred vessel [should be made only by the Mandate of Heaven], and not covet that which is impossible to obtain ... then the fortune and blessing he accumulates will flow to his descendants and [he himself] will be able to enjoy the reward of Heaven to the end of his life.[24]

The ' strong man ' concept referred to here is a recurring theme in the *Han-chi.* It appeared many times in Pan Piao's dialogue with the warlord Wei Hsiao. In the *Han-chi hsü,* the term alluded to is the ' powerful minister ' (*k'ang-fu*) and, in the concluding section of the *Han-chi,* the ' strong and virtuous ministers ' (*chiao-chiao tsün-ch'en*).[25] It is obvious that the author implies a specific comparison here. Pan Piao's warning to Wei Hsiao was not only appropriate to the strong men who controlled the provinces and commanderies at the end of the Former Han; it also served as a historical lesson (*chien*) to the new strong men, Ts'ao Ts'ao and others, who controlled the provinces and commanderies in just the same way by the end of the Later Han Dynasty.

Pan Piao's counsel to Wei Hsiao dealt with two historical issues: the political situation of the Ch'un-ch'iu period (8th–5th centuries B.C.) when the Chou court had declined and the feuding states divided the realm, and the notion of dynastic rule as an open game of 'chasing the deer'. These were also issues frequently mentioned by Hsün Yüeh's contemporaries in their political dialogues.[26]

By repeating Pan Piao's counsel, Hsün Yüeh adroitly dismissed the possibility of the empire's continuing fragmentation. Unlike the 'feudalistic' Chou rule, the imperial institutions of the Ch'in and the Han were seen to be so firmly established that a retrogression to a divided empire and flagrant feudalism was impossible. But the continuation of the empire as the form of government did not necessarily mean the continuation of the Han dynasty in particular. Thus, to counter the appealing notion of 'chasing the deer', that the succession to control of the empire could be achieved purely by force of arms and conquest, a mystical interpretation of the Mandate of Heaven as expounded in Pan Piao's 'Discourse on the Mandate of an Emperor' (which constituted the backbone of Later Han conservatism) was reiterated. The lengthy quotation of the *Wang-ming lun* thus properly concluded the *Han-chi* chronicles.

The Chinese believed in precedents and historical parallels. Hsün Yüeh, born some two hundred years later than Pan Piao, was provided with a much stronger argument for the Han cause than the mere expectation on which Piao had based his prophecy of a Han restoration. The restoration of the Liu house by Emperor Kuang-wu was an established and well-remembered fact in Hsün Yüeh's time.[27] This historical precedent became the strongest argument for a further 'restoration', and is a basic postulate in the *Han-chi* apologia.

Hsün Yüeh's *Han-chi* means 'Chronicles of the Han' and yet it covers only the Former Han period.[28] Nonetheless, Hsün Yüeh himself wrote in the epilogue of *Han-chi* that the Chronicles were compiled 'in this four hundred and twenty-sixth year of the Han dynasty', referring to the Former and the Later Han dynasties as a single unit, i.e. from *c.* 206 B.C.–A.D. 200.[29] The same specific remark was made also in the *Han-chi hsü*, in which the year was referred to as 'the four hundred and sixteenth'. Inevitably one asks the question: Why did the *Han-chi* then cover only the two hundred-odd years of the Former Han rule?

Historiography provides an apparent explanation: The *Han-chi* was a 'mere condensation' of the *Han-shu*, which was the 'History of the Former Han Dynasty' ending with Wang Mang's reign. But, just as the court's modest declaration accounts for only the ostensible purport of the undertaking, historiography gives only an apparent answer to the question concerning the contents of the *Han-chi*. For, so far as historiography was concerned, Hsün Yüeh could easily have avoided the confusion by omitting the misleading statement about 'the four hundred odd years' from the foreword and the epilogue.

Whether Hsün Yüeh had the time or indeed the means to expand the *Han-chi* beyond the scope of the *Han-shu* is a separate problem to be dealt with later.[30] However, in an official apologia for the Han rule, the present scope of the *Han-chi* provides a definite advantage. For one thing, if Han rule was to continue after the Chien-an 'restoration' as Hsün Yüeh and other Han loyalists hoped, then the dynasty in Hsün Yüeh's time would still be in continuing existence, not at a terminus justifying a, terminal dynastic history; and, in that sense, no matter how the scope of the *Han-chi* might be expanded, it could not by definition cover the entire time-span of an existing dynasty. In addition, as an historical exemplum, the present scope of the *Han-chi*, containing a complete cycle of the rise, decline and restoration of the Han dynasty in its first 'two hundred odd years', would be an ideal unit for presentation. The Han restoration at the end of this cycle was an accomplished fact, whereas the Chien-an 'restoration' manipulated by Ts'ao Ts'ao remained but a pious fantasy at the time of the compilation of the *Han-chi*. The inclusion of the Later Han period in this work would therefore have reduced rather than enhanced the effect of vindicating the dynasty.[31]

The implied parallels between the Former Han and the Later Han rule, particularly between the Emperor Kuang-wu's restoration in A.D. 25 and the Emperor Hsien's 'restoration' in A.D. 196, as well as between Pan Ku's compilation of the *Han-shu* after the first restoration and Hsün Yüeh's compilation of the *Han-chi* after the Chien-an 'restoration' were skilfully indicated in Hsün Yüeh's epilogue to the *Han-chi*. The epilogue reads in part as follows:

I produced ... this *Han-chi* ... by rewriting the *Han-shu* ... to give a summary view of the past with the expectation that the coming generation will have *chien* [lessons to learn].[32] My epilogue reads:
    ... The Great Han establishes the great lineage... [We should forever] remember the two *Tsu* [Great Ancestors], and the six *Tsung* [Distinguished Ancestors].[33]
    Our enlightening Emperor [Hsien] succeeds to this great lineage, and although he had suffered sorrowful disasters and is harrassed by bitterness, he is born with the heavenly virtue and is destined to establish a great rule. The strong virtuous minister [34] should only be an assistant to the state and help [our emperor] to the very end in pacifying the realm so that virtue shall bring forth blessings.
    When the rebellion is quieted and proper order restored, the great institution will be set to order again. When once military objectives have been achieved, we then ascend to civil programmes.

Following the ritual precedents of the ancients, the emperor commands me, his humble servant, conscientiously to write historical documents to commemorate the meritorious deeds of the past and to recount by-gone events so as to make them clear to those to come and to show a warning lesson to future generations.[35]

In these passages, the parallel is established by the mention of the two *Tsu* (Great Ancestors of the dynasty, i.e. the Emperor Kao-tsu of the Former Han and the Emperor Kuang-wu, with the temple title Shih-tsu, of the Later Han), the six *Tsung* (Distinguished Ancestors of the dynasty, i.e. T'ai-tsung, Emperor Wen; Shih-tsung, Emperor Wu; and Chung-tsung, Emperor Hsüan, all of the Former Han; Hsien-tsung, Emperor Ming; Shu-tsung, Emperor Chang; and Kung-tsung, Emperor An, all of the Later Han), and the compilations of the *Han-shu* and the *Han-chi* respectively.

The effect of these suggestions is clear: now, after the coming of a second restoration, the dynastic history is rewritten to point out the varied courses of action taken by leaders in the past, who either became traitors and perished or remained loyal and prospered; whether the Han empire will have a second true restoration or another tragic usurpation will depend upon the course taken by the present strong man (Ts'ao Ts'ao), to whom the Han loyalist makes his appeal.

The last, but not the least, significant effect of the *Han-chi* as a device for dynastic vindication lies in its annalistic structure, which is a con-scientious imitation of the canonical *Ch'un-ch'iu* (Spring and Autumn).[36] Some critics have pointed out that in abandoning the ' composite ' format of the standard histories (*cheng-shih*) devised by Ssu-ma Ch'ien in the *Shih-chi* and adopted by Pan Ku in the *Han-shu*, and in reverting to the annalistic format similar to that of the archaic *Ch'un-ch'iu* chronicles, Hsün Yüeh represents a profound conservatism in Chinese historio-graphy.[37] In assimilating the *Han-chi* with the *Ch'un-ch'iu*, which was assumed to have been written by Confucius and had the status as a Con-fucian canonical book, Hsün Yüeh intended to impute to his Chronicles much of the mystique of the canonical scriptures.

Like the other historical parallels used by Hsün Yüeh, discussed above, the parallel between the *Han-chi* and the *Ch'un-ch'iu* went much deeper than mere adoption of the annalistic structure. The late Chou epoch (*Ch'un-ch'iu*) as a period of dynastic decline was often alluded to by Hsün Yüeh's contemporaries in their discussions on the Chien-an political situation.[38] Besides, there was in Han times a strong belief that Confucius himself was a ' loyalist ' who wrote the *Ch'un-ch'iu* in a time of utter political turmoil in anticipation of a ' restoration ' of good order to the realm, an anticipation taken by many of the Han Confucians as a prophecy of the rise of the Han.[39]

While the parallel with the *Ch'un-ch'iu* is mainly a matter of mystique, there were other historiographical considerations which caused Hsün Yüeh to revert to the annalistic genre for his *Han-chi*. One of the reasons which Hsün Yüeh stated was that the 'composite' format of the *Han-shu* was too complicated. In the *Han-shu*, the accounts of a single event would appear separately in many different sections of the work, such as the Basic Annals (*pen-chi*), the Tables (*piao*), the Treatises (*chih*), and the Biographies or Memoirs (*chuan*). While the Basic Annals were supposed to provide a coherent outline of the most important accounts of the period, the other individual sections (particularly the biographical sections) tended to be semi-independent, each having a centre of interest of its own. This arrangement was acceptable to the sophisticated historian in the sense that it gave the multiple facets of a particular event. Accordingly, a major event which involved many persons would appear in the Basic Annal (with minor but still important events registered in the Tables, and those which could not be chronologically recounted described in the Treatises); the different viewpoints of those persons about, or their involvement in, the event would be separately assessed in the biographies of different individuals.[40]

Furthermore, following Ssu-ma Ch'ien's own principle in the *Shih-chi*, each individual (except the most infamous ones) would be presented in the most favourable light in his own biography. In such a biography would be found almost all the complimentary accounts or comments on the biographee, while the uncomplimentary ones were likely to be entered elsewhere (for example in the biographies of his critics or enemies). Thus the 'composite' format polarized both factual accounts and value-judgements on historical events.[41] To Hsün Yüeh, the dynastic vindicator, this confusion in the application of praise and blame seemed most urgently in need of rectification.

By adopting a unitary annalistic format in the *Han-chi*, Hsün Yüeh not only simplified the factual narrative by deleting the repetitive accounts in the *Han-shu* but also avoided the complication of a system of multiple value judgments. After all, the *Han-chi* was supposed to be the 'Chronicles of [Our] Emperors' (*Ti-chi*, which was probably the original title of the work), hence the Han emperors and the court constituted the only foci in the narration and evaluation of the political developments of Han China.

The simplified annalistic 'plan' of the *Han-chi* had one definite advantage. In this work, the 'merits' of the Han rulers were recounted in a continuous dynastic succession, thus producing a 'cumulative' effect.

By comparison, the 'marvellous counsels and good words' of the 'meritorious ministers and renowned worthies' were entered as coming from isolated individuals.[42] This tended to reinforce Pan Piao's (and implicitly Hsün Yüeh's) argument that the Liu house of the Han, though declining, still possessed a powerful legacy in its 'cumulative merits', far stronger than that which might be claimed by any of its potential challengers.[43]

All in all, it becomes quite evident from this examination of the format and the conception of the *Han-chi* that Hsün Yüeh's execution of his official role as an apologist for the Han dynasty was exemplarily successful, particularly when one takes into account the pressure of divided loyalty arising from his own personal background and family connections and the political climate of his time.

THE HISTORIAN'S DISCOURSES (*shih-lun*)

Hsün Yüeh was not a mere apologist for the Han court. As he said in the Foreword to the *Han-chi*, the chronicles which he compiled would contain:

1. Ordinances and Precedents; 2. Warning Lessons; 3. Dangerous and Disorderly Situations; 4. Balanced and Just Measures; 5. Military Strategies; 6. Civil Administration and Educational Programmes; 7. Favourable and Good Omens; 8. Disastrous and Abnormal Occurrences; 9. Events of the Cultured Chinese; 10. Events concerning the Four Barbarians; 11. Permanent Ways; 12. Expedient and Unusual Measures; 13. Counsels and Plots; 14. Subversive Persuasions; 15. Arts and Scholarship; 16. Literary Expositions.[44]

Included in this list are certain kinds of material which were often considered dangerous or even seditious, i.e. the 'Dangerous and Disorderly Situations', the 'Disastrous and Abnormal Occurrences', the 'Expedient and Unusual Measures', 'Plots', and 'Subversive Persuasions'.[45] The inclusion of this material in the Chronicles contradicted the aim of the *Han-chi* as a simple apologia for the court. In fact, the original version of the *Han-chi* contained certain commonly tabooed material which was ultimately expurgated from the text by its later editors but was preserved in the T'ang dynasty commentary on the *Han-shu*.[46]

According to Hsün Yüeh's own words, all this material was included in the *Han-chi* because these were matters 'which may be examined against facts and verified; and they rightly constitute counsels of lasting value which may be applied in myriad situations without becoming an inflexible dogma (*pu-ni*)'.[47] This statement deserves special notice. First of all, it indicates Hsün Yüeh's willingness to examine and describe different facets of the Han rule and his intentions to be a conscientious historian whose work would stand the test of verification. If he accomplished this, the *Han-chi* would be almost superior to the canonical classics – not only would it be similar to the Canons in its effect, but it would be more versatile and more readily verifiable. Secondly, the statement illustrates a peculiar Chinese concept of history (*shih*) and of the nature of 'historical lessons' (*chien*). According to the first part of the statement, the *Han-chi* would contain nothing but history – matters which had been established as fact. However, according to the second part of the statement, these matters would not be merely past events; they were matters also concerning the present and the future; they constituted the 'counsels' and 'lessons' applicable to myriad situations – matters transcending space and time (*pu-ni*).[48]

As I have said, the Chinese believe in precedents and historical parallels. Historical events are not merely facts of the past, connected to the present in rigid temporal sequence. They manifest certain patterns which constitute the truth (*tao*, the Way; *kuei*, the rule; or *chien*, the lesson) of the hidden inner world. It is this notion of recurrent patterns of history that gave rise to the traditional Chinese emphasis on historical didacticism, the application of praise-and-blame to events of the past, offering a lasting lesson for the present and the future.[49]

This notion of transcendency in historical didacticism was reinforced by the mixture of classical learning and historical scholarship in Chinese traditional education. Moulded in the tradition of Confucian humanistic learning, the Chinese literati tended to follow two lines of scholarly pursuit. The more dogmatic mind usually looked to the canonical scriptures (*ching*, classics, scriptural authority) for inspiration, while the more realistic mind reflected upon the changing world in the recent past (*shih*, history, archives, factual record). These two lines constituted the broad field of humanistic studies, i.e. 'history' – the 'history' both of remote antiquity (tradition of the Canons providing the idealistic and dogmatic standard for criticism) and the recent past (the mundane affairs of the contemporary world sustaining much of the criticism and re-affirming the superiority of the classical ideals or dogmas). The convergence of these two lines seemed a necessary process, for no one praising Golden Antiquity could forget recent troubles and no one studying recent troubles could avoid contrasting them with antiquity.[50]

The writings of Hsün Yüeh serve as a good example of this convergence of interests. His uncle Hsün Shuang was both a great master of the canonical classics and a highly polemical historian of the Han. In his no longer extant work, the *Han-yü* (Remarks on Han Affairs), he put together his criticism, based on the criteria established by the classics, of the events of the Han dynasty.[51] This work probably formed the background for Hsün Yüeh's *Han-chi*, particularly for the *lun* sections, which gave authoritative judgements on Han events, especially on the conduct of the rulers.[52]

In fact, of the thirty-nine discourses (*lun*) included in the present *Han-chi*, thirty-four were strictures directly or indirectly aimed against the Han throne. The nature and the contents of the thirty-nine *lun* may be classified under four categories:

(a) Discourses on topics of general importance, implying no criticism of the Han throne – total 5 *lun*.

(b) Critical comments on an event, an historical situation, or society at large, implying mild criticism of the Han throne – 11 (or 10) *lun*.

(c) Critical comment on the policy or administrative measures of the court, indicating strong criticism of the Han rulers – 17 *lun*.

(d) Severe and direct criticism of the personal conduct or the character of a Han ruler – 6 (or 7) *lun*.

Tabulated No.	In *Han-chi*	Content or nature of *lun*
1	2: 12b: 14a	a
2	3: 12b	c
3	4: 2a	c
4	5: 4b	c
5	5: 12b–14a	c
6	5: 14ab	c
7	6: 4b–6b	a
8	7: 5b	b
9	7: 5b–6a	b
10	8: 3a–4b	c
11	8: 8b–9a	d
12	8: 16b	d
13	9: 9a	c
14	9: 16b	c
15	9: 17a	c
16	10: 2b–4b	b
17	12: 4b	c
18	13: 13b–14b	d
19	15: 5ab	b
20	16: 13a–14b	d
21	17: 10a	b
22	20: 5b	c
23	20: 11ab	c
24	22: 6ab	d
25	22: 8ab	b
26	23: 6b	b
27	23: 9b–10b	c
28	23: 10b–11b	a
29	24: 13ab	a
30	25: 4a–5b	a

Tabulated No.	In *Han-chi*	Content or nature of *lun*
31	25: 6b–7a	d
32	26: 5b–6a	b
33	27: 8b	c
34	27: 12a	b
35	28: 5b	c
36	28: 5b–6a	c
37	28: 7ab	c
38	28: 9b–10b	b
39	29: 2ab	b (d)

Concerning these *lun*, Hsün Yüeh remarked in his Epilogue to the *Han-chi*: ' In the *Han-chi* . . . when a passage is introduced by the word *lun*, it is your minister Yüeh's own comment which gives a summary evaluation of or provides broad perspective to an important event.'[53] However, in the *Han-chi* as we now have it, only one such passage is introduced by the word *lun* (No. 35 in the table above); another passage bears no introductory word or phrase (No. 29); the other discourses are all introduced by the phrase: ' Hsün Yüeh says ' (*Hsün Yüeh yüeh*). This indicates some alteration of the text by its later editors.[54]

Generally, the discourses in the (c) and (d) categories (those constituting strong or direct criticism on the Han rulers) are quite short; they rarely exceed the length of one half-page (in the double-paged woodblock prints); and all of them are directly relevant to the historical events recounted in preceding passages in the Chronicle. On the other hand, the discourses in the (a) and (b) categories are relatively long; most of them are more than half a page long, and some of them cover several half-pages (No. 1, more than 2 half-pages; Nos. 7, 19, each of about 4 half-pages in length); some of these discourses are not directly relevant to the preceding historical entries in the Chronicles, but appear to be independent essays arbitrarily inserted in the text.

Because of the complicated textual problems involved, it is thus rather difficult to discuss Hsün Yüeh's conception of ' historical discourse or commentary ' on the basis of the longer *lun* passages in the *Han-chi*, particularly those in category (a). This leaves some thirty-four shorter *lun* in category (b), (c), and (d), all of which contain Hsün Yüeh's strictures, directly or indirectly aimed against the Han régime or its rulers. As I have already suggested, some of these criticisms of the Han rulers and their favourites (i.e. *Lun* 2, 3, 4, 11, 12, 20, 24, 31, 32, 34, 37) were probably the product of Hsün Yüeh's personal suffering under the imperial persecution. Others were probably written in his capacity as a conscientious historical commentator and critic.

There was, within the orthodox tradition, some precedent justifying Hsün Yüeh, the court historian and the official apologist, in including these criticisms in the *Han-chi*. The most significant justification came from the *Ch'un-ch'iu* canonical tradition which strongly influenced Hsün Yüeh's work in the *Han-chi*. According to the *Ch'un-ch'iu* tradition as it was established in Han Confucian orthodoxy, Confucius was a 'loyalist' but his loyalty was due neither to the Chou (the legitimate but purely titular monarch in Confucius' time) nor to the Lu royal house (the rulers of Confucius' native state); it was rather to a myth of royalty – an abstract ideal of authority and unity. Thus it was said that in the *Ch'un-ch'iu* Confucius had exalted as well as censured the régimes both of the Chou and of Lu. And it is this exaltation-and-censure which established the authority for the exercise of praise-and-blame (*pao-pien*) in later historical tradition.[55]

Confucius' exaltation of the Chou and of Lu was said to have been made in the 'form' of the *Ch'un-ch'iu*; that is, in compiling the *Ch'un-ch'iu* annals he had followed the official calendars of both the Chou court and of the state of Lu. His censures were said to have been made in the 'substance' of the *Ch'un-ch'iu*; that is, by the use in the entries in the annals of particular terminology with established ethical overtones to describe events and the selection or rejection of items of information for the record.[56] If this had been true of the praise-and-blame tradition in the *Ch'un-ch'iu*, Hsün Yüeh's *Han-chi* was certainly a significant departure from that tradition. For Hsün Yüeh's vindication of Han rule was explicitly stated in the panegyrics in the *Han-chi*, while his censure of the rulers and other prominent personages of Han times was equally explicit in the *lun* discourses. Such plain statements and explicit judgements diverged widely from the assumed tradition of implicit criticism.

As may be seen from the extant works of the Han and pre-Han periods, the exercise of praise-and-blame commentary by historians had in fact been quite limited. The *Ch'un-ch'iu* classic itself contains no explicit comment on the events it recorded; all the implied 'praise' or 'blame' in the work was extrapolated by later Confucians reading between the lines.[57] In Ssu-ma Ch'ien's *Shih-chi* and Pan Ku's *Han-shu*, praise-and-blame were more strongly implied or stated. But their author's comments were mainly directed at an historical personage or an institution, and were seldom made about an event itself.[58] It is Hsün Yüeh who seems to have become the first conscious commentator on historical events themselves by developing the *lun* discourses into a specific genre. After Hsün Yüeh, comment or critique (*lun* or *p'ing*) on historical events (*shih*) was much in vogue; authoritative personal comment or evaluation of past events, known as *shih-lun* or *shih-p'ing*, became an important genre in traditional Chinese historiography.[59] This type of comment demonstrates the peculiar Chinese conception of history with its inherent notions of transcendence, of parallel and recurrent pattern of events, and of historical didacticism. These motifs already found their expression in the full range of Hsün Yüeh's *lun* discourses, ranging from his censorious short comments on strictly historical events in the categories (c) and (d) above to his long essays on semi-historical or non-historical topics in the categories (a) and (b).

In the *Han-chi*, the sense of temporal transcendence was suggested not only in the author's juxtaposition of recorded fact and inserted allusion within the discourse, but also in the implications of such a discourse for contemporary issues. Although the *Han-chi* deals only with the history of the Former Han dynasty and Hsün Yüeh's censorious comments are made about specific personages of that dynasty, in these comments he often imported a reference to events which had happened long before or after Former Han times. Furthermore, while these comments were all ostensibly made about the historical events of the Former Han, their implications for the affairs of Hsün Yüeh's own time could be clearly seen.

For instance, in an entry under the sixth year of the Emperor Kao-tsu's reign (201 B.C.), Hsün Yüeh recorded that, on the advice of a Confucian official, the emperor had received homage paid to him by his own father. Hsün Yüeh appended the following censorious comment:

The *Classic of Filial Piety* [*Hsiao-ching*] stated that even the Son-of-Heaven should necessarily submit [his homage] to a superior...[60] [The rulers of the Chou dynasty] had worshipped Hou-chi [the legendary ancestor of the Chou] together with their worship of Heaven... King Yü [the legendary founder of the Hsia dynasty, traditionally believed to have existed from the 22nd to the 18th centuries B.C.] had not assumed superiority over K'un [his legendary disreputable father]. King T'ang [founder of the Shang dynasty, *ca.* 1766–1111 B.C.] had not assumed superiority over Hsieh [the legendary forefather of the Shang]. King Wen [of the Chou] had not assumed superiority over Pu-ch'ü [legendary forefather of the Chou]. This was the Way of ancient times.[61] The superiority of the son should not be imposed on his own father. The advice [given to the emperor] by the Prefect of the Imperial Household [*Chia-ling*] was therefore improper (*Lun* 2).

The sanction behind this censure is derived from the canonical *Classic of Filial Piety* as well as from the historical precedents which were presumed to have been established in remote antiquity. In criticizing the conduct of the Emperor Kao-tsu and the advice of his Confucian official, however, Hsün Yüeh was strongly influenced by the ideology of his own times – especially by the greatly increased emphasis on family ties and family morality among the emerging élite as instanced in the teaching of Hsün Shuang, Yüeh's uncle and intellectual mentor.[62]

In the discussion below, Hsün Yüeh's comments on those of the political and social problems of the Former Han which had significant bearings on the issues of his own time will be briefly reviewed. These include most of the *lun* in the categories (b), (c) and (d) and two others (Nos. 27–8) in the category (a). Hsün Yüeh's important discourses on Cosmology, Canonical Authority, and Historical Situations (*Lun* 1, 7 and 30, all in category (a)) will be studied in more detail in the next section.

Hsün Yüeh's writing reveals a basic concern for the sacrosanctity of the imperial order which by his time was rapidly approaching ultimate dissolution. To Hsün Yüeh and his contemporaries, the collapse of the imperial government was an acknowledged fact. What was less obvious was the breakdown of the Confucian world-view, the synthetic cosmic-moral order as an underlying dogma of the Han imperial institution. While Hsün Yüeh admitted that imperial administration on the old lines was no longer viable, he tried to salvage what was left of the Han Confucian synthesis by projecting imperial sovereignty as an abstract principle, an ideal of unity, and a moral force for coherence amidst the political chaos and disorder of his own times.[63]

According to this conception, the imperial sovereignty was not an ' omnipotent ' political power; its authority lay rather in the spheres of ideological guidance, ritual observance, and moral or intellectual example and persuasion. Hence Hsün Yüeh submitted that a sovereign might err on a point of practical worldly policy, but never on a point of moral (*tao*, *te*) or nominal (*ming*, *i*) rectitude.

Thus in *Lun* 2 Hsün Yüeh criticized the Emperor Kao-tsu for violating the principle of filial piety by accepting homage from his father, though the homage helped solve the problem of the position of the emperor as against that of his father in the hierarchical system. In *Lun* 3, he further criticized the Emperor Kao-tsu for pardoning the chancellor of a regional principality who had been disloyal to the empire but had courageously and gracefully defended his prince from imperial inquisition;[64] according to Hsün Yüeh, personal allegiance and obligation could never compensate for the crime of disloyalty to the empire. In *Lun* 6, he said that confusion within the official hierarchy must be rectified; official salaries could be adjusted according to need, but confusion between official income and private profit, which showed a state of moral corruption, must be prohibited.

In *Lun* 8, commenting on the economic measure adopted in 178 B.C. by the Emperor Wen to induce the rich to contribute surplus grain to the throne in exchange for noble rank so that the government might make use of the grain to relieve the poor,[65] Hsün Yüeh wrote the following reproof: ' The institution of a sage-ruler should aim solely at elucidating the Way and the principle of justice [*tao-i*]. All other calculative measures [i.e. economic or financial measures] must be subject to the consideration of the public good [*kung-i*] and of their appropriateness to the times [*shih-i*]; and they should be adopted only under compelling circumstances.'

In *Lun* 13, Hsün Yüeh repeated Confucius' saying that the ' rectification of Names ' (*cheng-ming*) should be a prime concern of the state, and that ' The Sacred Vessel [*ch'i*] and Name [*ming*] are the two things that should never be ceded to others ' [66] – one may yield in almost anything that constitutes worldly benefit – money, power, or land – but one should never yield on the principle (name, *ming*) concerning moral rectitude, or violate the symbols (sacred vessel, *ch'i*) of hierarchical authority.

A similar rigidity in Hsün Yüeh's conception of the sovereign's authority may be found in *Lun* 9, 14, 15, 16, 17, 22, 23, 33, and 34. It is also intimated in his discussion of six types of rulers and ministers in *Lun* 20. To Hsün Yüeh, the best rulers were those embodying moral rectitude (*cheng*), the ideal of humanity (*jen*), or the precept of righteousness (*i*), while those who diligently exerted themselves in administration were called ' mere rulers for the time being '; the best ministers were those who helped in the emperor's moral enlightenment, while those who diligently attended to their duties were called ' mere office holders '.

The dogmatism and idealism conveyed by Hsün Yüeh in his discourses were, however, constantly compromised by considerations of ' expediency ' in particular situations. In a sense, his dogmatic pronouncements about personal morality, particularly that of the sovereign and usually of a sovereign long dead, were rhetorical – they were intended to be standards, but he seems to have understood them to be unattainable ideals. He was much more flexible in his evaluations of government policies and administrative measures in particular situations, especially those of some immediate relevance to his own times.

He used the concept of ' timeliness ' (*shih*) in judging an historical event or in evaluating a past institution in *Lun* 5, 6, 8, and 10, ' expediency ' (*ch'üan*) in *Lun* 9 and 26, and the standpoint of ' considering the timeliness of an expedient measure ' (*ch'üan-shih chih-i*) was explicitly stated in *Lun* 23 and 25.[67]

Hsün Yüeh wrote these comments in a period of dissolution. Absoluteness was threatened on all levels. And a principle providing more alternatives in the solution of the myriad problems of the day seemed necessary. Hsün Yüeh's concession to ' expediency ' represented not only a retreat on purely political grounds but also a retreat from the dogmatic Confucian moral-ethical stand. It is in Hsün Yüeh's discourses on 'expediency' that one may find a true reflection of the changing conditions in the Chien-an era and some of the most thoughtful counsels given by Hsün Yüeh in the *Han-chi*.

Hsün Yüeh's concept of actual public administration was that power was delegated to the government bureaucracy in its successive hierarchies, each of them having limited autonomy in its own respective delimited sphere of action. Thus he favoured the Later Han system of Ducal Ministers (*San-kung*, in which three or more senior ministers shared the responsibility of the Chief Minister, *Ch'eng-hsiang* or Lieutenant Chancellor), despite the many abuses inherent in the system (*Lun* 35).[68] Hsün Yüeh probably advised against the reinstitution of the Chief Minister because of his concern about Ts'ao Ts'ao's possible arrogation to himself of all the administrative powers of the court (a move which Ts'ao eventually did make in A.D. 208).[69] But his view was also in basic accord with the Confucian ideal of a holistic state in which power and responsibilities should be more equitably shared by all members of the state.[70]

Hsün Yüeh's concept of sovereign authority and bureaucratic administration was inconsistent with his advocacy of a return to *feng-chien* 'feudalism'. His actual concept of *feng-chien* 'feudalism' was peculiar to himself, but it also reflected the political conditions of early medieval China and again accorded with the Confucian ideal of a holistic state. This may be seen in Yüeh's discourses on 'Feudal Lords' (*Chu-hou*) in *Lun* 5, on 'Land-holding' in *Lun* 10, and on 'Local Government' (*Chou-mu*) in *Lun* 36.

Hsün Yüeh's support for *feng-chien* feudalism was based on the familial concept of the state and the ideal of shared and delegated political authority and responsibilities. He thought that the *feng-chien* system would strengthen the personal, familial, or clan relationship between the ruler and the ruled, thus basing the political structure on a benevolent patriarchy. And he criticized the centralized local government system (*chün-hsien*, commandery and district) of the Ch'in and Han times, as a system designed to enable the imperial ruler to monopolize the powers and profits of the realm. Many early Confucians had been opposed to the hereditary rights of the nobility, but Hsün Yüeh as a spokesman for the new élite strongly supported such rights and considered these to be the backbone of *feng-chien* feudalism.[71]

In his review of the pre-Ch'in (pre-imperial) history of China in the same *lun*, Hsün Yüeh mentioned that the size of fiefs in pre-Chou times (before the twelfth century B.C.) had been relatively small, and this had had the advantage of producing a decentralized administration centred on the clan at the local level. It was in Chou times that the territory of the feudal lords was greatly expanded; this led to centralization of power within the feudal states and resulted in further territorial expansion and serious inter-regional warfare which eventually destroyed the *feng-chien* system. Hsün Yüeh therefore argued that fiefs should be kept small, that the feudal lords should enjoy local administrative autonomy, but that they should be put under an 'authoritarian' control by the imperial sovereign who was responsible for maintaining inter-regional peace and order and for the over-all guidance of the moral, intellectual, and ideological rectitude of the realm.

Although Hsün Yüeh's support of the *feng-chien* system reflected the political fragmentation developing in his time, his support of the system was conditional. Not only were the feudal lords to be subjected to control from above, but Hsün Yüeh thought that they were entitled only to the hereditary right of land-holding in their fiefs; they could not have 'ownership' of the people living in their domains – 'Land may be divided and owned [*yu fen-t'u*], but people should not be divided and owned [*wu fen-min*].' Although these feudal lords were to be subject to guidance from above in general moral principles and ideological matters, they should not be subjected to interference in their actual local administration by a regional power mediating between them and their sovereign. Hence in *Lun* 36, Hsün Yüeh severely censures the provincial governors-general (*Chou-mu*), a censure which applied to many governors-general who posed as regional warlords in Hsün Yüeh's own time.[72]

While Hsün Yüeh's conception of the sovereign's authority and his disapproval of 'regional' administrative power may be seen against the background of the Chien-an period, his peculiar attitude toward the 'small feudal lords' raises some interesting questions. According to Hsün Yüeh, these 'small lords' were those 'whose domain ideally did not exceed one hundred *li*' (about 22 miles), and 'who should have a hereditary right to their landholding but not to the governing [enslaving?] of the people'. Although here Hsün Yüeh was commenting on an historical institution, he seems to have conceived the image of a new nobility – the Chinese élite in the Age of Disunity.

This image of a new nobility may explain Hsün Yüeh's view of the élite in his other discourses. Ideally, the élite would submit to the sovereign's control in moral, ritual, and ideological matters, but they should have full powers in their own affairs – their leadership in the local communities, which were to be patriarchal, their structure highly personalized and based on the family. The élite should not transgress the rules of propriety, lest they become as unruly as the three *yu* (the disorderly stalwarts, the intriguers, and the treacherous partisans) who are specifically singled out for censure by Hsün Yüeh in *Lun* 16.[73]

The élite should neither 'enslave' others, nor should they be excessively rich, lest they become like the unruly local magnates or big landlords censured by Hsün Yüeh in his discourse on 'Land-holding' in *Lun* 10. These latter were those 'who possessed excessive land-hold-ings, up to several hundred or even one thousand *ch'ing*' (one *ch'ing* equals approximately 13 acres), 'who were wealthier than the feudal lords and were in fact self-styled feudal lords', 'who had benefited from the light land tax in Han times', and 'who arrogated to them-selves power and privileges which belonged to the ruler'. Hsün Yüeh further explained that the 'feudal lords' enjoyed hereditary and exclusive right to land-holding but did not have absolute authority within their domain; i.e. they could not by themselves dispose of their domains or subdivide their lands by creating new sub-fiefs (*chuan-feng*); the lesser nobility (*Ta-fu*) did not even have hereditary and exclusive right to land-holding (*chuan-ti*). However, the local magnates im-properly styled themselves 'lords' with the usual hereditary apparatus, and they were in the habit of disposing of land-holding by themselves in free buying and selling, so implying absolute authority over their possessions; obviously, they were 'more powerful than the feudal lords'.

Local magnates and landlords had posed serious problems to society and the state throughout Han times. (In the age of disunity and bar-barian conquest, local magnates and great landlords became almost the sole holders of local power over the Chinese communities.[74]) To con-trol these great land-holders, Hsün Yüeh suggested that the government should limit the size of land-holding as an interim measure, which would be the preliminary to the development of policy.

Hsün Yüeh's view on land policy was in part a reiteration of the proposals of the famous Han Confucian Tung Chung-shu (176–104 B.C.) and of the reform programme worked out by Wang Mang.[75] In part it reflected the Ts'ao régime's concern for the vital importance of agricultural production and its experiment with 'military colonies' and 'land colonies' (*ping-t'un* and *t'un-t'ien*).[76] But its central theme lies in Hsün Yüeh's ideal of the new nobility – an élite who would be neither too poor nor too rich, but between the extremes.[77]

Finally, the new élite should be noble not only in terms of their worldly possessions (money, land, power), but also in terms of their spiritual or cultural refinement. They should be endowed with lofty ideals (the Confucian moral virtue, *te*). They should also be flexible in establishing and maintaining their leadership – this, in times of difficulty, would call for stern measures and practical realist approaches (the Legalist emphasis on constraints, *fa*).

Thus in *Lun* 27–8, Hsün Yüeh combined the Confucian ideal of education and moral influence (*te-chiao*) and the Legalist emphasis on administrative and judicial control (*hsing-fa*). In this *lun*, Hsün Yüeh first made a summary review of the policies and accomplishments of four important Former Han rulers, the Emperors Kao-tsu, Wen, Wu, and Hsüan. He then categorized the disputes between Confucians and Legalists on the principles of government in the following schema:

1. Those who emphasize *chiao-hua* (education and moral persuasion).
2. Those who emphasize *hsing-fa* (administrative and judicial control).
3. Those who argue that *chiao-hua* must precede *hsing-fa*.
4. Those who argue that *hsing-fa* must precede *chiao-hua*.
5. Those who hold that *chiao-hua* must be detailed in government programmes.
6. Those who hold that this must be summary and concise.
[7. Those who hold that *hsing-fa* must be detailed.] (This does not appear in the present *Han-chi*, probably due to textual corruption.)
8. Those who hold that *hsing-fa* must be summary and concise.
9. Those who hold that this should be lenient.
10. Those who hold that this should be severe.

Hsün Yüeh stated that 'each of these categories had gravitated to one extreme and had not comprehended the essence of government [*chih-t'i*] or the greatest virtue of the Sage'.

According to Hsün Yüeh, 'the Way of the Sage was modelled after Heaven and Earth, regulated by the Five Elements, so as to transcend changes; it is therefore versatile and never becomes fixed [dogmatic, *ni*].' Hsün Yüeh postulated: (1) The Ways of Heaven and Earth prescribe that both *chiao-hua* and *hsing-fa* exist in parallel, but this refers to their metaphysical and non-moral existence only. (2) The Way of the Sage-ruler, on the other hand, puts *chiao-hua* above *hsing-fa* and cultural accomplishment above military achievement, and this should be the moral ideal for human society (*i*). (3) In actual historical situations, however, this ideal is complicated and compromised by 'chance' elements (*yü*), which dictate whether *chiao-hua* should precede *hsing-fa* or *vice versa*; and these 'chance' elements make up the different historical situations (*shih*) and different historical 'times' (*shih*), which cannot be dogmatically, or systematically, or simplistically provided for.

In the same *Lun*, Hsün Yüeh advocated a flexible and realistic approach to the issues of education (moral persuasion) and administrative-judicial control. He advocated a gradual and evolutionary approach:

Education must be used sparingly at the beginning; administrative and judicial control also must be delicately employed at the beginning. Gradually, when education and moral persuasion are in full swing and everyone has been exalted to good conduct, then you may demand a complete and perfectly detailed programme; when administrative and judicial control is established and everyone has been warned to avoid offences, then you may tighten the control.

He criticized those who arbitrarily set an impossibly high moral standard and failed to consider the people's incapacity to attain it; this, he thought, was categorically trapping the people in immorality, and would be as bad as arbitrarily devising a rigid and harsh law code without considering the people's actual conditions.

The same emphasis was laid on flexible judicial action in *Lun* 19, in which Hsün Yüeh criticized the Emperor Wu's harsh punitive measures.[78] He said that, if the government was too rigid in its law enforcement and did not give people a chance to repent and rehabilitate themselves, it would force wrong-doers to persist in their evil courses and become worse. In *Lun* 25, Hsün Yüeh repeated that the relative severity of law enforcement should be related to the needs of different times (*shih*); he pointed out that the relatively lax implementation of law in early Former Han times had been devised to mitigate government cruelty in the preceding Ch'in régime; he said that judicial control needed to be tightened when disorder appeared, as it had been in mid-Han times; but when dynastic misrule led to widespread uprisings, or when over-harshness in law enforcement led to general unrest, it would be timely to relax judicial measures so as to change the situation.

In all these discourses, Hsün Yüeh emerged as a spokesman of the new élite – a moderate who counselled ' compromise, moderation, and tolerance ' to all the warring factions in an age of disunity.[79]

COSMOLOGY, CANONICAL AUTHORITY, AND HISTORY

In the discourse on ' Education versus Legal Action ' (*Lun* 28) mentioned in the preceding section, Hsün Yüeh referred to the three important principles to be considered in policy deliberations: (1) the cosmological ' Ways of Heaven and Earth ' (*t'ien-ti ch'ang-tao*); (2) the moral ' Way of the Sage-ruler ' (*hsien-wang chih tao-i*); and (3) the contingent elements in a particular situation (*yü*, chance; *shih*, determining conditions; *shih*, time). But it was to the third principle, the consideration of the contingent in a particular situation, that Hsün

Yüeh gave his first and most consistent attention, thus showing his own insight into human history. This is clearly indicated in three other lengthy discourses in the *Han-chi*: *Lun* 1, 7 and 30, in which Hsün Yüeh examined in turn the problems of 'historical situations', 'cosmology', and 'canonical authority'.

In his discourse on 'Astronomy and Cosmic Omens' (*Lun* 7), Hsün Yüeh began by reiterating the popular Han Confucian thesis on the correspondence between cosmic and human phenomena.[80] He wrote:

When misrule occurs here [in human society], change will appear there [in the cosmos]; this is like a shadow simulating the shape [of the subject which cast the shadow] or like an echo reflecting the sound. Therefore, an enlightened ruler must observe the cosmic occurrence and comprehend [its related significance]; he must rectify himself, acknowledge his fault, and repent his wrong-doing; then evil occurrences will be averted and fortunate occurrence will be generated. This is the natural relationship.

However, Hsün Yüeh warned that the cosmos belonged to the infinite and the intangible; so cosmic occurrences were not a reliable guide to human affairs. He repeated Wang Ch'ung's disparaging criticism of the thesis of cosmic-human correspondence by pointing out that even the Sage-rulers in remote antiquity, like Yao and T'ang, had suffered natural disasters like great floods and drought, and that even Confucius' most virtuous disciple, Yen Hui, had suffered an untimely death.[81]

But Hsün Yüeh also criticized those who denied outright any correspondence between cosmos and man. In his opinion, those who negated the thesis were somehow confused by the apparently contrary evidence mentioned by Wang Ch'ung and failed to note other complexities involved in the correspondence. These complexities included the law of nature and the condition of man. Some parts of the law of nature could be influenced by human efforts; other parts could not. Similarly, the human condition had three categories:

1. Those natural tendencies which were self-fulfilling and needed no effort from men.

2. Those which could be furthered by human effort; or those which could not be accomplished without human effort.

3. Those which could not be affected or accomplished by human effort.

Acording to this conception, the thesis of the correspondence between cosmos and man should be modified as shown in the diagram.

Hsün Yüeh gave human disease and medication as examples. Some diseases needed no medication but would be cured naturally; some diseases could be cured by medication and would not be cured without it; and some diseases could not be cured in spite of medication. He gave

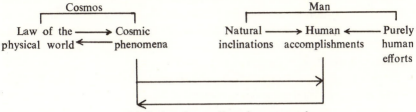

Limited and complicated correspondence

education and human improvement as another example. Some geniuses needed no education to perfect themselves; some men needed education to improve themselves; others could not be improved in spite of education.

Hsün Yüeh severely criticised simplistic thinking. He held that Heaven, Earth, and Men each had different 'Ways'; and to investigate these, one should be flexible in approach:

One must comprehend the law of nature and examine the nature of men; peruse the canonical classics and cross-examine [these against] the records of past and the present events; take heed of the three different conditions of men [82] and penetrate into their subtlest details; avoid the two extremes and grasp the mean; take reference from the Five Elements in their mutations; and place these in different combinations and sequences; then one may dimly envisage an approximation of truth (*Lun* 7, continued).

Hsün Yüeh seems to have been sceptical about men's ability to learn ultimate truth. He concluded his discourse with the moral that 'the superior man must exert to the uttermost his mental and physical capacity [to comprehend and to accord with the truth]; after that, you may resign yourself to Fate.'

Fate, however, was beyond human control. What men could do was to rely on the authority of the Sages, on the wisdom of those who had 'exerted their mental and physical capacities to the uttermost', in the attempt to comprehend and conform with the Way. Therefore, Hsün Yüeh tended to rely on the authority or dogmas of the canonical classics. Quotations from the Confucian classics appear as the validating authority in many of Hsün Yüeh's discourses in the *Han-chi*.[83]

But even in this last recourse, Hsün Yüeh had his reservations and doubts. Imperial Confucianism, instituted in the heyday of Han rule, had long degenerated into a scholasticism of quarrels and hair-splitting over the interpretation of texts; and, as an institution, it was shaken by the power-struggle between the ruling house and the defiant élite during the deterioration of the imperial order. In his own lifetime, Hsün Yüeh had seen how the Confucian canonical scriptures were differently inter- preted by different authorities for diverse political purposes. The more reflective minds had turned to the unorthodox teachings of Taoism and Logico-Legalism for inspiration. The ultimate authority of the Canons had therefore been seriously undermined.[84]

From his discourses in the *Han-chi*, Hsün Yüeh seems to have been quite conversant with the unorthodox Taoist and Legalist teachings, as well as with some of the anti-orthodox theses expounded by Wang Ch'ung. Although Hsün Yüeh did not lose faith in the authority of the Confucian Sages, he seems to have lost his confidence in the correctness of the Han Confucian interpretation of the canonical scriptures and in the degree to which later ages correctly understood the Way of Golden Antiquity. This is clearly shown in Hsün Yüeh's discourse on ' Con- fucian Canonical Scholarship ' (*Lun* 30). After a review of Han Con- fucianism,[85] Hsün Yüeh remarked:

The Sage-ruler [fearing that Men would lose their good nature,] followed the Fundamental Principles of Heaven and the Basic Principles of Earth to set up regulations for the instruction [of Men] in accordance with the mean. When this was practised at the time, it became the Moral Way [*tao-te*]; when this was recorded and transmitted to later generations, it became Canonical (*Lun* 30).[86]

But, Hsün Yüeh continued:

Coming to the later degenerate ages, the heretical branches grew and the various philosophers produced their own teachings to confound these im- portant principles. Thenceforward, the subtle teaching [of the sage-rulers] ceased and the various discourses went astray. Therefore, Confucius, who had feared and worried about this situation, sighed and lamented [the cor- ruption of] the [sacred] teachings (*Lun* 30, continued).[87]

In the same comment, Hsün Yüeh sharply criticised the anti-scholas- tic tendency of his time – the teachings of those who advocated a return to nature, and to the primitive condition of man (*chih*), a concept which was to become dominant in the intellectual life of the Wei and Chin times.[88] But neither did he favour mere erudition for its own sake. He asserted:

As to the sayings of Chi Lu: ' Why should one read books to become learned? '[89] and of Chi Tzu-ch'eng: ' A superior man should only [count on his moral] quality; why should he care for ornamental accomplishments [or literary refinement]? '[90] – These are like those, hiding themselves in caves, who cannot see the bright sky; or those, who hold themselves fast in the [bleak] woods in winter and cannot understand the flourishing summer; these are not the ways of illuminating understanding. On the other hand, those men who are widely read fail also to discriminate rubbish and take every-thing as good; [their knowledge] is like a vast paddy-field where weeds and rice-plants grow together – a lamentable scene to the good farmer... There-fore, Confucius said: 'By extensively studying all learning, and keeping oneself under the restraint of the Rules of Propriety, one may thus not err from what is right.' (*Lun* 30, continued).[91]

But since the Sage had long been dead, who on earth was to establish the Rule of Propriety? In Han times, it was the imperial authority which had posed as the grand patron and the ultimate arbiter between competing schools of thought – here lay both the political strength and the intellectual weaknesses of Han Confucianism. Hsün Yüeh observed:

During the Emperor Hsiao-wu's reign, Tung Chung-shu promoted and exalted Confucianism and suppressed the hundred schools. Later, Liu Hsiang and his son were in charge of editing and collating the classical writings. From that time on, old and new canonical teachings were discriminated, the nine streams of scholarship were distinguished, and the classical works became better known. But [these scholars, i.e. Tung, Liu and others] were themselves not as honourable as the Sage. How could they prevent the suspicions of all under Heaven? (*Lun* 30, continued).[92]

In this comment, Hsün Yüeh paid tribute to both Tung Chung-shu, representative of the official Modern Text School of the Han ortho-doxy, and Liu Hsiang's son, Liu Hsin, spokesman of the unofficial and unorthodox Ancient Text School in the Han Confucian controversy. During the conservative Later Han, the Modern Text School was up-held as the state orthodoxy, but it was the unofficial teaching of the Ancient Text School which attracted many of the talented scholars in antiquarian studies and which eventually outlived and displaced the official teaching of the Modern Text School in post-Han times.[93] Then, in discussing the development of Confucian learning in Later Han times, Hsün Yüeh observed:

[As a result of the controversy arising from the Former Han], later scholars differed in their opinions, and each changed or added something [in their interpretations of the canons]. After the Han restoration [i.e. in the Later Han], the Grand Minister of Agriculture [*Ta-ssu-nung*], Cheng Chung [died A.D. 114], and the Palace Attendant Chia K'uei [30–101] each produced a commentary on the *Tso-chuan* tradition of the *Ch'un-ch'iu* Canon;[94] during the reign of Emperor Huan, the former Grand Administrator of Nan-chün, Ma Jung [79–166] produced an interpretation of the *I-ching* Canon and introduced some strange expositions.[95] Your Majesty's minister [Hsün] Yüeh's uncle, Hsün Shuang, also wrote a Commentary on the *I-ching*...[96] From then on, in the area of Yen and Yü [roughly the middle Yellow River and the Huai river valleys], those who studied the *I-ching* all followed Hsün's teaching (*Lun* 30, concluding paragraph).

The way in which Hsün Yüeh mentions the unorthodox *I-ching* teaching of Hsün Shuang in this passage is a strange one. Granted that Hsün Shuang's teaching was both popular and intellectually significant in the last years of the Later Han rule, it is still surprising that Hsün Yüeh should suddenly assume such an air of arrogance. Is it not possible that Hsün Yüeh, in concluding his discourse on Han Confucianism with this unique reference to his uncle's subversive teaching, meant to indicate the flagrant political motives behind the interpretations of the Canons – ranging from Tung Chung-shu's work, which had helped to build up imperial orthodoxy, to Hsün Shuang's propagandism which undermined the Later Han? [97]

It is quite clear from the passage above that the authority of the Canons had been seriously undermined by controversy about their proper interpretation. And more importantly, the Han court in the Chien-an era was no longer in a position to make an authoritative or normative judgement on the controversy. Hsün Yüeh ended his discourse with the lament: 'The present time is far from that of the Sages; the precept of the Way [*tao-i*] has become very difficult for us to comprehend' (*Lun* 30, concluding paragraph). In other words, it was no longer feasible for the Chien-an élite to look to the Canons as their only source of inspiration or as an infallible guide to the 'Rules of Propriety' for human affairs. So Hsün Yüeh turned his attention elsewhere, specifically to historical studies.

Was not history the record of good examples? And was it not a Confucian precept that a kingly administration was upheld not by force, but by good example? Hence the *Han-chi* was pronounced to be a record of the good examples achieved by the Han dynasty, such as 'the regulations and ordinances'; 'fair and just measures'; military, administrative, and educational programmes; the patterns of sino-barbarian affairs; meritorious counsels and admonitions; scholarly and literary accomplishments, and so on: all these rightly constituting the 'Rules of Propriety' for the current reign.

Unlike the Canons, which also purported to be a record of good examples, history could be verified. This may partly explain why Hsün Yüeh did not follow the precedent of his uncle Hsün Shuang by adding new commentaries to the Canons, but was content with compiling the Han Chronicles. In his work, he gave historical writing importance and rationale.

In addition to its verifiability, Hsün Yüeh was also impressed by history as a reservoir of variegated human experience, in which the complex nature and ever-changing conditions of men defied any dogmatic solution or simplistic approach. This he discussed in his first discourse in the *Han-chi* (*Lun* 1). Here he subdivided historical situations (as illustrated by the struggle for imperial domination between Liu Pang, founder of the Han dynasty, and his arch enemy, Hsiang Yü) into three basic elements:

1. *hsing* – the general condition;
2. *shih* – the special situation at the time;
3. *ch'ing* – mental states, including the state of the mind, the heart, and the intentions of men.

In Hsün Yüeh's own words:

What is called *hsing* refers to the general situation [or overall condition, *ta-t'i*] favourable or unfavourable [to those involved in the situation]. What is called *shih* refers to the adjustment [one must make] to an immediate situation and the opportunity [which one is offered in this situation] to advance or retreat. What is called *ch'ing* refers to one's mind [or heart, *hsin*], one's long-range goal [or ideal, *chih*], which determines one's positive or negative attitude [or inclination, wish, *i*] towards a decision (*Lun* 1, continued).

Hsün Yüeh gave as an instance the same policy, planned for comparable occasions but leading to different results because of the variation in the combination of the three elements.

Following this line of argument, Hsün Yüeh went on to show how the operation of these three elements had brought about such different results in the series of civil wars in the Ch'in–Han transition, *c.* 209–201 B.C., leading to the very different fates of the various groups of anti-Ch'in insurgents.[98] Significantly, this important long discourse was appended to an entry in the *Han-chi* concerning the Emperor Kao-tsu's decision against the full-scale reinstitution of *feng-chien* feudalism.[99] The relevance of this discourse to Hsün Yüeh's time has been discussed in detail earlier.[100]

In the conclusion to this discourse, Hsün Yüeh pointed out that 'What is contingent [*ch'üan*, expedient] cannot be predicted; what is ever-changing cannot be foreseen. To follow the shifting times [*shih*] and to respond to the changing environment is the key to effective planning' (*Lun* 1, concluding sentence). What is important in this concluding sentence is Yüeh's view of history and human affairs. According to this view, every historical occurrence is unique, and any parallel or analogue drawn between these unique occurrences, like those drawn by Hsün Yüeh between the Han restoration in the first century A.D. and the Chien-an 'restoration' of his own time, could only be illusory. Hsün Yüeh the realist thus repudiated Hsün Yüeh the court apologist.[101]

HISTORIOGRAPHY

The above analysis shows the striking tension between Hsün Yüeh's ideal of historical study and his official duty as a court historian. In the *Han-chi*, this tension was aptly resolved by the author's manipulation of the contradiction between 'form' and 'substance'. As we have seen, Hsün Yüeh's vindication of the Han dynasty was accomplished, first by the choice of his subject matter (i.e. the record of the rise, decline and restoration of the Han, *c.* 206 B.C.–A.D. 23;[102] second by the formal panegyrics which he wrote in the Foreword, the Introduction, and the Epilogue of the *Han-chi*;[103] and third by the parallel which he continually suggested between the two dynastic restorations in A.D. 25 and 196, which coincided respectively with the compilation of the two historical works, the *Han-shu* and his own *Han-chi*. He needed to say no more.

Hsün Yüeh was perhaps too much imbued with the old tradition of Chinese historiography to let the bias inherent in his official mission jeopardize the factual account.[104] His own 'Biography' mentions that the *Han-chi* was a conscientious imitation of the *Tso-chuan* tradition of the *Ch'un-ch'iu*, rather than of the canonical *Ch'un-ch'iu* itself.[105] While the *Ch'un ch'iu* was supposed to be a Canon devoted to 'praise-and-blame', the *Tso-chuan* consisted mainly of factual details added to the terse entries in the *Ch'un-ch'iu*, with the supposed intention of 'letting the facts account for the moral'.[106] This would have been in basic accord with Hsün Yüeh's ideal of history as a reservoir of facts illustrating the subtle nature and condition of men in complex situations.

Unfortunately, the ideal of Hsün Yüeh, like the similar ideal of a later historian Cheng Ch'iao (A.D. 1108–66),[107] was largely unfulfilled. Not only was Hsün Yüeh's ideal of history compromised by his official brief, the vindication of the Han dynasty; he also lacked time and adequate means to complete his intended study of history. The *Han-chi* compilation was decreed by the Emperor Hsien in 198 and finished in 200.[108] The dispatch with which it was completed indicates the Han court's urgent need of dynastic vindication. Two years were barely sufficient for the mere compilation of the *Han-chi*, comprising as it did thirty *chüan* and several hundred thousand characters,[109] let alone for a thorough study of the complex events and human conditions which it recorded.

The *Han-chi hsü* mentions that the emperor ordered the Imperial Secretariat to supply papers and writing brushes and the Guards As

Rapid As a Tiger to act as copyists in compiling the *Han-chi*.[110] This reveals the very limited resources which the court could assemble for the task; it also intimates that Hsün Yüeh's own secretariat (i.e. the *Mi-shu chien* or office of the Custodian of the Secret Archives) was essentially a one-man office, lacking even an adequate supply of paper and writing brushes or a staff of copyists. The general poverty of the court may be glimpsed in the statement in the dynastic history which mentions that merely three years before this (in the early months of A.D. 196) the various court officials 'had had to cut down the wild thorns and lived beside the bare walls of the ruined city '.[111]

The impressive collection of books and other documents in the imperial library had been repeatedly plundered and destroyed during the preceding years of civil turmoil. The *Hou-Han shu* mentioned that

When Tung Cho moved the imperial court to Ch'ang-an [in A.D. 190] after the destruction of Loyang, the officials and the masses were thrown into turmoil. They took the important documents and literary works treasured in such imperial academies and libraries as the P'i-yung, the Tung-kuan, the Lan-t'ai, the Shih-shih, the Hsuan-ming, and the Hung-tu Halls; they cut and defaced these books. Of those books made of silk-cloth, the large-size ones were matted together to make curtains and carriage covers, and the small pieces were made into bags and containers. As for those collected and conveyed by Wang Yün to the western capital [Ch'ang-an], they amounted to only seventy-odd cart-loads; the journey was long and difficult, and during it half of the books had to be abandoned. Later, when Ch'ang-an fell into disorder [A.D. 192–5], all these were burned and destroyed. Nothing survived.[112]

The *Han-shu* was probably one of the very few books available to Hsün Yüeh in the imperial library at that time. Under these circumstances, it would have been extremely difficult in 198–200 for Hsün Yüeh to write a good history of the dynasty even if he had the time and the independence to do so – and he had neither. So his modest claim that he was merely condensing and simplifying Pan Ku's *Han-shu* into the *Han-chi* in order to produce a shorter history of the dynasty for easier reference was, in this sense, a plain statement of fact.

Hsün Yüeh's historiographical accomplishment in the modest *Han-chi*, however, was truly remarkable. The work was highly regarded both by his contemporaries and by later historians.[113] Some traditional critics even considered it to be better than the *Han-shu*.[114]

A complete and detailed analysis of the historiography of the *Han-chi* is beyond the scope of the present study. The following preliminary survey of its contents and the principal sources is intended to indicate only some of the essential features of the work.

Some basic statistics : numbers of chüan, *pages, and characters in the* Han-chi

The *Han-chi hsü* mentions that Hsün Yüeh condensed the *Han-shu* into a work of 30 *chüan*, totalling several hundred thousand characters. As we now have it the number of *chüan*, pages, and total characters of the Chronicles of the various Former Han emperors in the now extant *Han-chi* may be tabulated as follows:

Chüan	Emperor	Years of Reign	Double-pages	Columns and characters [a]		Characters (1) (in *lun*)	(2) (in Chronicle)
1	Kao-tsu	11	12	244	4880	240 [b]	4640
2			15	337	6740	580	6160
3			14	290	5800	100	5700
4			11	233	4660	80	4580
5	Hui-ti	7	15	311	6220	840	5380
6	Empress Lü	8	10	205	4100	900	3200
7	Wen-ti	23	16	335	6700	220	6480
8			17	363	7260	760	6500
9	Ching-ti	16	18	385	7700	220	7480
10	Wu-ti	54	13	282	5640	860	4780
11			18	375	7500		7500
12			14	292	5840	80	5760
13			14	300	6000	340	5660
14			17	364	7280		7280
15			13	272	5440	40	5400
16	Chao-ti	13	15	310	6200	680	5520
17	Hsüan-ti	25	13	275	5500	120	5380
18			12	246	4920		4920
19			14	299	5980		5980
20			15	308	6160	280	5880
21	Yüan-ti	16	11	228	4560 [c]		4560
22			12	259	5180	500	4680
23			12	246	4920	1000	3920
24	Ch'eng-ti	26	15	314	6280		6280
25			15	316	6320	880	5440
26			12	259	5180	340	4840
27			13	264	5280	200	5080
28	Ai-ti	6	12	243	4860	1100	3760
29			14	296	5920	380	5540
30	P'ing-ti	5	7	137	2740		2740
	(Wang Mang)	18	14	317	6340		6340
	(Epilogues)		6 [d]	167	3340	3340 [e]	
Total	Down to P'ing-ti		409		171,760	10,740	161,020
	including Wang Mang		423		178,100	10,740	167,360
	including Epilogues		429		181,440	14,080	

[a] Estimated by columns; 1 column = 20 characters.

[b] Hsün Yüeh's Prolegomena (*hsü*) in the introductory paragraph.

[c] Corrupt; the entry for one year (45 B.C.) is totally missing, see *Han-chi* 21.10a. An entry of 82 characters under this year is to be found in editions other

than the Huang edition (later the *Ssu-pu ts'ung-k'an* photolithographic edition) used here.

d I.e. Pan Ku's Epilogue to the *Han-shu* and Hsün Yüeh's Epilogue to the *Han-chi.*

e Containing Hsün Yüeh's note to the Han restoration, quotation of Pan Piao's *Wang-ming lun*, and Epilogues.

The figures above are based on the *Han-chi* in the *Ssu-pu ts'ung-k'an* edition, printed in the traditional 'double-pages', each double-page consisting of twenty-two columns and each column containing twenty Chinese characters. The total number of *chüan* is thirty, the same number given in the *Han-chi hsü*. But, even by the most generous method of counting, that is, by the total page-number multiplied by the number of characters per page including the blank columns, the total number of characters in the *Han-chi* including the Prolegomena and the Epilogues is about 188,760 (429 × 440), which is far less than the 'several hundred thousand characters' mentioned in the *Han-chi hsü*. And if the blank columns are excluded, the number of characters is still less, about 181,440. This seems to indicate that the text of the *Han-chi* in its present form is seriously corrupt.

A preliminary survey of the contents of the *Han-chi* may be made by comparing the length (expressed as the number of characters) of these Chronicles with that of two other standard chronological accounts of the Former Han period. The two works taken for comparison are Pan Ku's *Han-shu*, the work on which the *Han-chi* was based, and Ssu-ma Kuang's (1019–86) *Tzu-chih t'ung-chien*, perhaps the best and most authoritative of all Chinese chronological histories, compiled in the eleventh century. The Basic Annals in the *Han-shu* are the shortest chronicle of events occurring in the reigns of the Former Han emperors, events which constituted the primary entries in the *Han-chi* chronicles. The Former Han section of the *Tzu-chih t'ung-ch'ien*, like the *Han-chi* itself, is a secondary compilation mainly based on the *Han-shu*, but was generally considered the most comprehensive chronological survey of the reigns of these emperors, both in detail and in depth.

Reign of emperor or empress	*Han-chi* Total length	*Han-chi* Chronicle only	*Han-shu* Total length [a]	*Han-shu* Difference [b]	*Tzu-chih t'ung-chien* Total length [c]	*Tzu-chih t'ung-chien* Difference [d]
Kao-tsu	22,080	21,080	12,432	−8,648	28,404	6,324
Hui-ti	6,220	5,380	1,140	−4,240	1,839	−4,381
née Lü	4,100	3,200	1,572	−·1,628	4,855	755
Wen-ti	13,960	12,980	4,764	−8,216	18,412	4,452
Ching-ti	7,700	7,480	2,388	−5,092	8,339	639
Wu-ti	37,700	36,380	8,088	−28,292	50,111	12,411

Reign of emperor or empress	*Han-chi* Total length	*Han-chi* Chronicle only	*Han-shu* Total length [a]	*Han-shu* Difference [b]	*Tzu-chih* Total length [c]	*t'ung-chien* Difference [d]
Chao-ti	6,200	5,520	2,352	−3,168	4,757	−1,443
Hsüan-ti	22,560	22,160	7,188	−14,972	25,605	3,045
Yüan-ti	14,660	13,160	3,372	−9,788	8,206	−6,454
Ch'eng-ti	23,060	21,640	3,900	−17,740	20,415	−2,645
Ai-ti	10,780	9,300	1,810	−7,490	14,787	4,007
P'ing-ti	2,740	2,740	2,160	−580	7,161	4,421
Wang Mang	6,340	6,340	37,300 [e]	30,960	20,726	14,386
Totals: through P'ing-ti	171,760	161,020	51,166	−109,854	192,891	21,131
+ Wang Mang	178,100	167,360	88,466	−78,894	213,617	35,517

[a] Based on the I-wen reprint of the Wu-ying tien ed.; each double-page consisting of 20 columns, each column containing 21 characters. This includes annotation and commentaries. To determine the average number of characters of the *Han-shu* text proper in each column, samples have been taken from *Han-shu* 1A.2, 16; 2.2,6; 4.2, 10; 5.2, 5; 6.2, 12, 22; 7.2, 6; 8.2, 7, 12, 19; 9.2, 7; 10.2, 11; 11.2 and 12.2, 7. The average number of characters is estimated at 12.50 per column; 0.50 is to be deducted from the average because of incomplete columns within each of these Annals. The average of 12 characters per column thus constitutes the basis of the estimate. Blank columns are excluded.

[b] Difference in length between the Chronicle proper of the *Han-chi* and the Basic Annals of the *Han-shu*.

[c] Based on the *Ssu-pu ts'ung-k'an* edition; each double-page consisting of 26 columns, each column containing 20 characters, including annotation. The estimated number of characters of the text proper is based on the average number of 14.7 characters per column in the sample pages: 9.2, 11.3, 13.4, 15.5, 20.6, 25.7, 28.8, 31.9, 35.10, and 38.11.

[d] Difference in length between the *Han-chi* (including *lun*) and the Former Han section of the *Tzu-chih t'ung-chien* (including *lun*).

[e] Based on the 'Biography of Wang Mang', *Han-shu* 99A–C; with an average of 16.6 characters per column from the sample pages: 99A.2, 99B.7, 99C.12 and 13.

An analysis of Hsün Yüeh's particular attention to
certain Former Han emperors

Several significant points emerge from this comparison. First, the length of the *Han-chi* (excluding Wang Mang's reign) is more than three times that of the Basic Annals of the *Han-shu*.[115] This means that more than two-thirds of the material in the *Han-chi* was drawn from elsewhere. And since the *Han-chi* is written in a terser style than the *Han-shu*, the proportion of additional material is even greater than a simple word-count would indicate. All this additional material had to be dated and chronologically arranged to fit the chronological format of the *Han-chi*, a task needing considerable research and meticulous care.

Secondly, the length of the *Han-chi* (excluding Wang Mang's reign) is quite close to that of the longer and more comprehensive *Tzu-chih t'ung-chien*. The difference in length between the two is only 21,131 characters, or slightly more than ten per cent of the total of the larger work. This shows that the *Han-chi* is nearly as comprehensive as the *Tzu-chih t'ung chien* as an account of the Former Han period.

Thirdly, so far as the reigns of the individual rulers are concerned, the emphasis (as measured by the length of the narrative) falls differently in the *Han-shu*, the *Han-chi*, and the *Tzu-chih t'ung-chien*. In the *Han-shu*, the emphasis is placed in the following order: Kao-tsu, Wu-ti, and Hsüan-ti;[116] in *Han-chi*, Wu-ti, Ch'eng-ti, Hsüan-ti, and Kao-tsu; in *Tzu-chih t'ung-chien*, Wu-ti, Kao-tsu, Hsüan-ti, and Ch'eng-ti. The overall importance of the Emperors Kao-tsu, Wu-ti and Hsüan-ti in all these accounts is quite clear: Kao-tsu, in connection with the founding of the dynasty and the many battles which he fought; Wu-ti and Hsüan-ti, for their long reigns which were the climax of Han imperial power, and for the important administrative measures which they introduced.[117] But the emphasis given to the Emperor Ch'eng-ti in the *Han-chi* was quite new, and in this case Ssu-ma Kuang in writing the *Tzu-chih t'ung-chien* seems to have followed the *Han-chi's* precedent, rather than the stated account in *Han-shu*.

The importance which Hsün Yüeh gave to Emperor Ch'eng-ti is difficult to explain. The relatively long reign of the emperor does not sufficiently explain the length of his Chronicle in the *Han-chi*. Emperor Hsüan-ti's reign was one year shorter than Emperor Ch'eng-ti's, but his chronicle (excluding Hsün Yüeh's *Lun*) is considerably longer than Ch'eng-ti's. (However, if Hsün Yüeh's *Lun* discourses as well as the basic Chronicles are included, Ch'eng-ti's reign receives more emphasis than Hsüan-ti's.) Emperor Yüan-ti's reign (16 years) was of the same length as Emperor Ching-ti's, but far shorter than Emperor Wen-ti's (23 years); however, the Chronicle of Emperor Yüan-ti slightly exceeds that of Emperor Wen-ti in length, and was nearly twice as long as that of Emperor Ching-ti.

The amount of source-material available to the historian was no doubt an important factor in determining the relative length of these chronicles of individual reigns. The sources of the *Han-shu* on the period from Emperor Kao-tsu to Emperor Ching-ti were mainly secondary materials taken from Ssu-ma Ch'ien's *Shih-chi*; whereas those on the period from Emperor Wu-ti to Emperor P'ing-ti were primary documentation gathered by the authors of the *Han-shu*. This may partly explain why in the *Han-chi* (which was mainly based on the *Han-shu*) the Chronicle of Emperor Yüan-ti is longer than that of Emperors Wen-ti and Ching-ti.

However, the amount of material available does not explain why in the *Han-chi* the Chronicle of Emperor Ch'eng-ti is longer than the Chronicle of Emperor Kao-tsu. The source-material on Kao-tsu available to the author of the *Tzu-chih t'ung-chien* in the eleventh century amounted to at least 28,404 characters (the length of the Kao-tsu section in the *Tzu-chih t'ung-chien*), but Hsün Yüeh in the early third century chose to use only about 22,080 characters in his account of Kao-tsu's reign. The fact that Kao-tsu, the founding emperor of the dynasty, was made fourth in order of importance among the Han emperors in the *Han-chi* (this also influenced the *Tzu-chih t'ung-chien* which placed Kao-tsu second to Emperor Wu) indicates a priority in Hsün Yüeh's selection of materials. In the case of Kao-tsu, it seems to indicate that Hsün Yüeh was not primarily interested in the story of founding the dynasty through victory in ' the blood-stained battlefields' or through ' chasing the deer on horseback'. This image was all too relevant to the situation of the Chien-an reign, with the strong man Ts'ao Ts'ao emerging on the horizon as a new victor on the battlefields and potentially as founder of a new dynasty.[118]

If we compare the length of the Chronicles in the *Han-chi* with that of the corresponding sections in the *Tzu-chih t'ung-chien*, we can see that the Chronicles in the *Han-chi* are generally shorter than those in the *Tzu-chih t'ung-chien*, with the exception of the Chronicles of the Emperors Hui-ti, Chao-ti, Yüan-ti and Ch'eng-ti. These four Emperors are generally considered the weak rulers of the Former Han, rulers whose reigns witnessed a decline in imperial authority.[119] An emphasis on these weak rulers suited not only the political situation during the Chien-an period, but also the politics of the ' restoration ' – that is, ' to support the declining, and to minister to the weak ', as Yüan Shu had said in his last letter to Yüan Shao.[120]

It is in the Chronicles of Emperor Ch'eng-ti and his predecessor Emperor Yüan-ti that we find Hsün Yüeh's most lengthy *lun* in the *Han-chi*. Since the reigns of Yüan-ti and Ch'eng-ti were considered to have been the beginning of the decline of Former Han imperial rule, and this downward trend was connected with the ultimate triumph of Han Confucianism,[121] Hsün Yüeh's emphasis on these two reigns probably originated in his attempt to study the decline in its relation to Confucianism.

This hypothesis may be confirmed by an analysis of the important discourses which Hsün Yüeh inserted in the Chronicles of Yüan-ti and

Ch'eng-ti, i.e. *Lun* 24, 27, 29, 30, 31, 32, and 33. *Lun* 27, which appears in the Chronicle of Yüan-ti's reign, contains Hsün Yüeh's important comment on the antithesis between the Confucian ideal of education and moral persuasion (*chiao-hua*) and the Legalist emphasis on law (*hsing-fa*). In this discourse, Hsün Yüeh specifically quotes the Emperor Hsüan-ti's criticism of the future Emperor Yüan-ti, observing that Yüan-ti was too favourably inclined toward Confucianism, an inclination which was to cause the Han decline.[122] Hsün Yüeh's *lun* was specifically intended to refute this viewpoint. Although Hsün Yüeh thought that the decision to give priority to education and moral persuasion or to law should depend on the situation of the time, thus implying that Emperor Yüan-ti's whole-hearted promotion of Confucianism might have been untimely, he nonetheless affirmed the ultimate priority of Confucianism, thus upholding the correctness of Yüan-ti's Confucian inclination.

Lun 29, which appears on the Chronicles of Ch'eng-ti, contains Hsün Yüeh's discourse on 'Confucian canonical scholarship'. Although he was critical of the controversial interpretation of the Canons by the Han Confucians, he suggested that this was due to the inability of the degenerate later ages to comprehend the truth expounded by the Sage, not to the fallacy of the Sage's teaching.

Thus the blame for Han decline was transferred to the general decline and moral corruption of the age. Hsün Yüeh substantiated this charge of general corruption of the age in other discourses included in the Chronicles of these two reigns. In *Lun* 24, he bitterly attacked Shih Hsien, the eunuch who attended Emperor Yüan-ti, and petty men involved in government in general; in *Lun* 33, he censured Chang Fang, the male favourite and confidant of Emperor Ch'eng-ti. In *Lun* 30, he expressed sympathy for the righteous officials and scholars who were wronged by their rulers or other groups in power. In *Lun* 31, he criticized the confusion of the line of succession to the Han throne. In all these things Hsün Yüeh probably saw further reasons for the Han dynastic decline.

Hsün Yüeh was consequently effective enough in vindicating Confucianism and the Confucian élite, but he failed to vindicate the dynasty and the other ruling groups. Whether Hsün Yüeh's advocacy of Confucianism and his diagnosis of dynastic corruption were an adequate statement of the case in the context of actual events is open to question. But he presented this case in explicit discourses, and substantiated it by the historical accounts in the *Han-chi*, so fulfilling his claim that everything 'may be examined in the actual facts and confirmed'.[123]

Other materials from the Han-shu

The difference between the length of the *Han-chi* and the Basic Annals section of the *Han-shu* indicates that more than two-thirds of the material in the *Han-chi* came from other sources. Hsün Yüeh's own statement, as well as the circumstances under which the *Han-chi* was compiled, make it quite certain that the work was based mainly, if not solely, on the materials in the *Han-shu*.[124] This means that more than two-thirds of the material in the *Han-chi* was taken from the other sections of the *Han-shu*, i.e. the Tables (*piao*), the Treatises (*chih*), and the Biographies and Memoirs (*lieh-chuan*).

Since the body of Tables in the *Han-shu* contains mainly the dates of persons and events, their usefulness is limited to establishing the correct dates for various entries in the *Han-chi*. The inclusion of material from this section extended only to a few summaries of the ' prolegomena ' (*hsü*) to the Tables (see the second item in the following list). It is the material derived from Treatises and Biographies of *Han-shu* that makes up the bulk of the *Han-chi*.

A comparison of the original *Han-shu* Treatises and their restatement in the *Han-chi* indicates that while some parts of the restatement are word-for-word quotations of the original, other parts present genera-lized accounts of the basic ideas of the original in somewhat different words. For instance, *Han-chi* 5: 4b-6a gives a concise but comprehen-sive abstract of the ' Treatises on the Five Elements ' (*Wu-hsing chih*) from *Han-shu* (27A, B, C). The first part of the *Han-chi* restatement of this material contains only 135 characters, enumerating the Five Elements, their corresponding natures and their correlations with the state of government.[125] This is quoted from *Han-shu* 27A (Treatise on the Five Elements, Section A). The original totals 24 double-pages or more than 10,560 characters (estimated on the basis of 12 characters per column excluding annotation and commentaries, with 20 columns per page) and is extremely difficult to read, whereas the *Han-chi* restate-ment is concise, straightforward and readily comprehensible. The second part of the *Han-chi* restatement contains 398 characters, enumerating the Five Activities of Man corresponding to the Five Elements (i.e. demeanour, speech, seeing, hearing, and thinking), the virtues necessary in the emperor with respect to these Five Activities, and their effects on natural phenomena; this is a restatement of *Han-shu* 27B, 27C, *and* 27D, the original totalling 88 copious double-pages or more than 21,120 characters. Only the first 17 characters of the *Han-chi* restatement appear to be a direct quotation from the original; the remainder has no word-for-word counterpart in the *Han-shu*; nonetheless, the basic postulates in the copious, confusing, and difficult *Han-shu* Treatise are aptly summarised in the *Han-chi* restatement – an excellent performance seldom achieved in historians' abstracts of abstruse Chinese texts.[126]

Other lengthy excerpts from the *Han-shu* Treatises in the *Han-chi* include:

Han-chi	*Han-shu*
5: 6b–9b	22 Treatise on Rites and Music
5: 9b–12b	19A Prolegomenon, Table of the Hundred Officials
6: 3b–4b	26 Treatise on Astronomy and Astrology
7: 4a–5a	24A Treatise on Food and Money
8: 4a–5b	24A
8: 5b–6a	23 Treatise on Law
13: 4b–6a	24A; 24B
14: 6a–8b	21A Treatise on Measurements and Calendars
24: 2b–5a	25A; 25B Treatise on the Sacrificial Liturgy
25: 1a–5b	30 Treatise on Literature
30: 26	28B Treatise on Geography

In addition, there are a number of short and fragmentary quotations, mainly of the *Han-shu* Treatises on Astronomy and Astrology (*Han-shu* 26), and on The Five Elements (*Han-shu* 27A–E), scattered in various entries in the *Han-chi*; these mainly deal with natural omens, portents and other strange occurrences during the reigns of the individual Han rulers and the interpretations of them given by contemporary authorities, such as Tung Chung-shu and Liu Hsiang.[127]

In most of these lengthy excerpts, there are minor variations between the *Han-chi* restatement and the *Han-shu* original which probably result from mistakes in transmission of one or other of the texts. The slightly different wording in the *Han-chi* résumé is thus often useful for textual collation. But there are parts of these excerpts which bear no word-for-word relationship to the original. These abstracts provide a concise and generalized restatement of the basic ideas of the *Han-shu* original; they are more useful as the summary review of the ideas and judgements of the *Han-shu* Treatises than for simple textual collation.

The placing of these lengthy excerpts abstracted from the *Han-shu* Treatises in the *Han-chi* Chronicles appears to have been quite arbitrary. But a general plan for their use in the *Han-chi* may be postulated. The founding of the dynasty by Emperor Kao-tsu as the result of numerous battles was followed by a period of relative peace during which the basic court institutions were set up; these included liturgical 'Rites and Music', 'Court Officialdom', and their justification by omens and astrological analogues; since the reign of Emperor Kao-tsu was a time of continual military troubles, accounts of these institutional arrangements and related matters were properly relegated to the reigns of his successors, the Emperor Hui-ti and the Empress *née* Lü; and these are found in *Han-chi* 5 and 6, the chapters covering this period of tentative peaceful settlement. Then came the reigns of Emperors Wen-ti, Ching-ti, and Wu-ti, a period of vigorous reform in economic, administrative, and financial matters; therefore the entries from the treatises on Food and Money, on Law, and on Measurements and the Calendar are to be found in *Han-chi* 7–14 dealing with their reigns. The last period of Former Han rule witnessed the court's accomplishments in liturgical and scholarly matters; these were recounted in the excerpts on Sacrificial Liturgy and Literary Works in the *Han-chi* 24–5.[128] The last Treatise included in the *Han-chi* is an excerpt of that on Geography of the *Han-shu*, which presents a restatement of the Han imperial domain and its regional administrative framework – a summary description of the extent of imperial power and the imperial administration at the climax of Han rule, which would have served as a timely reminder to the readers of the Chien-an reign, when effective Han power was territorially limited and exiguous.[129]

Even more important than the excerpts from the Treatises were the materials in the *Han-chi* derived from the Biographical Sections (*Lieh-chuan*) of the *Han-shu*. In the *Han-chi*, any account of the career of an individual other than the dynastic ruler was entered in connection with some event involving that individual in the affairs of the state or society at large – a meritorious deed or some memorable counsel which he had given, or conversely a serious crime he had committed. Thus, the sum of the material concerning any individual was ordinarily scattered in several entries; however, a biographical résumé was usually included either in the entry in which the individual made his first appearance or in the entry which noted his death (if his death was specifically dated).

More complicated than the problem of where to insert such biographical information was the problem of determining the amount of such information which was to be included in the concise and primarily chronological *Han-chi*. A preliminary survey of the biographical material on individual persons in the *Han-chi* indicates that Hsün Yüeh was quite sparing in his use of biographical data on high-ranking officials of the Former Han régime, no matter how important or meritorious they might have been. For instance, in the entry for the first year of the Second Emperor of the Ch'in (i.e. 209 B.C.), an account was given of the future Emperor Kao-tsu's first armed insurrection,[130] and this included a biographical résumé of Kao-tsu's five important comrades-in-arms during the insurrection: Hsiao Ho (future first Chief

Minister, *Hsiang-kuo*, at the Han Court), Ts'ao Ts'an (Hsiao Ho's successor as Chief Minister), Hsia-hou Ying (a Han General), Chou Po (the future Grand Commandant and Chief Minister of Han), and Fan K'uai (Kao-tsu's lieutenant).[131] The résumé included in the *Han-chi* consisted of only 33 characters (fewer than 7 characters per person), and read: 'Hsiao Ho was formerly a clerk in charge of the prison at the P'ei [district]; Ts'ao Ts'an was an assistant in that office; Ying, a stableboy at the P'ei [district office]; Po lived by mat-making; and K'uai was a dog-butcher; they were all [Kao-tsu's] old acquaintances.' [132]

On the other hand, Hsün Yüeh was very generous with his references to the literati; the *Han-chi* contains not only many lengthy quotations from the 'marvellous counsels' given to the court by individual members of the literati, but also some relatively detailed biographical résumés of the lives of these counsellors. For instance, the biographical résumé on Chang Liang, the Taoist adviser to Kao-tsu, has some 180 characters[133]; the account of Li I-chi, a lesser Confucian adviser of Kao-tsu, contains a biographical résumé of 17 characters, supplemented by 50 additional characters describing his first meeting with Kao-tsu and 41 characters of direct quotation from his first counsel to Kao-tsu.[134] Some of Hsün Yüeh's accounts of the literati were not even directly related to the political events recorded in the *Han-chi*. For instance, in an entry under the first year of the Yung-shih reign period of the Emperor Ch'eng-ti (16 B.C.), a lengthy account is given of a Taoist eccentric named Yang Wang-sun of Emperor Wu's time, who left a will expressing the desire to be buried naked.[135] The account implies criticism of the extravagance of the time, particularly the sumptuous burial projects undertaken by the court; but it has no direct relevance to Ch'eng-ti's rule.[136]

Generally, it is the account of the lives of the individual members of the literati together with quotations from their political counsels and scholarly or literary works rather than the treatises on administrative matters, accounts of battles, and such things, which makes up the bulk of the *Han-chi*. In this respect, the *Han-chi* became largely a presentation of the literati's ideas of their own role in the state, and of their striving towards a perfect society and state in Former Han times, under the far from perfect rule of the house of Liu.[137]

In addition to the biographical data on individuals, certain specific social groups which were described in Collective Biographies (*lieh-chuan*) in the *Han-shu* were also given attention in the *Han-chi*. These included accounts of the local magnates and the wandering stalwarts (*yu-hsia*) from *Han-shu* 92, which were summarized in *Han-chi* 10 : 2

and 28:9; accounts of the 'money-makers' (*huo-chih*) from *Han-shu* 91, which were summarized in *Han-chi* 7 : 6a–7b; and accounts of the Confucian scholars (*ju-lin*) from *Han-shu* 88, which were summarized in *Han-chi* 10 : 9a and 25 : 1a–3a.

Hsün Yüeh also gave space in the *Han-chi* to the tribesmen living on the Chinese border. In *Han-chi* 8: 9–12a, a lengthy quotation of Ch'ao Ts'o's counsel on defence strategy against the Hsiung-nu tribes was taken from *Han-shu* 49. In *Han-chi* 11 : 5a–8b, an excerpt of the 'Memoir on Hsiung-nu' was taken from *Han-shu* 94A, followed by a quotation from Chu-fu Yen's counsel against the war with the Hsiung-nu which is preserved in *Han-shu* 64A. In *Han-chi* 10 : 10a–12a, the counsel of the Prince of Huai-nan against an expedition into south and southeast China against the people of Min-yüeh was summarized from *Han-shu* 64A. In *Han-chi* 11 : 12a–14b, an excerpt from the 'Memoir on the Southwestern Aborigines' (*Hsi-nan-i*) was taken from *Han-shu* 95, followed by a quotation from Ssu-ma Hsiang-ju's counsel to the people of Szechuan (Pa and Shu) from *Han-shu* 57B. In *Han-chi* 12 : 6b–9a, an excerpt from the 'Memoir on the Western Regions' (*Hsi-yü*) was taken from *Han-shu* 96A. Finally, in *Han-chi* 15 : 8b–11b, two lengthy quotations from Pan Ku's criticism of the Emperor Wu-ti's general policy of frontier expansion and the adverse effects this had upon the Chinese economy were produced from *Han-shu* 96B and 94B.

Hsün Shuang's influence on the Han-chi

From this survey, it becomes quite clear that the *Han-chi* is not a mere court apologia nor merely the result of 'scissors-and-paste'. In his Discourses, Hsün Yüeh had expressed his ideals of society and the state as well as his comments on subjects like the Canons and historiography; none of these was entirely compatible with simple court apologia. Besides, many of Yüeh's ideological postulates in the Discourses were woven into the historical narration in the *Han-chi*, first through his selection of materials for inclusion and then by the way in which these materials were organized into the chronicles of successive reigns. Although one may question Hsün Yüeh's political ideals and historical methodology, one cannot but agree that the *Han-chi* was the product of deep thought and scholarly sophistication.

This reminds us of the question raised at the beginning of this section: how could Hsün Yüeh in his one-man office, with nothing but a supply of paper and writing brushes from the Imperial Secretariat and a few copyists selected from among the emperor's body-guards, produce such a work in two years? Even if the *Han-chi* had been based entirely on the *Han-shu* and there had been many experienced copyists to assist in the work, it would still have taken many years to finish such a compilation. Besides, many of the excerpts made from the *Han-shu* were rewritten and did not exactly correspond with the original and could not have been made by mere copyists.

The surmise is that though the compilation of the *Han-chi* was officially decreed by the emperor in A.D. 198, the preliminary work had probably been begun privately by Hsün Yüeh some years before. Since he had been interested in the *Ch'un ch'iu* and other historical works from his early boyhood, he may well have begun compiling the chronicles of the reigns of the various Han rulers as a scholarly pursuit during the period of obscurity in his life before the Chien-an 'restoration'. This might at least account for some of his severe strictures on the Han rulers, discussed above.[138]

Furthermore, some of the material in the *Han-chi* may have been drawn from the *Han-yü* (Remarks on Han Affairs), the historical work compiled by Yüeh's uncle Hsün Shuang, and also probably based mainly on the *Han-shu*.[139] This it seems may account for some of the textual discrepancies or disparities between the *Han-chi* and the text of the *Han-shu* as it now exists. An illustration of this may be found in the record of the mourning service for Emperor Wen in *Han-chi* 8 : 16 and *Han-shu* 4 : 19b respectively. The *Han-shu* versions reads: '[During the mourning period for Emperor Wen] . . . All those who should serve in the mourning and present themselves in mourning costumes should not *chien*.' In the commentary, the character *chien* was glossed by Fu Yen, as: 'reading *chien*, [whole phrase] meaning not to *chan-ts'ui* [cut and fray the edges of coarse, hempen garments expressing deepest mourning]'.[140] This gloss was repudiated by Meng K'ang who thought that the character *chien* in *Han-shu* should be interpreted as *hsien* 'bare feet'.[141] In a third gloss, Chin Cho (a scholar of the Chin dynasty) mentioned that the reading in a corresponding passage in the *Han-yü* was indeed *hsien* or 'bare feet'.[142] The corresponding reading in the *Han-chi* is *hsien-tsu* 'to bare [their] feet', which appeared to be an elaboration of the *Han-yü* reading.

Some critics have suggested that the textual discrepancies between the *Han-shu* and the *Han-chi* were due mainly to the fact that Hsün Yüeh, compiling the *Han-chi* in the early third century, had based his work on an earlier and less corrupt version of the *Han-shu*.[143] This suggestion is not borne out by the different readings in the two works in the above case, because the *Han-shu* reading of *chien* had already been glossed by Meng K'ang, a scholar of the third century and a younger contemporary of Hsün Yüeh; the date of the earlier commentator Fu Yen, is not known, but his gloss in the *Han-shu* clearly antedates that of Meng K'ang. So this variant reading in the *Han-shu* could not have been due to corruption after Hsün Yüeh's time.

The relationship between the different readings and the glosses in this passage may be shown in the diagram.

Dates	*Authorities*
1st century	*Han-shu: Chien* (?)
2nd c.	*Han-yü: hsien* (bare feet)
	Fu Yen's gloss: *chien* (cut and fray)
3rd c.	*Han-chi: hsien-tsu* (to bare the feet)
3rd c.	Meng K'ang's gloss: *hsien*
	Chin Cho's gloss referring to the *Han-yü*
579–645	Yen Shih-ku's Commentary upholding the *hsien* gloss
17th–19th centuries	Other commentators in the Ch'ing dynasty upholding the *chien* reading according to the context in the *Han-shu* statement

This suggests that the possible sources of the *Han-chi's* material may be postulated as in the diagram below.

Other documents or historical works

Pan-Ku's *Han-shu*

Hsün Shuang's *Han-yü*

Hsün Yüeh's *Han-chi*

6

Hsün Yüeh's works:
The *Shen-chien* (Extended Reflections)

The 'Biography of Hsün Yüeh' mentions his having written, in addition to the *Han-chi*, a second major work entitled *Shen-chien*, and tens of discourses (*lun*) including one entitled *Ch'ung-te cheng-lun* (Impartial Discourse in Exaltation of Moral Virtue).[1] Of these, only the *Han-chi* and the *Shen-chien* now survive.[2] According to Yüan Hung's (328–76) *Hou-Han chi*, the *Shen-chien* was completed and submitted to the Han throne by Hsün Yüeh in the eighth lunar month of the tenth year of Chien-an (2–30 September A.D. 205), that is, about five years after Yüeh's completion of the *Han-chi*.[3]

During the five years intervening between A.D. 200 and 205, the situation of the Chien-an reign had greatly changed. The compilation of the *Han-chi* had been intended by the titular Han throne as a commemoration of the dynastic 'restoration' at Hsü. The work was, however, completed in a year extremely inauspicious to Han rule. In the first lunar month of that year (3 February–2 March A.D. 200), a plot against Ts'ao Ts'ao was uncovered. The plot involved Tung Ch'eng, the brother-in-law of Emperor Hsien, and Liu Pei, a member of the Han imperial family and an army officer supporting the loyalist cause. As a result, the whole family of Tung Ch'eng were put to death and the forces of Liu Pei were routed by Ts'ao Ts'ao. The loyalist cause suffered a severe blow.[4] From 200 to 205, Ts'ao Ts'ao won a series of battles against his military rivals in north China. The triumph of the Ts'ao faction thus contrasted sharply with the declining position of the Han loyalists under the Chien-an régime. By 205, it had become quite clear that any hope of a second glorious restoration of Han rule had been merely wishful thinking.[5] These circumstances made a profound impact on Hsün Yüeh's life and thought, as is shown by the content and the literary style of his second major work, the *Shen-chien*.

The *Shen-chien* as we now have it comprises five chapters (*chüan*) of reflective essays, in contrast with the essentially historical accounts and discourses in the *Han-chi*. The first chapter, entitled *Cheng-t'i* or

127

'The Essence of Government', contains a number of relatively meaty, substantial and well-reasoned essays, some of which appear to be restatements of Hsün Yüeh's *lun* discourses included in the *Han-chi*. The second chapter, called *Shih-shih* or 'Current Affairs', contains discourses on nineteen itemized topics, some of which are only briefly discussed. The third chapter, called *Su-hsien* or 'Common Superstitions', and the fourth and the fifth chapters, called *Tsa-yen* or 'Miscellaneous Dialogues, I–II', contain many expositions in question-and-answer form, their contents ranging from metaphysics, religion, and pseudo-science, to problems of human nature, politics, and literature. While some of these expositions follow a logical and systematic sequence of inquiry and explanation, others are quite arbitrarily set out and cursorily treated. In fact, some of the passages in the *Shen-chien* are so laconic and inconsistent in style that they appear to have been extemporized.[6]

The title *Shen-chien* means 'lengthening', 'extending', or 'reiterating' the *chien* (mirror, reflection, lessons of history).[7] The Chinese character *chien* had a highly complex meaning. The archaic script of the word (the ideograph *chien* without the metal *chin* radical, as the one which appeared in the *Han-chi* Epilogue) signified a man looking into a container of water; from this seemed to evolve the idea of 'overseeing' and 'watching for a warning'[8]; it also acquired the connotation of 'precedent' or 'historical lesson', as the word was used in the Confucian classics.[9] When the bronze mirror came into use, it was called *chien* (usually with the metal *chin* radical, as the ideograph in the title *Shen-chien*), something from which one took reflections.[10] More importantly, on some bronze mirrors there were engraved certain sacred diagrams or mottos on state affairs which the ruler might readily peruse or reflect upon. Inscriptions on the bronze tripod, the tortoise-shell, and the mirror *chien* were mentioned as three important ways of commemorating the ordinances or canons of the court.[11] *Chien* as a sacred article of the court, or an historical lesson left behind by the sage-rulers, thus came to symbolize not only the political power of the state but also the religious sanction for it.[12] And the loss of *chien* – the ability to see correctly and interpret the models and lessons provided by history – often connoted the loss of the Mandate of Heaven.[13]

The Prefatory Section of the *Shen-chien* may be 'paraphrased' as follows:

The foundations of the Way are nothing but humanity [*jen*] and righteousness [*i*]. These are woven into the Five Classics and other writings like warp and woof. They are manifested in the odes and hymns, and in the music and dance. The mirror of history [ch'ien-chien or former chien] is already clear.[14] It need only be reiterated [shen] through time. Therefore, the ancient Sage-rulers only devoted themselves to the reiteration [shen] and stressing of humanity and righteousness. Faithfully following [the Way] continuously is what I call Shen-chien.[15]

In other words, truth itself may be timeless, but its specific meaning to men – its significance as the lesson of history – needs constantly to be restated; the chien needs to be continually reflected upon. Hence the writing of the Shen-chien.

The view that the canonical writ needed to be continually extended and brought up to date was shared by many scholars in Han times.[16] Ts'ai Yung (A.D. 133–99), an older contemporary of Hsün Yüeh's, in a commentary on Pan Ku's treatise Tien-yin, wrote: ' Tien refers to the canons and ordinances; yin means to extend and lengthen. The Shu-ching canon [The Book of Historical Documents] expounded the ordinance of [the Sage-ruler] Yao in the chapter Yao-tien [Canon of Yao] [17]; the Han dynasty continues the lineage [of Yao], extending and lengthening it [to the present time].' [18] According to Han tradition, both the sacred teaching of the legendary Sage-ruler Yao and his familial line were continued and lengthened through Han rule.[19] Hidden behind this view of the canonical writ was a mysterious notion of piety: by following the sacred teaching of the ancient Sage-ruler Yao, the Han dynastic ruler would seem to secure the continuation of Yao's sacred lineage both philosophically and as a matter of family duty. To a Han loyalist like Hsün Yüeh, no blessing greater than this could descend on the dynasty. So by calling his second major work Shen-chien, which was synonymous with Tien-yin, Hsün Yüeh seems to have drawn another deliberate parallel between himself and Pan Ku (the author of the Tien-yin) whose Han-shu had successfully commemorated the glorious restoration of the Han in the first century A.D.

The style of the Shen-chien is very difficult, especially when it is compared with the lucid style of the earlier work, the Han-chi. Generally, Hsün Yüeh's discourses in the Han-chi are fluent, high-sounding, well conceived and lucidly reasoned, and otherwise written in a straightforward manner; those in the Shen-chien are obscure, ambiguous, and extremely terse or laconic in style. In fact, the difference in style between the Han-chi and the Shen-chien is so obvious that it may even be detected in those few pieces rendered into English in this book.[20]

It may be remarked that, in both the Han-chi and the Shen-chien, Hsün Yüeh's direct comments on historical events are more straightforward and to the point, while his discourses on non-historical topics tend to be relatively difficult and obscure. However, the more obscure or laconic style of the *Shen-chien* shows itself in those passages in the *Han-chi* and the *Shen-chien* which are nearly identical in purport, meaning, or content.[21] These provide us with examples for critical comparison between two works by the same author.

The abstractness of Hsün Yüeh's writing in the *Shen-chien* is evident in his formal eulogy of Han rule in the second paragraph. The paragraph may be paraphrased as follows:

The sacred Han receives the Mandate from Heaven.[22] It reveres and assists in Heaven's work,[23] resulting in merits encompassing the whole universe.[24] There are valiant ministers who bring order out of disorder.[25] Waste and ruin are restored according to a grand plan.[26] Its institutions follow the model of the Three Dynasties.[27] The Emperor sincerely leads in his moral excellence.[28] His meritorious deeds accumulate with time.[29] The heavenly Way is here.[30] The Emperor need only exert himself toward it.[31] Grace will extend high and low.[32] Peaceful prosperity will prevail in the myriad states. Oh, how far-reaching.[33]

This second paragraph, with the first paragraph quoted earlier, constitute Hsün Yüeh's Prolegomena to the *Shen-chien* and set the style of the whole work, which contrasts sharply with the style of the *Han-chi* as illustrated by its prolegomenon, which was translated and discussed in the preceding chapter. In the two passages in the *Shen-chien* Hsün Yüeh has used only 124 characters to restate the basic themes which he had set forth in the lengthy Foreword and Introduction of the *Han-chi*. In the matter of style, the abstractness and terseness of the *Shen-chien* were mainly effected by the omission of many proper names and specific historical allusions which had found their way into the corresponding passages in the *Han-chi*.

The only proper name in the two passages quoted above from the *Shen-chien* is the name of the Han dynasty; all other terms which might be expressed by a number of proper names or by historical references have been exchanged for 'weaker' abstract, common, or collective nouns, as shown in the tabulation on p. 131.

The passage from the *Shen-chien* which contains Hsün Yüeh's formal eulogy of Han rule (the second passage quoted above) is not only extremely laconic in style but also ambiguous in meaning. In fact the Chinese text of this passage is utterly untranslatable. The English rendering of this passage as given above is only a paraphrase of the original, coming as close to its meaning as can be managed through the labyrinth of classical quotations and historical allusions, which may be deciphered with the clues provided by the commentator of the *Shen-chien*.[34]

Transliteration of terms from the *Shen-chien*	English rendering	Abstractness	Proper names and historical reference involved
wu-tien	the five classics	C	*Shu-ching*, *Shih-ching*, *Ch'un-ch'iu*, etc.
ch'ün-chi	various writings	C	Historical works such as the Chronicles of Ch'u and Chin, the *Ch'un-ch'iu* of Lu, *Han-shu*, and philosophical works such as *Mencius* and *Hsün-tzu*
chien	lesson of history	A	As found in *Ch'un-ch'iu*, etc.
sheng-wang	sage-rulers	B or C	King Yao, King Shun, King Yü, etc.
san-tai	the three ancient dynasties	C	The Hsia, the Shang, and the Chou Dynasties

Abstractness of terms: A. abstract noun; B. common noun; C. collective noun.

Ostensibly, this passage constitutes an eulogy of Han rule. It contains many quotations from the *Shu-ching* canons. Taken together, these quotations allude to the achievements by a series of sage-rulers of remote antiquity: 'the valiant ministers' and those who 'bring order out of disorder' refer to the reign of the sage-ruler King Wu of the Chou dynasty; the 'restoration of waste and ruin' refers to the merit of the legendary sage-ruler King Yü of the Hsia dynasty, and so on. To traditional Chinese scholars, this difficult passage has seemed to convey a suggestion that Han rule may be compared to the sacred reigns of Golden Antiquity, and to be intimating a warning to Ts'ao Ts'ao, implicitly one of the 'valiant ministers' (*hu-ch'en*) in Hsün Yüeh's time (just as Ts'ao was implicitly referred to as the *k'ang-fu*, 'over-powerful minister', and *chiao-chiao tsün ch'en* 'strong and virtuous minister', in the Foreword and Epilogue of the *Han-chi*).[35]

The actual Chinese text of the passage, however, is far more intriguing. First of all, the so-called quotations from the *Shu-ching* were not quotations in the usual sense, but were characters taken out of their context from the *Shu-ching*; in the *Shen-chien*, these archaic characters were put together in expressions; each of these expressions referred to one aspect of Han rule, while their component characters each alluded to a whole passage in the *Shu-ching* canons.[36] Furthermore, each of these expressions presented a literal meaning diametrically opposite to the import of the classical allusions in their component characters.[37] By this literary manipulation, each of the five compact expressions in the third, fourth, and fifth sentences of the passage presented a literal meaning antithetic to its historical allusion.

Transliteration of the Chinese expression	Literal meaning	Antithetic meaning
hu-ch'en	tiger ministers	valiant or obedient ministers
luan-cheng	disorderly government	orderly government
huang	desolation	cultivation
pi	ruins	establishment
yin	obstruction	construction

These expressions all appear in those sentences which depict the general historical condition from which the sacred Han rule emerged. Literally, these sentences read: ' There were *hu-ch'en* [tiger ministers], *luan-cheng* [disorderly government]. And the time was nothing but *huang* [desolation], *pi* [ruins], and *yin* [obstruction] . . .' Taken literally, this appears to be an appropriate description of the difficult conditions in 209–202 B.C. or in A.D. 22–9, when popular rebellions had just overthrown the imperial government and China was ravaged by civil wars – the situation out of which the Former and the Later Han dynasties were to rise triumphantly.[38]

However, as the commentator of the *Shen-chien* pointed out, the terms *hu-ch'en*, *luan-cheng*, *huang*, *pi*, and *yin* each bore a connotation completely different from its literal meaning, as rendered above. Accordingly, the statement conveyed by these terms has a double meaning: its dark side depicts the preceding gloom; its bright side connotes the resulting felicity. This double meaning would be particularly pertinent to Hsün Yüeh's own time. The literal reading of the statement depicted the real conditions of the time: there were the tiger ministers (Ts'ao Ts'ao and his group), and the time was nothing but desolation and ruin. The literary allusions in the passage, on the other hand, accorded well with the Han loyalist's pious anticipation: given another miracle of ' restoration ', a third Han dynasty would appear, just as glorious as the preceding two (the Former and the Later Han dynasties, which had emerged from equally difficult and unpropitious conditions).[39] The key to this miracle lay in the hands of the ambivalent *hu-ch'en* – whether the strong man Ts'ao Ts'ao wished to make good his administration by identifying himself with the ' valiant minister ' or to let the state fall into disorder, becoming himself a ' tiger minister ', would depend upon his own judgement. Hsün Yüeh could only hope for a miracle.

The obscurity and vagueness of the style of the *Shen-chien* has aroused the suspicion of some Chinese critics. Huang Chen (flourished 1256–70) thought that the literary style of the *Shen-chien* was 'humiliatingly weak' (*pei-jo*) in comparison with that of the *Han-chi*; he doubted whether the existing *Shen-chien* was really from Hsün Yüeh's own hand.[40] However, a detailed study of the textual history of the *Shen-chien* seems to prove the authenticity of the present text beyond doubt.[41] A more plausible explanation of the stylistic difference between the *Han-chi* and the *Shen-chien* must be sought elsewhere.

Another critic, Yang Ch'i-kuang of the Ch'ing dynasty, thought that the corrupt state of the *Shen-chien* might have been due to the political pressure brought to bear on Hsün Yüeh by the Ts'ao régime.[42] As mentioned earlier, Ts'ao Ts'ao's attitude toward the dignitaries at the titular Han court hardened considerably after his military successes in north China in 200–5. Yüan Hung noted in the *Hou-Han chi* that Hsün Yüeh was politically frustrated when he wrote the *Shen-chien*.[43] A similar statement in Yüeh's 'Biography' reads:

By that time [*c.* 205], state power had shifted to the hands of the Ts'ao clique. The [Han] Emperor could only humble himself [by maintaining a non-committal attitude toward government affairs]. Yüeh wished to make his recommendations and censures on current affairs, but he soon found that his counsels could not be adopted by those in authority. He then wrote the *Shen-chien*.[44]

Political pressure and his own disillusionment thus had a definite effect on the later writing of Hsün Yüeh. Of the three notables who attended on and lectured to Emperor Hsien, only Hsün Yüeh died a natural death. In his *Han-chi* discourses, Hsün Yüeh had discussed in detail the difficulty of surviving under unfavourable conditions; to do this, one would have 'to grind the square and make it round' or 'bend the straight and make it crooked'.[45] He had probably learned the lessons of history too well to risk himself in any unnecessary blunders. The 'humiliatingly weak' style of the *Shen-chien* might therefore be one indication of the author's way of self-preservation in a dark age.

Hsün Yüeh was, however, not a mere escapist. Although he adopted a vague and elusive style in writing the *Shen-chien*, he nonetheless remained steadfast in his basic stand as a Confucian.[46] What was changed was probably the 'appearance' rather than the 'substance' of his work, his approach to the issues of his time rather than his basic conviction concerning them. Hsün Yüeh himself seems to have admitted and apologized for this. In a dialogue in the *Shen-chien*, he posed the question: if what the Sage had to say should be simple and straight, then why were the canonical classics written (presumably by the Sage) in such an obscure and difficult style? The answer which he gave was: truth or reality itself is neither simple nor straight; to express adequately the truth or reality which is obscure and subtle, the Sage could not but adopt an equally subtle style.[47] Beneath the change in Hsün Yüeh's political attitude and literary style as seen in the *Shen-chien*, there seems to be an important change in his intellectual orientation: a deeper insight into the ' truth or reality that is obscure and subtle '.

The Chien-an élite felt the complex tension between their opposition towards and a conflicting loyalty to the imperial order equally in their political, moral, and intellectual worlds. They were bitterly aware of the shortcomings of the imperial authority as represented by the ruling dynasty and the court. But they were even more fearful of the consequences of the imperial downfall – the political and moral disarray which the élite's previous activism had helped to foster. In their reflective self-criticism and their intellectual pursuit of a remedy, the cultivated élite in this transitional period searched the canonical classics and the history of the remote and the recent past for inspiration. To some of them, the best remedy lay in a restoration of the imperial order (now represented by the house of Liu and the Han court), an order which had been tested and strengthened by the lessons of the dynastic decline and resurrection. Thus after the Tung Cho disaster in A.D. 189–95, many of the former dissident élite had become loyalists toward Han rule, the only stable imperial institution of which they had knowledge and experience.[48]

In writing the *Han-chi*, Hsün Yüeh had resolved the basic conflict between his pious hope for a Han restoration and his bitter knowledge of the shortcomings of the dynasty in its past performance. In this work, he re-examined the history of the Han dynasty through its cycle of rise, decline and restoration between *c.* 206 B.C. and A.D. 23. Within this cycle, the dynasty had undergone a real fall under the reigns of its mediocre rulers but it had also experienced a real revival with the arrival of a virtuous restorer, the Emperor Kuang-wu. This implied that the merit and mandate of the dynasty was so strongly established that no petty usurper properly deserved its legacy. Thus the sixteen years of Wang Mang's reign (A.D. 8–23) were but a small cycle of trial within the greater cycle, in which the usurper merely cleared the way for the meritorious restorer. Within this frame of reference in the *Han-chi*, Hsün Yüeh was free to express his criticisms of the Former Han rulers and ministers and to assess their merits or faults.[49]

The concept of historical cycles passing through a time-span contains a theoretical difficulty, for it provides arguments which may be used against the existing dynasty. After all, the time-span of two hundred years of the Former Han (or even the four hundred years of the Former and the Later Han taken together) is but a small stretch measured against eternity. To prove the enduring strength of an 'everlasting dynasty' through such a limited time-span would appear like an experiment on something finite used to infer something infinite – a fallacy noted by Hsün Yüeh himself in one of his reflections in the *Shen-chien*.[50]

This theoretical difficulty, coupled with his awareness of the futility of the attempted Han restoration at Hsü, seemed to force Hsün Yüeh to abandon his limited plan of historical investigation and deal with something more indefinite. His aim in the *Shen-chien* was to prove the permanence of the imperial order itself, an order now not necessarily associated with any particular dynasty. This he accomplished by ascribing a transcendent order to human affairs, by correlating the immutability of the Way of Heaven with the immortality of man's institutions.

Hsün Yüeh's orientation toward the transcendent becomes evident in the third paragraph of the *Shen-chien* – the beginning of the chapter on 'The Essence of Government' (*Cheng-t'i*). In the prolegomenon to the *Han-chi*,[51] Hsün Yüeh had explicitly glorified the tradition of Han rule. But now, in this part of the *Shen-chien*, he expressed a much more subtle concept than that of the 'rule of propriety' vested in the imperial power.[52] He postulated a Way of Heaven inherent in the reciprocating forces of *yin* and *yang*; this was correlated with the Way of Earth, consisting of relative softness and hardness (*kang* and *yu*, fluidity-solidity) in the myriad things on earth; this was further correlated with the Way of Men, consisting of *jen* (kind-heartedness, humanity) and *i* (justice, righteousness). These three Ways determine man's actions in the political, social, and moral spheres, extending from the sovereign ruler to the masses. The eternal Way of Heaven thus sanctioned the immortality of the Way of Men.[53]

In this redirection of his intellectual interest – from the concrete to the abstract, from the limited scope of dynastic history to the indefinite realm of reflective thinking – Hsün Yüeh was aided as well as hindered by the specifically Chinese concept of history, with its inherent notion of temporal transcendency.[54] In his commentary on historical events Hsün Yüeh had never lost sight of the transcendental meaning of the lessons which he drew from these events. Hsün Yüeh's *lun* discourses in the *Han-chi* were reflections (*chien*) upon groups of events which were distant from one another in time but inter-related by the author's didactic postulates. Similarly, Hsün Yüeh's reflections in the *Shen-chien* were mainly based on his own observation of human affairs, affairs disconnected in time and not limited by the span of the Han dynasty. Hsün Yüeh's exercise in abstract or metaphysical thinking was therefore restricted by his primary concern with man.[55] In this sense, Hsün Yüeh the historian had prepared as well as defined Hsün Yüeh the philosopher. And the *Shen-chien* was but a complementary volume to the *Han-chi*, expounding and extending the lessons which Hsün Yüeh drew from historical studies. Thus when Hsün Yüeh wrote in the Prefatory Section of the *Shen-chien* that ' the mirror of history [*ch'ien-chien*, the former *chien*] is already clear; it need only be reiterated [*shen*] through time ', by ' the mirror of history ' he probably meant the *Han-chi* – the historical work which he had completed some five years before. Accordingly, the title of *Shen-chien* itself seems to have a double meaning, of which Hsün Yüeh himself might or might not have been aware.

CONFUCIANISM AND TAOISM IN ' CH'ING-T'AN '

Chinese bibliographers have generally classified Hsün Yüeh's *Shen-chien* as a Confucian (*ju-chia*) philosophical work.[56] Hsün Yüeh, as he expresses himself in his *Han-chi* and more so in his *Shen-chien*, was, however, a Confucian in a very special sense. Like many of his Confucian predecessors, Hsün Yüeh absorbed many non-Confucian elements into his work.[57] But unlike those Confucians who rose with the high tide of Confucian popularity in the early Han and constructed elaborate systems of synthesis sanctioning the emerging imperial order,[58] Hsün Yüeh lived in a time of imperial decline, with Confucian doctrine itself at a low ebb. He had been searching for a remedy for the evils of his time in both Confucian and non-Confucian sources, but after prolonged reflection returned to an essentially Confucian stand. He found that he had to serve the needs of his time in ways significantly different from those of his predecessors.

The old grandiose Confucian synthesis was no longer meaningful.[59] But Hsün Yüeh was convinced that Confucianism still contained valuable truths about the universe, the nature of men, and all the elements of human experience. In his own words, he was transmitting the old Way, not creating a new one. Thus the *Shen-chien* is an assemblage of old sayings, but addressed to a new audience. The novelty of his restatement or synthesis is evident in the style of the *Shen-chien*, as we have seen, as well as in certain shifts of emphasis and the orientation of its contents.

Hsün Yüeh's concept of the Way or *tao* was central to his concerns. In pre-Han times, *tao* or the Way had been used by the Taoist in its predominantly metaphysical sense, referring to ' nature ' or the cosmos, immanent and transcending the entire physical universe.[60] *Tao* was also an important term used by the Confucians, though its reference had often been confined to the human sphere: for them *tao* was the ultimate truth or basic postulate in men's social, political, moral and religious life.[61] In Han Confucianism, the Taoist idea of the trans-cendent cosmic Way was absorbed into a grandiose synthesis to supple-ment the pragmatic Confucian social teaching and to become the linking element in the postulated Heaven–Earth–Men triad which sanctioned the holistic imperial order.[62] *Tao*, as postulated by these Taoists and Han Confucians before Hsün Yüeh, transcended not only the spheres of the supernatural, the natural, and the human, but also the temporal spans of the past and the present, thus providing a mystic force unifying the changed and the unchanged (or the changing and the non-changing).[63]

In comparison, Hsün Yüeh's concept of *tao* was narrower. He was mainly interested in bringing the omnipresent into the present or extending the finite into the infinite. His efforts in this direction may be seen in the use of certain peculiar terms or categories of *tao* in the *Shen-chien*, such as *tao-pen* (Trunks of the Way),[64] *tao-ching* (Warps of the Way),[65] *tao-ken* (Roots of the Way),[66] and *tao-shih* (Fruits of the Way).[67] This play of words deprived the *tao* of much of its trans-cendent potential. His characterization of the Way of Heaven, Earth and Men, as nothing but *yin*-and-*yang*, softness–hardness, and *jen*-and-*i* respectively, was also more restrictive than that of the early Han Confucians.[68] This indicates that Hsün Yüeh was essentially a prag-matic historian and mainly concerned to reflect on the manifest and the particular. Even though he conscientiously attempted to abandon mundane history and to orient himself towards the transcendental, he could not help exposing his real concern – the preservation of order in human society.

However, if Hsün Yüeh the particularist failed fully to espouse the omnipresent and transcendent Way, he compensated by vigorously exploring the particular Way of Changes, the interaction between the universal and the particular.[69] To Hsün Yüeh the historian and classical thinker, the Way of Changes might be comprehended dialectically and by analogy. The canonical Confucian *Classic of Changes* (*I-ching*) provided him with both the inspiration and the authority for this pursuit.[70]

According to ancient Chinese metaphysical and scientific thinking, as preserved in the *Classic of Changes*, the cosmos presented itself as a myriad 'beings', mutually dependent and forever changing, which were reducible to certain basic elements or roots according to numerological formulae. These elements or their 'numbers' (*shu*), though potentially infinite, may be comprehended and distinguished by the mind through analogical and dialectical reasoning. By analogical reasoning, one may always reduce the apparent multiplicity of the myriad to a basic binary polarity, i.e. *yin-yang*, or reverse the process from these two to the myriad. These two processes of reasoning, that is, from the concrete and specific to the abstract and universal and *vice versa*, may be illustrated by the following examples:

(1) knives – knife – metal – hardness – *yang* (and in the reverse direction);

(2) *yin* – weakness – softness – water – rivers (and in the reverse direction).

By dialectical reasoning, one may infer the unknown and thus the infinite from the known, or create a new synthesis to subsume the differences which cannot be merged by analogical reasoning alone. These may be illustrated by the following examples:

(1) *yang* (the positive) – non-*yang* (the not positive) – *yin* (the negative);

(2) *yin*-and-*yang* (the discriminative negative and positive) – *t'ai chi* (the non-discriminant Unique One, that which is definitely neither negative nor positive) – *wu-chi* (the non-discriminant indefinite, the unresolvably infinite).[71]

Numbers are themselves both unique and common, independent and inter-related. They imply the dialectical antithesis by being particularist, restrictive and finite in themselves as units, but universalistic, transcendent and infinite in their quantification and in their combinability. Their restrictive uniqueness enables men to assign them to their particular lots (*shu*), which are immutable in themselves. But the universality and combinability of numbers at least projects a nuance of transcendency, which helps men to identify their particular lot (*shu*) with the abstract number (*shu*) and thus to forget their finiteness, or to relate each man's limited lot (*shu*, number, lot, such as the length of life-span, the contour of a man's environmental conditions, special visitation of bad or good fortunes) to a Greater Number (*ta-shu*) whose immensity is the same as the Universe.[72]

To the *I-ching* numerologist, numbers demonstrate one special knowable essence: the antithesis between the odd and the even, which is equated with the antithesis between the *yang* and the *yin*. Like the *yin-yang* antithesis which may be transcended by dialectical reasoning, the odd-even antithesis may be transcended in numerological manipulations:

> *yang* (one extremity) *yang* (in extreme) produced
> *yin* (another extremity)
> odd + odd = even.

By manipulating analogical and dialectical reasoning, the *I-ching* numerologist is thus able to define and at the same time transcend all things – both the known and the unknown.[73]

In the *Shen-chien*, both analogical and dialectical reasoning are vigorously pursued, though not to the theoretical extreme. The *I-ching* postulates of 'change' (*pien*), 'numbers' (*shu*), and 'transcending' (*t'ung*) are recurrent themes in Hsün Yüeh's reflections.[74] And, as pointed out by the critic Huang Chen who considered the *Shen-chien* an imitation of the *Fa-yen* written by Yang Hsiung (53 B.C.–A.D. 18), a famous *I-ching* numerological theoretician,[75] Hsün Yüeh's infatuation with numbers is manifest in his use of the many 'numerological categories' in the *Shen-chien*, such as the 'two means',[76] the 'five virtues',[77] the 'six tempers',[78] the 'three primal spheres',[79] the 'five human businesses',[80] the 'hundred officers',[81] the 'six principles' of the government of the ancient sage-rulers,[82] the 'four evils'[83] and the 'five basic government programmes',[84] and many others.

Hsün Yüeh's manipulation of dialectical reasoning can also be seen in a number of antithetical terms in the *Shen-chien*, such as happiness-worry (*lo-yu*),[85] obeying-opposing (*shun-ni*),[86] injuring-benefiting (*shun-i*),[87] bending-stretching (*ch'ü-shen*),[88] discord-accord (*wei-shun*),[89] fortune-calamity (*hsing-tsai*),[90] 'trouble that begets more troubles' and 'trouble that mitigates troubles' (*yu-nan chih nan, wu-nan chih nan*),[91] and 'offences that constitute real crimes' and 'offences that constitute no real crimes' (*yu-tsui chih tsui, wu-tsui chih tsui*).[92]

Number-mysticism seems to offer some relief to the mind in despair. Frustrated and confined as he was in the Chien-an milieu, Hsün Yüeh found little consolation in his studies of Confucian dogma or of recent history.[93] The only hope which he might entertain seemed to lie in changes in the future. Concerning the future, an agnostic might console himself with the thought: though the future may be uncertain, the present is equally unsure – can one be certain that the evil present would not come to pass? To the *I-ching* dialectician, a greater consolation might be found in the following reasoning: history (the ever-changing past) shows that all glories, good fortunes, and happinesses had taken their course and been succeeded by humiliations, calamities, and sufferings; would not the reverse also be true: that present evil would be followed by better things? This seemed to be the solution which Hsün Yüeh found in his dialectical reflections: submit to the Way (of change) in times of misfortune and wait for the Way to reverse its cycle.[94] To use a conventional *I-ching* precept: 'When calamity [symbolized by *P'i*, the 12th hexagram in the *I-ching*] goes to the extreme, good fortune [symbolized by *T'ai*, the 11th hexagram in the *I-ching*] arrives.'[95]

There is a relativism underlying this dialectic numerology, and it posed a logical difficulty for Hsün Yüeh's Confucian thinking. The dialectical infinite transcends not only good and bad fortune, but all man-made dogmas as well. What is taken to be fortunate or unfortunate at this moment may be reversed in the next moment, and this is susceptible to further reversals in the next moment still. Thus what is certain in a limited sphere would become uncertain in a wider arena, and one might well doubt whether any specific and ultimate fortune can be called good or bad. By implication one would be led to question the identity of good and bad as such – a grave offence against Confucian moral dogmatism.[96]

This implied moral relativism seems to have troubled Hsün Yüeh, and this may account for the fluctuation of his position between the Confucian and the Taoist stands on moral issues. The difference between the Confucian and the Taoist conceptions of *tao* or the Way lies not in the idea of the transcendent or of 'nature' *per se*, but in the relation between the transcendental (nature) and the particular (Men). To the Taoist, *tao* or 'nature' is omnipresent; it is one and the same in the world of men and of animals, and in the inanimate world. Thence comes the precept of 'returning to nature', to the amoral original state of indifference and indiscrimination, which gives rise to libertinism (the return to the animal nature) and quietism (the return to the inanimate state).[97] The Confucian, on the other hand, observes the oneness as well as the multiplicity in the Universe, in which the myriad spheres of being share their oneness or communion with the Unique One (*t'ai-chi*) but each of them follows its particular nature (the human differentiated from the animal which is further differentiated from the inanimate). It is this particularistic nature of man's accomplished state (*te*, virtue or morality in a broad sense) that was emphasized by the Confucian as a complement to the *tao*. And this particular nature or state of men is defined by the Confucianist as 'naturally' moral (*te*, moral virtue in a narrower sense), or at least morally conditioned by the conflict between the moral and the immoral elements inherent in the nature of animate beings.[98]

Although Hsün Yüeh acknowledged the existence and operation of amoral forces greater than man (i.e. the amoral *yin-yang* or *kang-yu* in the Way of Heaven and Earth,[99] the cyclical working of fate or 'numbers',[100] the influence of changing times and environments,[101] or incomprehensible apparitions),[102] he nevertheless defined the Way or *tao* as being moral from the viewpoint of man (*tao-te*).[103] At birth, man is endowed with his particular nature by Heaven, but the development of this nature needs nourishment from education and constraint by law.[104] Thus Hsün Yüeh rejected libertinism.[105] According to him, although man's life-span was predetermined and could not be lengthened by human effort, one might nevertheless cultivate and make full use of one's life within the given limit;[106] one was able to do this because it was in accordance with one's nature, not because of influence from the extraneous supernatural.[107] The working of fate is uncontrollable, but in acknowledging it one ought not try to evade it either through superstitious practices or by escape into libertinism; one must play one's assigned role and fulfil the moral obligations arising from it, so that good fortune may be properly accorded and bad fortune mitigated.[108]

However, even with these elegant postulates, the gloomy issue of relativism cannot be entirely removed from Hsün Yüeh's thought, particularly where human fortune or misfortune are concerned. Explicitly, Hsün Yüeh reiterated the Confucian conviction that one is capable of knowing what is morally right and wrong and so must uphold the right within the human sphere although one may not know what is ultimately to be fortunate or unfortunate. However he tempered the severity of adhering to the right in the human sphere by making allowance for contingency or expediency (*ch'üan*) as determined by elements of temporal change. His recurrent injunction to 'acknowledge and comprehend the changing lot' (*i pien-shu tso t'ung*) together with his emphasis on reciprocity in the *Shen-chien* thus show a covert tendency toward moral relativism which later became predominant among the eccentric individualistic élite during the Age of Disunity.[109]

Inherent in Hsün Yüeh's modified attitude toward moral dogmatism is his new conception of human nature. Here the emphasis was shifted from the early Confucian assertion of a morally defined human nature (*hsing*) to a more favourable consideration of the more primitive condition of human feelings (*ch'ing*). In his brief review of pre-Han and Han Confucian ideas of human nature, Hsün Yüeh criticized in turn the theses of Mencius that human nature is all good, of Hsün-tzu that human nature is all bad, of Kung-sun-tzu that human nature is neither good nor bad, and of Yang Hsiung that human nature is a mixture of good and bad.[110] Hsün Yüeh contended that all these theses were one-sided.[111]

He further criticized the Han Confucian thesis which separated human nature (*hsing*) from human feelings (*ch'ing*) and which contended that the first would be all good and the second explicitly or implicitly evil.[112] He argued that by holding human nature to be all good and human feelings to be all bad, one made the bad man devoid of nature and the Sage devoid of feelings.[113] He admitted that 'kind-heartedness and righteousness' (*jen-i*) which come from human nature were always good, whereas 'likes and dislikes' (*hao-wu*) which come from human feelings were sometimes good and sometimes bad. But he contended that this did not prove that human nature itself is always good and human feelings themselves sometimes bad. For what is called 'kind-heartedness or righteousness' implies a moral judgement passed on the accomplished action, whereas the feelings of 'like or dislike' precede the action and judgement and are therefore morally indeterminate.[114]

Hsün Yüeh further argued that to do good it was not necessary to mitigate one's *ch'ing* (feelings, passions) by one's *hsing* (moral nature) or that one's *hsing* must be stronger than one's *ch'ing*; it rather depended on how strong the extraneous 'stimulus' would be which determined what 'response' one was induced to make. To illustrate this point, he wrote:

Some one said: 'Man's [feelings] are such that once he sees a profitable course he immediately likes it. That he can be restrained by [the precept of] kind-heartedness and righteousness [jen-i] is because his moral nature [*hsing*] suppresses his feelings [*ch'ing*]. But when his moral nature is weaker than his feelings and cannot suppress them, then his feelings will have their own way in evil-doing.'

I said 'It is not so ... if there is a man who likes both wine and meat, then when the [attraction of] meat wins he will eat and when the [attraction of] wine wins he will drink. The two [attractions] contend with each other; that which wins will have its way. It is not because by his feelings he wants wine and by his nature he wants meat.' Now if there is a man who likes both profit and righteousness, then when the [attraction of] righteousness wins he seeks righteousness and when the [temptation of] profit wins he seeks profit. These two elements also contend with each other; that which wins will have its way...[115]

The thesis which Hsün Yüeh challenged was the one accepted by many Confucians, particularly the Neo-Confucians;[116] Hsün Yüeh's antithesis, equating 'righteousness' and 'profit' with 'meat' and 'wine' both as outside attractions, is so daringly unconventional that it seems anti-Confucian.

Concerning such extraneous elements working in 'historical' situations, Hsün Yüeh posed an interesting question: Granted that the people in Golden Antiquity were all primitive and good and so was the government under the Sage-rulers, was not this due to the inborn moral nature (*t'ien-hsing*) of men? Hsün Yüeh seems to answer 'no'. The people of Golden Antiquity might seem to have been primitive and good while those in a corrupt age (i.e. under the despotic Ch'in rule) seem corrupted. But this, according to Hsün Yüeh, was due to the influence of the different times; and these influences comprised several elements. People living in the mountains seem more primitive, while those living in the market-places seem more sophisticated; this is due to environmental influences. People ruled by wicked rulers become disorderly, while those ruled by good rulers are orderly; this is due to political persuasion. In explaining the difference in environmental influences, Hsün Yüeh was aware of the economic factors: the people in Golden Antiquity were few in number, hence they were primitive and yet good-natured. All this, he argued, has nothing to do with man's inborn nature.[117]

It is human feeling, *ch'ing*, the immediate state of the human mind, rather than the morally defined and cultivated human nature (*hsing*), that underlay Hsün Yüeh's conception of man, of moral conduct, and of good government.[118] He stated that feeling likes and dislikes, being basic to all men, would be the same for the ruler and the ruled; this 'same-feelingness' constituted the essence of sympathy which, more than the intellectual aspect of moral exhortation, would bind together the ruler and the ruled in a holistic state.[119] The duty of the sage-ruler should be to extend happiness to all-under-heaven, while the privilege of the ruler should lie in the 'reward of happiness' which all-under-heaven extended to him.[120]

As a general principle, Hsün Yüeh asserted, the ruler should be absolutely honest in his likes or dislikes.[121] In specific situations, however, the feelings of the ruled must be sympathetically but intelligently considered.[122] Thus, a superior man may be inspired to do good through an appeal to his noble feelings; the feelings or desires of an inferior man, on the other hand, can be neither solely relied upon nor dogmatically suppressed – they need to be properly guided and skilfully regulated;[123] in the administration of justice, human feelings should be considered and made manifest.[124] And Hsün Yüeh warned those in power that 'when people are not afraid of death, they cannot be intimidated by punishment; when people find no happiness in living, they cannot be exhorted to do good.' In these cases, Hsün Yüeh concluded, 'no government measures can avail'.[125]

In his reflections on human nature and moral conduct, Hsün Yüeh anticipated the intellectual interest of the post-Chien-an élite in the relationship between 'intellect' (*ts'ai*, lit. ability, talent) and 'moral conduct' (*hsing*, lit. conduct) or 'conscience' (*hsing*, the moral nature of men); these are touched on in two discourses in the *Shen-chien*.[126] In one of these discourses, Hsün Yüeh postulates a moral quality in human intellect by distinguishing two types of intellect: one is inborn (*pen*) and incorporated in man's primal nature and thus inseparable from man's moral conduct; the other was cultivated (*mo*) and can be separated from moral conduct.[127] In the other discourse, he stated that 'intellect' of the latter category was secondary in importance to 'moral conduct'.[128]

All these shifts in emphasis and orientation show the Taoist influence pervading Hsün Yüeh's thinking. Within the tradition of Taoist thought itself, two tendencies may be found. One, embodied in the *Lao-tzu*, is characterized by its cool condescension toward man, its concept of nature as a supreme and inhuman force, and its postulating *tao* as the *raison d'être* or the mechanism of nature. The other, embodied in the *Chuang-tzu*, is characterized by its compassion for man and its emphasis on *tao* as a mystic force working inside the human mind, transforming men and elevating them from their low condition.[129] It was mainly this latter tendency in Taoism, with its affinity to the 'romantic spirit' of the neo-Taoists, which prevailed in post-Han élite circles.[130] Although Hsün Yüeh rejected the Taoist concept of *tao* as an amoral law of nature, he seems to have accepted the romantic Taoist notion of man – that man, even reduced to his bare 'instinctive' feelings, still has something good in his nature.

There was a third tendency in Taoism, its emphasis on magic and physical immortality; the so-called religious *hsien* (immortal) Taoism which represented a mixture of corrupt Taoist ideas and the folk religion of Han times.[131] Being conversant with philosophical Taoism, Hsün Yüeh was in a better position to single out this particular branch of Taoism for criticism. From his studies of history, Hsün Yüeh could not but accept the evidence of historical documents concerning the apparition of superhuman beings. But he held that these so-called *shen-hsien* 'immortals' were merely the prodigies and monsters such as those occasionally found in far-away lands like 'the pygmy in the southern jungles'.[132] He had no faith in the alchemist's formula of elixir; he said that alchemistic experiments must accord with the law of nature and that it would be self-deception to infer a supernatural element from experiments conducted on the principles of natural law.[133]

Hsün Yüeh discussed in some detail the Taoist method of cultivating longevity through breathing exercises. Such exercises, he thought, were like taking medicine, good only for remedial purposes; when the body and the mind are in harmony, one need not resort to it.[134] According to Hsün Yüeh, the ideal way of attaining long life was to follow the Confucian precept and achieve harmony of body and mind.[135] He also severely criticized as self-deception the superstitious practice of healing sickness or avoiding danger by magic.[136]

Hsün Yüeh's criticism of superstition was, however, much inhibited by his formal Confucian stance. Although he did not quite believe in personified supernatural beings, he nevertheless upheld the Han state rituals of sacrifice and prayer to the spirits.[137] He also tolerated divination and *yin-yang* mysticism, even though he doubted the intervention of the supernatural in human affairs.[138] He approved the practice of physiognomy, which was much in vogue in his time, on the explicit ground of the natural relationship between the physical and mental condition of men,[139] but the deeper reason may well have been the earlier endorsement given to such practices by Confucius and Mencius.[140]

In all these areas of interest, from his infatuation with *I-ching* numerology to his encounter with vulgar Taoism, Hsün Yüeh simply reflected the intellectual currents of his time, currents which culminated in the pursuit of ' pure conversation ' (*ch'ing-t'an*) and ' dark learning ' (*hsüan-hsüeh*) in Wei and Chin élite circles. Many topics in the *Shen-chien*, such as the relationship between human nature (*hsing*), human feelings (*ch'ing*), and human intellect (*ts'ai*), the problem of ' arriving at ' the ultimate truth (*chih*), and the equivalence or disparity between our concept of the truth and our ability to express it in words, were all later to become important themes both in *ch'ing-t'an* conversations and *hsüan-hsüeh* pursuits.[141] In addition, the very terse and laconic style as well as the complex and ambiguous meaning of many of Hsün Yüeh's statements in the *Shen-chien* were to serve as models for later *ch'ing-t'an* works.

In fact, some of the writings or conversation pieces produced by Yüeh's uncle, Hsün Shuang, during the earlier *ch'ing-i* protest movement, were also later greatly admired by the *ch'ing-t'an* pioneers. In A.D. 219, when Sun Ch'üan, head of the regional state of Wu in the lower Yangtze river valley, temporarily acknowledged the supreme sovereignty of the Han–Ts'ao régime, Chung Yu (151–230), a dignitary of the Han–Ts'ao régime and a notable figure in the Chien-an élite circles, sent the following letter to Ts'ao P'i (Ts'ao Ts'ao's son, who became the Emperor Wen-ti of Wei in 220):

The late Ducal Minister [*Ssu-k'ung*] Hsün Shuang from my native commandery once remarked: 'Man should lead a passionate [way of life]; how endearing are those who endear themselves to me and how despicable are those who despise me!' When I think of Sun Ch'üan [with Shuang's words in my mind], [I cannot but] consider [Sun Ch'üan despicably] endearing.

In reply, Ts'ao P'i wrote:

From your letter, I know that you have been enchanted by that southern state [i.e. Wu]. As to the *ch'ing-t'an* of the Ducal Minister Hsün and [your calling] Sun Ch'üan 'despicably endearing', [holding your letter], sighing and laughing I cannot let it out of my hand. Should [the intriguing] Sun Ch'üan be lapsing into his intrigues again [i.e. reversing his attitude of submission], we should humiliate him by Hsü Shao's 'Monthly Comments on Personality' [*yueh-tan-p'ing*]. Sun Ch'üan has lived comforably as the [head of a] buffer state between two [hostile] states [i.e. the Han-Ts'ao and the Shu-Han, with which Sun Ch'üan had alternated his alliance]. Looking up and down to Hsün and Hsü is enough.[142]

Two points are noteworthy in these letters. First, they specifically relate Hsün Shuang's saying and Hsü Shao's 'Monthly Comments on Personality' to the *ch'ing-t'an*. Secondly, the style and meaning of these letters are quite as elliptic and gnomic (as indicated by the words which have had to be added in the translation) as many of Hsün Yüeh's statements in the *Shen-chien*, and represent the literary fashion of the time.[143]

Hsün Yüeh's 'Biography' mentions that Yüeh and other Attendants of the Emperor Hsien 'engaged in dialogues day and night', and that by the time when Yüeh wrote the *Shen-chien* 'state power had shifted to the hands of the Ts'ao clique and the emperor had to humble himself [by maintaining a non-committal attitude toward government affairs]'. This suggests that all the discourses made by Yüeh and his fellow Attendants were no more than verbal exercises – like the two witty pieces of badinage written by Chung Yu and Ts'ao P'i. One piece of such talk between Hsün Yüeh and his colleague K'ung Jung has been preserved in the *Fu-tzu*, presumably written by Fu Hsüan (217–78). This dialogue was said to have been prompted by a special event:

Toward the end of the Han dynasty, a certain person named Kuan Ch'iu-yang and his younger brother had travelled together with another companion. In a snow-storm, their food supply had been exhausted. Thereupon, Kuan and his younger brother killed and ate their companion in order to be able to continue their journey. Later both Kuan and his brother were pardoned [by the government] in a general amnesty.

A moral question thus arose, which probably became a conversational topic among the Chien-an élite. The question was: despite the government amnesty, should Kuan and his brother be considered morally liable for the death of the companion? K'ung Jung was recorded to have answered 'no', saying: 'Kuan loved his own body [and the body of his younger brother] which he owed to his father. In order to preserve his and his brother's lives, he had to devour his companion. There was nothing [morally] wrong in this action.' Hsün Yüeh differed and said: 'Kuan selfishly preserved [his own] life [*t'ou-sheng*] by destroying the life of others [*sha-sheng*]. Is not this a crime?' To this K'ung Jung was recorded as making the cold rejoinder: 'This companion was [just a casual companion and] not a friend of Kuan's... What Kuan destroyed was only a talking animal. It is just as if a dog had devoured a fox and the fox had swallowed a parrot. Why should you feel indignant about it?'[144]

The authenticity of this dialogue is questionable. But the terse and laconic style of Hsün Yüeh's rejoinder, which consists simply of the antithetic expression 'selfishly preserving life [*t'ou-sheng*] and destroying life [*sha-sheng*]' seems to match his style as used in the *Shen-chien*. In his expostulations, K'ung Jung is made to stand for anarchic sentimentalism of the kind expressed in the saying of Hsün Shuang cited above (about the 'passionate way' of liking those who like me and despising those who despise me); he also stands for the moral indifferentism (men are simply talking animals; their destruction calls for no special moral indignation) into which the world has sunk. Hsün Yüeh, on the other hand, remains a Confucian, concerned with the moral integrity of his fellow men.

Probably to counter-balance the implication of moral relativism in some of his other reflections,[145] Hsün Yüeh set an extremely high moral standard in a few passages in the *Shen-chien*, particularly in the last three paragraphs. In the first of these he wrote: 'Superior men have their permanent communion with righteousness and their permanent vow to faithfulness [i.e. as the supreme moral good]. If people must communicate [with one another in the mundane manner] before they can establish friendship and must take vows [in the mundane manner] to ensure this friendship, is this not narrow?'[146] This emphasis on righteousness and faithfulness as the supreme good, above and beyond the mundane relationships between communicating friends, contrasts sharply with the attitude attributed above to Hsün Shuang and K'ung Jung. Continuing his exhortation, Hsün Yüeh wrote: 'Highest is the one who makes no discrimination between the past and the present; next the one who makes no discrimination among those living within the [four] seas. If one's ideal is in union with all-under-heaven, how great a virtue! ' [147] While quantitatively the mind of the great man encompasses the multitude of all men, qualitatively it is beyond the multitude of common men. Thus Hsün Yüeh continued: ' The ideal of a great man is incomprehensible [to the masses]; its immensity is in union with the Way. The ideal of the masses of people is manifest; it conforms distinctly with the vulgar [social conventions]. Thus only when one's ideal is in union with the Way, will he not flow and sink amidst the vulgar.' [148]

In the second passage, Hsün Yüeh proposed an approach toward moral perfection (*chih*) in three ascending stages. First, the cultivation of moral conduct from the feeling of shame (*ch'ih*) toward the outside world; second, the cultivation of moral conduct from the feeling of shame toward the Divine Intelligence (*shen-ming*); third and the highest, to do this from the feeling of shame toward one's own self.[149] In the third and last paragraph, he went on to eliminate even the ' feeling of shame ' (an important Confucian criterion of moral virtue) from the supreme moral standard. He contended that ' one's ideal or virtue should come naturally from within and have nothing to do with shame ' (which still has an extraneous element in it).[150]

By setting a moral standard beyond the reach of ordinary men, Hsün Yüeh tended to undermine the pragmatic Confucian teaching which emphasized conformism, social conventions and social institutions. His concept of the moral absolute came close to the Taoist ideals of the Way and of the ' Superman ' in its contempt for the ordinary world. Probably with this in mind, Hsün Yüeh in the same last paragraph of the *Shen-chien* offered a compromise by stating that ' In moral virtue, one must compare oneself with the supreme; in desire, one must compare oneself with the lower men ... Thus one may approach towards the Sage and the Worthy.' Concluding the *Shen-chien*, he further stated: ' The best is the purest of the pure; the second best only approximates to this. Nowadays there is none who does better than to approximate to this. But if one can approximate to this, there will be no evil – this is good enough.' [151] From the absolute, Hsün Yüeh thus returned to the relative.

CONFUCIANISM, LEGALISM, AND HSÜN YÜEH'S COUNSELS

While the Taoist and the Han Confucian both postulated ' nature ' as a transcendental force underlying and sanctioning human society, they differed in their emphasis. For the Taoist, the end of human perfection lay in man's return to nature; for the Confucian, the ideal was man's elevation from his natural state to an advanced form of civilization. Although in philosophical matters Hsün Yüeh continued to vacillate between Confucianism and Taoism, his basic Confucian stance may be found in his concern with the kind of political programme needed to perfect men in society. This deep interest in government policy separated him from the pure Taoists and placed him among the Confucian-Legalists.[152]

The Legalists occasionally drew on the Way or *tao* to justify social order, but their chief emphasis was on political institutions and power within men's civilized society.[153] *Fa*, or methods, man-made rules and law, represented this basic orientation of the Legalists or *Fa-chia*.[154] Where the Confucian and the Legalist differed was not on law (*fa*) or coercive rules (*hsing*) as essential means of administration, but in the ideal of government. The Legalist considered ' peace and public order ' achieved by political force to be the means as well as the end of the state. The Confucian, admitting law and coercive power to be necessary for the maintenance of public order in a corrupt age, insisted that the ideal state under the sage-rulers should aim at the moral perfection of human society. Legalists are therefore often called ' realists ', and Confucians ' idealists '.[155]

For more than a century of its early history, the Han régime had followed the Legalist government system and statecraft which it inherited from their predecessors the Ch'in, so much so that Emperor Hsüan (reigned 74–69 B.C.) was said to have remarked that the Han tradition was founded on a mixture of Legalist and Confucian teaching.[156] And long after its overt conversion to Confucianism the Han régime was generally labelled: ' outwardly Confucian and inwardly Legalist ' (*yang ju, yin fa*).[157] The decline of the Legalist tradition, at least in the highest echelons of the court, came in the latter half of the first century B.C., when a number of doctrinaire Confucians rose to high positions in the civil bureaucracy while imperial centralism disintegrated as a result of the upsurge of regionalism reinforced by rampant nepotism in the provinces. Legalism fell to an even lower ebb under the highly conservative Later Han rule while Confucianism and neo-Taoism prevailed in the élite circles.[158]

As the Han régime deteriorated, an increasing number of critics began to peer through the veil of Confucian idealism in order to examine the evil conditions of the time. Some of these critics, particularly those from the lower ranks of officialdom – men with practical experience in administration and bitter personal knowledge of the social and political ailments of the realm – began to advocate sterner and more radical measures which approached the teaching of Legalism.[159] It was, however, not until the downfall of the Later Han had dismantled the facade of unity provided by the Confucian aegis that overt advocates of Legalism found an eager patron in the strong man Ts'ao Ts'ao.

The rise of Ts'ao Ts'ao's personal power during the Chien-an régime was a gradual development spread over more than a decade. The evolution of the Legalistic tendency in the Ts'ao leadership proceeded at the same rate. Although the pro-Han Confucians at the Chien-an court were steadily losing ground so far as real political power was concerned, they continued to be able to withstand the pro-Ts'ao Legalists on ideological issues.[160] The divergence between these two groups can be traced clearly in the works of Hsün Yüeh, whose equivocal Confucianism represented a compromise between the pro-Han and the pro-Ts'ao factions in the Chien-an régime and a transition from a Confucian to a Legalistic orientation in political theory.

The Confucian idealists always looked to the canonical classics for authoritative precepts, while the realistic mind was prone to search for stimulating lessons in the history of the recent past. Hsün Yüeh's distrust of canonical authority and his devotion to the study of history implied, to some degree, a flexible approach to the ideological and political issues of his time – an approach which made him more receptive to realist Legalist theories. Although Hsün Yüeh upheld the Confucian authority as the ultimate sanction in the state, he also acknowledged the changing needs of different times. In his discourse on ' morality [*te*] versus law [*fa*] ' in the *Han-chi*, he affirmed that the moral perfection of man should be the highest goal of society and the state, but he never denied the validity of the Legalist argument that law constituted the very basis of the state on which the moral elevation must raise itself.[161]

In the *Shen-chien*, Hsün Yüeh found a further link with Legalism. He identified ' legal restraint ' (*fa*) and ' moral education ' (*chiao*) as the reciprocal *yin* and *yang* elements, both being essential to the governance of men (1.1b). Of the ' five basic government programmes ' which he advocated, three were in the category of *Realpolitik*, namely economics and finance, military preparation, and legal control; only two, leadership by example and moral education, represented the moral Confucian ideal.[162] In his comment on legal control, Hsün Yüeh affirmed the Legalist doctrine that reward and punishment (*shang-fa*) were the essential means of such control and constituted the pivots of government. He wrote: ' The ruler must make clear the principle of reward and punishment in the administration of law ' (1.3). ' He must distinguish good from evil through merit made manifest and crimes committed' (1.4a), so that 'All good actions should be made known; all evil deeds should be openly denounced' (1.4b), and that 'rewards be made with wisdom, and punishments be made inescapable' (1.5b). All this appears strongly Legalistic, although Hsün Yüeh mitigated the harshness of his injunctions by relapsing into the conservative Confucian postulate that a superior man (chün-tzu) should not himself incur humiliation, least of all legal punishment, and that law should be effective only in restraining the petty man (hsiao-jen) and those in the middle (chung-jen). He reiterated that it was education and moral persuasion which should be the means of raising men from their lowly condition.[163]

Even Taoism, particularly in the work attributed to Lao-tzu, was said to have contained an embryo of Legalist doctrine.[164] Most often-quoted in this connection was Lao-tzu's saying: 'The Sage rules by emptying the people's hearts and filling their bellies, weakening their wills and toughening their sinews, and ever striving to make the people without knowledge and without desire.'[165] and 'The Sage is ruthless; to him the people are but straw dogs.'[166] In a similar vein, Hsün Yüeh compared the governing of the masses to fishing,[167] horse-breaking,[168] the rearing of fowls,[169] and, in a less derogatory image, damming up water.[170] All these similes, which primarily concern the method of governance, come close to the Legalist point of view.

Legalism, in its extreme formulation, was an ideology of political despotism. It was the Legalist advocacy of despotism under the disastrous Ch'in rule that brought lasting infamy on the School of Legalism in the traditional Chinese mind. However, with his basic Confucian convictions Hsün Yüeh was able to adopt many of the key doctrines of Legalism without actually lapsing into the advocacy of Legalist despotism. This led to the combination of Confucian idealism and Legalist realism in many of Hsün Yüeh's political counsels in the Shen-chien, which show a 'liberal' inclination rarely achieved either by the dogmatic Confucians or by the hardheaded Legalists.

In the first two chapters of the Shen-chien, Hsün Yüeh considered a number of administrative measures, practical or expedient, for the Chien-an régime. These included:

Training of militia (1.5; 2.3b–4)
Legal procedure (1.8–9a; 2.5b–7a)
Pardon and amnesty (1.9a; 2.14b–15a)
Taxation (1.10b–11, 13b)
Merit system of promotion (1.4, 5b, 6b–7a; 2.2b–3a)
Appointment of provincial officials (2.3)
Local governments (2.4b–5)

Prohibition of blood-vengeance (2.7–8a)
Official emoluments (1.14b–15a; 2.8)
Restriction of land ownership (2.8b–9a)
Monetary system (2.9–10)
Expenditure on sacrifices (2.10b–11)
Court assembly (2.12)
Re-establishing the Official Erudites (*Po-shih*) (2.13b–14a)
The *shang-chu* institution (2.15)
The Bureau of Historiography (2.15b–16)

Hsün Yüeh's view about blood feuds had a special meaning for the time. The strength and belligerence of the local magnates and big clans in Han times continued to be an important element in the general un-ruliness of the local leaders described by the Han historians.[171] With the decline of imperial authority towards the end of Han rule, regional and local belligerence posed a serious threat to public order. Blood feuds, which emerged as an integral part of local and clan militarism, became a special concern of the Chien-an régime, as Hsün Yüeh's writings show.[172]

His counsel on the issue of blood feuds was a compromise between upholding an ancient tradition and a concern for contemporary social needs. He affirmed the tradition of the blood feud, but asserted that such actions by private parties must be properly regulated by govern-ment. He wrote:

[Someone posed] a question on vengeance and I answered: 'Taking ven-geance was a right [*i*] in ancient times.' He then asked: 'Should we let the people be free to take revenge?' I said: 'No.' And he said: 'What should we do about it?' I answered: 'There should be both freedom and restric-tion [of such actions]. There should be both chances [for people] to stay alive and [for people] to be killed. These should be stipulated according to right [*i*] and adjudicated according to law [*fa*]. This is called "establishing both the right and the law"'.[173]

He went on to reiterate the canonical precept of 'voluntary avoidance of vengeance' which required a person on whom blood revenge was being sought to move away from his native place and resettle in a distant region.[174] He proposed a new criterion to determine the legality of actions involving vengeance. Such actions, he wrote, should be judged on the basis of whether or not the party involved had complied with the stipulation of avoidance. It would be legitimate to kill an enemy who did not avoid revenge as prescribed; it would be law-break-ing to kill a person who had complied with the stipulation of avoidance. The only exception would be that those who acted (whether they moved or stayed) in official capacities (i.e. carrying out administrative orders, fulfilling official duties, and so on) should not be considered as not complying with the stipulation.[175]

In this counsel, Hsün Yüeh gave due consideration to the clan concept of righteousness (i), the judicial basis of justice (fa), and the supremacy of governmental administrative power. In a sense, he was trying to reconcile the conflicting interests of the local magnates, the court literati, and the holder of emergency political power (i.e. the Ts'ao military high command).

His comment on the ritual institution of shang-chu (lit. serving the imperial princess) also showed the conflict between the interests of the declining imperial house and the triumphant élite of his time. According to the shang-chu ritual of Han times, a person who wedded an imperial princess was to be accorded the status of a dependant of the imperial family. He would be treated not as an equal partner in the marital relationship but as a dependant who was adopted into the imperial family to serve the princess.[176] This ritual, which originated from pre-Han times, was possibly a remnant of the matriarchal customs of a much earlier date. The ritual was given Confucian sanction in the Kunyang school of orthodoxy so as to elevate the newly-emerged imperial family to the status of sovereign supremacy.[177] In patriarchal Han society, the institution of shang-chu generated many abuses and led to serious friction between the imperial family and other social groups.[178] With the decline of the imperial authority and the rise of Confucian critics of absolute state power or despotic monarchy in middle and later Han times, shang-chu as a symbol of monarchic absolutism and as a remnant of matriarchal rituals came into direct conflict with the interest of the influential élite who advocated the principle of moderate monarchical power and were in this supported by the patriarchal great clans. The ritual was implicitly censured by Ching Fang (84–44 B.C.) and Ying Shao (c. A.D. 178–96) and was explicitly denounced by Wang Chi (d. 48 B.C.) and Hsün Shuang (Yüeh's uncle).[179] Wang Chi's discussion of the practice was quoted in the Han-chi, where Hsün Yüeh appended a discourse, expounding the grounds for its condemnation in more detail.[180]

Hsün Yüeh's reiterated criticism in the Shen-chien of this time-worn practice was not without its practical meaning. Marital relationship with the imperial family, once considered an exceptional privilege by the élite, had become more and more perilous in times of political instability. The number of regents of state who fell through the intrigues of the eunuchs during the second century and those of Emperor Hsien's relatives by marriage who died by Ts'ao Ts'ao's sword are ample evidence of this.[181] The peril continued after Hsün Yüeh's time.

A famous anecdote recounts how the poet Juan Chi (210–63) feigned drunkenness for sixty days so as to avoid responding to a proposal of marriage from the house of Ssu-ma, future rulers of the Chin dynasty.[182] The danger which he thus avoided may be seen in the tragic fate which befell the equally famous poet Hsi K'ang (223–62), who had the bad luck to marry a princess of the Ts'ao house in the Wei dynasty and consequently fell under the sword of the Ssu-ma usurpers.[183] Several notables from later generations of the Hsün family also contracted marital relations with the house of Ts'ao and later with the house of Ssu-ma of the Chin dynasty, although they managed to survive the dangers arising from the relationship.[184] One of them, Hsün Hsien (321–58), tried to evade a marriage proposal from the house of Ssu-ma by running away from the imperial capital, only to be caught in the provinces by local officials and brought back to the wedding ceremony.[185] So the irony of Hsün Yüeh's pedantic counsel is sufficiently evident.

Hsün Yüeh's realistic and cautious approach to other sensitive issues of his time may be seen in his counsel on the re-establishment of the Official Erudites at the Imperial Academy. The offices of the Erudites and the Imperial Academy were important ingredients in the myth of all-encompassing imperial rule; their re-establishment was therefore fervently advocated by Hsün Yü and K'ung Jung, the grand patrons of the Confucian élite during the early Chien-an period.[186] But though Hsün Yüeh was in a position to give the proposal crucial ideological support, he avoided a grandiloquent proposal, and in his counsel made a colourless statement consisting of only nine characters: ' Install Official Erudites [*pei Po-shih*]; expand the Imperial Academy [*kuang T'ai-hsueh*]; worship Confucius [*ssu K'ung-tzu*] '; concluding with the moral ' these are in accord with the ritual [*li-yeh*] ' (2.13b).[187] Hsün Yüeh's coolness in this matter stemmed partly from his disillusionment with Han Confucianism and partly from his assessment of the political situation of the Chien-an era. The subsequent tragic deaths of K'ung Jung and Hsün Yü indicates Hsün Yüeh's moderation that reflects his shrewdness in the matter of political survival.[188]

He exercised the same caution in putting forward some of his liberal ideas on the administrative problems of his time, particularly in his counsels on legal and financial issues. The struggle between the pro-Han Confucians and the pro-Ts'ao Legalists had its impact on the enforcement of law in the Chien-an era. One major controversy concerned the reinstitution of the punishments by mutilation (*jou-hsing*) which had been officially abolished by the Former Han court in 167 B.C.[189] The Confucians, represented by K'ung Jung, strongly opposed the measure, which was enthusiastically proposed by Ts'ao Ts'ao's Legalist-inclined advisers. Although Hsün Yüeh did not favour outright reinstitution of mutilation, he admitted that in individual cases such punishments might be imposed in lieu of the death sentence so as not to decrease further a population already decimated by the civil war. Hsün Yüeh's counsel implied that the Confucians' opposition to mutilation was based upon the doctrine of the dignity of the human body as a corollary of the ideal of human dignity and the precept of filial piety (one received one's body from one's parents and should therefore do the utmost to preserve it intact); hence, death was preferred to bodily mutilation. Ts'ao's advisers, on the other hand, were interested in the economical use of man-power. And Hsün Yüeh's counsel was a compromise between these two attitudes.[190]

Contrary to contemporary opinion, which was against the frequent declaration of general amnesties (*she*), Hsün Yüeh considered that recourse to this measure was sometimes necessary in order to win back the people's hearts, although he warned against the excessive use of it.[191] Hsün Yüeh pointed out five categories to be considered for specific pardons (*wu-she*) but refrained from elaborating on the rules for a general amnesty; he re-asserted the principle that what is expedient cannot be set out in rules – a mild rebuttal of the Legalist emphasis on statutes. Hsün Yüeh considered that, to mitigate the harshness of the law, it is necessary that criminal charges, verdicts, and sentences be carefully reviewed at several levels of court hearings. This was a restatement of the injunction in the *Chou-li* canon, a work of uncertain date in which Confucian and Legalist ideas are inextricably mixed.[192]

The economic and financial difficulty of the Chien-an régime may be seen in Hsün Yüeh's counsel on 'Official emoluments'. To ensure loyalty and to curb corruption among the ruling bureaucracy, official emoluments needed readjustment, but this must be controlled by the budget. Here Hsün Yüeh modified his earlier approval of salary increases which he had incorporated in a *lun* discourse in the *Han-chi*. He now considered the institution of a sound financial system more important than raising salaries.[193]

The three-fold government establishment under the Chien-an régime, with its overlapping offices and functions not only caused endless friction but also imposed a tremendous financial burden on the state. The friction between the Han Court and the Ts'ao administration over budgetary matters is shown in Hsün Yüeh's counsel on 'Expenditure on sacrifices'. In order to ensure the sacerdotal prestige of the Han house, sacrificial rites needed to be properly carried out by the court. But, Hsün Yüeh wrote, expenditures under this head should be controlled by the budgetary revenue, which was under the charge of the Ts'ao administration.[194]

To reduce friction and the financial burden, Hsün Yüeh argued, the ruling establishment needed to be restructured and integrated. An expanded regular 'court assembly' would be an initial step in co-ordinating at least the Palace Court and the Imperial Secretariat, and, with Ts'ao Ts'ao's participation, the military high command.[195] Many official sinecures, particularly those in the Imperial Secretariat, might be abolished without causing further friction if their occupants could be appointed to administrative posts in local government in accordance with an enlightened merit system.[196] And the position of the central government could be strengthened by creating a unified bureaucracy in charge of militia forces.[197] All these were pragmatic measures reasonably argued, but unfortunately with serious partisan implications. The proposed court assembly would not only have tended against Ts'ao Ts'ao's method of 'divide and rule' but would inconvenience and humiliate Ts'ao Ts'ao by calling for his regular audience with the Son-of-Heaven.[198] The other two measures would have directly cut into the power base of Ts'ao Ts'ao's command, that is, in local administration and the army. These were proposals which Ts'ao Ts'ao could never accept.

The dilemma of Ts'ao Ts'ao thus becomes clear. The financial burden on his administration in maintaining cumbersome court sinecures was a price he had to pay for the support which his leadership needed among the elder dignitaries and the young élite. In these circumstances, the development of the uncommitted and apolitical habit of *ch'ing-t'an* among the parasitic courtiers who had turned their sinecure offices into intellectual centres of retreat was probably much welcomed and even encouraged by the Ts'ao leadership. Here lay part of the *raison d'être* of the political patronage given to literature and scholarship by Ts'ao Ts'ao and later by his successors in the Ts'ao-Wei dynasty.[199]

Hsün Yüeh's insistence on the institution of separate controls over the revenue and expenditure of the state and of the emperor's private household (1.11) was another synthesis of Confucian and Legalistic elements. Under early Han rule, a tentative separation had been made between the financial needs of the emperor's household and those of the state. The former was administered by the Small Treasurer (*Shao-fu*) and the latter by the Grand Minister of Agriculture (*Ta-ssu-nung*). Revenue for state expenditure came mainly from land-and-household taxes, which were later supplemented by the income from certain government monopolies (the production of salt and iron, etc.). Revenue for the private expenditure of the emperor and his household came mainly from special imperial reserves (the products of ' mountains, seas, pools, and the marshes ') and tribute gifts.²⁰⁰ The demarcation, however, became less distinct in the declining years of the Later Han when the revenue of the state dwindled as a result of growing landlordism in the provinces, and special revenues from some ' secondary pursuits ' such as ' trade, mining, and industry ' were put under the charge of eunuch-appointed agents representing the emperor's private household.²⁰¹ This collection of revenues by the eunuch-appointed agents was bitterly denounced by the dissident élite during the *ch'ing-i* protest movement.²⁰² Hsün Yüeh's insistence on a clear separation between the revenue and expenditure of the emperor's private purse and those of the public service of the state probably reflected his own earlier traumatic experiences under eunuch exploitation.

Hsün Yüeh's criticism of ' private profit-seeking ' by imperial agents (1.11a) would seem to undermine still further the economic basis of the Han imperial house. But, since the titular Han emperor in the Chien-an era had already lost whatever control he had had over state finance, the real target of Hsün Yüeh's criticism might well have been the Ts'ao administration, which was in complete control of financial matters. In the mind of many of the Han loyalists who came from former *ch'ing-i* circles, the Ts'ao administration was no more than a privately controlled agency under Ts'ao's charge, and many of Ts'ao's extortions were as ruthless as those of the eunuchs. Hsün Yüeh's criticism of these extortions thus appears double-edged, being directed both against the eunuchs of the past and Ts'ao's followers in the present. So his historical moral was aptly applied to contemporary issues.

His objection to high-handed administrative measures induced him to advocate a lenient tax policy which displayed a strong Taoist influence. He denounced heavy taxes and profit-seeking by the administrative agencies as theft and banditry committed by the government against the people. In his words:

The highest [authority? virtue? *t'ai-shang*] would be not to exhaust the market [*k'ung-shih*]²⁰³ the next, not to commit theft; still next, not to commit robbery... If one 'exhausts the market', the people will not stand idly by; if the people will not stand idly by, he [the one in power] must get it [profit, revenue] through deceitful means; this is theft. If one commits theft, the people will prepare against it; when the people prepare against it and he cannot get it [through deceitful means], he must oppress the people hard

and seize it; this is robbery. In this case, the people will fight back and riots
and disaster will ensue (13b).

The term *t'ai-shang* and the similes of 'theft' and 'robbery' in this
passage are distinctively Taoist.[204]

Related to Hsün Yüeh's objection to high-handed governmental
regulation of the economy was his counsel on the monetary system.
In contradiction to the deepset Confucian bias against 'precious
metal' and against commerce, Hsün Yüeh upheld the positive value
of trade and the monetary system which were noticeably declining
during the Chien-an era.[205] He affirmed the usefulness of money as
the medium of exchange facilitating trade, and the contribution of
trade to the coherence of the state. He supported a 'free market'
system and opposed governmental measures of restriction. He argued
that, even in times of emergency, the government should restrict the
export of only a few items of vital importance to the state: in Hsün
Yüeh's time, such items consisted of horses and cattle, the one for
military and the other for agricultural needs. As for commodities in
daily use, no restriction should be imposed on their circulation, which
should be determined by market supply and demand. Here, Hsün Yüeh
seems to have postulated a law of economics which, he thought, would
operate according to its own dynamism and defy all governmental
regulation (2.9–10).

A more complex counsel with far-reaching impact on later Chinese
economics was that on land policy. The problem of land-encroachment
had harassed many a ruler of the Former Han dynasty, and had been
instrumental in bringing about the downfall of Wang Mang, the Confucian usurper-reformer who tried first to restrict the size of private
landholdings, and later to nationalize all land.[206] After the restoration
under the Later Han, scholars continued to criticize the evil of landlordism, but they were generally silent on the practicability of governmental restriction of landownership, an issue which gained increasing
importance during the Age of Disunity.[207] Hsün Yüeh's counsel on
land policy appears to be the first extant discourse on restriction and
equalization of landholding in the Han–Wei transition era, and is thus
worthy of special attention.

Hsün Yüeh had earlier expounded his opinion on land system in a *lun*
in the *Han-chi*, in which he gave a review of the land-tax system and
its inherent evils in the past. He wrote: 'During Emperor Wu's reign,
Tung Chung-shu had proposed that there should be some restriction
on people's landholdings. Coming to Emperor Ai's time [6 B.C.–A.D. 1],
there had been a restriction that people should not hold land in excess

of 30 *ch'ing*. Although the regulation had been formulated, it was not put into effect.' [208]

However, Hsün Yüeh said that mere restriction was not sufficient. What was needed was a positive land policy. In this connection, he gave a penetrating discussion of the Confucian ideal of the 'Well-field' (*ch'ing-t'ien*) system, an ideal of equal land-allotment to the peasant households which was supposed to have been realized by the Sage-rulers during the period of Golden Antiquity.[209] While adhering to the ideal of economic equality and social justice inherent in the myth of the 'Well-field' system, Hsün Yüeh pointed out with genuine insight that this system, considered as an economic measure, was good only for intensive cultivation and, considered as social legislation, was needed only in a time of over-population. However, from his study of the disaster of Wang Mang, he also saw the practical difficulty of carrying out the equitable legislation that was needed in a time when society had become settled and the pressures of population growth, land scarcity, and land-encroachment produced a vicious circle. He wrote:

The Well-field system should be set up in [a time of] over-population. When there is plenty of land but few people, the system may be disregarded. But if the system is abolished in [a time of] scanty population and reintroduced in a time of over-population, the situation will be that when [we come to a time of over-population] the richly yielding fields will all be in the hands of the magnates, and if this situation is abruptly rectified, they will resent this, and troubles will follow. The difficulty of instituting an [equitable] system thus becomes manifest.[210]

With this dilemma in his mind, the importance of 'gradualism', 'timeliness', 'farsightedness', and 'long-range planning' is obvious. Hsün Yüeh lamented that the Emperor Kao-tsu (founder of the Former Han) and Emperor Kuang-wu (founder of the Later Han) had both lacked the good sense to set the land policy straight at the beginning of their dynasties (in a time when it was within their capacity to do so). As for his own time, Hsün Yüeh was not enthusiastic in pushing the idealistic 'Well-field' system forward, but he insisted that a start should be made in this direction with the hope that a full realization of the higher goal would be attained gradually. He counselled:

Even if we cannot fully implement the detailed Well-field system now, we should at least regulate the *per capita* land-holding [*k'ou-shu chan-t'ien*] and set up restrictive standards. People should be allowed to cultivate land but not to buy or sell it [i.e. although the government is unable actively to restrict landownership, it should passively withhold recognition of ownership resulting from land-encroachment]. This will relieve the plight of the impoverished and discourage private land-encroachment. It will also pave the way for future legislation.[211]

After his disillusionment with the Confucian canonical authority, Hsün Yüeh had become distrustful of the ideal provided by the 'Well-field' system (an ideal institution much praised in the canon) by the time when he wrote the *Shen-chien*. After reiterating some of his statements from the *Han-chi*, he added a new comment in his *Shen-chien* counsel: 'Absolute right of landownership was not an ancient [tradition]; the Well-field system is not a [proper] modern [institution]' (2.9a).

Being aware that the Chien-an régime was incapable of enforcing any restriction on private land-holding (a restriction which would immediately have antagonized the majority of the privileged élite), Hsün Yüeh omitted the clause on restriction of land-holding from his *Shen-chien* counsel. But he still insisted that the government was morally bound to withhold recognition of unlimited and unjustified landownership, thus reserving its position; then future regulations could be enacted when the government was in a position to enforce them.

Hsün Yüeh's counsel on land policy reflected the interest of other groups in the power structure of the Chien-an régime. While he was writing his comments on land policy at the palace, similar counsels on the land system were being submitted through different official channels by Ssu-ma Lang (Ts'ao Ts'ao's own Chief Clerk, *Chu-pu*), Tsao Chih and Han Hao (both high officials at the imperial court), and Hsü Kan and Chung-ch'ang T'ung (both literary assistants in Ts'ao's administration).[212] Meanwhile, Ts'ao Ts'ao's army officers were experimenting with the system of 'military-agricultural colonies' (*t'un-t'ien*) in the provinces.[213] Theoretically, all these counsels and reports would have needed the emperor's formal endorsement, which means that everything on this matter would ultimately have gone through Hsün Yüeh's office.

According to the historical records, the establishment of 'military-agricultural colonies' originated in the proposals made by Tsao Chih and Han Hao in A.D. 196. Tsao Chih at that time held the title of Inspector of the Palace Guards (*Yü-lin chien*). His proposal therefore would have had to go through Hsün Yüeh's office at the Palace Court first.[214] Besides, the first experiment with such 'colonies' was made in an area surrounding the new capital at Hsü, which had formerly been a district town in Hsün Yüeh's own native Ying-ch'uan Commandery where the local magnates, including Hsün Yüeh's clansmen, had set up a number of fortified estates (*t'un*) during the Tung Cho crisis. Hsün Yü, travelling back to Ying-ch'uan in his effort to organize the anti-Tung Cho campaign, might have seen at first-hand these self-sufficient defence units organized by his fellow countrymen.[215]

His observations seem to have constituted the basis of his counsel to Ts'ao Ts'ao in 195 on economic self-support. At that time he was vigorously supporting Ts'ao in the Han 'restoration' at Hsü, where the system of 'military-agricultural colonies' was tried.[216] The experience of Hsün Yüeh's peers, and the reasoned endorsement given by Hsün Yüeh and Hsün Yü to such a policy of self-sufficiency thus jointly contributed to the economic well-being of the régime.

Finally, Hsün Yüeh's dissatisfaction with the condition of his times seems to have made him project far into the future his ultimate hopes for the resurrection of an ideal political and social order, the accomplishment of better 'legislation', and the moral elevation of all men. This reinforced his conception of 'time', 'change', and the 'lessons of history', expressed in the last counsel in the list above, that is, the establishment of an official Bureau of Historiography. Here Hsün Yüeh expounded his broad view of history: all the deeds of men, from the emperor to the masses, for better or worse, should be put on record, so that men might have a sense of permanence in the fleeting world of change (2.15b–16).

As secretary of the Palace Court and the Custodian of imperial archives, Hsün Yüeh was at least in a position to make this last counsel a partial reality. The keeping of a daily record, the 'Diaries of Activity and Repose' (ch'i-chü chu), probably dated back to early Han times. But the practice seems to have been interrupted amidst the turmoil towards the end of the second century. During the reign of Emperor Hsien, the titular Son-of-Heaven in the Chien-an era, a 'Diary of Activity and Repose of Emperor Hsien' (Hsien-ti ch'i-chü chu) was once again kept, and fragments of it still survive.[217] Hsün Yüeh, though disillusioned with Confucian canons, kept his faith in 'history' – 'history' as a didactic record of the past, expressing the hope of the present, and providing a mirror for the future.

7

Conclusion: The world after Hsün Yüeh

Hsün Yüeh's life and thought were marked by many contradictions. He was a precocious child, born and 'orphaned' in a large, wealthy, and influential family whose status was undergoing rapid changes. In barely three generations (from Hsün Shu to Hsün Yüeh), the family had risen from being that of a local magnate to that of a top-ranking court aristocrat. Yüeh's own life went through two distinct stages: that of a persecuted recluse, and that of an eminent courtier. He witnessed the collapse of a great imperial dynasty. He weathered a dangerous political storm, beginning with the court's persecution of the dissident élite and ending with the élite's triumph over the court. He also experienced the dramatic change in the political attitude of the élite, from that of indignant agitation against the court to that of loyal support of the dynastic 'restoration', and from that of vigorous activist political involvement to that of disillusionment, withdrawal and resignation. Hsün Yüeh's two important works, the *Han-chi* and the *Shen-chien*, each epitomized a stage in his own changing attitudes and also an important phase in the élite's political and intellectual re-orientation during this transitional era. The *Han-chi* was the last major product of the *ch'ing-i* positive political endeavour in the Later Han; the *Shen-chien* marked the beginning of the *ch'ing-t'an* evasion and withdrawal from active involvement in the Age of Disunity.

The breakdown of the Han imperial order was accompanied by the disintegration of the grand Confucian synthesis as an orthodox state ideology. Legalism and Taoism, which in Han times had been absorbed into the Confucian synthesis, now tended to go their own ways. Their breaking away was slow. Although there were upheavals and intrigues with strong ideological implications in the early years of the Chien-an reign, these were constantly restrained or reconciled by the Confucian advocate of compromise. Men like Hsün Yüeh and Hsün Yü, with ambivalent political inclinations and flexible ideologies, were able to maintain at least a tenuous facade of unity.

With the passing away of Hsün Yüeh's generation, this facade of unity among the Chien-an élite disappeared. Ts'ao Ts'ao's military success completely over-shadowed the pro-Han sentiment at the court. The hope of a genuine Han restoration evaporated. The eventual take-over of the Han throne by the Ts'ao leadership was but a matter of time. The influx to the court of the literati from Ching-chou as a result of Ts'ao Ts'ao's conquest of that region in A.D. 208 strengthened the trend among the fringe élite toward Taoism and ch'ing-t'an escapism. Equally conspicuous was Ts'ao Ts'ao's own leaning toward the rigorist solutions of Legalism, and his determination to find 'new men' of practical knowledge and administrative talent to serve his régime, a determination which he revealed in his decrees in A.D. 210 and 214.

Meanwhile, preparation for Ts'ao's usurpation of the throne was being made by his close associates, who requested from the titular court a series of concessions of ritual forms symbolizing Ts'ao Ts'ao's advancement toward the throne.[1] Hsün Yü, the last senior Confucian dignitary at the court, refused to endorse the granting of such concessions and was compelled to commit suicide in A.D. 212.[2] In the following year, Ts'ao Ts'ao was ennobled as the Duke of Wei with the 'Nine Honoraria' (chiu-hsi) which were usually granted to a dynastic usurper before his final ascent of the throne.[3] In A.D. 216, Ts'ao Ts'ao became King of Wei, but he died before he could finally assume the title of emperor. In A.D. 220, ten months after Ts'ao Ts'ao's death, Emperor Hsien of the Later Han performed the official rite of abdication of the throne in favour of Ts'ao Ts'ao's heir, Ts'ao P'i, who then founded the Wei dynasty.[4]

Thus the death of Hsün Yüeh in A.D. 209 coincided with the beginning of the end of the myth of the second Han restoration conceived by the Confucian dignitaries at Hsü. And Hsün Yü's suicide in A.D. 212 virtually sounded the death knell of titular Han rule. The fact that Yüeh had died three years earlier probably saved him from a crucial test of his own divided loyalty and his ambivalent ideology at the time when the symbolic existence of Han sovereignty was threatened by Ts'ao's administration.[5]

But the political and ideological dilemma which confronted the ruling élite as a whole persisted long after the official demise of the Han dynasty. An indication of the tenacious hold of the imperial legacy on the élite may be found in the rival claims to legitimacy made by the Wei dynasty and the splinter state in Szechuan. Liu Pei, an avowed loyalist to the Han cause, had been driven from northern China after his forces were routed by Ts'ao's in A.D. 200–1. He gained control over the Szechuan region in A.D. 214. After Ts'ao P'i's assumption of the imperial title, Liu Pei declared himself to be the true emperor and successor to the Han dynasty, naming his dynasty Han (generally known as the Shu-Han, literally the Han régime in Szechuan), and thus reviving once again the myth of 'restoration'.[6]

Ts'ao P'i's claim to legitimacy was based on the ritual of abdication by the last Han emperor. Liu Pei's was based on his family's lineage (which was descended from the house of Liu) and on a secret edict which he was said to have received from the last Han emperor when his forces had revolted against Ts'ao Ts'ao in A.D. 199–200.[7] Although the other splinter state, the Kingdom of Wu in southeastern China, far excelled the Shu-Han state both in resources and in man-power, its ruler was far more cautious about assuming the imperial title or antagonizing either the Wei or the Shu-Han. One of the reasons for this was probably his lack of any legitimate claim on the imperial throne.[8]

The founding of the Wei dynasty did not represent a sharp departure from the tradition of the past. As the ritual of abdication implied, imperial rule continued in spite of the change of dynasty.[9] The new régime inherited from the expired Han not only the throne but also its cumbersome bureaucratic establishment and its fragmented élite.[10] But it lacked the cohering force of Han Confucianism to sustain the facade of unity. The difficulty of maintaining unitary imperial rule without the support of the Confucian synthesis was vividly illustrated in Ts'ao P'i's discussion with his counsellors on how the realm could be effectively ruled in the absence of a 'Sage-ruler'. In other words, how could a Confucian imperial order survive when Confucianism was dead? [11]

Of course, Confucianism was not totally dead. It survived, first of all in the mystique of imperial rule, and secondly as the heritage of culture in the new élite circles, a cultural continuity sustained by classical education, family traditions, and the clan mores of the great aristocratic households in the Age of Disunity. The difference was that, with the obliteration of a strong imperial rule as an embodiment of the Confucian political ideal of Grand Unity, the élite now turned to search for a 'smaller unity' within themselves. They were now more concerned about the well-being of themselves, their families and clans, and other private relationships, than about the well-being of the state and society as a whole. The status and accomplishments of members of the new élite were judged not so much by their successes in an official career or services to the state as by their social prestige, personal influence, landed property, and intellectual refinement. Many of these celebrities were known as the neo-Taoists, or more properly the Confucian Taoists; they had the education and family background which befitted a Confucian élite, but they were now distinguished by an 'apolitical' and therefore fundamentally un-Confucian attitude; and they were principal adepts of the new movements of 'pure conversation' (ch'ing-t'an) and 'dark learning' (hsüan-hsüeh).[12]

These élite groups continued to constitute a burden upon as well as a menace to the new régime. To mollify the élite, the Wei court continued the multi-channelled bureaucratic structure of the Chien-an régime. To ensure adequate financial support for the cumbersome corps of officials and to exert a minimal but vital control of the centre of power in the multi-channelled bureaucracy, the Ts'ao rulers continued to favour Legalism, particularly its emphasis on 'reward and punishment' as the means of political control. Legalism, now lacking the grandeur of an imperial platform (which it had in Han times) or the security of despotic power (as it once had in the Ch'in dynasty), soon degenerated into a dubious practice of vexatious rules and of acrimonious fault-finding. In the hands of those petty officials trusted by the Wei rulers, Legalism served more to alienate the fringe élite than to ensure effective exercise of authority.[13] A court dignitary, Ssu-ma I, with the support of the fringe élite groups, gradually usurped the power of the Wei ruler. Toward the end of the Cheng-shih era (240–8), the Wei régime under its third ruler relapsed into a three-fold establishment similar to that in the Chien-an period. Now it was the turn of the Wei ruler to become the figurehead at a titular court while Ssu-ma I became the de facto dictator, with the various coteries of the élite clustered on the fringe of the court as before.[14]

The manner in which Hsün Yü met his death in A.D. 212 indicates the weakness as well as the strength of these court dignitaries during the Age of Disunity. Influential as he had been, Hsün Yü failed completely to put up any effective resistance to Ts'ao's advance toward the throne. As a seasoned intriguer, Hsün Yü knew that the combined strength of his supporters from the Hsün clan and from élite circles could not withstand Ts'ao's onslaught. The Hsün clan had long lost its home base in Ying-ch'uan. The strength of the Hsün clan, their relatives and close associates, had been decimated in the warfare between Yüan Shao and Ts'ao Ts'ao. A similar fate had befallen many other families of the Chien-an élite. They had all been uprooted from their local bases and were now dependent on the support of the court bureaucracy, which in turn depended upon Ts'ao Ts'ao's military power.

However, from the historical records, it seems quite evident that

Ts'ao Ts'ao would have hesitated to order Yü's open execution at Hsü. Yü's prestige and influence among his fellow élite had been so high that such a drastic action might have led to serious troubles. The fact that Yü's death generated such strong anti-Ts'ao propaganda in the splinter states in Szechuan and the lower Yangtze region indicates that this danger was real. What Ts'ao Ts'ao did was to summon Yü to a military headquarters in the south and detain him there, and Yü ended his life with poison.[15]

Hsün Yü's suicide gave the Ts'ao faction a chance to conceal the conflict. And all was forgiven.[16] Yü's children were well-treated by the Wei court. One of his sons had married Ts'ao Ts'ao's own daughter, later entitled the Princess of An-yang.[17] Although the political power and influence of the extended Hsün family as a whole suffered an eclipse after the deaths of Hsün Yüeh and Hsün Yü, many of the Hsün descendants had higher status and prestige than ever before in the Wei and later the Chin élite circles.[18] Several members of the family were closely involved with the Ssu-ma faction in its move against the Wei throne and in the founding of the Chin dynasty. Many of them received higher titles of nobility and important official posts from the early Chin court. As an aristocratic house, the Hsün attained their highest noble status in the last quarter of the third century.[19]

This resurgence of the political influence of the Hsün lineage indicates that, while none of the aristocratic families individually could withstand the direct challenge of a military dictatorship, their combined strength could not be wiped out by any such dictator through purges. The influence of the entrenched élite continued to undermine each new régime founded by such dictators until its replacement by yet another strong man.[20] During these centuries of disunity, it became a general tendency for an emerging strong man to follow the Legalist persuasion in exercising his *de facto* power, and for a titular ruler and the élite group surrounding the throne to defy such a strong man by withholding the traditional Confucian sanction for his *de facto* rule, or by adopting the Taoist attitude of evasion toward his *ad hoc* authority. The stalemate in the strife between the entrenched élite families and a series of short-lived autocratic dynasties thus led to a continuation of the rivalry between the Confucian-Taoists and the Confucian-Legalists in the Age of Disunity, which kept the three ancient traditions of thought – Confucianism, Taoism and Legalism – alive.[21]

The historical record makes no mention of Hsün Yüeh's descendants. Consequently, we know nothing about this particular branch of the Hsün family.[22] But the scholarly tradition of the family was upheld by the offspring of the other branches. Many of Yüeh's agnate nephews were well-known Confucians. One of them, Hsün Hung, distinguished himself in a coterie of famous Confucian scholar-officials such as Chung Yu, Wang Lang, and Yüan Huan.[23] Another of them, Hsün I (died 264), was famous for his polemical comments on the *I-ching* (Book of Changes) and on the moral precepts of *jen* (human-heartedness) and *hsiao* (filial piety).[24] Still another, Hsün Ts'an, produced several subtle comments on human nature (*hsing*), personal ideal (*chih*), knowledge and wisdom (*shih*), ability and intellect (*ts'ai-chih*), and their relationship with an individual's other achievements (*kung*, deeds; *ming*, prestige, etc.).[25] A significant dispute between the Taoist-inclined Hsün Ts'an and his Confucian brother Hsün Wu on the *I-ching* is still extant. In this argument, four basic categories for analyzing the *I-ching* were established: (1) abstract idea (*i*); (2) concrete image (*hsiang*); (3) written presentation (*tz'u*); and (4) verbal exposition (*yen*). Ts'an's comments on human nature were said to have been highly prized by P'ei Hui and Fu Ku (209–55), two outstanding Confucians of their times; his analysis of the *I-ching* had a considerable influence over Wang Pi's (226–49) famous reinterpretation of this Confucian canonical classic.[26] Hsün Jung, the son of Yüeh's agnate nephew, also distinguished himself equally in the study of the Confucian *I-ching* and of the Taoist classic *Lao-tzu*; he was said to have had a prestige in his own day equal to that of Wang Pi and Chung Hui (225–64).[27] Hsün Yüeh's Confucian-Taoist synthesis was thus well preserved within the family circle.

Hsün Yüeh's interest in government policies, which produced the Legalist tinge in his writings discussed in the preceding chapters, also had its followers within the Hsün family. Yüeh's agnate nephew, Hsün I, was an influential figure in the Ssu-ma faction which founded the Chin dynasty. Hsün I rose to the top position of a senior Ducal Minister (*T'ai-wei*) at the new court. Under the Chin dynasty, the sinecure office of the Custodian of the Secret Archives (*Mi-shu chien*) once headed by Hsün Yüeh was reorganized into the pivotal Palace Secretariat (*Chung-shu chien*) which was now headed by Hsün Hsü (died A.D. 289), a grandson of Yüeh's agnate cousin. And Hsün Hui, another grandson of Yüeh's agnate cousin, helped devise a new set of rituals for the use of the Chin court. All three of these men also appear to have been instrumental in the drafting of important administrative and legal ordinances, probably including the famous 'Land-ownership Restriction' (*chan-t'ien*) and 'Land-allotment' (*k'o-t'ien*) acts proclaimed in early Chin times. The Chin dynasty's land policy represented not only a systematization of the fragmentary experiments in the field which had been attempted from Ts'ao Ts'ao's time, but also the fruition of continual scholarly deliberations among the official élite on land policy and the regulation of property.[28]

Hsün Yüeh's thinking and conduct as a court bureaucrat seemed to have significantly affected members of later generations of the extended Hsün family. A study of two notable members of the family, Hsün I and Hsün Hsü, may serve to illustrate this point. Hsün Hsü had received the title of marquis from the Ts'ao–Wei court. When the Chin dynasty was founded, he was given another marquisate. He declined it but accepted the office of Superintendent of the Palace Secretariat (*Chung-shu chien*) at the Chin court. It was said that he always hid himself behind the secrecy of the government bureaucratic apparatus. Whenever a new policy was formulated, he would announce it as the decision of the court and avoid any reference to his own contribution to it. Once Hsü's cousin suggested that he ' should make known some of his activities in the bureaucracy so that those who had benefited from his influence might cherish grateful memories '. Hsü's son-in-law also suggested that he should cultivate close contacts with those who had received his favour so that they might become his personal followers. Hsü rejected these suggestions and said that ' to cultivate a private following against the public interest would be most undesirable conduct in an exemplary official '.[29]

Hsün I was said to have adopted a similar attitude at court. He, too, had received the title of marquis from the Ts'ao–Wei dynasty and was given the title of duke by the Chin ruler. He served consecutively in the various Ducal Ministries, *Ssu-k'ung*, *Ssu-t'u*, and *T'ai-wei*, at the early Chin court. At his death in A.D. 274, the court issued an edict to the effect that Hsün I had never taken an interest in his private household and that he had not even possessed a private mansion. As a result, two million copper coins were granted by the emperor to build a mansion for his household.[30] In this respect, Hsün Yüeh's ideal of a model official, his insistence on the separation of public and private interests, and his censure of unprincipled partisanship in government, found a clear echo.

However, Hsün I and Hsün Hsü were not entirely as upright and self-denying as suggested above. Hsü's biography in the *Chin-shu* mentions that when he was transferred from the office of the Palace Secretariat to be the acting Prefect of the Imperial Secretariat (*shou Shang-shu ling*) he became so angry that he openly complained that he had been deprived of the ' dragon's pool '.[31] In other parts of the *Chin-shu*, both Hsün Hsü and Hsün I were described as cowards, flatterers, and men without principle, who had earlier betrayed the Ts'ao–Wei dynasty in favour of the Ssu-ma usurpation and later sided with the notorious faction led by the Chia family whose treachery eventually caused the downfall of the unified Chin empire.[32] This conflict of historical judgements cannot be solved in simple moralistic terms and there are other complicated factors in the lives of these later Hsün notables.[33] What is clear is that these members of the Hsün lineage not only reaffirmed Hsün Yüeh's ideal of imperial bureaucratic rule but also inherited the dilemma of conflicting loyalties, a dilemma which had determined Hsün Yüeh's political and ideological ambivalence as expressed in the *Han-chi* and the *Shen-chien*.

Beyond the extended Hsün family circle, the power struggle and ideological rivalry raged on among different factions and coteries of the élite. The over-lapping ideological and factional affiliations which characterized the Hsün notables in successive generations continued, in a sense, to epitomize the life and thought of the élite. New turmoil following the Chin downfall and the barbarian invasions of north China during the fourth century further complicated the situation. However, as a tentative generalization, it may be said that the effort made by the Confucian Hsün Yüeh to reconcile the rival factions and ideologies of his time was later emulated by numerous notables from both the Confucian-Taoist and the Confucian-Legalist coteries. Though these men differed in their precise political convictions they always shared a basic cultural unity which characterized them as an essentially Confucianized élite.

Hsün Yüeh's effort to effect a rapprochement or a balance of power between the rival factions was continued by Li Feng in the court bureaucracy during the Wei–Chin transition. Like Hsün Yüeh, who had been installed by Ts'ao Ts'ao at the titular Han court but who later transferred his loyalty to the Han, Li Feng was a protégé of Ssu-ma Shih (*de facto* ruler at the Wei court in 251–5) who installed Feng as Palace Secretary (*Chung-shu ling*, a successor to the *Mi-shu chien* formerly headed by Hsün Yüeh) at the titular Wei court. And Li Feng later transferred his allegiance to the Wei throne. In his attempt to effect a balance of power between the pro-Wei and the pro-Ssu-ma factions so as to forestall Ssu-ma's usurpation of the throne, Li Feng gave his support to Hsia-hou Hsüan, the surviving leader of the decimated pro-Wei faction. Ssu-ma Shih discovered that he was betrayed, and in A.D. 254 he executed both Li Feng and Hsia-hou Hsüan. According to the historical record, Li Feng and Hsia-hou Hsüan were exemplary Confucians of their times; they were both self-composed and unpresumptuous. Their deaths at Ssu-ma Shih's hand indicates how ruthless the power struggle had become within half a century after Hsün Yüeh's death.[34]

A close parallel to Hsün Yüeh's erudite interests in letters and in government policy was Chung Hui's (225–64) versatile achievement in scholarship and in real politics. Hui came from the Chung lineage of Ying-ch'uan. (Hui's father, Chung Yu, had been one of Hsün Yü's protégés and earlier the Chung family had been one of the outstanding families of Ying-ch'uan depicted in the *Hou-Han shu* which also included the collective biographies of Hsün Shu, Hsün Shuang, and Hsün Yüeh, alongside that of Ch'en Shih and his descendants.) Like Hsün Yüeh, Hui was a precocious child, prolific and diligent in learning, who achieved considerable fame in his early years. He wrote several important treatises on the *I-ching* and on human nature and intellect (*ts'ai-hsing*), as well as a book in twenty *chuan* entitled *Tao-lun* (Discourse on the Way) which was said to be Legalist-inclined. His prestige among his contemporaries equalled that of Wang Pi. He served in several offices of the Palace Secretariat and the Imperial Secretariat at the Wei court and was later appointed commander-in-chief of the Wei forces that finally conquered the Shu–Han state in A.D. 263. Once in control of Szechuan, Hui tried to raise an armed revolt against the Ssu-ma faction at court but was killed by mutinous soldiers the next year.[35]

Similar to Hsün Yüeh's eclectic Confucian attitude was the posture taken by Hsü Kan (170–217), Wang Su (195–256), Tu Shu (198–252), Fu Hsüan (217–78), and P'ei Hsiu (224–71), in addition to Fu Ku and P'ei Hui mentioned earlier. The position of P'ei Wei (267–300), on the other hand, represented a more conservative Confucian reaction to his time.[36] The most explicit emulation of Hsün Yüeh's attempt to effect a rapprochement of Taoism and Legalism through Confucianism was made by Wang Ch'ang (died A.D. 259). Ch'ang had served as Ts'ao P'i's Literary Attendant (*T'ai-tzu wen-hsüeh*) and later became a high-ranking general in Ssu-ma's *de facto* régime. He wrote a *Chih-lun* in which he analyzed several ancient traditions which might be used as guidelines to current affairs (*shih-wu*).[37] This work is now lost, but the five-point proposal which Ch'ang submitted to Ssu-ma I in A.D. 249 showed the marked influence of Hsün Yüeh's political counsels in the *Han-chi* and the *Shen-chien*.[38] Ch'ang also left a family instruction to his two sons, in which several points made by Hsün Yüeh in the *Shen-chien* were reiterated almost *verbatim*.[39]

Many of these Confucians were both outstanding scholars in their times and also great patrons of letters and scholarship. P'ei Hui and

Fu Ku had given patronage to the precocious Wang Pi.[40] The prestige of these Confucians which was fairly high among their contemporaries was, however, later much overshadowed by that of Wang Pi and other celebrities in the Taoist 'pure conversation' and 'dark learning' groups. For instance, Chung Hui, whose fame equalled that of Wang Pi in contemporary élite circles, later came to be known most unfavourably for his alleged encounter with the eccentric Hsi K'ang.[41] This indicates that while the Confucian-Legalists maintained their hold on the world of reality they had long yielded to the Taoist eccentrics and individualists in the realm of ideas. The criticisms later made by some of the conservative Confucian-Legalists against the Confucian-Taoists only helped to spread the notoriety of the eccentrics.[42]

However, some of the leading Taoist celebrities did make attempts to reconcile their position with the Confucian-Legalists or to synthesize the rival ideologies of their times. Wang Pi's argument that the Sage Confucius excelled Lao-tzu and Chuang-tzu in embodying the Taoist precept of 'non-action' (wu-wei) and Juan Chan's ambivalent statement that Confucius' emphasis on moral order (ming-chao) and Lao-tzu's emphasis on naturalness were 'dissimilar and yet similar' are well-known.[43] Equally well-known are Wang Pi's new Commentaries on the Confucian Canons and Kuo Hsiang's reinterpretation of the Confucian moral order in Taoist terms.[44] Even Ho Yen (190–249), notorious leader of an eccentric 'pure conversation' group in the Cheng-shih period (240–9), was said to have a deep concern with Confucian moral teaching.[45]

This survey is far from exhaustive, but it suffices to show the wide range of Hsün Yüeh's attributes and justifies our using his life and thought as an epitome of those of the élite in early medieval China. In Yüeh's life and thought one finds a reflection not only of the world of his immediate contemporaries but also of that of several succeeding generations.

Partly because of the intrinsic value of his works, and partly because of the wide range of his scholarly interests and the high prestige of the aristocratic Hsün lineage as a whole, Hsün Yüeh had a very high reputation during and after his lifetime. Ch'en Ch'ün (died 236), the powerful Minister of Civil Service Personnel (Li-pu shang-shu) at the early Wei court, had once said that Hsün Yü, Hsün Yüeh, and their nephew Hsün Yu each had no equal in his time.[46] Yüeh as an historian was highly praised by Yüan Hung (328–76), author of the Hou-Han chi, and Fan Yeh (398–445), author of the Hou-Han shu. Chang Fan of the Chin dynasty also mentioned that Yüeh's *Han-chi* was very popular in Chin times.[47]

Yüeh's prestige remained exceptionally high till the middle of the T'ang dynasty. The second T'ang ruler, Emperor T'ai-tsung (reigned: 629–49), was said to have specifically ordered that a copy of Hsün Yüeh's *Han-chi* be sent as a gift to one of his provincial administrators with the following edict: 'This book contains many illuminating narrations and penetrating, versatile discussions [of state affairs]; it perfectly encompasses the essence of government and the proper relationship between the ruler and the ruled. Now I bestow it on you. You should always read and refer to it.'[48]

Even the famous critic Liu Chih-chi (661–721), whose *Shih-t'ung* (Comprehensive Historiography) is the earliest systematic study of Chinese historiography now extant, praised Hsün Yüeh lavishly. He considered Hsün Yüeh to be the father of dynastic chronicles in the post-classical (i.e. post-Chou) age. He also stated that Yüeh's *Han-chi* was better received than the original *Han-shu* itself from the Wei dynasty on through mid-T'ang times.[49] According to the Bibliographical Résumé of the *Imperial Library Catalogue of the Ch'ing Dynasty* (*Ssu-k'u ch'üan-shu tsung-mu t'i-yao*, compiled in 1782), the *Han-chi* together with Ssu-ma Ch'ien's *Shih-chi* and Pan Ku's *Han-shu* constituted a special subject in the civil service examination during the T'ang dynasty.[50] The prestige of Hsün Yüeh's work then reached its climax.

Hsün Yüeh's works, which are in a sense all historical reflections as defined by Yüeh himself in his prefaces to the *Han-chi* and the *Shen-chien*, stimulated a series of similar compilations under the imperial aegis or from private hands during and after the T'ang dynasty – works which were called *Chien* or 'Mirrors' ranging from serious political treatises to commonplace occult manuals.[51] The influence of Hsün Yüeh's works on the famous historian Ssu-ma Kuang (1016–86) may be attested by the title which the latter adopted for his masterpiece, the *Tzu-chih t'ung-chien* (Comprehensive Mirror for Aid in Government).[52]

Before Hsün Yüeh, historical works were classified in the Chinese catalogue of books or official bibliographical treatise under the section of the *Ch'un-ch'iu* (Spring-and-Autumn) canons.[53] After Hsün Yüeh, historical writing had developed so energetically that a new system of classification was needed. In the 'Bibliographical Treatise' (*Ching-chi chih*) of *Sui-shu* (History of the Sui Dynasty) which was completed in c. 656, 'Historical works' (*shih*) became one of the four main sections in the catalogue of books, the remaining three sections being 'Canonical scriptures' (*ching*), 'Philosophical works' (*tzu*), and 'Collections of literary pieces' (*chi*). The section 'Historical works' itself contained thirteen sub-sections, totalling 817 entries and 13,264 *chüan*.[54]

Of course it would be an exaggeration to ascribe all these to Hsün Yüeh's influence, but his contributions to these developments may nevertheless be traced along several lines. Hsün Yüeh's *Han-chi* set a specific example for the compilation of dynastic chronicles in later times.[55] The *Han-chi* had been intended as an official apologia for the Han court but was actually written in accordance with Hsün Yüeh's own values and polemical criteria, in defence of Confucianism and the Confucian élite. This polemical undertone seems to lie behind most of the prolific historical works produced in the Age of Disunity. In this 'dark' age, the wish of the monarchs to panegyrize their abortive reigns, the wish of the provincial notables to glorify their families or their places of origin, and the desire of the dishonest to whitewash their careers all tended to intrude into the writing of new 'histories'. There were histories of the peripheral dynasties (*tsai-chi*), histories of the provinces and regions (*fang-chih*), and histories of the celebrated families (*chia-chuan*), written for different purposes but with a similar polemical motivation.[56] Among them, the *History of the Toba Wei Dynasty* (c. 424–556, *Wei-shu*) – often called the 'foul history' (*hui-shih*) – written by Wei Shou (506–72) was a notorious testimony to the historian's 'crooked brush' (*ch'ü-pi*).[57]

Even the new system of classification, the quadripartite catalogue which emerged in the Age of Disunity and is still used by many modern Chinese libraries and bibliographers, may be traced to the influence of Hsün Yüeh. The system as preserved in the 'Bibliographical Treatise' of *Sui-shu* may be traced through the catalogue compiled by Li Ch'ung in A.D. 317–22 to the earlier catalogues of the imperial library collections compiled by Hsün Hsü (the grandson of Hsün Yüeh's cousin) in A.D. 264 and by Cheng Mo in the middle of the third century. Both Hsün Hsü and Cheng Mo served in the office of Custodian of the Secret Archives (*Mi-shu chien*, later renamed *Chung-shu chien*, Palace Secretariat), and their catalogues were based on the checklists of library collections in the custody of that office.[58] Hsün Yüeh himself had served as the Custodian of that office for more than ten years from about A.D. 198 to 209. During his tenure, he had shown a conspicuous interest in written records and had repeatedly counselled the last Han court to collect lost books and documents and to preserve existing archives. Furthermore, he had, in unambiguous terms, declared the independence of historiography from the authority of the antiquarian canonical learning. His attitude seems to have had a considerable influence on the separation of the historical works (*shih*) from the section of canonical scriptures (*ching*), in the new quadripartite classification system (*ssu-pu*).

In contrast to the important influence of Hsün Yüeh's historical work on later Chinese historiography, the influence of his philosophical work on Chinese thought seems to have been slight. The *Shen-chien* was in fact seldom mentioned in later ages.[59] The reason is that, in the ideological rivalry between Taoism and Legalism (or more appropriately between Confucian-Taoism and Confucian-Legalism) during the Chinese medieval ages, Confucianism as such had increasingly receded into the background. Although the Confucian classics continued to be studied and Confucianism still permeated the familial traditions of the aristocratic houses, the Confucian Canons no longer represented the orthodox dogmas of the state. And the Confucian persuasion, because of its emphasis on compromise and reconciliation, lacked the polemical sharpness which characterized the Taoist and the Legalist persuasions in ideological disputes.[60]

The tenuous facade of ideological and political unity erected by Hsün Yüeh and his followers, a facade which was based on compromise, ambivalence and vague synthesis, proved too weak to weather the subsequent turmoils. Since Confucianism survived mainly in the education and the family heritage of the medieval élite, its influence lay in the field of classical scholarship and erudition. Accordingly, it seems natural that, while Hsün Yüeh's influence on historical scholarship remained outstanding, his moral reflections received little attention during the later part of the Age of Disunity.

Modern scholars differ in their opinion about when the medieval age in Chinese history ended. Although the Age of Disunity came to an end in the seventh century with the regeneration of the unitary empire, divisive trends along ethnic, cultural, political, and socio-economic lines remained strong long after imperial reunification. The absence of a strong Confucian ideology as the cohesive dogma of the state together with the predominance of an entrenched élite, which had characterized the Age of Disunity, continued to undermine the unified Sui and T'ang empire.[61] The situation gradually changed after mid-T'ang times, as the position of the aristocratic households descending from the Age of Disunity was weakened by the new 'lesser gentry' and, as much later still, a new ideology of political and moral absolutism was gradually formulated by the neo-Confucians.[62] For this reason, some scholars have tentatively set the ending of the Chinese middle ages at the time of the T'ang-Sung transition (tenth to eleventh centuries) and called the Age of Disunity early medieval.[63]

With the end of the 'medieval' age after mid-T'ang times Hsün Yüeh, as an epitome of the medieval élite, suffered a serious eclipse in his posthumous reputation. His shortcomings, his political compromise, his ideological ambivalence, and the vagueness of his intellectual synthesis came under stern criticism by the scholars of Sung times with their new unprecedentedly vigorous conception of orthodoxy. Cheng Ch'iao (1102–60) testified that although Hsün Yüeh's *Han-chi* had been very popular in former times it had fallen into obscurity after the T'ang dynasty.[64]

Huang Chen, who lived in the middle of the thirteenth century, severely criticized the *Shen-chien*. He wrote: 'In general, this book is wordy and inconsequential [*tz'u-fan li-kua*]; its style is inconsistent... The discussion of human nature [*hsing*] and feeling [*ch'ing*] runs through many sections, but makes few good points. The literary style is vulgar and weak [*pei-jo*].'[65] Huang Chen's criticism of Hsün Yüeh's discussion of human nature and feeling indicates the essential difference between the old Confucian and the neo-Confucian conceptions of man and his moral attributes. To the old Confucian, the moral nature (*hsing*) and the amoral feelings (*ch'ing*, emotion, including the potential *yü*, desires) were coherent parts of man's inborn, 'physiological', nature. This implied a moral relativism in the inter-relation and inter-action between the moral and the amoral forces within man. And moral relativism was abhorred by the neo-Confucians, to whom the difference between right and wrong, good and bad, or virtue and vice, tended to be absolute.[66]

The strongest criticism of Hsün Yüeh was written by the Ch'ing scholar Yang Ch'i-kuang, probably echoing the Sung neo-Confucians' censure of Yüeh. Yang Ch'i-kuang wrote:

Yüeh and his cousin Yü had both been recommended by Ts'ao Ts'ao to attend [to the Han ruler] at the inner palace. Yü was later killed by Ts'ao because of his straight speaking, while Yüeh was able to save his neck. For this, some people praised Yüeh's wisdom and capacity for self-preservation. In the end, this only proved that Yüeh was less loyal to the Han and not as honourable as Yü.

Yüeh's service to a usurper's régime was as infamous as Yang Hsiung's [service under the régime of the usurper Wang Mang]. But later gentlemen were more strict in censuring Yang... Yüeh spent his last years comfortably and escaped Ts'ao's jealousy or persecution. Would this not have been due to Yüeh's skill in flattering [Ts'ao]?

Furthermore, Yüeh's book was entitled *Shen-chien* [Extended Reflections and Warnings]. But he had not put in it a single word of 'hidden warning' [*yin-yü*] to enlighten his master... Probably he had wished to enlighten the Han emperor so that the enlightenment would extend indirectly to the other side [i.e. Ts'ao, Yüeh's real master]. Or perhaps Yüeh may have made some covert strictures against Ts'ao. But after he learned the lesson of Yü's tragedy he may have cut these out [from his finished work]...

This was no doubt a way of self-preservation. But to preserve his pure integrity he ought to have retired himself in seclusion [from the Ts'ao régime]; or better still have sacrificed his life for the sake of the Way [*tao*]. Unfortunately, Yüeh could do neither of these.[67]

The pointlessness of this criticism, quite apart from its applying to Yüeh a concept of 'loyalty' which had not existed before Sung times, lies in the fact that Yang Ch'i-kuang not only fails to study Yüeh's works carefully but also seems not to have noticed that Yüeh had died three years before Yü's tragic death and therefore did not have a chance to face the final test of his loyalty to the Han. This kind of arbitrary moral verdict seems to characterize many of the so-called 'comments on history' (*shih-lun*, *shih-p'ing*, or *lun-shih*) written by the neo-Confucians.[68] It was partly in reaction to this blatant disregard of historical facts by the neo-Confucians that a new school of 'Han Learning' (*Han-hsüeh*) with its emphasis on textual, philological, and historical studies developed in the seventeenth, eighteenth, and nineteenth centuries.[69]

Hsün Yüeh, in writing his explicit discourses on historical events and personages, had helped to develop the genre of moralizing comment on history (*shih-lun*), but he had supported his didactic discourses with his careful study of history. Many of the second-rate neo-Confucian moralists, on the other hand, were poor historians but were bold in commenting on the moral virtue of others. The result was not only that Hsün Yüeh's posthumous fame came under the direct personal attacks of such second-rate hacks but also that, as the genre of such 'comments on history' steadily degenerated, the intrinsic value of Yüeh's own scholarship in historiography (including his well-founded *Lun* discourses on history) was gradually neglected by the school of 'Han Learning'.[70] Thus to the scholars of 'Han Learning', Hsün Yüeh's *Han-chi* became merely a secondary compilation based on the *Han-shu*, valued only as a basis for collation with the *Han-shu*.[71]

To conclude the study, Hu San-hsing's (*c.* 1230–1302) enlightened opinion of Hsün Yüeh may be mentioned here. Hu San-hsing also criticized the weaknesses of Hsün Yüeh as a statesman. But he had a fairer as well as a more sympathetic judgement on Yüeh's life and thought. He said that the significance of Yüeh's life and the value of his works must be assessed against the background of his times.[72] In other words, in order to grasp the true meaning of Yüeh's life and thought, one must understand the world in which he and the medieval Confucian élite lived – a theme which I have attempted to pursue in writing this study.

Notes to the text

Notes to chapter 1

1 Okazaki's extensively documented history of the Wei, Chin, and the Northern and Southern Dynasties (1932), remains an outstanding work on the period. For studies in English on the decline and fall of the Later Han, see L. S. Yang, in Etu Zen Sun (1956), 103–34; Wright (1959), 3–28; Balazs (1967), 173–254.

2 'The Biography of Hsün Yüeh' in *HHS* 62 (*lieh-chuan* 52), 8–11a. For previous studies of Hsün Yüeh, see Busch (1945), 58–90; Yoshinami (1956), 68–86; Hihara (1959), 9–20. For detailed discussions of the various editions and textual problems of Hsün Yüeh's works, see Chi-yun Chen, *Monumenta Serica* 27 (1968), 208–32.

3 Cf. Chapter 7.

4 Chi-yun Chen, *Monumenta Serica* 27 (1968), 208–32.

5 For instance, see *Wen-hsien t'ung-k'ao* 193.1631; *Jih-chih lu* 8 (*chüan* 2b), 99; *Ssu-k'u ch'üan-shu tsung-mu* [*t'i-yao*] 47.6–8a. Cf. Chin Yü-fu (1944), 44–5; Hulsewé, in Beasley and Pulleyblank (1961), 33–4, 39, 43.

6 See Chapter 5, note 143. Chi-yun Chen, *Monumenta Serica* 27 (1968), 211, 222–7.

7 See Chapter 4 and Chapter 5. Chi-yun Chen, *Monumenta Serica* 27 (1968), 213–21.

8 *HHS* 62 (*lieh-chuan* 52), 8a–11a.

9 Chi-yun Chen, *Monumenta Serica* 27 (1968), 227–8.

10 For a discussion of the nature of the Chinese dynastic histories, see Bielenstein (1950), 21–81; Michael C. Rogers, *The Chronicle* (1968), 32–73. For discussions of traditional Chinese biographical writings, see D. C. Twitchett, in Beasley and Pulleyblank (1961), 95–114, also Wright and Twitchett (1962), 24–39; John Garraty, in Boorman (1962), 487–9.

11 A famous collection of anecdotes concerning the *ch'ing-t'an* celebrities of this time is the *Shih-shuo hsin-yü*. For English studies of this work, see Yoshikawa tr. by Baxter (1955), 124–41; Mather (1956), 58–70; (1964), 349–51. For general accounts on the eccentrics, see Fung Yu-lan II (1953), 168–236; also (1960), 217–40. For special studies cf. Ho Ch'i-min (1966).

12 Bodde, in Coulborn (1956), 83–92, indicates that certain feudalistic phenomena appeared in China during the Age of Disunity. In his review of Coulborn, Lattimore points out a 'relapse' form of feudalism in traditional China (1962), 542–51. A brief comment on the term 'feudalism' as used in Chinese history has been made by L. S. Yang, in Hucker (1969), 1–10. Cf. also Zürcher (1959), 43–5, 57–9, 81–6.

13 In the absence of a simpler and more appropriate term, the word 'feudalistic' is used here with some reservation. It refers to those non-bureaucratic elements and tendencies generally known as *feng-chien* feudalism in its post-Chou usage. This includes general political decentralization and disunity, the

178

upsurge of regionalism and localism, rampant landlordism, as well as clannish, familial, and predominantly personal influences in politics. The conflict between bureaucratic centralism and 'feudalistic interests' in the Age of Disunity can be found in the land policy of the Ts'ao-Wei and the Chin dynasties, L. S. Yang (1963), 131–48; also (1966). The Chinese traditional historians themselves had viewed the upsurge of landlordism as a development toward *feng-chien* feudalism; see Hsün Yüeh's discourses on landlordism and self-styled nobility in pages 101–4, 158–60; compare this with the term 'untitled nobility' discussed by L. S. Yang (1963), 90–1.

14 Marxist Chinese historians generally reject Marx's label of 'Asiatic Society' and consider Chinese society in post-Chou times (from the third century B.C. to the mid nineteenth century) as 'feudal variants' based primarily on landlordism; Feuerwerker (1968), 16–31; for more details, see Eberhard (1965), 66–74. In the west, Marx's idea of 'Asiatic Society' has been elaborated by Wittfogel (1957), but Max Weber's theory of bureaucracy (1951), seems to have wider currency; cf. especially Balazs (1967), 3–27; Wittfogel's theory has been criticized by Eberhard (1965), 53–66, 69, 74–88. The generalization made by Wittfogel and Balazs may be modified by a number of studies on non-bureaucratic elements and trends of traditional China; cf. C. K. Yang, in Nivison and Wright (1959), 209–43; T. Masabuchi (1966), 316–33. See also Houn (1965), and Ping-ti Ho (1968), 1–92. The tenacious tradition of bureaucracy in the Age of Disunity surprised Balazs, in his study of the judicial system of early medieval China. He specifically pointed out how slowly change in the law codes reflected the socio-political reality, such as the rise of the aristocratic families or the influence of Buddhism during this period: (1954), 6–26. The symbiosis of monarchical autocracy and gentry aristocracy in the Wei and Chin periods is an intriguing phenomenon which has led to many controversies among Chinese and Japanese scholars. In general, we may say that the aristocratic families (*meng-fa*) in medieval China achieved their political triumph after the early years of the Chin rule (the fourth century). During the third century, political power was wielded by leaders of divergent and mixed backgrounds who had yet to entrench themselves in their aristocratic status. In a pioneering work, L. S. Yang identified the active leaders in the last years of the Later Han, i.e. 'leaders of the Pures', as coming from the big families, who were 'learned but not necessarily extremely wealthy', in Etu Zen Sun (1956), 125–33. Yang's view has generally been substantiated in later studies by both Chinese and Japanese scholars. For the various opinions expressed by Chinese scholars during the 1959 controversy over the nature of the Ts'ao-Wei régime in medieval China, see the articles in the collection *Ts'ao Ts'ao lun-chi* (1962). For Japanese works on this point, see Utsunomiya's review article (1962), 6–23. For other related Japanese works, see Ochi's review article (1962), 93–103.

15 For traditional critics, see Fan Yeh's comment in *HHS* 67 (*lieh-chuan* 57), 2; Kan Pao's comment in *Chin-shu* 5.31–2. Cf. also *Jih-chih lu* 5 (*chüan* 12), 39–43, 55; *Nien-erh-shih cha-chi* 8.148–51. The intrinsic value of the literature, thought, and scholarship of this period has been re-assessed by many modern scholars; Ho Ch'ang-ch'ün (1947), T'ang Yung-t'ung (1956) and (1957); Liu Ta-chieh (1957); Mou Chung-san (1962); Ho Ch'i-min (1966) and (1967); Okazaki (1932), 423–541; Mori (1954), 225–328; Kaga (1964).

16 Mather (1964), 349–51; Balazs (1967), 233–5, 239–42; Zürcher (1959), 45–6. These non-eccentrics were the first to censure incursions from the eccentric fringes. It was probably due to these contemporary strictures that many of the eccentrics achieved their notoriety. See Chao I, *Nien-erh shih cha-chi*· 149–51. Some of the non-eccentrics are considered to be Legalists by Etienne

Balazs (1967), 250–54; they are called 'the conservatives' or 'the straitlaced Confucians of the old school' by Michael Rogers, *The Chronicle*, 61–2, 68.

17 Balazs in his discussions of the Chinese thinkers in the Han–Wei and Wei–Chin transition periods devoted only a few lines to the conservative Confucianists (1967), 195–6, 197, 250, 253–4. What Balazs described as Legalists were more likely to be Confucianists or Legalist-Confucianists. For the struggles between the Taoist-Confucianists and the Legalist-Confucianists in the Wei and Chin times, see Michael Rogers, 'The Myth' (1968), 58–63; also *The Chronicle*, 61–2. Cf. Zürcher (1959), 45–6 and also 86–90.

18 *SKC* 2.1–74. An interesting remark on the Legalist inclination of the Wei rule was made in A.D. 243 by Ts'ao K'an, a member of the Ts'ao ruling house; *Wen-hsüan* 52.1129–34. See also Okazaki (1932), 508–9, 519.

19 *SKC* 21.20–2. Holzman (1956) and (1957), *passim*. Ho Ch'i-min (1966), 16–38.

20 *Wen-hsüan* 52.1128.

21 *Wen-hsüan* 23.491. English translation by Robert Payne (1947), 128. 'History' (*Shu* or *Shang-shu*) and 'Odes' (*Shih*) refer to two of the Confucian canonical classics (*ching*).

22 Cf. Balazs (1967), 155.

23 The importance of the Han legacy in the Age of Disunity and early T'ang period has been amply borne out by Michael C. Rogers' studies of 'exemplar history' of those periods; *The Chronicle*, 1–4, 32–73. For dynastic 'revival' or 'restoration', see L. S. Yang (1963), 3–5.

24 Hsün Yüeh's *Shen-chien* was the only Confucian writing of the Chien-an era listed in Chang Chih-tung's highly selective bibliography, *Shu-mu ta-wen*, 3.4a; the *Chung-lun* by Hsü Kang, a junior contemporary of Hsün Yüeh, was listed separately under the Wei dynasty. See also the editor's comment in *Ssu-k'u ch'üan-shu tsung-mu t'i-yao*, 91.20b–21a.

Notes to chapter 2

1 For general accounts of the Later Han decline, see note 1 in Chapter 1. On the dates of Hsün Yüeh's birth and death, see Chapter 4 below. On the state and society during the reigns of the sixth and seventh emperors of the Later Han, see Kano (1964), 304–23; also (1961), 11–21. For intrigues at the court, see Goodrich (1964–5), 165–77, and (1966), 187–210. For events which occurred in A.D. 181–220, consult De Crespigny (1969), which is an English translation of *Tzu-chih t'ing-chien* 58–88.

2 *HHS* 6.14–15a. It was said that Emperor Chih had been poisoned by the Regent of State, Liang Chi, *ibid*. 18a. Also *HHC* 19.230–4.

3 *HHS* 7.1. *HHC* 20.234–5.

4 *HHS* 7.1–2; 34 (*lieh-chuan* 24), 9b–15. *HHC* 20.234–21.249.

5 *HHS* 7.8b–9; 34 (*lieh-chuan* 24), 15b–16; 78 (*lieh-chuan* 68), 9b–14, 18b–19a. *HHC* 21.249–52.

6 Michaud (1958), 48–75. See also note 1 above.

7 An excellent analysis of the antagonism between centralism and localism in traditional empires was made by Weber (1951), especially 16–17, 26, 47–50, 64–75, 79–83, 86–95. A more recent study of this problem is in Eisenstadt (1963). Balazs (1967), 152, was of the opinion that the state of equilibrium in the permanent bureaucratic society of China was actually 'generated by conflicting pulls' which 'tended to cancel each other out'. Cf. also Houn (1965); Ping-ti Ho (1968), 1–92.

8 The problem of land settlement had been raised as early as 202 B.C. in two edicts issued by Emperor Kao-tsu of the Former Han, *Han-shu* 1B.4b–5, tr. by Dubs (1938), 103–6. The crisis of private land encroachment was discussed by Tung Chung-shu in c. 120 B.C., *Han-shu* 24A.16–17, tr. by Swann (1950), 179–84; cf. L. S. Yang (1963), 134. The Emperor Wu-ti's (reigned 141–87

B.C.) moves toward centralization of power and economic reform, though quite successful at first, eventually led to widespread unrest in the provinces when his high-handed officials (*ku-li*) upset the local equilibrium, *Han-shu* 6.34; 24A.17a; 90.6b–12; cf. Dubs (1944), 7–13, 16–25; Watson (1961), II, 438–47. The uprising in 99 B.C. indicated the strong opposition to the emperor's measures, so that the historian noted that 'crowds of robbers . . . obstructed the mountain [passes] and attacked cities', that 'many Inspectors, Commandery Administrators, and lower [officials] suffered execution', and that 'many of the braves and stalwarts [i.e. the local magnates] have relationships at a distance and attached themselves to the groups of bandits', Dubs (1944), 106. Although the insurgents were denounced by the court as 'robbers and bandits', they seemed to have had the strong support of the local leaders and the sympathy of the provincial administrators. As a result, the Emperor Wu-ti rescinded some of the harsh measures in the last years of his reign, *Han-shu* 24A.17a; 66.5–6. Other measures were withdrawn or relaxed during the reigns of his successors, Emperor Chao-ti (87–74 B.C.) and Emperor Hsüan-ti (74–48 B.C.), *Han-shu* 7.5a, 10; 8.6b–7a, 8b–9a, 11a, 12b–13a, 19a, 20b, 21b, 23a, 24a; Dubs (1944), 147–8, 187–90. Cf. Creel (1960), 241–2. Strong criticism of the Emperor Wu-ti's policies was voiced by representatives from the provinces at the court assembly recorded in the *Yen-t'ieh lun* (Discourses on Salt and Iron), tr. by Gale (1967); see especially his Introduction, 17–30. Cf. Yoshinami (1968), 138–59.

9 For a critical reappraisal of Wang Mang, see Bielenstein (1954), 82–165.

10 L. S. Yang, in Etu Zen Sun (1956), 103–11. For detailed studies of Liu Hsiu's rise to power, see Bielenstein (1954), 87–165; (1959), 1–287.

11 *HHS* 1B.12–13a, 22b–23a; also 2.1b *chi-chieh*. Cf. *Nien-erh shih cha-chi* 4.71–2; L. S. Yang, in Etu Zen Sun (1956), 108. Other measures of compromise and retreat included the reduction of imperial garrison forces in the provinces and changes in the army conscription system: Ho Ch'ang-ch'ün (1962), 96–115; Hamaguchi (1966), 291–325, 326–35.

12 *HHS* 49 (*lieh-chuan* 39), 19–21a. *HHC* 17.201–2. For details, see Chi-yun Chen (1958), 109–31; (1960), 139–52. Chien Po-tsan (1969), II, 173–82.

13 Wang Yü-ch'uan (1949), 166–73.

14 *HHS* 43 (*lieh-chuan* 33), 11b–12a; 78 (*lieh-chuan* 68), 2–3a; (*chih* 26), 4–12a and *chi-chieh*. See also Ch'en Ch'i-yün (1960), 127–57; Yoshinami (1968), 138–59; Kamada (1968), 113–37.

15 Michaud (1958), 67–75. L. S. Yang, in Etu Zen Sun (1956), 122–5. Balazs (1967), 174–5, 188–92, 227. Wright (1959), 22–4. Chi-yun Chen, *T'oung-pao* 54 (1968), 77–8.

16 The most thoroughly documented study of the Han regional and local government system is Yen Keng-wang (1961); see his Preface, 3–5; I, 74–97, 216–18, II, 271–97, 409–26. Cf. also De Crespigny (Nov. 1967), 65–6.

17 'Ch'üan Hou-Han wen', (in *Ch'üan shang-ku san-tai Ch'in-Han san-kuo liu-ch'ao wen*, 2), 46, 12a.

18 Wang Yü-ch'uan (1949), 136, 142. Yen Keng-wang (1961), I, 102–46, 221–44; II, 305–15.

19 Weber (1951), 47–50, 91–5. Houn (1965), 17–25, 45–8. De Crespigny (Nov. 1967), 57–71. For the crisis in the local sub-bureaucracy of later times, see James T. C. Liu (1959), 80–5; Hucker (1961), 58–60; and T'ung-tsu Ch'ü (1962), 36–73. One of the most important differences between the local government sub-bureaucracy of Han times and that of the later periods is that in Han times the staff of the sub-bureaucracy had much higher status and prestige in the state and society at large. In the staff of the Han local government sub-bureaucracy, there were at first many literati of promising calibre who constituted the élite in the locality. In later times, the quality of these men

was affected by a full-blown civil service system based on literary examinations; the local government sub-bureaucracy then drew their staff mainly from those who failed to pass these examinations and were looked down upon by the graduate literati. *Jih-chih lu* 3 (*chüan* 8), 69–80. *Han-kuan ta-wen* 5.11a. Yen Keng-wang (1961), Preface 5, 10–11; I, 119, 121–4; II, 332–4, 404, 408.

20 Yen Keng-wang (1961), II, 409–23. See the many cases recorded in 'The Biographies of Reasonable Officials' (*Hsün-li chuan*) in *Han-shu* 89. Even some of the notorious high-handed administrators sent by the Emperor Wu to the provinces in pursuance of his policy of centralization had to cultivate strong local support by co-operating with one faction of the local élite against the others: *Shih-chi* 122.30–1, 35–6, 38–9, tr. by Watson (1961), 440–5. *Han-shu* 90.3b–4, 6b, 7b–10a, 11b, 14, 15b–20.

21 Yen Keng-wang (1961), II, 419–26. See also pages 21–3.

22 Weber's study of the Chinese literati remains standard (1951), 40–7, 107–41. For Confucius' ideals of reform and his influence on the Chinese literati, see Creel (1960), 25–253. The literati of pre-Han and Han times constituted a loose group of learned and politically active individuals; their scholarship, which gave them prestige as well as access to government offices, was yet to be subjected to a rigidly formulated civil service examination: Houn (1956), 138–64. This accounts for the fluid status, complex ideology, and diverse social background of the pre-Han and Han literati, in contrast to the 'mandarin' or the 'gentry-as-degree-holders' in later times; Chung-li Chang (1955), the Introduction by Franz Michael. Balazs (1967), 154, used the composite terms 'scholar-official gentry' and 'cultivated literati' in a single page with reference to such an élite; elsewhere, he referred to the pre-Han 'revolutionary intelligentsia', 18, in contrast to the Han and post-Han 'intellectual aristocracy', 7, or 'traditional intelligentsia', 159.

23 Weber (1951), 25–32, 36–43. Creel (1953), 22–44, 98–131. Fung Yu-lan (1960), 178–90. Bodde, in Wright (1953), 19–80. Cf. Bodde (1954), 47–55.

24 Weber (1951), 44–7, 138–41. Creel (1953), 130–42.

25 Weber (1951), 107–41. Dubs (1938), 15–22, 216–17; (1944), 20–5, 196–8, 271–4, 285–6, 292–8, 341–53, 365. Tjan Tjoe Som (1949), 82–5, 95–7. Fung Yu-lan (1952), I, 402–7. Creel (1960), 242–5.

26 The transformation of the literati as individual idealists into an upper social stratum consisting mostly of cultivated and privileged households and clans took place under the Han rule with the office-holders entrenching their position in society through nepotism and the Confucianization of the local magnates and big clans. Dubs (1944), 292–4. Yü Ying-shih (1956), 209–16.

27 For instance, Tung Chung-shu and Shih Tan in the Former Han, *Han-shu* 56 and 86.15b–20a. Cf. Ch'ien Mu (1956), 269–91.

28 Cf. Fung Yu-lan (1953), II, 1–132; (1960), 178–216. Dubs, I (1938), 14–22, 216–17; II (1944), 20–5, 196–8, 271–4, 285–6, 292–8, 341–53. Tjan Tjoe Som (1949), 82–145. Wright (1959), 8–17.

29 Bielenstein (1954), 131. Jao Tsung-i, on the other hand, compiled a substantial collective biography of those who had criticized, opposed, or refused to serve Wang Mang (1955), 157–208. Bielenstein concluded that Wang Mang's reign had been accepted by the ruling class (gentry) with the exception of the Former Han imperial family of Liu and that the new dynasty might have survived but for the natural disaster caused by flooding of the Yellow River; (1954), 82–7, 145–52, 165. This conclusion has been challenged by Yü Ying-shih (1956), 272–80. Yü's study shows that the rise of the Later Han was closely related to the strength of the literati-as-gentry (or Confucianized local magnates and big clans), 222–56; cf. also L. S. Yang, in Etu Zen Sun (1956), 106–11. The conclusions of Bielenstein and Yü can be reconciled. Wang Mang, especially in the early years of his reign, seems to have had the support

of the literati-as-idealists, the career bureaucrats, and the literati-as-gentry, Yü (1956), 216–18; and his reform measures including many anachronistic elements seem in basic accord with the demands of the literati-as-idealists; cf. Ch'ien Mu (1956), 269–91. The failure of the reform, natural disasters, and rebellions (first the starved peasants and later, the local magnates and big clans) put an end to the reign; Bielenstein (1954), and the authorities cited in 82–4; Yü (1956), 222–6. Many of the literati-as-idealists and career bureaucrats were frustrated not just because of Wang Mang's downfall but more importantly because of the failure of a reform which they initially supported.

30 *HHS* 79A (*lieh-chuan* 69A), 2. P'i Hsi-jui (1959), 113–14, 117–18, 148–60. Tjan Tjoe Som (1949), 164–6. Even the selection of civil service personnel by court examination was later discontinued; De Crespigny (Nov. 1966), 67–78.

31 P'i Hsi-jui (1959), 113–40. Tjan Tjoe Som (1949), 120, 146–54, 164–5.

32 *Nien-erh-shih cha-chi* 4.76–8. P'i Hsi-jui (1959), 109–13. Tjan Tjoe Som (1949), 100–28. Bielenstein (1959), 232–48. See especially *HHS* 36 (*lieh-chuan* 26), 4, 17a; 79A (*lieh-chuan* 69A), 10.

33 See note 23 above. Also note 123 below.

34 Ku Chieh-kang (1955). Eberhard, in Fairbank (1957), 33–70. For its application to Wang Mang's reign, see Bielenstein (1954), 156–9. For its influence on later rebel ideologies, see Y. Muramatsu, in Wright (1960), 241–67. Chi-yun Chen, *T'oung-pao* 54 (1968), 111–12.

35 This theory was formally expounded by Pan Piao in his *Wang-ming lun*, cf. Chapter 5, pages 87–9, below. For the influence of this theory on Later Han historiography, compare Ssu-ma Ch'ien's depiction of the origin of the Liu house in *Shih-chi* 8.2–4, tr. by Watson (1961), II, 77, with Pan Ku's in *Han-shu* 1B.25–6a, tr. by Dubs (1938), 147–50.

36 See above, note 32.

37 P'i Hsi-jui (1959), 127, 134, 139, 141–59. Tjan Tjoe Som (1949), 137–54. The Modern Text School eventually perished after the fall of the Later Han and it was in the late nineteenth century that its teaching was resurrected by some polemical Confucian reformers. Liang Ch'i-ch'ao, tr. by Immanuel C. Y. Hsü (1959), 85–7.

38 *HHS* 36 (*lieh-chuan* 26), 5a, 6a, 7b–11a, 13–16; 79A (*lieh-chuan* 69A), 2a, 10, 11a, 14b; 79B (*lieh-chuan* 69B), 6, 12b, 15a.

39 *HHS* 49 (*lieh-chuan* 39), 1–2a. *Lun-heng*, especially 1.1–2.4, 17.14–19a; tr. by Forke (1962), I, 136–55, 313–17; II, 9–15, 30–42. Cf. Fung Yu-lan (1953), II, 150–67.

40 *HHS* 52 (*lieh-chuan* 42), 14–18a. Balazs (1967), 196–7, 205–13.

41 *HHS* 49 (*lieh-chuan* 39), 16, *chi-chieh*.

42 *HHS* 83 (*lieh-chuan* 73), 2a, 5a, 5b–7a. *Jih-chih lu* 5 (*chuan* 13), 39–40.

43 See Wang Ch'ung's comments in *Lun-heng* 3.6–12a; tr. by Forke (1962), I, 304–12. Shryock (1937), 2–6, 10–19, 37–43. Balazs (1967), 227–30.

44 *Nien-erh-shih cha-chi* 5.89–91. See the two collective biographies of the eccentric (*tu-hsing*) and the recluses (*i-min*) in *HHS* 81 (*lieh-chuan* 71) and 83 (*lieh-chuan* 73). Cf. Yoshinami (1968), 138–59.

45 See L. S. Yang's discussion of the antagonism between the 'Pure' and the 'Turbid', in Etu Zen Sun (1956), 122–9. Also Goi (1954), 22–30; Kawakatsu (1967), 23–50.

46 *HHC* 13.159–60, 163–4; 14.171; 17.203–4; 18.209, 215, 216–17; 19.227–8, 231; 20.236–7; 21.239, 250, 251–2. L. S. Yang, in Etu Zen Sun (1956), 122–5.

47 *HHC* 13.163–4; 17.199, 206–7; 21.249.

48 *HHS* 78 (*lieh-chuan* 68), 2–3, 4a, 5–7, 9–10a, 18b–19a. Michaud (1958), 67–75.

49 *HHS* 69 (*lieh-chuan* 59), 1–3a, 6–8.

50 L. S. Yang, in Etu Zen Sun (1956), 124–5, 129–33. Cf. Kawakatsu (1967), 23–50.

51 See notes 46–50.
52 *HHS* 7.14b–15a; 66 (*lieh-chuan* 56), 4b–7a; 67 (*lieh-chuan* 57), 3b. Chi-yun Chen *T'oung-pao* 54 (1968), 77–8.
53 *HHS* 67 (*lieh-chuan* 57), 3b–5. Chi-yun Chen, *T'oung-pao* 54 (1968), 78.
54 *HHS* 67 (*lieh-chuan* 57), 2b.
55 *HHS* 67 (*lieh-chuan* 57), 2–6. *Jih-chih lu* 5 (*chuan* 13), 47. *Nien-erh-shih cha-chi* 5.93–5. L. S. Yang, in Etu Zen Sun (1956), 123–9. Balazs (1967), 190–1, 229–32. *Tang-lung* as local public opinion, *Miyazaki* (1956), 106, 280; Ochi (1962), 96.
56 *Tang* as village community, *Chou-li*, 9.2a–3, of 500 households, 10.22b; in Confucius' *Analects*, Legge (1960), I, 227. Confucius' criticism of *tang* partisanship, Legge (1960), I, 205, 300.
57 The eunuch's criticism of the *tang* partisans, *HHS* 67 (*lieh-chuan* 57), 3b, 4b, 15b–16a; the literati's justification of *tang* partisanship, *HHS* 8.3a, 67 (*lieh-chuan* 57), 5ab; also *HHC* 23.273, 24.283. Masabuchi (1960), 727–46.
58 *HHS* 67 (*lieh-chuan* 57), 2b.
59 Chi-yun Chen, *T'oung-pao* 54 (1968), 80; see Hsün Yüeh's own comments in *HC* 9.9a; 20.5b, 11; 22.6; 27.12; 28.7. Cf. Chapter 4, pages 70–1.
60 *HHS* 67 (*lieh-chuan* 57), 2b–3a.
61 Fan P'ang was one of the 'Eight Guides' (*pa-ku*), and Ch'en Chih one of the 'Eight Aides' (*pa-chi*) in the partisan leadership, *HHS* 67 (*lieh-chuan* 57), 4a, 14b–17a, 19b–20.
62 For the relation between the high literati in the imperial bureaucracy and the lesser literati in the local sub-bureaucracy, see notes 16, 19 and 20.
63 *HHS* 67 (*lieh-chuan* 57), 2–4.
64 Chi-yun Chen, *T'oung-pao* 54 (1968), 73–115.
65 According to L. S. Yang, this group represented 'the great families of the intellectuals' who were 'learned but not very wealthy', in Etu Zen Sun (1956), 115–21, 123–9. According to Eberhard, this represented the 'city branch' of the gentry clans: (1965), 44–6. See also Yano (1958), 23–31; Utsunomiya (1962), 6–23; Masabuchi (1966), 316–33.
66 *HHS* 67 (*lieh-chuan* 57), 3b, 7, 10a, 11, 13b–14a, 16, 18b–19a, 20b, 22b, 23a.
67 Chi-yun Chen, *T'oung-pao* 54 (1968), 78–83. Cf. Kawakatsu (1967), 23–50; Yoshinami (1968), 138–59.
68 Kawakatsu (1950), 47–63.
69 *Han-shu* 76.1b–2a, 8b. Utsunomiya (1955), 439. Chi-yun Chen, *T'oung-pao* 54 (1968), 78.
70 Ying-ch'uan and its neighbouring Nang-yang and Ju-nan commanderies produced more than 25% of the élite whose names and places of origin were recorded in the *HHS*, Künstler (1966), 22–3. Cf. Chang Chung-tung (1964), 17–20; also Kano (1967), 101–12.
71 *HHS* 67 (*lieh-chuan* 57), 10.
72 *HHS* 67 (*lieh-chuan* 57), 7a, 10a.
73 *HHS* 62 (*lieh-chuan* 52), 11a and *chi-chieh*.
74 'Ying-yin Hsün-shih-p'u', in *Shih-shuo hsin-yü*, 731. *Yuan-ho hsing-chuan* 3.20.
75 *HHS* 39 (*lieh-chuan* 29), 11a.
76 *HHS* 62 (*lieh-chuan* 52), 1b–2a.
77 *HHS* 70 (*lieh-chuan* 60), 15b.
78 *HHS* 62 (*lieh-chuan* 52), 1 and *chi-chieh*.
79 For the local magnate's (or *yu-hsia*, local stalwart) modest attainment as a Confucian gentleman, see *Shih-chi* 124.16; Watson (1961), II, 461. For the Hsün as local magnates, see Yoshinami (1956). Certain members of the Hsün clan still behaved in the manner of a stalwart (*hsia* or *yu-hsia*) by the end of the second century A.D., *Shih-shuo hsin-yü* 1.3b (p. 6). For a discussion of *yu-hsia's* social status, see Ping-ti Ho (1963), 176–80. The relation between the

yu-hsia tradition in pre-Han and early Han times and the activities of the persecuted partisans in the second half of the second century A.D. was clearly noted by the historian in *HHC* 22.264–5, and *HHS* 67 (*lieh-chuan* 57), 2a.

80 For the literati-bureaucrats' persecution of the local stalwarts, see *Shih-chi* 124.9–16. Watson (1961), II, 457–61.

81 *Shih-shuo hsin-yü* 1.2b–3a (pp. 4–5). The meetings between the Hsün and the Ch'en were publicized in the élite circles of Wei and Chin times and variably recorded in different sources; see note 87. It is unlikely that they were entirely groundless. The dates of the meetings pose some difficult problems. These also affect the dates for Hsün Shu's birth and death. According to Shu's biography in the *HHS*, Shu died in the third year of Chien-ho (A.D. 149) at the age of sixty-seven (Chinese reckoning); hence he would have been born in A.D. 83. Ch'en Shih had served as an Administrative Assistant (*Kung-ch'ao*) at Ying-ch'uan after the eunuch Hou Lan had become a Palace Attendant (*Chung ch'ang-shih*) sometime after A.D. 149. Ch'en Shih served as the Magistrate of T'ai-ch'iu after receiving a special recommendation by the Ducal Minister (*Ssu-k'ung*) Huang Ch'iung. And Huang Ch'iung served twice as *Ssu-k'ung* in A.D. 151–2 and 161 respectively. It was after Shih's retirement as the Magis-trate of T'ai-ch'iu that he frequently visited the Hsün. The meeting must have happened sometime after 151. By that time Hsün Shu would have long been dead. Also in A.D. 149 Hsün Yü (163–212) was not yet born and could not have sat on Shu's lap. Accordingly, the dates for Shu's birth and death have to be revised tentatively as ?100–?167, as given on p. 24. The revised date of Shu's death may also account for Hsün Shuang's first retirement from office in A.D. 167. In 166, however, Hsün Yüeh's father had long been dead (Yüeh's father died when Yüeh was still young). But all the eight sons of Hsün Shu were said to have been present at the meeting. It is possible that the Ch'en and the Hsün frequently exchanged visits in the long period between 152 and 166. At the earlier meetings, Shu's eight sons were present but not Hsün Yü; at the later meetings, the infant Yü was present but some of Shu's sons had died; hence, the confusion of the events and the dates. The dates for other *tang-ku* incidents as recorded in the *HHS* also pose serious problems. For instance, see *HHS* 67 (*lieh-chuan* 57), *chiao-pu* 1–5.

82 *HHS* 62 (*lieh-chuan* 52), 1b, 12b.

83 *HHS* 62 (*lieh-chuan* 52), 12b–13.

84 *HHS* 62 (*lieh-chuan* 52), 1.

85 Yoshinami (1956), 68–86. Cf. Kano (1967), 98–118.

86 *HHS* 62 (*lieh-chuan* 52), 13b.

87 *HHS* 62 (*lieh-chuan* 52), 1b, *chi-chieh*.

88 Chi-yun Chen, *T'oung-pao* 54 (1968), 80–3, see especially note 2 in 81.

89 *HHS* 62 (*lieh-chuan* 52), 2b–6. See Chi-yun Chen, *T'oung-pao* 54 (1968), 80–1 and notes.

90 *HHS* 62 (*lieh-chuan* 52), 2a.

91 For the local partisans' ruthless attack on the eunuch clique, see *HHS* 67 (*lieh-chuan* 57), 3b, 9a, 12b, 17b, 20a, 21b.

92 *HHS* 8.2–3a; 67 (*lieh-chuan* 57), 5a. *HHC* 23.270–1, 273.

93 *HHS* 8.4b.

94 *HHS* 8.6b. *HHC* 24.283.

95 *HHS* 62 (*lieh-chuan* 52), 1b, 8a. Hsün's involvement in the second *tang-ku*, *HHS* 62 (*lieh-chuan* 52).2a, 6b.

96 *HHS* 62 (*lieh-chuan* 52), 8. Other 'underground' notables, *HHS* 62 (*lieh-chuan* 52), 6b; 67 (*lieh-chuan* 57), 13b, 16b, 18b–19a, 20b, 22b, 23a.

97 *HHS* 67 (*lieh-chuan* 57), 13b, 14b, 16b–17a, 18b–19a, 23a.

98 *HHS* 67 (*lieh-chuan* 57), 23a. Chang Fan, *Han-chi*, cited in *SKC* 10.28a, *chi-chieh*. Ho Yung, Yüan Shao, and Ts'ao Ts'ao were all known for their *yu-*

hsia activities when they were young, *HHS* 74A (*lieh-chuan* 64A), 1b and *chi-chieh*; *SKC* 1.8b; 10.28b; *Shih-shuo hsin-yü* 3.75b (p. 532). For the relation between *yu-hsia* and the persecuted partisans, see above, note 79. Yüan Shao, Ts'ao Ts'ao, and Hsün Yü later became important political leaders in the civil war during the early years of the third century.

99   *HHS* 62 (*lieh-chuan* 52), 7b.
100 Chi-yun Chen, *T'oung-pao* 54 (1968), 73–115; H. Wilhelm (1967), 31–57.
101 *HC* 25.5a.
102 *HHS* 67 (*lieh-chuan* 57), 23b. *chi-chieh*; *SKC* 10.27b–29a, *chi-chieh*.
103 *HHS* 70 (*lieh-chuan* 60), 1a.
104 Chi-yun Chen, *T'oung-pao* 54 (1968), 82–3, 112–15.
105 *Ibid.* 73–115. The different attitudes of the dissident high literati and the bellicose local leaders in the anti-eunuch league may be seen in the consultation between Tou Wu (the Regent of State in A.D. 168) and his followers, *HHS* 69 (*lieh-chuan* 59), 3b, between Ho Chin (the Regent of State in A.D. 189) and his militant supporters, 7b–9, and between Huang-fu Sung (the commander of the Han army in A.D. 184–5) and Yen Chung (a local magnate from the Han-yang Commandery), *HHS* 71 (*lieh-chuan* 61), 3b–4. Cf. Kawakatsu (1967), 38–45; Chi-yun Chen, *T'oung-pao* 54 (1968), 113–14.
106 *HHC* 22.259–60, 262; 23.271–3, 276, 279, 282; 24.287–8. HHS 7.14–15; 8.2b, 3b, 4b–5, 8b; 66 (*lieh-chuan* 56), 4b–5, 9b, 10a; 67 (*lieh-chuan* 57), 5a, 9a, 13 14b, 20, 21b, 23a; 72 (*lieh-chuan* 62), 1b. Cf. Ho Ch'ang-ch'ün (1959), 33–4. Tada (1968), 160–80.
107 *HHC* 24.290–1. For events after A.D. 181, De Crespigny's (1969) English translation of the *Tzu-chih t'ung-chien* 58–68 may be consulted.
108 Levy (1956), 1; Michaud (1958), 54–7, 67–75. Balazs (1967), 174–6, 187–94, 227, 232. Wright (1959), 17–20, 22–4. Pokora (1961), 64–79, 448–54. Stein (1963), 1–78. Maspero (1967), I, 57–60; II, 44–50; 151–6. Tada (1968), 176–80.
109 Fung Yu-lan (1960), 180–90. Bodde, in Wright (1953), 19–20, 46–51; also Bodde (1954), 46–54.
110 *Lao-tzu* 1 (*chang* 25), 14. *Chuang-tzu* 4 (*pien* 11), 14–22, particularly 20b and 22a; 5 (*pien* 13), 12–14, particularly 15a. *Hsün-tzu* 3.10a; 4.9a; 5.2a, 7; 7.7b; 14.1b. *Han-fei tzu* 8.9b; 20.3a. *Lü-shih ch'un-ch'iu* 1.8a; 5.3b, 7a; 13.3b. *Li-chi* 21.1–3; 50.23–4a. See especially the 'Great Learning' in Legge (1960), I, 357–9; 384–5; and the *Li-yün* in Legge (1967), I, 364–6. Cf. Bodde (1954), 51–2.
111 *Han-shu* 56.8b, 11b; 72.5b–6b, 15; 81.5b. *Kung-yang chu-shu* 1.8b, 23, 26.1a; cf. Fung Yu-lan, II (1953), 82–5; (1960), 201–3. For a modern exposition of this theme, see K'ang Yu-wei, *Ta-t'ung shu* (Shanghai 1935); cf. Howard, in Wright and Twitchett (1962), 295–6. The influence of the *t'ai-p'ing* ideal on religious thought in Former Han times may be seen in Emperor Ai's change of reigning title to that of *t'ai-p'ing* at the urge of the magician Hsia Ho-liang who possessed a religious tract entitled *Pao-yuan T'ai-p'ing ching*, *Han-shu* 75.31b–32; Dubs (1955), III, 6–8. Cf. Ho Ch'ang-ch'ün (1959), 36; Vincent Shih (1956), 163; Pakora (1961), 448–54. For the residual influence of the *t'ai-p'ing* ideal on the Taiping Rebellion in nineteenth-century China, see Vincent Shih (1967), 338–42.
112 Ho Ch'ang-ch'ün (1959), 35–9.
113 Or Metal—Wood—Earth—Water—Fire according to the cycle of destruction. Fung Yu-lan, I (1952), 159–69, II (1953), 20–3; (1960), 191–4, 199. Bodde, in Wright (1953), 22–3, 29.
114 There had been an earlier controversy on whether the Han dynasty possessed the virtue of the element Water (colour Black) or the element Earth (colour Yellow), *Shih-chi* 26.9–12; by the middle of the first century B.C. it was believed that the Han possessed the virtue of Fire (colour Red), *Han-shu* 21B.

72b; 25B.23b; it was not until A.D. 26 that the Han court settled the issue by officially proclaiming Fire as the dominating virtue of the dynasty, *HHS* 1A. 18b–19a and *chi-chieh*; *Han-shu* 1B.26a; *HC* 1.1–2a. Bielenstein (1959), II, 233.

115 *Han-shu* 99A.36b. Dubs III (1955), 103–4, 106–12, 258–9. *HHS* 13 (*lieh-chuan* 3), 16b.

116 Bielenstein, II (1959), 232–48.

117 See above, note 111. Cf. Kawakatsu (1967), 23–48.

118 Weber (1951), 178–9, 181–90; Fung Yu-lan (1960), 60–5, 102–3, 106–7; Creel (1953), 81–97; Waley (1939), 59–79; Gernet (1968), 118–20. The doctrine of Chuang-tzu was more anarchistic than that of Lao-tzu, for instance, see Fung Yu-lan (1952), I, 170–91, 221–45.

119 Weber (1951), 187, 193–4. Fung Yu-lan (1952), I, 190; (1960), 102–3. For the implication of this on the conservative teaching of Kuo Hsiang (died A.D. 312), de Bary (1964), 243–7.

120 These were called the Huang-Lao Taoists, see *Shih-chi* 55.2–6, 28–30; 56.23; Watson (1961), I, 134–6, 149–50, 167.

121 Taoist predominance at the Han court lasted from 193 to 140 B.C., *Shih-chi* 12.3; 24.13–19; 107.8; 121.7, 8, 15, 19; Watson (1961), I, 422–6; II, 114. Cf. Dubs (1938), I, 210, 272–5, 333; (1944), II, 21. Creel (1956), 141–2, and *passim*. Morgan (1935), xliv. de Bary (1964), 157–9. See Hsün Yüeh's comment in *HC* 23.9b–10a. Cf. Ch'ien Mu (1956), 73–4; Fung Yu-lan (1960), 213–14.

122 See Hsün Yüeh's comment in *HC* 8.3b.

123 See the canonical writ on dynastic revolution, in Legge (1960), III, 173–5, 300–4, also 381–42 and *passim*. Cf. Creel (1953), 21–4. Mencius on regicide, Legge (1960), II, 167, on revolutionary uprising, 271–4, 280–1, 292–4, 299–300; on dynastic changes, 354–61. Cf. Bodde (1954), 47–52. See also above, page 16.

124 Dubs (1938), I, 15–16, 18–22; (1944), II, 341–2. Creel (1960), 235–6, 241–2.

125 *Shih-chi* 121.5–6; Watson (1961), II, 396–7.

126 *Shih-chi* 121.16–17; Watson (1961), II, 403–5.

127 Dubs (1944), II, 341–53. See also above, note 121.

128 Fung Yu-lan (1960), 181–90; Creel (1953), 132–51; also (1960), 242–5. The Han orthodoxy emphasized the study of a body of ancient classics (canonized as the Five Classics, *wu-ching*) rather than Confucius' personal teachings *per se*. Confucius' sayings (the *Analects*) were not even included in the orthodox curricula in the Imperial Academy. Cf. Dubs (1944), II, 32. According to Han thought, the Five Classics were a repository of ancient traditions established by the Sage-rulers of Golden Antiquity (i.e. the Hsia, Shang, and particularly the Chou rule), while the Hundred Schools of Philosophy including Confucianism (*ju*) represented different branches of learning emanating from these ancient traditions. The emphasis in Han thought was on devotion to studies of these Classics while making eclectic use of various Schools of Philosophy. *Han-shu* 30.4b–5, 7–8, 9b–10a, 12b–13, 14b–15a, 18b–19, 26b–27a, 33, 38, 41b–42a, 42b–43a, 44, 45b–46a, 48, 49b, 51a, especially 51b–52a. For a modern view of this theme, see Fung Yu-lan (1960), 30–41.

129 See the activities of the Huang-Lao Taoists and the *yu-hsia* stalwarts in the provincial areas, as well as the connection between these two groups, *Shih-chi* 118.14–15; 120.3–4, 14–15; Watson (1961), II, 344–55, *Han-shu* 35.5a–12a; 36.4b–5a, 6b; 37.1–3a; 4b–5; 39.11a; 40.a–3a; 44.8b, 9a; 45.5–11a; 47.2b–6; 50.5a; 51.9a, 13a, 20b–22. Cf. Morgan (1935), xliv. Lao Kan (1950), 237–52; Masabuchi (1951), 555–97; also in Mikami and Kurihara (1954), 233–55; James J. Y. Liu (1967), 12–13.

130 For the mysticization of Confucius and his teaching, see Fung Yu-lan (1960), 206–7; the Taoist inclination in the Confucianists, 207–16. Taoism as a

philosophy and as a religion, Creel (1956), 139–52. Later Han mysticism, Pokora (1961), 64–79.

131 *HHS* 57 (*lieh-chuan* 47), 2b–3.

132 See notes 79 and 98.

133 *HHS* 30A (*lieh-chuan* 20A), 6a; 30B (*lieh-chuan* 20B), 1b–21. Hsün Shuang, 62 (*lieh-chuan* 52), 2b–6b.

134 *T'ai-p'ing ching ho-chiao*, especially Wang Ming's preface, 1–3, 9–11. Cf. Pokora (1961), 448, 454; Hsiung Te-chi (1962), 8–25.

135 *HHS* 30B (*lieh-chuan* 20B), 15b–21. Cf. Hsiung Te-chi (1962), 8–15; Michaud (1958), 82–7; Ying-shih Yü (1965), 84.

136 Hsiung Te-chi (1962), 15.

137 Some dubious sources traced the pedigree of the Chang leadership of the *T'ai-p'ing* Taoists to their origin in high literati families; see the citations in *SKC* 8.42, *chi-chieh*. Cf. Hsiung Te-chi (1962), 24–5 and notes; Li Kuang-pi, in Li-shih chiao-hsüeh yueh-k'an-she (1954), 3–4.

138 *HHS* 30B (*lieh-chuan* 20B), 15b–21. Both Hsün Shuang and Cheng Hsüan had earlier suffered under the *tang-ku* persecution; Cheng Hsüan was said to have been well-treated by the Yellow Turban insurgents; *HHS* 35 (*lieh-chuan* 25), 10.12.

139 Ssu-ma Piao, *Chiu-chou ch'un-ch'iu*, cited in *SKC* 1.14b–15a *chi-chieh*; also *HHS* 30B (*lieh-chuan* 20B), 21b *chi-chieh*.

140 *HHS* 56 (*lieh-chuan* 46), 1–9. Ch'en Fan, a Ducal Minister in A.D. 168, had been honoured as one of the 'Three Lords' (*san-chün*) of the dissident literati; 57 (*lieh-chuan* 47), 4a.

141 *HHS* 71 (*lieh-chuan* 61), 1. Cf. Levy (1956), 216–17.

142 *HHS* 54 (*lieh-chuan* 44), 17b Michaud translated the term *ch'iang-fu* as 'carrying their children on their back' (1958), 96. However, *ch'iang* also means 'money' (lit. the string which fastens together the coins; *Kuan-tzu* 20.5b, 6a, 6b. *Han-shu* 58.12a *pu-chu* has a detailed discussion of the two meanings of this term and their confusion in Han usage.

143 *Pao-p'u-tzu, nei* 9.3a. Based on this and probably other sources, *Tzu-chih t'ung-chien* presents the following account of Chang Chüeh: 'People from the eight provinces [*chou*] . . . all responded to him. Some even deserted or sold their treasures and properties, moving and running to follow him'; 58.1864.

144 *HHS* 57 (*lieh-chuan* 47), 7b.

145 *HHS* 54 (*lieh-chuan* 44), 17b. Cf. Miyagawa (1956), 6.

146 *HHS* 71 (*lieh-chuan* 61), 1b.

147 *HHS* 57 (*lieh-chuan* 47), 8–9a; 58 (*lieh-chuan* 68), 7–8a, especially 19; 71 (*lieh-chuan* 61), 2a; 78 (*lieh-chuan* 68), 17b–18a, 19a; 81 (*lieh-chuan* 71), 21. *HHC* 24.291, 292, 293.

148 *HHS* 78 (*lieh-chuan* 68), 19; 81 (*lieh-chuan* 71), 21.

149 Chang Chün, Hsiang Hsü, Liu T'ao, Lü Ch'iang and Wang Yün who accused the eunuchs were all counter-accused by the eunuchs and convicted; see above, notes 147 and 148; also *HHS* 66 (*lieh-chuan* 56), 10. Fan Yeh, author of the *HHS*, had a strong bias for the partisans, Yoshikawa T. (1967), 158–63.

150 For instance, see *HHS* 71 (*lieh-chuan* 61), 2a.

151 *HHS* 9.9b; 50 (*lieh-chuan* 40), 6a, 6b, 9a; 55 (*lieh-chuan* 45), 6b, 9b. In the case of Prince Ch'ung of Ch'en (in the middle Huai river valley) it was specifically mentioned that his countrymen knew that he was a good soldier and dared not revolt; 50 (*lieh-chuan* 40), 3a.

152 *HHS* 35 (*lieh-chuan* 25), 12a; 45 (*lieh-chuan* 35), 8a; 79A (*lieh-chuan* 69A), 7a. Cf. Kawakatsu (1967), 39–40.

153 *HHS* 8.10b; 78 (*lieh-chuan* 68), 17b–18a.

154 Hsün Yüeh's uncle, Hsün Shuang, a persecuted partisan, was recruited into government service by Wang Yün, the Commissioner of the Yü province having jurisdiction over the Ying-ch'uan Commandery; K'ung Jung, another persecuted partisan, was also recruited by Wang Yün; *HHS* 66 (*lieh-chuan* 56), 10a; 70 (*lieh-chuan* 60), 4.

155 Of the three top leaders of the rebellion, Chang Chüeh had died earlier and his body was captured and destroyed by the Han forces in the tenth lunar month (21 November – 20 December A.D. 184); his brother Chang Liang was captured in the same month; Chüeh's other brother, Chang Pao, was killed in the following month (21 December 184 – 18 January 185); *HHS* 8.10b–12a. However, other branches of the Yellow Turbans remained active and later uprisings continued to harass the realm; *HHS* 8.12–15.

156 *HHS* 64 (*lieh-chuan* 54), 10–13.

157 *HHS* 66 (*lieh-chuan* 56), 10; 71 (*lieh-chuan* 61), 2–3a, 8–9a.

158 See above, note 157. Cf. Chi-yun Chen, *T'oung-pao* 54 (1968), 113–14.

159 *HHS* 66 (*lieh-chuan* 56), 10. Cf. Miyagawa (1956), 8.

160 *HHS* 66 (*lieh-chuan* 56), 10; 78 (*lieh-chuan* 68), 19b.

161 *HHS* 8.15b. Cf. Yen Keng-wang (1961), I, 31–2; II, 290–2. Only a few *chou-mu* were actually appointed in that year; others retained the title of *tz'u-shih* but their power was similarly augmented. De Crespigny (Nov. 1967), 59.

162 *HHS* 8.14b and *chi-chieh*.

163 *HHS* 69 (*lieh-chuan* 59), 6b–7; 74A (*lieh-chuan* 64A), 2a and *chi-chieh*. *HHC* 25.301, 303, 304–5.

Notes to chapter 3

1 *HHS* 8.15b. For many of the events described in this chapter, the English translation of *Tzu-chih t'ung-chien* 58–68 by De Crespigny (1969) may be consulted.

2 *HHS* 8.16a; 69 (*lieh-chuan* 59), 7–10a; 70 (*lieh-chuan* 60), 1. *HHC* 25.305–6.

3 *Tzu-chih t'ung-chien* 59.1901–2, based on *HHS* 8.16, 69 (*lieh-chuan* 59), 10, and *HHC* 25.307.

4 *HHS* 8.1 and *chi-chieh*; *chih* 26.4a–6a, *chi-chieh*; *chih* 27.3a.

5 *SKC* 10.4b and *chi-chieh*.

6 See Yen Chung's advice to the general Huang-fu Sung, page 51. The frontier general Tung Cho's encounter with the humiliated boy emperor of Han is vividly described in *HHS* 72 (*lieh-chuan* 62), 4a; *SKC* 6.5b–6 *chi-chieh*.

7 *SKC* 6.4–7.

8 *HHS* 72 (*lieh-chuan* 62), 4b; 74A (*lieh-chuan* 64A), 2b. *SKC* 6.39 and *chi-chieh*.

9 *HHS* 74A (*lieh-chuan* 64A), 2–3. *SKC* 6.39b–40a.

10 *HHS* 70 (*lieh-chuan* 60), 15b. *SKC* 10.4b.

11 *SKC* 1.16b–17 and *chi-chieh*.

12 *HHS* 67 (*lieh-chuan* 57), 23.

13 Translated from *HHS* 72 (*lieh-chuan* 62), 5–6, with some omissions.

14 *HHS* 9.2–6; 72 (*lieh-chuan* 62), 6–18a.

15 Translated with some omissions from *HHC* 28.333–5. Cf. also *HHS* 72 (*lieh-chuan* 62), 12b–13a and *chi-chieh*.

16 *HHC* 28.335–7. *HHS* 72 (*lieh-chuan* 62), 13b–14a.

17 Translated with some omissions from *HHS* 72 (*lieh-chuan* 62), 14b–15a.

18 *HHS* 9.7a.

19 *HHS* 74A (*lieh-chuan* 64A), 3–7; *SKC* 6.40–8.

20 *SKC* 1.17b–33a.

21 *SKC* 10.4b.

22 *SKC* 6.48 and *chi-chieh*.

23 *SKC* 1.33a.

24 See pages 49–58.
25 See Ts'ao's numerous announcements in *SKC* 1.65, 78b–81, 97b, 99b–100a, 125, *chi-chieh*.
26 *SKC* 1.33–5. There were some discrepancies concerning Ts'ao's role in the change of the reigning title to Chien-an. According to *HHS* 9.7a, the new title was adopted on 23 February A.D. 194, six months before the emperor's arrival at Loyang and seven months before Ts'ao came into contact with the court. *HHS*, however, was strongly biased against Ts'ao Ts'ao. According to *SKC*, Ts'ao's contact with the court was established *c*. 17 February–16 March of the same year.
27 *SKC* 10.8; *HHS* 62 (*lieh-chuan* 52), 8b; 70 (*lieh-chuan* 60), 6a.
28 *HHC* 29.344–6. *HHS* 9.7b; 70 (*lieh-chuan* 60), 17b–18a. *SKC* 1.35–7 Cf. Kuo Mo-jo *et al.* (1962), 22, 40, and *passim*.
29 See Chapter 4.
30 *SKC* 1.23b–32 and *chi-chieh*; also 10.5–7.
31 *HHC* 29.344–5. *SKC* 1.35–42 and *chi-chieh*; 10.8b–15a and *chi-chieh*. See also pages 58–65, 77–8, 80–1, 155–6.
32 *SKC* 1.41–6, 49b–52a.
33 Cf. notes 26, 27, 28, and 31.
34 *SKC* 1.36b–37a and *chi-chieh*; 16.1b–2 and *chi-chieh*. Also *Chin-shu* 26.5a, 6b–7a, tr. by L. S. Yang (1963), 158, 163. Cf. Li Chien-nung (1963), 20–5.
35 *Chin-shu* 47.5a. Cf. L. S. Yang (1963), 140; Li Chien-nung (1963), 24–5.
36 *SKC* 28, 29b–30. Also *Chin-shu* 26.9b–10, tr. by L. S. Yang (1963), 106–70. The full scale of these works was reached in *c*. 243–65 but their beginning probably dated back to the Chien-an era. Cf. Li Chien-nung (1963), 21–2; Chao Yu-wen (1958), 29–46; Ochi (1961), 1–24; Fujiie (1962), 71–101; Kuo Mo-jo (1962), 44–5, 50–1, and *passim*; Nishijima (1956), 1–84; Sogabe (Dec. 1967), 1–35.
37 *SKC* 1.60 *chi-chieh*. Also *Chin-shu* 26.5a; tr. by L. S. Yang (1963), 159; see also 140. Cf. Li Chien-nung (1963), 118–22.
38 *HHC* 30.355–60. *SKC* 1.70–7a and *chi-chieh*; 32.10b–18; 47.5–6a.
39 The dependence of the prominent 'aristocratic households' (*men-ti*) or gentry in the Age of Disunity on the bureaucratic institutions of the state has been pointed out in a number of studies by Japanese scholars; Kawakatsu (1950), 47–63, also (1958), 175–218; Goi (1956), 14–23; Yano (1958), 23–47; Moriya (1951); Miyagawa (1956), 263–398; Miyazaki (1956), 8–16, 27–8, 30–2, 89–91, 97–100, 253–61, 283–300, 528–44 and *passim*; Ochi (1962), 97–103; Utsunomiya (1962), 17–18. Similar views have been expressed by many Chinese authors on the Ts'ao Ts'ao controversy; see Kuo Mo-jo *et al.* (1962). Cf. Balazs (1967), 7–8.
40 See Chapter 2. This point may be supplemented by the studies of genealogies of the Wei-Chin new élite, Kawakatsu (1950), 47–63; Yano (1958), 23–47.
41 *HHC* 26.311; *SKC* 1.18–21. Ts'ao Ts'ao's name was replaced by that of Chang Ch'ao, Grand Administrator of the Kuang-ling Commandary, in *HHS* 74A (*lieh-chuan* 64A), 3a.
42 *SKC* 1.18–21, *chi-chieh*; 7.4b.
43 See the fate of the local magnates in Ying-ch'uan discussed below; also *SKC* 10.7a and *chi-chieh*.
44 *HHS* 62 (*lieh-chuan* 52), 7. Hsün Yüeh's nephew Hsün Yu was in Shuang's company, *SKC* 10.27–9a and *chi-chieh*. For Hsün Yüeh's close relationship with Hsün Shuang, see Chapter 5 below.
45 *HHC* 26.319; *SKC* 10.4b–5a; *HHS* 70 (*lieh-chuan* 60), 15b.
46 *HHC* 25.309; 26.312; *SKC* 6.10; *HHS* 72 (*lieh-chuan* 62), 5–6.
47 *HHS* 62 (*lieh-chuan* 52), 7a.
48 *HHS* 66 (*lieh-chuan* 56), 11.

49 *Ibid.* 11b–13.
50 *HHC* 27.326–7; 28, 333–8; *HHS* 72 (*lieh-chuan* 62), 11b–16.
51 *HHS* 9.4b–5.
52 See the proclamation of the anti-Tung Cho alliance in A.D. 190, *HHC* 26.313. Other loyal utterances by these leaders were recorded in the sources cited in the *chi-chieh* of *SKC* 1.18 and *passim*, 6.7b and *passim*; 7.6b and *passim*, 8.6a and *passim*; 10.8 and *passim*; also *HHS* 74a (*lieh-chuan* 64a), 5, 8b–17.
53 *Shih-chi* 97.16; 99.2–5, 14–15; tr. by Watson (1961), I, 277, 286–7, 293–4.
54 *Shih-chi* 92.40; tr. by Watson (1961), I, 231.
55 *Han-shu* 77.3b–4a. For similar views held by the adherents of Taoism or *Yin-yang* cosmology, see 75.1b–2a, 20–2; 85.15. For the influence of these views on the Han court, see 75.31–3. Cf. Eberhard, in Fairbank (1957), 33–70.
56 See *Han-shu* 100a.7b, 11b; also *HC* 30.22a, 24b.
57 See Chapter 2, pages 15–16, 31–2.
58 See Chapter 2, pages 23, 26–30.
59 *SKC* 13.48 and *chi-chieh*.
60 *HHS* 71 (*lieh-chuan* 61), 3b–4a.
61 See above, note 52.
62 See, for instance, Hsün Yü's various counsels to Ts'ao Ts'ao, *SKC* 10.8, 20–2, and *chi-chieh*. *HHS* 70 (*lieh-chuan* 60), 17, 20b.
63 See above, note 41.
64 *HHC* 26.314; *HHS* 73 (*lieh-chuan* 63), 2b.
65 *HHC* 27.325; *HHS* 75 (*lieh-chuan* 65), 6; *SKC* 6.72–4.
66 *HHS* 74ᴀ (*lieh-chuan* 64ᴀ), 7b–8a; *SKC* 6.48 and *chi-chieh*.
67 *SKC* 1.32–5 and *chi-chieh*.
68 *HHS* 70 (*lieh-chuan* 60), 17; *SKC* 10.7b–8 and *chi-chieh*; *HHC* 29.343–4.
69 *SKC* 10.14a.
70 *SKC* 6.48b–51a and *chi-chieh*.
71 *HHC* 28.341–2; *SKC* 6.75.
72 *SKC* 6.75b–77a; *HHC* 29.347–8.
73 *SKC* 6.77.
74 *SKC* 6.77b *chi-chieh*.
75 *Ibid.*
76 *SKC* 6.48b–61, and *chi-chieh*; *HHS* 75 (*lieh-chuan* 65), 66–9.
77 *HHC* 29.350.
78 Cf. L. S. Yang (1969), 3–23, also in Fairbank (1957), 291–309.
79 Legge (1960), I, 256.
80 *Han-shu* 43.10b–11a, 15a; 48.26b–27a; 56.3b–4, 7a, 9b, 13b–15a; 58.4a; 71.9b–10a; 75.20; 85.4a. The theory culminated in Pan Piao's *Wang-ming lun*, cited in *Han-shu* 100ᴀ.8, 10a. Though Wang Ch'ung repudiated many theories concerning the correspondence between nature and men, wisdom and morality, virtue and physical well-being, or personal attainment and external condition, he tacitly accepted the effect of long-range 'accumulated virtue' on an individual's 'fate', which could not be changed by short-term efforts, *Lun-heng* 3.12–13; 5.1–3. Cf. L. S. Yang (1969), 10–11.
81 See notes 53, 54 and 55.
82 Cf. Chi-yun Chen, *T'oung-pao* 54 (1968), 73–115.
83 See Chapter 2, pages 19–30.
84 For Shu's and Shao's anti-eunuch activities, see pages 28, 39–40.
85 *HHC* 28.341; *SKC* 6.36, 40a, 44b, 75b, and *chi-chieh*.
86 *HHC* 28.339; 29.348; *HHS* 75 (*lieh-chuan* 65), 8a; *SKC* 6.42, 48a *chi-chieh*, 52b *chi-chieh*, 76b *chi-chieh*.
87 *HHC* 28.342; 29.347; *HHS* 74ᴀ (*lieh-chuan* 64ᴀ), 12a; 75 (*lieh-chuan* 65), 7a, 8a; *SKC* 6.39 *chi-chieh*, 73a *chi-chieh*, 75.
88 See Chapter 5, pages 85–93. A similar emphasis on the cumulative virtue of the Han in comparison with that of the regional warlords was made by Pan

Piao in his *Wang-ming lun* cited in *Han-shu* 100a.7b and reiterated by Hsün Yüeh in *HC* 30.22a.

89 *SKC* 1.35 and *chi-chieh*, 40a *chi-chieh*; 6.42b, 47b–48a *chi-chieh*, 75; 10.7b–8a.

90 *SKC* 10.14a, also 15a.

91 *SKC* 10.19.

92 *HHS* 74A (*lieh-chuan* 64A), 7a, 12–14a, 17b–20.

93 *HHC* 28.338–9.

94 On the contrast between Ts'ao Ts'ao and Yüan Shao, see Okazaki (1932), 17–25, 432–9, 451–74; Miyagawa (1956), 16–21, 25–30; and especially Kuo Mo-jo *et al.* (1962), 42–6 and *passim*. Cf. Balazs (1967), 227–30.

95 *HHC* 26.313; the text reads that 'he failed to protect the people's [landlords, local magnates?] fortified [manors]'. Cf. Miyagawa (1956), 10–11.

96 See the fate of the local magnates in Ying-ch'uan mentioned above. Also the case of Cheng T'ai in *HHC* 27.324–5.

97 *HHC* 30.357.

98 *HHC* 27.328; *SKC* 11.10b–16.

99 For brief discussions on these regional states in the southwest, see Miyagawa (1959), 21–5, 30–3, 211–61. Kano (1959), 85–102. Ueda (1967), 1–22. For the Chinese Communist historian's views, see Kuo Mo-jo *et al.* (1962), 43–4 and *passim*.

100 Wan Sheng-nan (1964), 2–11; Ho Ch'ang-ch'ün (1964), 208–9; Okazaki (1932), 453–63.

101 The pro-Han faction was led by Emperor Hsien's relatives (the Tung and the Fu families) and the court dignitaries (K'ung Jung and others). The pro-Ts'ao faction emanated from the nucleus of Ts'ao's military command, including Hsün Yu, Hsün Yüeh's nephew, who served as Ts'ao's principal military adviser (*chün-shih*); a list of Ts'ao's other military advisers may be found in *SKC* 1.39b *chi-chieh*.

102 See notes 14 and 16 in Chapter 1.

103 *SKC* 1.13 and *passim*. For the appraisal of Ts'ao Ts'ao by his contemporaries, see 11–12a, 127–32, and *chi-chieh*. For appraisal by modern Chinese and Japanese scholars, see note 94. Cf. Balazs (1967), 173–86, 227–30.

104 See above, pages 45–7; also Chapter 4, pages 80–1.

105 Kuo Mo-jo *et al.* (1962).

106 *HHC* 29.344–5.

107 *HHC* 29.345.

108 *HHC* 29.345. A similar counsel was given to Ts'ao Ts'ao by Chia Hsü, *SKC* 10.41.

109 See Chapter 4, pages 79–82; also Chapters 5 and 6.

110 *HHS* 62 (*lieh-chuan* 52), 8b.

111 *SKC* 10.8b.

112 *SKC* 10.29b–32.

113 See pages 136–161.

114 The bias against Yü may be seen in *SKC* 10.27b–29a *chi-chieh*. Yü's Taoist tinge is hinted at in 32a and *chi-chieh* (where Ts'ao compares Yü with Chang Liang, a Taoist adviser to Emperor Kao-tsu of the Former Han); his Legalist inclination is shown in 33a *chi-chieh*.

115 *HHS* 70 (*lieh-chuan* 60), 15b–21a; *SKC* 10.3–22, 42–4a, *chi-chieh*. See Hu San-hsing's comment on the three Hsün in a commentary in *Tzu-chih t'ung-chien*, 64.2065.

116 *SKC* 1.30–1 and *chi-chieh*; 10.5, 7.

117 *SKC* 10.7–17 and *chi-chieh*; 11.2–4 and *chi-chieh*.

118 *HHS* 54 (*lieh-chuan* 44), 20 and *chi-chieh*; *SKC* 26.1b.

119 The adherents included: Hsün Yu, *SKC* 10.32a, and 33a *chi-chieh*; Hsing Yung, 12.25; Pao Hsün, 12.28–30a; Ssu-ma Chih, 12.30b–31; Tung Chao,

14.18a, 21; Chia K'uei, 15.27b–28a; Wei Chi, 21.34b–35a; Man Ch'ung, 26.1.
Cf. Okazaki (1932), 453–5, 460–3, 464–8; Balazs (1967), 187–225.

120 On the abolition of punishment by mutilation, see Dubs, I (1938), 225. During
the Chien-an period and later, many well-intended Confucianists who were
otherwise opposed to Legalism also favoured re-instituting mutilation as a
substitute for capital punishment; see Hsün Yüeh's *SC* 2.5; also *SKC* 13.9b–11;
22.6b–7a and *chi-chieh*; *chin-shu* 30.8–11.

121 *Ch'uan Hou-Han wen* (in *Ch'uan shang-ku san-tai Ch'in-Han san-kuo liu-
ch'ao wen*) 81.11b–12a. *T'ung-tien* 168.887–8. *Cf.* Hamaguchi (1966), I, 667–83.
HHS 70 (*lieh-chuan* 60), 7–8. *SKC* 12.10 *chi-chieh*. There were many others,
some Legalist-inclined, who opposed the measure for practical reasons, 11.20b;
12.15b–17; 13.11 and *chi-chieh*. See also note 120.

122 See notes 120 and 121.

123 *HHS* 70 (*lieh-chuan* 60), 6–14a and *chi-chieh*; *SKC* 12.6–12 and *chi-chieh*.

124 *HHS* 62 (*lieh-chuan* 52), 8b.

125 *HHS* 62 (*lieh-chuan* 52), 11a.

126 See note 103.

127 See Chapters 5 and 6.

128 See notes 5, 6, and 7 in Chapter 1. Cf. Zürcher (1959), 45–6, 86–95.

129 See notes 1, 5, and 6 in Chapter 1.

130 *HHS* 9.8; 10b.12a. For Tung Ch'eng's status, see *SKC* 32.8a *chi-chieh*.

131 *HHS* 9.11a; 10b.12b–13a. One year before this, Ts'ao Ts'ao was enfiefed as
the Duke of Wei, *HHC* 30.361–3; Hsün Yü refused to endorse the measure
and was compelled to commit suicide, *SKC* 10.20–2 and *chi-chieh*; *HHS* 70
(*lieh-chuan* 60), 21a. Later two more plots against Ts'ao Ts'ao, one planned
by Chi P'ing and Keng Hsï in 218, the other planned by Wei Feng in 219,
also failed, *HHC* 30.264, 266.

132 *HHS* 9.9b; *SKC* 1.69 and *chi-chieh*.

133 *SKC* 1.70–3, and *chi-chieh*. Many of these Ching-chou literati were mentioned
in 6.83–91 and *chi-chieh*; 21.1–63 and *chi-chieh*.

134 Liebenthal (1947), 124–61. For the influence of the Ching-chou literati on
Confucian classical learning, see Kaga (1964), ' Preface ', 11–14; 48, 51–69,
194–9, 244–7, 316–18, 757–8 and *passim*.

135 See notes 133 and 134.

136 See notes 106 and 107.

137 *HHC* 29.344.

138 See note 133.

139 See note 134.

140 For Ts'ao's encounter with K'ung Jung and Hsün Yü, see notes 123 and 131.

141 For the intellectual trend after the middle Chien-an period, see Balazs (1967),
230–42. Cf. Chapter. 7.

142 See notes 5, 6, and 7 in Chapter 1.

143 *SKC* 1.77 and *chi-chieh*. Two similar orders were issued in A.D. 214 and 217;
106b, and 119a *chi-chieh*.

144 See notes 103 and 119.

Notes to chapter 4

1 *HHS* 62 (*lieh-chuan* 52), 1–2a, ' Biography of Hsün Shu '; 2b–8a, ' Biography
of Hsün Shuang '; 8–11a, ' Biography of Hsün Yüeh '; 11a,b, ' Biography of
Han Shao '; 11b–12b. ' Biography of Chung Hao '; 12b–14, ' Biography of
Ch'en Shih '; 14b–16a, ' Biography of Ch'en Chi '; 16b, ' Eulogy '.

2 *Ibid*. 11a.

3 *HHS* 34 (*lieh-chuan* 24), 7b–16a.

4 See Chapter 2, pages 23–7. Cf. Yoshinami (1956), 68–75.

5 *HHS* 62 (*lieh-chuan* 52), 1b, 8a.

6 *Ibid.* 8a.
7 See Chapter 2, pages 23–7.
8 Hsün Shu, see Chapter 2, pages 23–5; Shuang, see *HHS* 62 (*lieh-chuan* 52), 2b.
9 The contact between Hsüun and Ch'en, see Chapter 2, pages 25–6.
10 *HHS* 62 (*lieh-chuan* 52), 1.
11 For Shuang's works, see Chapter 2, pages 28–9.
12 *HHS* 62 (*lieh-chuan* 52), 8a.
13 See Chapter 2, pages 27–9.
14 *HHS* 62 (*lieh-chuan* 52), 1b–2a, and *chi-chieh*.
15 *Ibid.*
16 *Ibid.* 14. Cf. Kano (1967), 106–13.
17 *HC* 10.3b, *Lun* 16.
18 This point will be discussed in Chapters 5 and 6.
19 See Chapter 2, pages 27–8.
20 *HHS* 62 (*lieh-chuan* 52), 6b.
21 *Ibid.* 8.
22 *HC* 16.13, *Lun* 20.
23 *SC* 1.7a–8a.
24 *HC* 16.14, *Lun* 20.
25 *HC* 28.7, *Lun* 37. The stricture was reiterated in 22.6a.
26 *HC* 8.8b–9a, *Lun* 11.
27 For the quotation, see Legge (1960), v, 317.
28 For the allusion to Ning-wu-tzu and Chieh-yü, see Legge (1960), I, 180–1 and 332–3.
29 See *Shih-chi* 84.2–20, tr. by Watson (1961), I, 499–508.
30 See *Shih-chi* 83.31–2 and annotation; also *Han-shih wai-chuan* 1.11, tr. by Hightower (1952), 35–6 and note.
31 This man was said to have lived at the end of the Chou dynasty; see *Shih-chi* 83.23–4 and annotation.
32 *Ibid.*
33 *HC* 25.6b–7a, *Lun* 31.
34 See Chapters 5 and 6.
35 See note 11.
36 *HC* 25.5a; *SC* 3.7b–8.
37 *HC* 25.5a, *Lun* 30; see Chapter 5, pages 109–10, for details.
38 Cf. Chapter 6, pages 137–40.
39 *HHS* 62 (*lieh-chuan* 52), 7b.
40 *HC shu*, 2; 1.1a; 30.27a.
41 Chi-yun Chen, *T'oung-pao* 54 (1968), 94 and note 4.
42 See Chapter 2, pages 38–9; Chapter 3, page 42.
43 *HHS* 62 (*lieh-chuan* 52), 7a.
44 *HHS* 70 (*lieh-chuan* 60), 15b; *SKC* 10.4b.
45 *SKC* 6.40–2a.
46 *HHS* 70 (*lieh-chuan* 60), 16a.
47 At least Hsün Yü's brother Shen was in Yüan Shao's camp as late as A.D. 200; *SKC* 6.52a.
48 *HHS* 70 (*lieh-chuan* 60), 15b; *SKC* 10.5a.
49 *HHS* 62 (*lieh-chuan* 52), 7b; *SKC* 10.27–9a.
50 Chapter 3, pages 41–4.
51 See notes 41–5, pages 43–7.
52 Hsün Hung, see *SKC* 10.18a *chi-chieh*.
53 This point has been discussed in some detail in my paper ' The Rise and Decline of the Hsün Family (*c.* 100–300 A.D.) – A Case Study of One of the

Aristocratic Families in the Six Dynasties' (Paper No. 37, International Conference on Asian History, Hongkong, 30 August–5 September 1964). Some of the material used in that paper has been included in this book; other information on the later history of the Hsün family may be found in *Chin-shu* 39, 10b–26a; 75.21b–29. For further discussion of the distinction between the local magnates and the aristocratic households in medieval China, see Miyazaki (1956), 536–44; Miyagawa (1956), 173–210; Ochi (1962) 100–2.

54 *HHS* 62 (*lieh-chuan* 52), 8b.

55 *SKC* 1.33–5 and *chi-chieh*.

56 See Goi (1954), 22–30; (1956), 14–23; Kawakatsu (1958), 175–218; Yano (1958), 31–47; Ochi (1962), 97–9. These studies attempt to show the subtle political relationships arising from favours (official patronage) exercised through official, semi-official, and private channels by political leaders on behalf of their followers in Wei and Chin times.

57 *HHS* 62 (*lieh-chuan* 52), 8b; *HC hsü* 1b–2a.

58 See Chapter 2, pages 11–12.

59 See notes 4 and 5 in Chapter 3.

60 *Han-shu* 30.1b, and *pu-chu*; 36.19a and 31a.

61 *HHS* 7.9b and *chi-chieh*. Since this was the first court office added by Emperor Huan shortly after he had liquidated the powerful Liang family, its office-holder seemed to be particularly privy to court power.

62 *Tung-tien* 21.125.

63 *HHS* 62 (*lieh-chuan* 52), 8b; *SKC* 10.8b.

64 *SKC* 10.21b *chi-chieh*; 13.1–13; 22.4–12a; 23.14–18a; *Chin-shu* 1.1–37. Chung Yu, Ch'en Ch'ün, and Tu Hsi were all from Ying-ch'uan Commandery, the Hsün clan's native place.

65 See note 63.

66 *SKC* 10.7b–12.

67 *SKC* 10.21a.

68 Cf. Chapter 2, page 11.

69 *Tzu-chih t'ung-chien* 64.2065.

70 See note 21.

71 *HHS* 62 (*lieh-chuan* 52), 8b, 10b; cf. *HC* 1.1a.

72 *HHS* 66 (*lieh-chuan* 56), 11b and *chi-chieh*.

73 *HHS* 9.4b–5a.

74 See Yüeh's statement in *HC hsü*; for further discussion, see Chapter 5, pages 85–93.

75 See pages 55–6, 100.

76 *SKC* 10.21a *chi-chieh*.

77 See pages 44–7, 58–61, 154–6.

78 *SKC* 10.8b–13, 21b, and *chi-chieh*.

79 *SKC* 10.21b *chi-chieh*.

80 *Ibid.*

81 *SKC* 10.33a *chi-chieh*. For Ts'ao's relationship with the two Hsün, see Chapter 3, pages 60–1.

82 See Chapter 5, especially pages 81, 112, 124–6.

83 For Shuang's political inclinations, see Chapter 2, pages 28–9. For Shuang's influence over Yüeh; see pages 66–8. For the relationship between Shuang's *Han-yü* and Yüeh's *Han-chi*, see Chapter 5, pages 124–6.

84 See Chapter 5.

85 *HC* 10.2b–3a, *Lun* 16.

86 See pages 102–3.

87 See Chapter 2, pages 19–39.

88 See note 98 in Chapter 2.
89 See note 79 in Chapter 2.
90 *HC* 10.3b–4a, *Lun* 16.
91 For Yüeh's view of family solidarity, see pages 68–9, 101. For Shuang's view, see Chi-yun Chen, *T'oung-pao* 54 (1968), 83–5 and *passim*. An additional piece of evidence of Shuang's view on family solidarity may be found in *Shih-shuo hsin-yü* 1.19 (pp. 37–8), which records that once Shuang was asked by another notable to comment on the cultivated élite of Ying-ch'uan. Shuang replied by commending all his brothers. The other notable smiled and asked him whether a gentleman should only care for his relations, and Shuang retorted by saying that a man who cared for others more than for his own relations would be violating the precepts of morality.
92 See Chapter 6.
93 *HHS* 70 (*lieh-chuan* 60), 14a and 21a.

Notes to chapter 5

1 *Han-chi*, lit. Chronicles of Han; it was after Yüan Hung (328–76) had produced the *Hou-Han-chi* (Chronicles of the Later Han) that later editors designated Yüeh's work *Ch'ien-Han-chi* (Chronicles of the Former Han). For editions and various textual problems of the *Han-chi*, see Chi-yun Chen, *Monumenta Serica* 27 (1968), 209–13, 222–7.
2 Implying Ts'ao Ts'ao; see following discussions.
3 For a discussion of these offices, see Chapter 4, pages 76–7.
4 *Han-shu* by Pan Ku (A.D. 32–92) was a collective work by several members of the Pan family. For comments on the historiography of the *Han-shu*, see Sargent (1944), 119–43; Dubs (1946), 23–43; Bielenstein (1954), 23–5, and *passim*.
5 Cf. pages 114–15 below.
6 For detailed discussion see Chi-yun Chen, *Monumenta Serica* 27 (1968), 227–32.
7 See also *HHC* 29.354; *HHS* 62 (*lieh-chuan* 52), 10b.
8 *HC hsü* 2a.
9 *HC hsü* 2a,b. For a similar view held by an important thinker and historian of the late eighteenth century, see Nivison (1966), 202–3 and *passim*. Cf. also Bodde, in Wright (1953), 27–36.
10 *HC hsü* 2a,b.
11 See Chapter 3, pages 50–6.
12 See pages 128–9 below. For the influence of Yüeh's view, see note 9.
13 *HC hsü* 2a.
14 *HC hsü* 1–2; *HC* 1.1–2; 30.22–7a.
15 *HC* 1.2b.
16 *HC* 30.19b–24.
17 *HC* 1.1b–2a. For the theory of the Five Elements, see Chapter 2, pages 31–2.
18 *HC* 1.2. The glorification of the Han dynastic genealogy in the *Han-shu* contrasted sharply with the modest statement of the *Shih-chi*, and constituted an important element of Later Han conservatism discussed in Chapter 2, pages 15–16, 31–2. In *Shih-chi* 8.2–3, the origin of the Han founding emperor was briefly stated as follows: ' Kao-tsu, a native of the Chung-yang community in the town of Feng of the district of P'ei; family name: Liu; polite name: Chi; his father was known as " Old Sire ", and his mother, Dame Liu.' Cf. Watson (1961), I, 77.
19 *HC* 30.20–1.
20 For the *feng-chien* feudal system in Chou times, see Bodde, in Coulborn (1956), 52–66.
21 Cf. *ibid.* 66–71; also Creel (1964), 155–84.

22 See Chapter 3, pages 50–2.

23 *HC* 30.21b–22a, quoted from *Han-shu* 100A.7–8a.

24 *HC* 30.24b, quoted from *Han-shu* 100A.11. Cf. de Bary (1964), 180.

25 *HC* 30.27a. Cf. Chapter 3, pages 52–3. See also note 34 below.

26 See Chapter 3, pages 52–4.

27 For the impact of the Han legacy on Chinese thinking in the Age of Disunity, see Rogers, *Chronicle* (1968), 1 and *passim*.

28 See note 1.

29 *HC* 30.26b. In *HC hsü* it reads 'four hundred and sixteenth'. In Yüeh's 'Biography', *HHS* 62 (*lieh-chuan* 52), 11a, it reads 'four hundred and sixth'. This seems to be the result of successive corruptions. The *keng-chen* year (A.D. 200) or the fifth year of the Chien-an is only the one hundred and seventy-fifth year of the Later Han, starting from the first year of Chien-wu (A.D. 25). If the Former and the Later Han reigns were combined, the *keng-chen* year would be the four hundred and seventeenth of the Han.

30 See pages 112–13, 124–6.

31 For the illusion of the Chien-an 'restoration', see Chapter 3, pages 58–65; and Chapter 6, page 127; and Chapter 7, pages 162–3.

32 For the meaning of *chien*, see Chapter 6, pages 128–9.

33 Two *Tsu*: Emperor Kao-tsu, founder of the Former Han, and Emperor Kuang-wu (Shih-tsu), founder of the Later Han. Six *Tsung*; Emperors Wen (T'ai-tsung), Wu (Shih-tsung), and Hsüan (Chung-tsung) of the Former Han, and Emperors Ming (Hsien-tsung), Chang (Shu-tsung), and An (Kung-tsung) of the Later Han. The *Tsu* and *Tsung* of the Former Han and those of the Later Han thus suggest parallels.

34 *Chiao-chiao tsün-ch'en*, implying Ts'ao Ts'ao.

35 *HC* 30.26b–27a. The epilogue was written in rhymed prose.

36 *HHS* 62 (*lieh-chuan* 52), 10b. *Ch'un-ch'iu*, tr. by Legge (1960), v.

37 *Shih-t'ung t'ung-shih* 2.14. *Wen-hsien t'ung-k'ao* 193.1631. *Jih-chih lu* 8 (*chuan* 26), 99. Chin Yü-fu (1944), 44–5. Chang Hsü (1962), 20, 22–4, 204–5, 215–16.

38 See Yüan Shu's letter to Yüan Shao in Chapter 3, page 53; also the quoted dialogue between Wei Hsiao and Pan Piao in *HC*, as mentioned above.

39 See the discussion of the Three Ages (*san-shih*), *viz.* Disorder, Approaching Order, and Great Peace, espoused by the Kung-yang School concerning the *Ch'un-ch'iu*, *Kung-yang chu-shu* 1.23; P'i Hsi-jui (Commercial Press), 4.1 and *passim*.

40 Cf. Gardner (1961), 87–8; Hulsewé, in Beasley and Pulleyblank (1961), 35–41. Watson (1958), 104–34; for the polarized system of praise-and-blame in the 'composite Standard Histories', see 95–8.

41 See note 40. The 'composite' format of dynastic histories was severely criticized by Hsiao Ying-shih of the T'ang dynasty, see *Hsin T'ang-shu* 202.20.

42 For the inclusion of materials from the 'Biography' section (*lieh-chuan*) of the *Han-shu* in the *HC*, see pages 122–3 below.

43 For cumulative merit and the legitimization of dynastic rule, see Chapter 3, pages 50–6.

44 *HC hsü* 1b.

45 Ssu-ma Ch'ien's *Shih-chi* had been considered dangerous by the Former Han court because of its inclusion of such vital information about the realm. Once the treacherous Prince Yü of Tung-p'ing (son of Emperor Hsüan) went to the imperial court requesting a copy of the *Shih-chi*; the court advised Emperor Ch'eng to refuse the request, saying that the *Shih-chi*, containing 'intriguing plots', 'disastrous and abnormal occurrences', and 'strategic information on geography', should not be in the possession of a regional prince; *Han-shu* 80.8.

46 Chi-yun Chen, *Monumenta Serica* 27 (1968), 222–3.
47 *HC hsü* 2b.
48 For a modern critic of this concept, see Levenson (1956), 399–404; also in Wright and Twitchett (1962), 317, 320–5. For a defence, see note 49.
49 A few recent discussions on the Chinese concept of time and history may be mentioned here: Marcus (1961), 123–39; Yoshikawa (1963), 14–19; Nakamura (1963), 44–59; Franke (1965), 6–22; Sivin (1966), 82–92. For a detailed case study, see Nivison (1966).
50 Cf. Nivison (1966), 139–90, and *passim.*
51 See pages 28–29, 73–4.
52 Cf. pages 70–3, 98–100 below.
53 *HC* 30.26b.
54 Chi-yun Chen, *Monumenta Serica* 27 (1968), 223–7.
55 See Ho Hsiu's (A.D. 129–82) *Hsü* and *Chieh-ku* in *Kung-yang chu-shu, hsü* 1–2a; 1.1–5a. Cf. P'i Hsi-jui (Commercial Press), 4.1 and *passim*; Legge (1960), v, Prolegomena, 1–22 and *passim*; Franke (1920), 1–86 *passim*; Gardner (1961), 12–14. For a critical analysis of this thesis, see Kennedy (1942), 40–8.
56 See note 55.
57 Kennedy (1942), 40–8. Cf. Watson (1958), 76–8.
58 See notes 40 and 41. Also Gardner (1961), 19–21.
59 Yüeh's initiation was followed by Yüan Hung in the *Hou-Han-chi* and Ssu-ma Kuang in his famous *Tzu-chih t'ung-chien.* The genre of *shih-lun* or *shih-p'ing* became a separate branch of historiography in Sung times when ' Comments and Notes on History' (*Shih-p'ing* or *Shih-ch'ao*) were classified into a special sub-section under the section of *shih* (history) in the *I-wen chih* (' Treatise of Literature', based on a bibliography or catalogue of books usually in the imperial library collections) of the dynastic history *Sung-shih* 202.9b–11a, *Shih-ch'ao.* Cf. Chin Yü-fu (1944), 313–14. The heading *Shih-p'ing* was adopted by Chao Kung-wu in his *Chün-chai tu-shu-chih* (compiler's preface dated 1151), 2B.147–51, followed by Ma Tuan-lin in *Wen-hsien t'ung-k'ao* 200.1671–7. Cf. Yao Ming-ta (1957), 96–7, table. Written comment on history culminated in Wang Fu-chih's (1619–92) *Tu T'ung-chien lun* and *Sung lun*; it declined under the Ch'ing dynasty, owing probably to the political implication of such comments and particularly Wang's racist feeling toward the Manchu rule; cf. Gray, in Beasley and Pulleyblank (1961), 189–97; see also criticism of the genre by the Ch'ing scholars in the *Ssu-k'u ch'üan-shu tsung-mu t'i-yao* 88.1; Liang Ch'i-ch'ao (1966), 35.
60 *Hsiao-ching chu-shu* 8.2a.
61 Cf. *ibid.* 5.1–4.
62 Cf. Chi-yun Chen, *T'oung-pao* 54 (1968), 83–6. Emperor Kao-tsu after receiving homage from his father offered the honorary title ' Supreme August Sovereign' (*T'ai-shan-huang*) to the latter, thus confoming to the traditional precept; *Shih-chi* 8.69; Watson (1961), I, 108–9.
63 Cf. Wright (1959), 7–20.
64 Cf. Watson (1961), I, 184–7, for the incident.
65 *Han-shu* 24A.10–15, tr. by Swann (1950), 158–70.
66 Cf. Legge (1960), I, 263–4; Fung Yu-lan, I (1952), 59–63, 113, 302–11, 323–5.
67 Cf. Hihara (1959), 10–12.
68 See Chapter 2, pages 11–12.
69 See Chapter 3, page 63.
70 Bodde, in Wright (1953), 46–51.
71 For a concise discussion of feudalism and bureaucracy in China, see Bodde, in Coulborn (1956), 49–92. See also notes 12–14 of Chapter 1.
72 See Chapter 3, pages 44–7, 57–8.
73 See Chapter 4, pages 69, 81–3.

74 See notes 12–13 of Chapter 1.

75 See notes 8, 9, 27, and 29 in Chapter 2.

76 Cf. Chapter 3, pages 46–7.

77 Cf. L. S. Yang, in Sun (1956), 125–33; on Hsün Yüeh as spokesman of the new élite, see Chapter 1; cf. Yoshinami (1956), 71–8, 81–2.

78 For a general description of Emperor Wu's reign, see Watson (1958), 30–5; Dubs, II (1944), 7–13. For the emperor's measure against the local magnates, see note 8 in Chapter 2.

79 Yoshinami (1956), 68–86; Hihara (1959), 9–20; Busch (1945), 85–90.

80 Cf. Fung Yu-lan, II (1953), 7–58; Eberhard, in Fairbank (1957), 33–70.

81 For Wang Ch'ung's thesis, see note 39 in Chapter 2.

82 I.e. the most intelligent who need no effort to fulfil themselves; the middle ones who need to make an effort to fulfil themselves; and the least intelligent, who cannot fulfil themselves in spite of efforts. This classification had been made by Confucius: Legge (1960), I, 191 and 318.

83 See the example given in pages 98, 100 and 109.

84 See Chapter 2, pages 14–16.

85 *HC* 25.1–4a, which was an excerpt of *Han-shu* 30 and 88.

86 This referred to the tradition or Way established by the Sage-rulers, Yao, Shun, Yü, T'ang, Wen, Wu, and the Duke of Chou, before Confucius' time.

87 This referred to Confucius as transmitter of the sacred tradition or Way.

88 See Chapter 1; also Chapter 7.

89 Chi Lu (Tzu-lu), one of Confucius' disciples; for the quotation, see Legge (1960), I, 246.

90 Chi Tzu-ch'eng, another disciple of Confucius, *ibid.* 254.

91 *Ibid.* 193.

92 For a detailed study of Han canonical exegesis and the controversies involved, see Tjan Tjoe Som (1949), 82–165.

93 See note 92; also Chapter 2, pages 15–17.

94 Biographies in *HHS* 36 (*lieh-chuan* 26), 5–6 and 12–16 respectively.

95 Biography in *HHS* 60A (*lieh-chuan* 50A), 1–14.

96 Cf. Chi-yun Chen, *T'oung-pao* 54 (1968), 73–115. See also Chapter 2, pages 28–9.

97 See note 96.

98 Cf. the biographies of the leaders of these groups, tr. by Watson (1961), I, Parts 1 and 2.

99 *HC* 2.11b–12. For the counsels for and against re-feudalization, see Watson (1961), I, 140–3.

100 See Chapter 1; also Chapter 3, pages 57–8.

101 Hsün Yüeh as court apologist, see pages 76–8, 84–93.

102 The time limit at the end of the *Han-chi* was left open. Its entries end with the death of Wang Mang in A.D. 23; its allusion to the restoration would lead on to Later Han rule.

103 This became the stereotyped stylistic convention in later historians, see Bielenstein (1954), 44–81; Gardner (1961), 81–5.

104 For the traditional Chinese historian's concern for meticulous factual accounts, see *ibid.* also Gardner (1961), 18–68. Cf. the classic example cited in Legge (1960), V, 514–15.

105 *HHS* 62 (*lieh-chuan* 52), 10b.

106 Legge (1960), V, Prolegomena, 22–53; Gardner (1961), 10–17; Beasley and Pulleyblank (1961), 24–30; also Pulleyblank, in Dawson (1964), 144–7.

107 Liang Ch'i-ch'ao (1966), *pu-pien*, 233–4; cf. Pulleyblank, in Beasley and Pulleyblank (1961), 150–1.

108 *HC hsü* 1b–2a.

109 *HC hsü* 2b. There is some question about the length of the work; see following discussion.

110 *HC hsü* 1b; *HHS* 62 (*lieh-chuan* 52), 10b.

111 *HHS* 9.7a, Cf. Chapter 3, page 44.

112 *HHS* 79A (*lieh-chuan* 69A), 3a.

113 Chang Fan's *Han-chi*, cited in *SKC* 10.18b; *Shih-t'ung t'ung-shih* 2.14; *T'ang-shu* 62.16a; *Ssu k'u ch'üan-shu tsung-mu t'i-yao* 47.6–8a; Liang Chi'-ch'ao (1966), 29–30.

114 *Shih-t'ung t'ung-shih* 2.14.

115 A complete English translation of the Basic Annals of the *Han-shu* is available, Dubs, I (1938), II (1944) and III (1955).

116 Cf. Dubs, I (1938), 27–150; II (1944), 27–120 and 199–265.

117 See note 116.

118 For the proverb of 'chasing the deer on horseback', see Chapter 3, pages 50–2. The same proverb may be recalled in the very first discourse made by Hsün Yüeh in the *Han-chi* (*Lun* 1 discussed on pages 100–1), in which Hsün Yüeh vigorously repudiates historical analogue by parallel. The warning seems to be that while Kao-tsu had founded the Han dynasty on horseback, Ts'ao Ts'ao might not succeed in doing the same because of the difference in *hsing*, *shih* and *ch'ing*. Ts'ao Ts'ao's son, however, succeeded in founding a new dynasty, though a short-lived one.

119 Cf. Dubs, I (1938), 167–87; II (1944), 143–75, 277–338, 356–418, respectively.

120 See Chapter 3, page 53.

121 Dubs, II (1944), 285–98.

122 *Ibid.* 299–301.

123 See above, pages 93–4; also the discussion below.

124 Beside the *Han-shu*, Hsün Shuang's *Han-yü* was a major work consulted by Hsün Yüeh; see the discussion below in pages 124–6.

125 For the theory of Cosmology and the Five Elements, see Chapter 2, pages 16, 31–2, Chapter 5, pages 106–7, and the authorities cited in notes therein.

126 Because of the peculiar nature of Chinese writing, most historical writings in traditional times were works of compilation based, almost word-for-word, on earlier documents or other writings. A clear example is those parts of the *Han-shu* covering the Han rule up to the reign of Emperor Wu which were reproduced, almost word-for-word, from corresponding sections in the *Shih-chi*. Cf. Dubs, I (1938), 1, 167, 214–15, 291–2; see also Bielenstein's comment on the *HHS* (1954), 44 and *passim*.

127 *Han-shu* 27A.2; cf. above, note 125.

128 The important events during the reigns of these rulers are mostly chronicled in Dubs' translation of the Basic Annals of the *Han-shu*, I (1938), II (1944), III (1955). The *Han-chi* section which covers the corresponding reign of these rulers has been tabluated above, page 114.

129 On the Chien-an situation, see pages 44–7. On the reminiscent notion of imperial unity, see pages 49–50, 52–8; for Hsün Yüeh's idea of imperial unity and local autonomy, see above, pages 99–103.

130 For an account of this in the corresponding *Han-shu*, see Dubs, I (1938), 37–41, also Watson (1961), I, 81–3. The *Han-chi* account was given in the following short statement: 'In the ninth month [of 209 B.C.], the people of P'ei killed their magistrate; Kao-tsu became the Lord of P'ei; Hsiao Ho, his Lieutenant Chancellor; Ts'ao Ts'an and Chou Po, his Attendant Guards; Hsia-hou Ying and Fan K'uai, members of his Suite . . . [Here follows the biographical data of these men as rendered in the text.] By that time, Kao-tsu, in Wai-huang [a district in southern part of the modern Honan province], had an army of several hundred men. Hsiao Ho and others wanted to respond to Ch'en Sheng [leader of the first anti-Ch'in uprising]; they therefore invited the Lord of P'ei and set him up [to be their leader], and recruited their followers at P'ei, gathering a force of three thousand men' (1.4a). This

finishes the account of Kao-tsu's rising, which led to the founding of the Han dynasty.

131 Biographies in *Shih-chi* 53, 54, 57, 95.1–13, 95.19–24; tr. by Watson (1961), I, 125–33, 421–6, 255–6 (résumé only), and 427–40.

132 *HC* 1.4a.

133 *HC* 1.6b–7a. From *Han-shu* 40.1–3; cf. *Shih-chi* 55.1–7, tr. by Watson (1961), I, 134–6.

134 *HC* 1.11a. From *Han-shu* 43.1–2; cf. *Shih-chi* 97.2–5, tr. by Watson (1961), I, 269–71.

135 *HC* 26.5b–6a; the will is now merged with Hsün Yüeh's *Lun* 32 which preceded it.

136 Yang's will was more pertinent to Emperor Wu's reign than to Ch'eng's.

137 For Hsün Yüeh's criticism of the Liu rulers, see pages 70–3 and 95–100.

138 See note 137.

139 For Shuang's *Han-yü*, see pages 28–9; for Shuang's influence on Hsün Yüeh, see pages 66–8, 76.

140 *Han-shu* 4.19b *pu-chu*.

141 *Ibid.*

142 *Ibid.*

143 See the comments in *Ssu-k'u ch'üan-shu tsung-mu t'i-yao* 47.6–8a, and the authorities cited therein. Cf. Beasley and Pulleyblank (1961), 34, 39, 43.

Notes to chapter 6

1 *HHS* 62 (*lieh-chuan* 52), 8b and 11a.

2 On the various editions of these two works, their textual problems, and the possible inclusion of some of Hsün Yüeh's other independent *lun* discourses in the present *Han-chi*, see Chi-yun Chen, *Monumenta Serica* 27 (1968), 208–32.

3 *HHC* 29.352–4. After recording Yüeh's submission of the *Shen-chien* to the throne, the *HHC* produced several lengthy excerpts from the *Shen-chien*, and concluded the entry with a biographical résumé of Hsün Yüeh including a reference to his compilation of the *Han-chi*. This entry in the *HHC* was closely copied by the author of the *HHS* to form the 'Biography of Hsün Yüeh'. As a result, the 'Biography' first mentioned Yüeh's writing of the *Shen-chien* and then recounted his compilation of the *Han-chi*, thus giving the erroneous impression to the casual reader that Yüeh had written the *Shen-chien* before his compilation of the *Han-chi*.

4 See Chapter 3, pages 62–5.

5 See Chapter 3, pages 62–5; also Chapter 7, page 163.

6 For instance, *SC* 1.10b–12a; 2.5b–6a, 14b; 3.1a, 3a, 3b–4a, 7a–b; 4.8b–9a.

7 *Shuo-wen chieh-tzu ku-lin* 3671 and 6260.

8 *Ibid.* 3671.

9 See Legge (1960), I, 160; III, 700 (under *chien*), 726 (*chien*); IV, 744 (under *chien*); 775 (*chien*); V, 135/137, 422/424, 697/700, 714/718, 761/763.

10 *Shuo-wen chieh-tzu ku-lin* 3671.

11 Legge (1960), V, 761/763. Many bronze mirrors with sacred diagrams or words of blessing on them have been preserved: L. S. Yang (1969), 138–42 and plate, and the authorities cited therein. More lengthy inscriptions bearing a motto on state affairs were probably made on the *p'an-chien* plates rather than on the mirrors.

12 See the expressions in *Chen-kuan cheng-yao* 4.16b, 17a; also in Emperor T'ai-tsung's Preface to *Ti-fan* (the Imperial Model) 1b–2a.

13 Legge (1960), V, 135/137; also *HHS* 49 (*lieh-chuan* 39), 3a.

14 This might also refer to *Han-chi*; see discussion below.

15 *SC* 1.1a.
16 See Ssu-ma Ch'ien's 'autobiography' in *Shih-chi* 130.18–27, tr. by Watson (1958), 49–54; also Pan Ku's in *Han-shu* 100B.1. Historical writings were in fact listed as an extension section of the *Ch'un-ch'iu* canonical writ and did not form a separate division in the Han catalogue of books; *Han-shu* 30.15–18.
17 See Legge (1960), III, 15–27.
18 *Wen-hsüan* 48.1066.
19 Ssu-ma Ch'ien in his *Shih-chi* made no mention of the ancestral origin of the imperial family of Liu. The glorification of the family by ascribing to it as ancestor the legendary Sage-ruler Yao was begun by Liu Hsiang (77–6 B.C.), who based his theory on a dubious statement in the *Tso-chuan*. Liu Hsiang's ascription was incorporated by Pan Ku in his Epilogue to the Basic Annal of Emperor Kao-tsu, *Han-shu* 1B.25–6a, tr. by Dubs, I (1938), 146–50. Cf. *Shih-chi* 8.2–3 and annotations; *HHS* 36 (*lieh-chuan* 26), 14b–15a and *chi-chieh*.
20 The English rendering of the two prefatory passages of the *Shen-chien* in the present section gives a paraphrase rather than a translation of the original. See following discussion.
21 In addition to the prefatory passages, other *Shen-chien* passages which resemble the *lun* discourses in the *Han-chi* include *SC* 2.5b8–8b4 (*HC Lun* 5), 2.8a4–8b4 (*HC Lun* 5), 3.1–7 and 5.1–8 (*HC Lun* 6), 2.8b5–9a6 (*HC Lun* 8), 2.2b5–3a5 (*HC Lun* 22), 2.14b6–15a1 (*HC Lun* 22). Besides, there are five *Shen-chien* passages which repeat the *Han-chi lun* almost verbatim: *SC* 1.4a6–8 and a passage not in the present *SC* text but preserved in a quotation in the *Ch'ün-shu chih-yao* 46.612 (*HC Lun* 16), *SC* 2.2a7–2b4 (*HC Lun* 16), 2.15a7–15b1 (*HC Lun* 21), 2.6a8–7a3 (*HC Lun* 28), 2.5a8–5b5 (*HC Lun* 36). For detailed discussion of the textual problems involved, see Chi-yun Chen, *Monumenta Serica* 27 (1968), 218–22.
22 The sentence '*sheng Han t'ung-t'ien*' literally means 'the sacred Han unified or commanded Heaven'; *t'ung-t'ien*, however, probably means *t'ien-t'ung* (heavenly lineage, or mandate), as in a comparable passage in *Shih-chi* 8.88, '*Han-hsing . . . te t'ien-t'ung*' ('The Han rises . . . acquires her lineage or mandate from Heaven'); cf. Watson's translation in (1961), I, 118–19.
23 The sentence '*wei* (to think, to think only, only) *tsung* (to honour, to worship one's ancestor, ancestral line) *shih* (time, this time, this) *liang* (to aid, brilliant, to illuminate)' consists of four archaic characters frequently used in the *Shu-ching* canons, cf. Legge, tr. (1960), III, 649, 667–8, 677, 684. The whole sentence appears to be a compressed quotation from the 'Canon of Yao' (*Yao-tien*), tr. by Legge (1960), III, 50 and *passim*.
24 The archaic character *ke* (to reach, to correct, most excellent) came from *Shu-ching*, cf. Legge (1960), III, 687. The whole sentence appears to be a compressed quotation from the 'Canon of Yao', tr. by Legge (1960), III, 15–17.
25 *Hu-ch'en* (valiant ministers) literally means 'tiger ministers'; *luan-cheng* (orderly administration) literally means 'disorderly administration'; for interpretation of these ambivalent terms, see following discussion.
26 *Huang* (waste, vast), *pi* (ruins), and *yin* (obstruction, destruction) allude to the great flood at the time of the legendary Sage-ruler Yao, cf. Legge (1960), III, 25, 323; for interpretation of these terms, see following discussion.
27 *Chien*, reflecting upon or learning from the past. Three Dynasties: Hsia, Shang, and Chou in the 'Golden Antiquity'. *Tien* (precedent, classic, canon) refers both to the model institutions of the past and to the canonical classics which were assumed to be ordinances or 'records' of these institutions.
28 Quoted from the 'Counsels of Kao-yao'; cf. Legge (1960), III, 68.

29 *Yu-shang*, an ambivalent expression, connotes something which is at its best but may still be improved or superseded.

30 A compressed quotation from the 'Counsels of the Great Yü'; cf. Legge (1960), III, 61, which reads: 'The determinate appointment of Heaven rests on your person.'

31 Alluding to the 'Counsels of the Great Yü' and the 'Counsels of Kao-yao'; cf. Legge (1960), III, 59 and 74.

32 The term *chih* (to ascend) *chiang* (to descend) is generally used in sacrificial hymns to praise the action of one's ancestors; cf. Legge (1960) II, 428–85 *passim*.

33 *SC* 1.1a7–1b3. The paragraph consists of many compressed quotations, allusions, and archaic expressions from the *Shu-ching* canons. Most of them are eulogies of the legendary sage-rulers of remote antiquity. The obscure meaning of these expressions and the ambivalence of their connotation in the *Shen-chien* make a direct translation of the passage almost impossible; for details, see following discussions.

34 Huang Hsing-tseng's annotation in *SC* 1.1a,b is particularly useful in identifying the ambivalent meaning of the terms *hu-ch'en*, *luan-cheng*, and *huang*; see above, notes 25–6.

35 *HC hsü* 1b, 30.27a; see Chapter 5, pages 84–8 and 90.

36 See above, notes 22–32.

37 See above, notes 25–6, and following discussion.

38 For the rise of the Former Han, see Dubs, I (1938), 2–150. For the rise of the Later Han, see Bielenstein, 3 vols. (1954), (1959), and (1967).

39 For the restoration of Han at Hsü and the pro-Han sentiment of the Chien-an régime, see Chapter 3, pages 44–6, 50–60; also Chapter 4, pages 79–81 and Chapter 5, pages 85–93.

40 *Ts'u-ch'i Huang-shih jih-ch'ao fen-lei* 57.6b–7a.

41 Chi-yun Chen, *Monumenta Serica* 27 (1968), 219–22.

42 *Po-tzu pien-cheng* 1.23.

43 *HHC* 29.354.

44 *HHS* 62 (*lieh-chuan* 52), 8b.

45 *HC* 25.6b–7, *lun* 31, tr. in Chapter 4, page 72.

46 See pages 136–61.

47 *SC* 5.3b–4a.

48 See note 39. The importance of the Han imperial legacy as a well-remembered reality in the post-Han period has been pointed out by Rogers, in *Chronicle* (1968), 1.

49 See Chapter 5.

50 *SC* 3.7.

51 See Chapter 5, pages 84–92.

52 See Yüeh's discussion on the 'rule of propriety' wielded by the imperial sovereign as the arbiter of 'right and wrong', in Chapter 5, pages 107–10.

53 *SC* 1.1b–2a.

54 Cf. Chapter 5 pages 98–9.

55 See pages 105–11, 140–4.

56 *Sui-shu* 34, '*Ching-chi chih*', 1b. *Wen-hsien t'ung-k'ao* 209, '*Ching-chi k'ao*', 1720. *Ssu-k'u ch'üan-shu tsung-mu t'i-yao* 91.20–1a.

57 See Chapter 2, pages 15–18, 28–9, 31–5.

58 Cf. Fung Yu-lan (1953), II, 1–87; (1960), 178–207; see especially the sections on Tung Chung-shu.

59 Cf. Wright (1959), 8–31.

60 Cf. Fung Yu-lan (1952), I, 172–5, 177–83, 223–5; (1960), 94–8. Waley (1949), 50–9. Welch (1965), 50–82. Creel (1956), 140–1.

61 Creel (1953), 34–7. See *tao* as referred to by Confucius and Mencius, in Fung Yu-lan (1952) I, 56, 59, 73, and 131.
62 Tung Chung-shu's reference to *tao,* Fung Yu-lan (1953), II, 44. *Tao* as expounded in the apocryphal books (*wei*) attached to the Confucian *Classic of Changes* (*I-ching*), ibid. 98–100. See also Fung Yu-lan (1960), 166–77, 191–203; Tjan Tjoe Som (1949), 71–82, 106–20.
63 See notes 60 and 62.
64 *SC* 1.1a4.
65 *SC* 1.6b2.
66 *SC* 1.10a6.
67 *SC* 1.6b5.
68 *SC* 1.1b.
69 Cf. note 62.
70 For a comprehensive discussion of the *I-ching*, see Wilhelm (1960). For brief discussions of *I-ching* symbolism and numerology, see Fung Yu-lan (1952), I, 379–99; also (1960), 138–42; Needham (1959) II, 304–45.
71 The complete system of the symbolic (*hsiang*) and numerological postulates of the *I-ching* masters of Han times had since been rejected and forgotten by scholars in post-Han times. Some fragmentary writings of these Han masters have been preserved and compiled in the works of several scholars of the Ch'ing dynasty; cf. the authorities cited in Chi-yun Chen, *T'oung-pao* 54 (1968), 73–5, notes. The numerological systems expounded by these Han masters have been reconstructed by Chang Hui-yen, and more importantly by Chiao Hsün, *ibid.* 103 and notes. Cf. also note 70 above. For post-Han interpretation of the *I-ching*, particularly rejection of the *hsiang-shu*, see Wright (1947), 75–88, and Liebenthal (1947), 124–61.
72 For instance, see Wang Ch'ung's reference to *shu* in determining the lot (fate) of individuals and states, *Lun-heng* 1.15b–16, 17.16b–18a, and *passim*.
73 See notes 70–1.
74 *SC* 1.6b5, 11a3; 3.1a7, 2b3, 3b4, 3b8, 4b4, 4b8; 4.4b6; 5.2b5; 7a1. Huang Hsing-tseng in his annotations pointed out many additional allusions to the *I-ching* from the *Shen-chien* text.
75 *Ts'u-ch'i Huang-shih jih-ch'ao fen-lei* 57.6b–7a. For Yang Hsiung's works, cf. Fung Yu-lan (1953), II, 136–50.
76 *SC* 1.2a3.
77 *SC* 1.2a3.
78 *SC* 1.2a4.
79 *SC* 1.2a5.
80 *SC* 1.2a5.
81 *SC* 1.2a7.
82 *SC* 1.2b.
83 *SC* 1.2b5.
84 *SC* 1.2b5.
85 *SC* 1.14a; also 4.11b and 5.4a.
86 *SC* 1.15a.
87 *SC* 4.4b–5a.
88 *SC* 4.6b–8a.
89 *SC* 4.11b–12a.
90 *SC* 4.9b10a.
91 *SC* 4.5b.
92 *SC* 4.5b.
93 See Chapter 4, pages 70–4; Chapter 5, pages 93–119.
94 *SC* 4.4b–5a.
95 *Chou-i chu-shu* 9.11b, 13b; tr. by Legge (1899), 434–7. Cf. Fung Yu-lan (1952), I, 388–90; also (1960), 19–20.

96 For the implication of relativism for the Confucian moral dogmas, see Fung
    Yu-lan (1953), ii, 228 and *passim*; also (1960), 223–40.
97 For pre-Han Taoist precepts, see Fung Yu-lan (1952), i, 177–91, 223–45; for
    post-Han Taoist trends, see Fung Yu-lan (1953), ii, 190–204; also (1960), 227–
    39. Most of the Taoist arguments were made by contrasting ephemeral human
    existence with the ever-changing but ever-lasting state of the inanimate. Cf.
    also Wing-tsit Chan (1963), 177–210; Waley (1939), 30–58.
98 For the Confucian concept of ' multiple ' *tao*, see Fung Yu-lan (1960), 166–7;
    for the Confucian idea of human nature, see Fung Yu-lan (1952), i, 66–75,
    119–27, 129–31, 284–8, 362–77. Cf. also Y. P. Mei (1955), 151–60.
99 *SC* 1.1b–2.
100 *SC* 3.1–2, 3b–4a; 4.4b–5a.
101 *SC* 1.11a, 14b–15a; 2.1b–2a, 5b, 6a, 8a–b.
102 *SC* 3.3b–4a, 4b; 4.4b–5a, 12b–13a.
103 *SC* 1.1a, 1b–2a, 6b, 10a, 14b; 3.1a; 5.4–6a.
104 *SC* 5.4, 5–6a, 7–8; also 1.4b–5a.
105 *SC* 1.2b–3a, 5a, 7b, 12a, 14b–15a; 5.2b–3a, 4b.
106 *SC* 3.3b, 6b–7a; 5.4.
107 *SC* 3.4–7a.
108 *SC* 3.1a, 2b, 3a, 3b; 4.8b–9; 5.4.
109 Cf. Hsün Yüeh's idea of *ch'üan* (expediency) and *shih* (timeliness) in Chapter
    5, pages 100–5; also discussions in the present section. For the trend of moral
    relativism in the Age of Disunity, see note 96 above; see also Chapter 1.
110 For the respective theories espoused by these Confucianists, see Fung Yu-lan
    (1952), i, 119–27, 286–7; (1953), ii, 150. The identity of the Kung-sun men-
    tioned in the text is not clear; according to the ' Hsiao Hsün-tzu ' (another
    title of the *Shen-chien*, for details, see Chi-yun Chen, *Monumenta Serica* 29
    (1968), 214, 217–18) in the *Tzu-hui* edition (Han-fen lou reprint of a Ming
    edition), Kung-sun reads Kung Tu (a disciple of Mencius); Kung Tu had
    participated in Mencius' discussion of human nature but did not state that
    human nature was neither good nor bad, which was the theory expounded by
    Kao-tzu, a contemporary of Mencius; cf. Fung Yu-lan (1952), i, 145–6.
111 *SC* 5.5.
112 *Cf.* Fung Yu-lan (1953), ii, 32–4.
113 *SC* 5.5b.
114 *SC* 5.5b–6a.
115 *SC* 5.6.
116 The neo-Confucians generally separated *ch'ing* from *hsing* (human nature in
    a narrow sense, morally conditioned), identifying *ch'ing* with *yin*, the potenti-
    ally evil, and *hsing* with the *yang*, the potentially or definitely good; cf. Fung
    Yu-lan (1953), ii, 516–20, 525–6, 556–8, 560–1, 614–16, and *passim*.
117 *SC* 2.2a.
118 *SC* 1.2a.
119 *SC* 1.10b.
120 *SC* 1.10b–11a. Also 1.14a.
121 *SC* 1.2b, 4a; 2.2b.
122 *SC* 1.3a, 4a.
123 *SC* 1.4b–5a, 12a–13.
124 *SC* 1.8–9a. The character *ch'ing*, as used in judicial terms, has a more com-
    plex meaning. It refers to the whole ' truth ' or reality involved in the case,
    including the ' various motives ' of the criminal in committing the offence.
    Considering and manifesting *ch'ing* in this sense means that the magistrate
    should have a sympathetic attitude toward the case and make an intelligent
    effort to seek the ' whole truth '.
125 *SC* 1.3b.

126 This theme was later best summarized by Chung Hui (225–64) in his *Ssu-pen lun* (Treatise on the Four Essentials) which commented on the four theories that *ts'ai* and *hsing* are (1) identical; (2) different; (3) combined; (4) separate. *SKC* 28.60a and *chi-chieh*. Cf. Mather (1964), 350, 353–4 and notes.

127 *SC* 5.1b–2a.

128 *SC* 5.2a.

129 The differences between Lao-tzu and Chuang-tzu are briefly discussed by Fung Yu-lan (1952), I, 172–4, and by Creel (1956), 140–2. Cf. also Waley's discussion of Lao-tzu's Taoism and its relation with political despotism in (1949), 50–9, 68–93, and of Chuang-tzu's Taoism in (1939), 3–79.

130 Cf. Fung Yu-lan (1953), II, 190–236; (1960), 231–40.

131 Creel (1956), 142–52.

132 *SC* 3.3b–4a, 4b.

133 *SC* 3.4a, 7.

134 *SC* 3.5–6.

135 *SC* 3.4, 6b–7a.

136 *SC* 3.3a. Hsün Yüeh's criticism of the vulgar Taoist practices resembled that which was contained in the ' Hsiang-erh Commentary on *Lao-tzu* ', a fragmentary manuscript which was discovered by Stein at the Tun-huang site (*MS* No. 6825), reprinted with annotations by Jao Tsung-i (1956). The ' Hsiang-erh Commentary ' was inconsistent in its criticism of vulgar Taoism. On the one hand, it subscribed to the Confucian moral precept by saying that the cultivation of moral virtue was the best way to achieve harmony of the body and the mind which in turn ensured longevity (6–8, 19, 23–5, 36–7, 47); it condemned the ' false Taoist teaching ' of ' sex formulae ' (12), ' magic talisman ' (12, 18, 21, 45), ' meditation ' (13), ' breath-control ' (33), or ' nourishing the physical inner self ' (15), and seemed to assert that ' immortality ' was ' pre-ordained ' and could not be achieved by ' artificial exertion ' (15, 21, 25). On the other hand, it criticized those who repudiated the ' immortality formula ' and those who asserted that ' immortality was pre-ordained and could not be achieved by exertion ' (25), and affirmed that ' longevity or immortality could be achieved by preserving *ching-shen* [vital energy] through certain sex formulae ' (9–10, 12–13, 21, 29–30, 38). Cf. also Ōbuchi (1966), 40–68; (1967), 97–129.

137 *SC* 2.10b–11; 3.2b–3a.

138 *SC* 3.1–2.

139 *SC* 3.3b. For the vogue of physiognomy in Later Han times, see Chapter 2, pages 17–18.

140 For Confucius' comment on sacrifice and prayer, see Legge (1960), I, 154, 158–9, 206. For Mencius on physiognomy, see Legge (1960), II, 306, 406.

141 *SKC* 10.18a *chi-chieh*; 10.23b–24 *chi-chieh*; 28.60–2 and *chi-chieh*. Cf. Fung Yu-lan (1960), 217, 238–9; Mather (1964), 348–91.

142 *SKC* 13.8b *chi-chieh*. The meaning of the last sentence in the passage is extremely fluid. For Hsü Shao's ' Monthly Comments on Personality ', see L. S. Yang in Etu Zen Sun (1956), 126; Balazs (1967), 229–30.

143 The vogue may be epitomized by Juan Chan's (died *c*. 312) elliptic and ambivalent reply to a cryptic question posed by Wang Jung (234–305). When asked whether Confucius' emphasis on morals and institutions (*ming-chiao*) would be the same as Lao-tzu's and Chuang-tzu's emphasis on the natural, Juan Chan simply answered: ' Are they not the same? ' For this equally cryptic reply, which in fact was not an answer at all but merely threw the question back to its originator, Juan Chan became very famous in *ch'ing-t'an* circles. *Chin-shu* 49.9, tr. by Fung Yu-lan (1953), II, 170. My rendering is slightly different from Fung's.

144 Shiba (1955), 227–40, interpreted Hsün Yüeh's lectures to Emperor Hsien solely in terms of *ch'ing-t'an* and produced the quoted dialogue as evidence. The source was mentioned as from both the *Fu-tzu* and the *Chin-lou tzu*. I have traced the source in *Fu-tzu* (Wu-ying-tien chü-chen pan edition) 3.12, which refers its origin to the *I-lin*. In *I-lin* 5.3b, the quoted piece is mentioned as from Yang Ch'üan's *Wu-li lun*.

145 See the discussion in pages 140–1.

146 *SC* 5.8b–9a.

147 *SC* 5.9a.

148 *Ibid.*

149 *SC* 5.9.

150 *SC* 5.9b–10a.

151 *SC* 5.10.

152 For the Confucian attitude toward 'nature' and 'civilization', see Confucius' remarks on 'the primeval and the cultivated' attributes of men, Legge (1960), I, 157; on 'quality and accomplishment', *ibid.* 190, 254–5; on 'man and the Way', *ibid.* 302; and on 'nature and learning', *ibid.* 318. For the Confucian-Legalists in Hsün Yüeh's time, see Chapter 1.

153 Waley (1949), 83–7; Fung Yu-lan (1952), I, 334–5.

154 Fung Yu-lan (1952), I, 312–30. Cf. Waley (1939), 151–96; Creel (1959), 199–211.

155 Creel called the teaching of Hsün-tzu, the moulder of Confucianism, 'authoritarian', (1953), 98–113, and the teaching of the Legalists, 'totalitarian', 113–32. Two of the famous Legalists, Han Fei and Li Ssu, happened to be Hsün-tzu's disciples, *ibid.* 116, 118, 121.

156 Dubs, II (1944), 299–301.

157 Kung-chuan Hsiao (1964), 108–21.

158 Dubs, II (1944), 285–6, 287–9, 292–4. See Hsün Yüeh's comment on Confucianism and the Han decline in Chapter 5, pages 118–19.

159 Balazs (1967), 196–225.

160 See Chapter 3, pages 45–6, 58–63.

161 *Lun* 27–8, also 19 and 25, discussed in Chapter 5, pages 100, 104–5.

162 *SC* 1.3.

163 *SC* 1.4b–5a.

164 See note 153.

165 Waley (1949), 145.

166 *Ibid.* 147.

167 *SC* 1.13a.

168 *SC* 1.13a.

169 *SC* 1.13.

170 *SC* 1.11b–12.

171 *Shih-chi* 124, tr. by Watson (1961), II, 452–61; cf. Ping-ti Ho (1963), 171–82. *Han-shu* 92.

172 See Chapter 2; cf. L. S. Yang, in Etu Zen Sun (1956), 103–33. For Hsün Yüeh's earlier comments on this, see Chapter 4, pages 69, 81–2; also Chapter 5, pages 101–4. The problem became more acute during early Wei rule, as indicated in the decree of A.D. 223, *SKC* 2.56b–57a.

173 *SC* 2.7a.

174 Cf. the canonical writ in *Chou-li chu-shu* 14.11–13a; 35.23b.

175 *SC* 2.7b–8a.

176 *Han-shu* 1B.22a *pu-chu*.

177 Mou Jun-sun (1952), 1–20; (1955) 381–421.

178 For examples, see *Han-shu* 52.4b; 68.2b–4; 97A.17b–18.

179 *Yü-hai* (1687–8 edition) 72.21b–22; *I-wei ch'ien-tso-tu* 1.21; 2.25; *Han-shu* 72.7a; *HHS* 62 (*lieh-chuan* 52), 4b–5a.

180 *HC* 17.10a, *Lun* 21.

181 *SC* 2.15. For the fate of the cognate relatives of Emperor Hsien, see page 63.

182 *Chin-shu* 49.3a.

183 *Chin-shu* 49.17a, 22–4.

184 Yüeh's nephew, Hsün Yün, married the Princess of An-yang (the daughter of Ts'ao Ts'ao); another nephew, Hsün Ts'an, married the daughter of Ts'ao Hung, Ts'ao Ts'ao's cousin; Hsün Yün's son, Hsün I, married the daughter of Ssu-ma I (posthumously honoured as Emperor Hsüan of the Chin dynasty); *SKC* 10.25b *chi-chieh*. Cf. Yano (1960), 14–18.

185 *Chin-shu* 75.27b–28a.

186 See pages 59–61, 79.

187 Appended to this terse counsel in the *Shen-chien* was a lengthy remark on Confucian classical scholarship in Han times, which appears to be a restatement of *Lun* 30 in the *Han-chi*, discussed in Chapter 5, pages 108–10.

188 This has been pointed out in three 'Prefaces' to the *Shen-chien* in Huang Hsing-tseng's annotated edition, Wang's *hsü* 1a; Ho's *hsü* 1b; and Huang's *hsü* 1b.

189 Cf. Dubs, I (1938), 255 and note 2.

190 *SC* 2.5b–6a. For other contemporary arguments concerning this issue, see notes 120–1 in Chapter 3. The decline in population during this period has been noted by L. S. Yang (1963), 125–6; cf. Bielenstein (1947), 125–63.

191 *SC* 2.14b–15a. For other contemporary opinions on this issue, see *HHS* 49 (*lieh-chuan* 39), 9b–10. General amnesties had been declared in A.D. 190, 191, 192 (three declarations in one year), 193, 194, 195, and 196 (twice in a year); *HHS* 9.2a, 2b, 3a, 3b, 4a, 5a, 6a, 7a.

192 *SC* 1.8–9a. Cf. the canonical writ in *Chou-li chu-shu* 35.2–36.3 and *chu-shu*.

193 *SC* 1.15a; also 2.8. The increase of official emoluments had been favoured by Hsün Yüeh in *HC* 5.14, *Lun* 6.

194 *SC* 2.10b–11. For the background of this counsel, see Chapter 3, pages 46–7.

195 *SC* 1.12; also 1.9.

196 *SC* 2.3. For the creation of many sinecures in the composite Han-Ts'ao régime, see Chapter 3, pages 45–6, 57–8, 62–5.

197 *SC* 2.3b–4. What Hsün Yüeh had in mind was the re-establishment of the imperial garrison forces in the provinces consisting mainly of conscript soldiers. The system had fallen into disuse in Later Han time; its replacement by professional soldiers was a major factor in the Later Han decline; see Chapter 2, note 11.

198 It was recorded that once Ts'ao Ts'ao had an audience with Emperor Hsien, and he found the circumstances threatening to his personal safety, since he was surrounded by the emperor's guards; thence-forth, Ts'ao never sought an audience with the emperor again; *HHS* 10B.12; *SKC* 1.38b *chi-chieh*.

199 Cf. Chapter 3, pages 45–6, 57–8, 62–5.

200 Cf. Yü-ch'üan Wang (1949), 155–6; L. S. Yang (1963), 88–9.

201 Ying-shih Yü (1967), 172–5, 217–19.

202 Balazs (1967), 189–92. Also L. S. Yang (1963), 86–9.

203 The meaning of *k'ung-shih* is not clear. Literally it means 'vain trade' or 'exhaust the market'. The word *k'ung* might be a corruption of *wang*. A passage in Mencius describes the origin of commercial tax in the following anecdote: 'Of old times, the market-dealers exchanged the articles . . . and simply had certain officers to keep order. It happened that a mean fellow made it a point . . . to catch in his net the whole gain of the market [*wang-shih-li*]. The people all thought his conduct mean, and therefore they proceeded to lay a tax upon his wares. The taxing of traders took its rise from this mean fellow.' Legge (1960), II, 227–8. Mencius had earlier spoken against taxing the traders (*ibid.* 162) and said that 'if in the market-place the official

merely levy a ground-rent on the shops but do not tax the goods or merely enforce the proper regulation without levying a ground-rent, then all the traders of the kingdom would be pleased and would store their goods in his market-place' (*ibid.* 199–200); cf. also Hightower (1952), 116. The precept seems to be in basic accord with Hsün Yüeh's attitude toward commerce and money.

204 *Lao-tzu* 17, 19, 38, 53, 57, 65, and 75, tr. by Waley (1949), 164, 166, 189, 207, 211, 223, and 235.

205 For the Han Confucian bias against money and trade, see *Han-shu* 24A.10–17a, tr. by Swann (1950), 154, 156–70. *Chin-shu* 26.15–21a, tr. by L. S. Yang (1963), 187–91. For the deterioration of the monetary system in Wei and Chin times, see L. S. Yang (1963), 129, 156–7, 191–7.

206 See Chapter 2, pages 11, 14–15.

207 Cf. L. S. Yang (1963), 129, 131–40.

208 *HC* 8.3b, *Lun* 10; cf. the discussion in Chapter 5, page 103. See note 212, below.

209 See Chung-shu Hsü, in Etu Zen Sun (1956), 3–17. Cf. Levenson, in Wright (1960), 268–87; L. S. Yang (1966), 295–300.

210 *HC* 8.3b.

211 *HC* 8.3b–4a.

212 *SKC* 1.36b–37a and *chi-chieh*; 9.5b *chi-chieh*; 15.7b; 16.1b–2 and *chi-chieh*. *Chin-shu* 46.20b. *HHS* 49 (*lieh-chuan* 39), 15b–16a. Hsün Yüeh's discourse in the *Han-chi* was the one quoted in its entirety in *T'ung-tien* 1.11–12 and in *Wen-hsien t'ung-k'ao* 1.33 where it was followed by lengthy comments by later scholars.

213 See Chapter 3, pages 46–7.

214 *SKC* 16.1b. Hsün Yüeh's discourses on land policy in the *Han-chi* and the *Shen-chien* were the most comprehensive, though not the most detailed, counsels on this issue, befitting Yüeh's role as the spokesman for the Palace Court.

215 Of those who counselled on the *t'un-t'ien* policy, Han Hao, Ssu-ma Lang, and Jen Chün all had had some experience in establishing local self-defence systems; *SKC* 9.5a *chi-chieh*, 15.6–7a, 16.1. Hsün Yü appeared to be the chief architect of the *t'un-t'ien* system; *SKC* 16.2b *chi-chieh*.

216 Cf. Chapter 3, pages 44–7.

217 *Sui-shu* 33.9–10. Cf. Beasley and Pulleyblank (1961), 4, 41, 61–2.

Notes to chapter 7

1 *HHC* 30.360. *HHS* 9.10b. *SKC* 1.81–2 and *chi-chieh*, 87 and *chi-chieh*, 89–101 and *chi-chieh*.

2 *HHC* 30.360–1. *HHS* 70 (*lieh-chuan* 60), 20b–21a. *SKC* 10.20 and *chi-chieh*.

3 *SKC* 1.87, 89–97a and *chi-chieh*. For Wang Mang's receipt of the *chiu-hsi* before his usurpation of the Han throne, see Dubs (1955), III, 201–12.

4 *HHC* 30.366–7. *HHS* 9.11b–12a. *SKC* 1.115–16 and *chi-chieh*; 2.13b–40a and *chi-chieh*.

5 *SKC* 10.22 *chi-chieh*. *HHC* 30.361. *HHS* 70 (*lieh-chuan* 60), 21–2a. Yoshinami (1956), 68.

6 *SKC* 32.10–35.

7 *SKC* 32.1b–2, and *chi-chieh*, 8–10.

8 *SKC* 47.12–59. Cf. Okazaki (1932), 25–59. Though the Wu state controlled a vast territory with abundant natural resources, the régime was undermined by a strong native southern élite and by the recalcitrant *Shan-yueh* aboriginals. This may also account for the conciliatory attitude of its ruler. Cf. Miyagawa (1956), 30–8, 233–61; Chou I-liang (1963), 51–2.

9 A detailed study of the ritual of 'abdication' and the weakness of a dynasty founded in this way was made by Miyagawa (1956), 73–172; see especially 89–110.

10 The problem of conflicting loyalties in the entrenched élite may be seen in the attitude of those notables who helped found the new dynasty, *SKC* 2.47 *chi-chieh*; 13.20–1 *chi-chieh*. The problem became more acute at the founding of the Chin dynasty, *Chin-shu* 33.3b–4, 14b; 37.5–6. Cf. Goi (1956), 14–23; Yoshinami (1957), 29–32.

11 *SKC* 15.8a and *chi-chieh*. Cf. T'ang Yung-t'ung (1957), 9–10.

12 See Chapter 1.

13 *SKC* 16.15–21; 14.34b–35. Cf. Okazaki (1932), 469–71; Liu Ta-chieh (1957), 63–79.

14 *SKC* 4.16–77. *Chin-shu* 1.28–3.4.

15 There were two different versions of the manner of Yü's death. The pro-Ts'ao version recounted that Yü had accompanied Ts'ao in a southern campaign, became sick and stayed at Shou-ch'un (in the middle Huai river valley) where he died of worry (*SKC* 10.20a), or that Yü had been summoned to Ts'ao's campaign headquarters in the south and was detained there where he died of worry (*HHC* 30.360–7). The pro-Han version mentioned that while Yü was detained by Ts'ao, the latter sent Yü an empty food-container for a gift, and after receiving it, Yü took poison and died (*Wei-shih ch'un-ch'iu*, cited in *SKC* 10.21a *chi-chieh*; also *HHS* 70 (*lieh-chuan* 60), 21a. There were different explanations of Yü's final conflict with Ts'ao Ts'ao. One source mentioned that Yü was implicated in Emperor Hsien's plot against Ts'ao and when the plot was uncovered Yü tried to save himself by denouncing the emperor's consort, born of the house of Fu, but he failed to regain Ts'ao's confidence and thus committed suicide. *Hsien-ti ch'un-ch'iu*, cited in *HHS* 70 (*lieh-chuan* 60), 21a *chi-chieh*. Another source mentioned that Ts'ao Ts'ao ordered Yü to kill the Empress *née* Fu but Yü refused and committed suicide. *SKC* 10.22a *chi-chieh*. The last allegation was made in an official proclamation by the ruler of the Wu state and publicized in the Shu state. The authors of the *SKC*, the *HHC*, and the *HHS*, and P'ei Sung-chih, commentator of the *SKC*, all reject these allegations and mention that Yü's final conflict with Ts'ao arose from the issue of the *chiu-hsi* ritual.

16 See note 15. The court observed formal mourning at Yü's death, and Yü received a posthumous title of Esteemed Marquis (*Ching-hou*), *HHS* 70 (*lieh-chuan* 60), 21a. Ts'ao Ts'ao's son, Ts'ao Chih, wrote a 'Eulogy' for Yü, *SKC* 10.20b *chi-chieh*.

17 *SKC* 10.19a, 22b.

18 *SKC* 10.18 *chi-chieh*. It was mentioned that Yü's son, Yün, supported Ts'ao's younger son Chih against Ts'ao's eldest son and heir-apparent P'i, the future Emperor Wen of the Wei dynasty. P'i therefore cherished some grievance against Yün but still showed Yün due respect. *SKC* 10.22b–23a, and 23–6a and *chi-chieh*.

19 *SKC* 10.23–6a and *chi-chieh*. The founder of the Ssu-ma clique had been a former protégé of Hsün Yü, 21b *chi-chieh*. *Chin-shu* 39.10b–26a and *chiao-chu*; cf. the Hsün Family Tree, p. xi.

20 Cf. Eberhard (1965), 42–7, 89–91; (1969), 72–5.

21 Okazaki (1932), 451–541. Ho Ch'ang-ch'ün (1947), 25–53. Liu Ta-chieh (1957), 1–17, 63–107. Balazs (1967), 187–254. Zürcher (1959), 86–95.

22 See The Hsün Family Tree, p. xi.

23 *SKC* 10.18a *chi-chieh*. Chung Yu had served as Chancellor of the Wei state, and later as Commandant of Justice (*T'ing-wei*) at the Wei court, *SKC* 13.1–16. Wang Lang was the father of the famous Confucianist Wang Shu (195–256); he became a Ducal Minister (*Ssu-k'ung*) at the Wei court, 25b–36a. For Yüan

Huan, see Chapter 3, pages 59–64. Huan served as Prefect of the Gentlemen of the Palace (*Lang-chung ling*) and acting Imperial Clerk Grandee (*Yü-shih ta-fu*) of the Wei state. 11.1–4.

24 *SKC* 10.23 *chi-chieh*.

25 *SKC* 10.23b–24 *chi-chieh*.

26 *Ibid.* Cf. Ho Ch'ang-ch'ün (1947), 54–81; T'ang Yung-t'ung (1957), 26–102. Liebenthal (1947), 124–61; Wright (1947), 75–88.

27 *SKC* 10.18a *chi-chieh*. For Wang Pi and Chung Hui, see note 26.

28 *SKC* 10.18a *chi-chieh*. *Chin-shu* 19.2b; 30.16; 39.10b–21a; Hsün I, Hsün Hsü, and Hsün Hui were mentioned as the principle collaborators of Chia Ch'ung (217–82) in producing the Chin ordinances, 40.3. Chia Ch'ung had been in charge of the financial administration at the central government even before the founding of the Chin dynasty; he was in charge of the imperial bureaucracy during early Chin times and was said to be responsible for instituting many reform measures, which favoured agricultural work and frugal government expenditure; his clique later came into serious conflict with other factions of the court aristocrats, culminating in the so-called 'rebellion of the eight regional princes'. For this, the *Chin-shu* nourished a strong bias against Chia Ch'ung and his clique. And Hsün Hsü was censured for his complicity in a conspiracy to keep the Chia clique in control of the Chin court. *Chin-shu* 40.1–23a.

29 *Chin-shu* 39.13b–14, 20.

30 *Chin-shu* 39.11–13a.

31 *Chin-shu* 39.20b.

32 *Chin-shu* 39.13a, 15a. See also note 28.

33 As indicated in note 28 above, the *Chin-shu* is biased against the Chia faction and its sympathizers, Hsün I and Hsün Hsü. In addition to the conflict of personalities in the struggle between the Chia clique and the other coteries of court aristocrats, certain policy differences and a conflict of economic interests may be inferred from the eventual confrontation between the Chia faction and the regional princes of Chin in A.D. 299–300 which led to the Chin downfall and the barbarian invasion of northern China during the fourth century. Many inner inconsistencies of the *Chin-shu* as an historical work have been pointed out by Rogers, *Chronicle* (1968), 32–73.

34 *SKC* 9.54–9 and *chi-chieh*. It was said that Ts'ao Ts'ao's father originated from the Hsia-hou family and was later adopted by the eunuch Ts'ao T'eng; both the Ts'ao and the Hsia-hou lineages were considered to be of equal status in the Wei dynasty. The pro-Wei faction at the court had been led by Ts'ao Shuang in 239–49. Ts'ao Shuang and his supporters were massacred by the Ssu-ma faction in a *coup d'état* in 249. Cf. Ho Ch'ang-ch'ün (1947), 32–8.

35 *SKC* 28.44–60. Ho Ch'ang-ch'ün (1947), 42–3. Ho Ch'i-min (1967), 144–5. Mather (1964), 353–4.

36 *SKC* 13.36–44; 16.13–24; 21.6–8 *chi-chieh*; 23.25–8a *chi-chieh*. *Chin-shu* 35.4b–18; 47.1–8. Cf. Ho Ch'ang-ch'ün (1947), 7, 42–3; Liu Ta-chieh (1957), 69–88. Balazs (1967), 250–4.

37 *SKC* 27.7–8a.

38 Compare Ch'ang's five-point proposal in *SKC* 27.14b–15a with *SC* 2.1–2a, 13b–14a (the first point in Ch'ang's proposal), 1.4, 2.2b–3a (second point), 1.15a, 2.3 (third point), 2.8 (fourth point), and 1.2b–3a, 3b–4a, 10b, 2.2 (fifth point); also *HC* 7.5b–6a, 10.2b–4 with the fifth point in Ch'ang's proposal.

39 *SKC* 27.8–13. For instance, compare Ch'ang's comments on *ch'ü* (yielding), *shen* (stretching-expanding), *huo* (calamity), *fu* (fortune), and *hui* (slander), *yü* (praise), with Yueh's as discussed in Chapter 6, page 139.

40 *SKC* 28.61a *chi-chieh*. Cf. Fung Yu-lan (1960), 219.

41 For Chung Hui and Wang Pi, see above, notes 26 and 35. *SKC* 28.60. Wang Pi's biography was appended to that of Hui's in the *SKC*. For Hui's infamous encounter with Hsi K'ang, see *SKC* 21.25 *chi-chieh*; *Shih-shuo hsin-yü* 3.49a (p. 479); *Chin-shu* 49.23b–24; Mather (1964), 350, 353–4.

42 See notes 5, 6, and 14 in Chapter 1.

43 Fung Yu-lan (1953), ɪɪ, 170; (1960), 219.

44 See note 26. Cf. Fung Yu-lan (1953), ɪɪ, 168–89, 205–36; also (1960), 220–30. T'ang Yung-t'ung (1957), 103–11. Zürcher (1959), 87–92.

45 Ho Ch'ang-ch'ün (1947), 70–5. T'ang Yung-t'ung and Jen Chi-yü (1956), 19–21. Liu Ta-chieh (1957), 22–3. Ho Ch'i-min (1967), 75–84.

46 *SKC* 10.17b–18a *chi-chieh*.

47 *HHC* 29.354. *HHS* 62 (*lieh-chaun* 52), 8a. *SKC* 10.18b *chi-chieh*. For Hsün Yüeh's influence on Yen Chih-t'ui's (531–91) view of the Confucian Canons and history, see Wright and Twitchett (1962), 55–6.

48 *T'ang-shu* 62.15b–16a. *Chen-kuan cheng-yao* 2.30b-31a.

49 *Shih-t'ung* 1.6; 2.14. For Liu Chih-chi and his work, see Beasley and Pulley-blank (1961), 136–51.

50 *Ssu-k'u ch'üan-shu tsung-mu t'i-yao* 47.6b.

51 For instance, the *Ti-fan* under the titular authorship of the Emperor T'ai-tsung of T'ang; the *Ch'en-kuei* under Empress Wu of T'ang (Chou); in these two works many echoes of Hsün Yüeh's ideas and counsels may be found, though Yüeh's authority was not specified. Also the *Li-tai chün-chien* and *Li-tai ch'en-chien* under the titular authorship of Emperor Hsün-tsung of Ming (reigned 1426–35). And the *Chien-chieh lu* by Ho Kuang-yüan in the Five Dynasties period (*c.* 907–60); the *T'ang-chien* by Fan Tsu-yü (1041–98). For the works of divination and physiognomy which bear the designation *chien*, see the fragmentary Sung Imperial Catalogue, *Ch'ung-wen tsung-mu* (compiled in 1034–8, *Lan-fen chai ts'ung-shu* edition), 4.6a, 7a, 21a, 23b, 24b, 26b, 27a, 28a, 30a.

52 Chin Yü-fu (1944), 44–5. Chang Hsü (1962), 204–5.

53 *Han-shu* 30.17–19. Cf. Wang P'i-chiang (1955), 18–22, 85–90; Yao Ming-ta (1957), 68–9. Ssu-yü Teng (1950), 13–14.

54 *Sui-shu* 33.1–30a. See also notes 53, 56.

55 See note 49. Also *Ssu-k'u ch'üan-shu tsung-mu t'i-yao* 47.8–48.23. Chin Yü-fu (1944), 44–5.

56 For studies of Chinese historiography in the Six Dynasties period, see Naitò (1955), 174–212; Chin Yü-fu (1944), 51–96; Cheng Ho-sheng (1925), two parts; Kobayashi (1954), 137–81; Shigezawa (1959), 1–16.

57 *Shih-t'ung* 7.94–7. For Wei Shou and his *Wei-shu*, see *Pei-shih* 56.1–18a. The scandal was chiefly due to Wei Shou's failure to satisfy the conflicting demands of the arrogant élite for self-glorification. *Ssu-k'u ch'üan-shu tsung-mu t'i-yao* 45.47b–49a. Chou I-liang (1963), 236–72.

58 According to Ssu-yü Teng (1950), 14, the new system of classification of books in the quadripartite catalogue was originated by Cheng Mo, an attendant at the *Mi-shu chien* during the Wei dynasty. According to *Sui-shu* 32.4a, ' Cheng Mo, the attendant at the *Mi-shu chien*, first produced a Catalogue of the Imperial Library [*Chung-ching*]; Hsün Hsü, the Custodian of Secret Archives [*Mi-shu chien*], then produced a New Catalogue [*Hsin-pu*], in which books were classified into four main sections'. Cf. Yao Ming-ta (1957), 70–3. Hsün Yüeh had been in charge of the *Mi-shu chien* for more than ten years, *c.* 198–209; he had long before begun collecting books and documents for the Imperial Library (*Mi-shu*). According to Wang Yin's *Chin-shu* (fragments quoted in *Chin-shu* 44.4a *chiao-chu*), what Cheng Mo did was merely ' to trim and delete some out-dated and superfluous statements in an old Catalogue', probably left by Hsün Yüeh.

59 Though Hsün Yüeh's reflections seem to have had considerable influence on Wang Ch'ang, Yen Chih-t'ui, and the Emperor T'ai-tsung and Empress Wu of T'ang, as mentioned earlier, Yüeh's *Shen-chien* was not cited on all these occasions.

60 For the continuation and extension of the Confucian social influence in southern China before, during, and after the Age of Disunity, see Miyagawa, in Wright (1960), 21–46. For the Confucian influence through later clan rules, see Hui-chen Wang Liu, in Nivison and Wright (1959), 63–96. A case study of a Buddho-Confucian in the Age of Disunity may be found in Dien, in Wright and Twitchett (1962), 43–64. The attempt of the Sui emperor to formulate a composite imperial ideology from elements of Confucianism, Taoism, and Buddhism at the close of the Age of Disunity has been studied by Arthur Wright, in Fairbank (1957), 71–104. For the development of Confucian classical scholarship during the Age of Disunity, see P'i Hsi-jui (1959), 141–92.

61 For the difficulty faced by the Sui ruler when he tried to formulate a new imperial ideology after his military unification of China in A.D. '589, see Wright, in Fairbank (1957), 71–104. For the divisive forces which undermined the T'ang empire, see Pulleyblank (1955), 24–81.

62 A number of studies of various aspects of this problem have been reprinted in James T. C. Liu and Peter J. Golas, ed., *Change in Sung China* (1969), with detailed suggestion for additional reading.

63 Whether the Sui and T'ang imperial age (589–906) should be called 'late medieval' would depend on whether one considers the Sung and post-Sung period (tenth century on) 'early modern', Reischauer and Fairbank (1960), 220–5. Cf. Eberhard (1969), 195–9.

64 *T'ung-chih* 65.772.

65 *Tz'u-ch'i Huang-shih jih-ch'ao fen-lei* 57.6b–7a.

66 This moral absolutism was clearly expressed by Chu Hsi (1130–1200) in his exhortation on suppressing 'human desires', Fung Yu-lan (1953) II, 559–61. For the neo-Confucian idea of absolute loyalty, see Mote, in Wright (1960), 202–40.

67 'Po-tzu pien-cheng' in *Wang-ch'uan ch'uan-chi*, 1.23. For the neo-Confucian emphasis on absolute loyalty and 'compulsory eremitism', see Mote, in Wright (1960), 229–40.

68 See note 59 in Chapter 5.

69 Cf. Freeman (1928), 78–110; Levenson (1954), 155–65; Fung Yu-lan (1960), 319–22. The important achievements of the school of Han Learning have been recounted in P'i Hsi-jui (1959), 295–349; cf. also Liang Ch'i-ch'ao, tr. by Immanuel Hsü (1959), 21–32 and *passim*.

70 Cf. note 59 in Chapter 5.

71 See note 34 in Chapter 1.

72 Hu's commentary in *Tzu-chih t'ung-chien* 64.2065.

Bibliography

I. *Basic sources and abbreviations*

HC   *Han-chi* 漢紀, by Hsün Yüeh 荀悅, *Ssu-pu ts'ung-k'an* edition.

HHC *Hou-Han chi* 後漢紀, by Yuan Hung 袁宏, Commercial Press: *Wan-yu wen k'u* edition.

HHS *Hou-Han shu* 後漢書, by Fan Yeh 范曄, I-wen yin-shu kuan reprint of Wang Hsien-ch'ien 王先謙, *Hou-Han shu chi-chieh* 集解 edition.

SC   *Shen-chien* 申鑑, by Hsün Yüeh, *Ssu-pu ts'ung-k'an* edition.

SKC *San-kuo chih* 三國志, by Ch'en Shou 陳壽, I-wen yin-shu kuan reprint of Lu Pi 盧弼, *San-kuo chih chi-chieh* 集解 edition.

II. *Other classical Chinese works*

Chan-kuo ts'e 戰國策, *Ssu-pu ts'ung-k'an* edition.

[*Chao-te hsien-sheng*] *chün-chai tu-shu chih* 昭德先生郡齋讀書志, by Chao Kung-wu 晁公武; and *Fu-chih* 附志, by Chao Hsi-pien 趙希弁; Commercial Press reprint edition, 1937.

Chen-kuan cheng-yao 貞觀政要, by Wu Ching 吳兢, *Ssu-pu pei-yao* edition.

Chin-shu 晉書, I-wen yin-shu kuan reprint of Wu Shih-chien 吳士鑑 and Liu Ch'eng-kan 劉承幹, *Chin-shu chiao-chu* 斠注 edition.

Chou-i chi-chieh 周易集解, by Li Ting-tsu 李鼎祚, *Hsüeh-chin t'ao-yuan* edition.

Chou-i chu-shu 周易注疏, I-wen yin-shu kuan reprint of the 1815 edition.

Chou-li chu-shu 周禮注疏, I-wen yin-shu kuan reprint of the 1815 edition.

Chuang-tzu 莊子, *Ssu-pu pei-yao* edition.

"*Ch'ien-Han chi chiao-shih*" 前漢紀校釋, by Niu Yung-chien 鈕永建, in *Nan-ch'ing cha-chi* 南菁札記, 1894 edition.

Ch'u-hsueh chi 初學記, by Hsü Chien 徐堅, Huang-shih 1888 edition.

Ch'uan shang-ku san-tai Ch'in-Han san-kuo liu-ch'ao wen 全上古三代秦漢三國六朝文, compiled and edited by Yen K'o-chün 嚴可均, Shih-chieh shu-chü reprint edition.

Ch'ün-shu chih-yao 群書治要, by Wei Cheng 魏徵, *Ssu-pu ts'ung-k'an* edition.

Fa-yen 法言, by Yang Hsiung 楊雄, *Han-Wei ts'ung-shu* First Series edition.

Fu-tzu 傅子, by Fu Hsüan 傅玄, Wu-ying-tien chü-chen pan edition.

Han-fei tzu 韓非子, *Ssu-pu pei-yao* edition.

Han-kuan ta-wen 漢官答問 by Ch'en Shu-yung 陳樹鏞, *Chen-i-t'ang ts'ung-shu* edition.

Han-shih wai-chuan 韓詩外傳, by Han Ying 韓嬰, *Han-Wei ts'ung-shu*, First Series edition.

Han-shu 漢書, I-wen yin-shu kuan reprint of Wang Hsien-ch'ien, *Han-shu pu-chu* 補注 edition.

Han-Wei liu-ch'ao po-san chia chi 漢魏六朝百三家集, compiled by Chang P'u 張溥, 1879 edition.

Han-Wei shih-ching k'ao 漢魏石經考, by Wan Ssu-t'ung 萬斯同, *Chao-tai ts'ung-shu* edition.

'Hou-Han i-wen-chih' 後漢藝文志, by Yao Chen-tsung 姚振宗, in *Erh-shih-wu shih pu-pien* 二十五史補編, K'ai-ming shu-tien edition.

Huai-nan tzu 淮南子, *Ssu-pu ts'ung-k'an* edition.

Hung-fan wu-hsing chuan 洪範五行傳, by Liu Hsiang 劉向, *Han-Wei i-shu ch'ao* edition.

Hsiao-ching chu-shu 孝經注疏, I-wen yin-shu kuan reprint of the 1815 edition.

Hsin T'an-shu 新唐書, I-wen yin-shu kuan reprint of the Ch'ien-lung wu-ying tien edition.

Hsün-tzu 荀子, *Ssu-pu pei-yao* edition.

I Han-hsueh 易漢學, by Hui Tung 惠棟, in *Huang-Ch'ing ching-chieh* 皇清經解, hsü-pien.

I-li 易例, by Hui Tung, in *Huang-Ch'ing ching-chieh*, hsü-pien.

I-lin 意林, compiled by Ma Tsung 馬總, *Ssu-pu ts'ung-k'an* edition.

I-wei ch'ien-tso-tu 易緯乾鑿度, *Ts'ung-shu chi-ch'eng* edition.

I-wen lei-chü 藝文類聚, by Ou-yang Hsün 歐陽詢, Wang-shih 1587 edition.

Jih-chih lu 日知錄, by Ku Yen-wu 顧炎武, Commercial Press: *Kuo-hsueh chi-pen ts'ung-shu* edition.

Ku lieh-nü chuan 古列女傳, by Liu Hsiang 劉向, *Ssu-pu ts'ung-k'an* edition.

Kuan-tzu 管子, *Ssu-pu ts'ung-k'an* edition.

K'un-hsueh chi-wen 困學紀聞, *by Wang Ying-lin* 王應麟, *Ssu-pu ts'ung-k'an* edition.

Kung-yang chu-shu 公羊注疏, I-wen yin-shu kuan reprint of the 1815 edition.

Kuo-yü 國語, *Ssu-pu ts'ung-k'an* edition.

Lao-tzu 老子, *Ssu-pu pei-yao* edition.

Li-chi chu-shu 禮記注疏, I-wen yin-shu kuan reprint of the 1815 edition.

Lieh-hsien chuan 列仙傳, by Liu Hsiang, *Ts'ung-shu chi-ch'eng* edition.

Lieh-tzu 列子, *Han-Wei ts'ung-shu*, Fourth Series edition.

Lü-shih ch'un-ch'iu 呂氏春秋, *Ssu-pu pei-yao* edition.

Lun-heng 論衡, by Wang Ch'ung 王充, *Han-Wei ts'ung-shu*, First Series edition.

Lun-yü 論語, I-wen yin-shu kuan reprint of the 1815 edition.

Meng-tzu 孟子, I-wen yin-shu kuan reprint of the 1815 edition.

Nien-erh-shih cha-chi 廿二史札記, by Chao I 趙翼, Commercial Press, 1958.

Pao-p'u tzu 抱朴子, by Ko Hung 葛洪, *Ssu-pu ts'ung-k'an* edition.

Pei-shih 北史, I-wen yin-shu kuan reprint of the Ch'ien-lung wu-ying tien edition.

Pei-t'ang shu-ch'ao 北堂書鈔, by Yü Shih-nan 虞世南, K'ung-shih 1888 edition.

Po-tzu pien-cheng 百子辨正, by Yang Ch'i-kuang 楊琪光, in *Wang-ch'uan ch'üan-chi* 枉川全集.

'Pu Hou-Han-shu i-wen-chih' 補後漢書藝文志, by Hou K'ang 侯康, in *Erh-shih-wu shih pu-pien*.

'Pu Hou-Han-shu i-wen-chih' 補後漢書藝文志, by Tseng P'u 曾樸, in *Erh-shih-wu shih pu-pien*.

'Pu Hou-Han-shu i-wen-chih' 補後漢書藝文志, by Ku Huai-san 顧懷三, in *Erh-shih-wu shih pu-pien*.

Sui-shu 隋書, I-wen yin-shu kuan reprint of the Ch'ien-lung wu-yin tien edition.

'Sui-shu ching-chi-chih k'ao-cheng' 隋書經籍志考証, by Yao Chen-tsung 姚振宗, in *Erh-shih-wu shih pu-pien*.

Sung-shu 宋書, I-wen yin-shu kuan reprint of the Ch'ien-lung wu-ying tien edition.

Shan-hai ching 山海經, *Ssu-pu ts'ung-k'an* edition.

Shih-chi 史記, Takikawa Kametarō's 瀧川龜太郎 *Shiki kaichu kōshō* 史記會注考證 edition.

Shih-ch'i-shih shang-ch'ueh 十七史商榷, by Wang Ming-sheng 王鳴盛, Kuang-ya shu-chü edition.

Shih-shuo hsin-yü 世說新語, I-wen yin-shu kuan reprint of the Sung edition.

Shih-t'ung [*t'ung-shih*] 史通通釋, by Liu Chih-chi 劉知幾, Shih-chieh shu-chü, 1956.

Shu-mu ta-wen [*pu-cheng*] 書目答問補正, by Chang Chih-tung 張之洞, Taiwan: Hsin-hsing shu-chü, 1956.

Shuo-wen chieh-tzu ku-lin 說文解字詁林, Taiwan: Photolithographic reprint of the 1931 edition.

Shui-ching chu 水經注, by Li Tao-yuan 酈道元, Wu-ying tien chü-chen pan edition.

Shuo-yuan 說苑, by Liu Hsiang, *Han-Wei ts'ung-shu*, First Series edition.

Ssu-k'u ch'üan-shu tsung-mu [*t'i-yao*] 四庫全書總目提要, I-wen yin-shu kuan reprint edition.

T'ai-p'ing yü-lan 太平御覽, Taiwan: Hsin-hsing shu-chü reprint of the Kanezawa bunko edition.

T'ang-shu 唐書, I-wen yin-shu kuan reprint of the Ch'ien-lung wu-ying tien edition.

Ti-fan 帝範, Tung-fang hsueh-hui, 1924.

T'ung-chih 通志, by Cheng ch'iao 鄭樵, Taiwan: Hsin-hsing shu-chü reprint edition.

T'ung-tien 通典, by Tu Yu 杜佑, Taiwan: Hsin-hsing shu-chü reprint edition.

Tso-chuan chu-shu 左傳注疏, I-wen yin-shu kuan reprint of the 1815 edition.

Tz'u-ch'i Huang-shih jih-ch'ao fen-lei 慈溪黃氏日鈔分類, by Huang Chen 黃震, Tz'u-ch'i Feng-shih keng-yü lou edition.

Tzu-chih t'ung-chien 資治通鑑, by Ssu-ma Kuang 司馬光, Chung-hua shu-chü, 1956.

Wen-hsien t'ung-k'ao 文獻通考, by Ma Tuan-lin 馬端臨, Taiwan: Hsin-hsing shu-chü edition.

Wen-hsüan 文選, Commercial Press, 1960.

Wen-shih t'ung-i 文史通義, by Chang Hsueh-ch'eng 章學誠, Shih-chieh shu-chü, 1956.

Yen-tzu ch'un-ch'iu 晏子春秋, *Ssu-pu ts'ung-k'an* edition.

Yü-hai 玉海, by Wang Ying-lin 王應麟, three editions: 1269, 1588, and 1687–88.

Yuan-ho hsing-chuan 元和姓纂, by Lin Pao 林寶, Hung-shih 1807 edition.

III. *Other works in Chinese and Japanese*

Akizuki K. 秋月觀暎, 黃巾の亂の宗教性. (The Religious Factors in the Yellow Turban Rebellion), *Tōyōshi kenkyū* 東洋史研究 15.1 (1956), 43–56.

Chang Chung-tung 張忠棟, 兩漢人物的地理分布. (The Geographical Distribution of the Han Elite), *Ta-lu tsa-chih* 大陸雜誌, 28.1 (Jan. 1964), 17–20.

Chang Hsü 張須, *T'ung-chien hsueh* 通鑑學, Hong Kong, 1962.

Chao Yu-wen 趙幼文, 曹魏屯田制述論 (A Preliminary Discussion on the Agricultural Colonies of the Ts'ao-Wei Dynasty), *Li-shih yen-chiu* 歷史研究 58.4 (1958), 29–46.

Ch'en Ch'i-yün 陳啓雲, 兩晉三省制度之淵源特色及其演變 (The Origins, Characteristics, and Development of the Triumvirate in the Central Government of the Chin Dynasty), *Hsin-ya hsueh-pao* 新亞學報 3.2 (1958), 99–229.
    畧論兩漢樞機職事與三臺制度之發展 (The Central Administration and the Development of the Triumvirate *san-t'ai* System in the Han Dynasty), *Hsin-ya hsueh-pao* 4.2 (1960), 127–157.

Ch'en Hsiao-chiang 陳嘯江, 魏晉時代之族 (Clans in the Wei and Chin Times), *Shih-hsueh chuan-k'an* 史學專刊 1.1 (1935), 153–94.

Ch'en Tao-sheng 陳道生, 重論八卦的起源 (A Re-examination of the Origins of the Eight Trigrams of the *I-ching*), *K'ung-Meng hsueh-pao* 孔孟學報 12 (1966), 1–28.

Ch'en Yin-k'o 陳寅恪, *Sui-T'ang chih-tu yuan-yuan lueh-lun-kao* 隋唐制度淵源畧論稿, Special Publication of the Institute of History and Philology, Academia Sinica, author's epilogue dated 1940.
    T'ang-tai cheng-chih-shih shu-lun-kao 唐代政治史述論稿, Special Publications of the Institute of History and Philology, Academia Sinica, author's preface dated 1942.

Cheng Ho-sheng 鄭鶴聲, 漢隋間之史學 (Historical Writings from Han to Sui, I), *Shih-ti hsueh-pao* 史地學報 3.7 (1925), 64–81; 3.8 (1925), 43–66.

Ch'ien Mu 錢穆, *Ch'in Han shih* 秦漢史, Hong Kong, 1956.
    Liang-Han ching-hsueh chin-ku-wen p'ing-i 兩漢經學今古文平議, Hong Kong, 1958.
    Chuang-tzu chuan-chien 莊子纂箋, Hong Kong, 1962.

Chien Po-tsan 翦伯贊, *Chung-kuo-shih lun-chi* 中國史論集 2 vols., Hong Kong: Lung-men shu-tien reprint, 1969.

Chin Yü-fu 金毓黻, *Chung-kuo shih-hsueh-shih* 中國史學史 Commercial Press, 1944.

Chou I-liang 周一良, *Wei-Chin nan-pei-ch'ao shih lun-ts'ung* 魏晉南北朝史論叢 Peking, 1963.

Chou Tao-chi 周道濟, 道儒法三家之君主無爲思想 (The Confucianist, Taoist, and Legalist Idea of Non-action as Applied to the Ruler), *Ta-lu cha-chih* 37.7 (Oct. 1968), 213–15.

Ch'ü Yueh-chih 瞿兌之, *Ch'in-Han shih-chuan* 秦漢史纂, Hong Kong: Lung-men shu-tien reprint of the 1944 edition.

Fan Ning 范寧, 論魏晋時代知識份子的思想分化及其社會根源 (The Differentiation of Intellectual Attitudes in the Wei and Chin Periods and Their Social Backgrounds), *Li-shih yen-chiu* 55.4 (1955), 113–31.

Fan Shou-k'ang 范壽康, *Wei-Chin chih ch'ing-t'an* 魏晋之清談, Commercial Press, 1936.

Fu Ssu-nien 傅斯年, *Hsing-ming ku-hsün pien-cheng* 性命古訓辨証, Commercial Press, 1940.

Fujiie R. 藤家禮之助, 曹魏の典農部屯田の消長 (The Development of Agricultural Colonies under the Agricultural Bureau of the Ts'ao-Wei Dynasty), *Tōyō gakuhō* 東洋學報 45.2 (1962), 71–101.

Goi N. 五井直弘, 後漢時代の官吏登用制「辟召」について (On the Special *p'i-chao* Selection System of the Later Han Dynasty), 歷史學研究, *Rekishigaku kenkyū*, 178 (1954), 22–30, 42.

    曹操政權の性格について (On the Character of the Ts'ao Ts'ao Regime), *Rekishigaku kenkyū* 195 (1956), 14–23.

Hamaguchi S. 濱口重國, *Shin-Kan Zui-To shih no kenkyū* 秦漢隋唐史の研究, Tokyo, 1966.

Hattori K. 服部克彥, 漢代の南陽郡 (The Nan-yang Commandery in Han Times), *Ryūkoku daigaku ronshū* 龍谷大學論集 387 (1968), 132–57.

Hihara T. 日原利國, 荀悅の批判意識について (On Hsün Yüeh's Critical Criteria) *Tōhōgaku* 東方學 18 (1959), 9–20.

Ho Ch'ang-ch'ün 賀昌群, *Wei-Chin ch'ing-t'an ssu-hsiang ch'u-lun* 魏晋清談思想初論, Shanghai, 1947.

    論黃巾農民起義口號 (On the Ideological Slogan of the Yellow Turban Peasant Insurrection), *Li-shih yen-chiu* 59.6 (1959), 33–40.

    東漢更役戌役的廢止 (The Abolition of Military and Corvée Conscriptions during the Eastern Han), *Li-shih yen-chiu* 62.5 (1962), 96–115.

    Han-T'ang chien feng-chien t'u-ti so-yu-chih hsing-shih yen-chiu 漢唐間封建土地所有制形式研究, Shanghai, 1964.

Ho Ch'i-min 何啓民, *Chu-lin ch'i-hsien yen-chiu* 竹林七賢研究, Taipei, 1966.

    Wei-Chin ssu-hsiang yü t'an-feng 魏晋思想與談風, Taipei, 1967.

Honda S. 本田濟, 范曄の後漢書 (Fan Yeh's *Hou-Han shu*), in *Handa Hakushi kanreki kinen shoshigaku ronshū* 神田博士還曆紀念書誌學論叢, Kyoto, 1957, pp. 299–309.

    魏晋に於ける儒玄の論爭 (Polemics between the Confucianists and the Mystics in Wei and Chin Times), *Kōdaigaku* 古代學 3.2 (1954), 102–14.

Hsiung Te-chi 熊德基, 太平經的作者和思想及其與黃巾和天師道的關係 (The Authorship of the *T'ai-p'ing ching* and its Relationship with the Yellow Turbans and the T'ien-shih Tao), *Li-shih yen-chiu* 62.4 (1962), 8–25.

Jao Tsung-i 饒宗頤, 西漢節義考 (Biographies of Chaste and Righteous Personages of the Former Han Dynasty), *Hsin-ya hsueh-pao* 1.1 (1955), 157–208.

    Lao-tzu hsiang-erh-chu chiao-tsan 老子想爾注校箋, Hong Kong, 1956.

Kaga E. 加賀榮治, *Chukoku koden kaiseki shi* 中國古典解釋史 *Journal of Hokaido Gakugei University* I A, Vol. 14, Supplement, 1964.

Kamada S. 鎌田重雄, *Kandai no shakai* 漢代の社會, Tokyo, 1955.

Kandai-shih kenkyū 漢代史研究, Tokyo, 1949.

漢代の尚書官 (The Emperor's Secretary in the Han Period), *Tōyōshi kenkyū* 東洋史研究 26.4 (Mar. 1968), 113–37.

Kano K. 狩野直禎, 蜀漢政權の構造 (Administrative Structure of Shu-Han), *Shirin* 史林 42.4 (July 1959), 85–102.

後漢時代地方豪族の政治生活―犍爲張氏の場合 (The Political Life of the Local Magnates and Big Clans in Later Han Times – The Case of the Chang Family in the Chien-wei Commandery), *Shisen* 史泉 22 (Oct. 1961), 11–21.

後漢中期の政治と社會―順帝の即位をめぐつレ (Politics and Society in the Middle of Later Han – as seen from the enthronement of Emperor Shun), *Tōyōshi kenkyū* 23.3 (Dec. 1964), 304–23.

陳羣傳試論 (A Note on Ch'en Ch'ün), *Tōyōshi kenkyū* 25.4 (Mar. 1967), 98–118.

Kawakatsu Y. 川勝義雄, シナ中世貴族政治の成立について (The Rise of Chinese Medieval Aristocracy), *Shirin* 33.4 (1950), 47–63.

魏晋南北朝の門生故吏 ('Household Disciples' and 'Former Subordinates' in the Wei, Chin, and Southern and Northern Dynasties), *Tōhōgakuhō* 東方學報 (Kyoto), 28 (1958), 175–218.

漢末のレジスタンス運動 (The Resistance Movement at the End of the Han Dynasty), *Tōyōshi kenkyū* 25.4 (Mar. 1967), 23–50.

Kobayashi N. 小林昇, 六朝時代の史學 (Historiography in the Six Dynasties Period), *Tōyōshisō kenkyū* 東洋思想研究 5 (1954), 137–81.

Ku Chieh-kang 顧頡剛, 潛夫論中的五德系統 (The Five Elements Theory in the *Ch'ien-fu lun*), *Shih-hsueh chi-k'an* 史學集刊 3 (1937), 73–92.

Ch'in-Han chih fang-shih yü ju-sheng 秦漢之方士與儒生, Peking, 1955.

Ku-shih pien 古史辨, vols. 1–5, Hong Kong: T'ai-p'ing shu-chü reprint, 1962–63.

Kuo Mo-jo 郭沫若, *et al.*, *Ts'ao Ts'ao lun-chi* 曹操論集, Peking, 1962.

Kurita N. 栗田直躬, 上代シナの典籍に現はれたる自然觀の一側面 (An Aspect of the View of Nature as Evidenced in Ancient Chinese Writings), *Tōyōshisō kenkyū* 5 (1954), 87–136.

Lao Kan 勞榦, 論漢代的游俠 (On the Wandering Knights of Han Times), *Wen-shih-che hsueh-pao* 文史哲學報 1 (1950), 237–52.

關於漢代官俸的幾個推測 (Some Conjectures on the Systems of Official Salaries during the Han Dynasty), *Wen-shih-che hsueh-pao* 3 (1951), 11–22.

漢代的豪彊及其政治上的關係 (Powerful Clans under the Han Dynasty and Their Influences), *Symposium in Honor of Dr Li Chi on His Seventieth Birthday*, Part 1, Taipei, 1965, pp. 31–51.

Li Chien-nung 李劍農, *Hsien-Ch'in liang-Han ching-chi shih kao* 先秦兩漢經濟史稿, Peking, 1962.

Wei-Chin nan-pei-ch'ao Sui-T'ang ching-chi shih kao 魏晋南北朝隋唐經濟史稿, Peking, 1963.

Li-shih chiao-hsueh yueh-k'an-she 歷史教學月刊社, ed., *Chung-kuo nung-min ch'i-i lun-chi* 中國農民起議論集, Peking, 1954.

Liang Ch'i-ch'ao 梁啓超, *Chung-kuo li-shih yen-chiu fa* 中國歷史研究法, Commercial Press: *Jen-jen wen-k'u* edition, 1966.

   Chung-kuo li-shih yen-chiu fa pu-pien 中國歷史研究法補編, Commercial Press: *Jen-jen wen-k'u* edition, 1966.

Liu Ju-lin 劉汝霖, *Han-Chin hsueh-shu pien-nien* 漢晉學術編年, Shanghai, 1932.

Liu Ta-chieh 劉大杰, *Wei-Chin ssu-hsiang lun* 魏晉思想論, Taiwan: Chung-hua shu-chü reprint, 1957.

Lung Shih-hsiung 龍世雄, 魏晉之一般苦悶 (The Prevalent Distress in the Wei and Chin Times), *She-hui k'o-hsueh lun-ts'ung* 社會科學論叢 4.8 (1933), 91–132.

Masabuchi T. 增淵龍夫, 漢代における民間秩序の構造と任俠的風俗 (The Lower Social Structure and the Convention of Knight-errantry of the Commoners in Han Times), *Hitotsubashi ronsō* 一橋論叢 26.5 (1951), 555–97.

   後漢黨錮事件の史評について (The *tang-ku* Incidents as seen by Chinese Critics), *Hitotsubashi ronsō* 44.6 (1960), 727–46.

Matsumoto M. 松本雅明, 後漢の逃避思想 (On the Idea of Seclusion and Escapism in the Later Han Dynasty), *Tōhōgakuhō* (Tokyo) 12.3 (1941), 381–411.

Mikami T. 三上次男, and Kurihara T. 栗原明信, ed., *Chukoku kodai-shih no chumondai* 中國古代史の諸問題, Tokyo, 1954.

Mitara M. 御手洗勝, 王充の王朝觀 (Wang Ch'ung's View of the Dynasty), *Hirojima daigaku bungakubu kiyō* 廣島大學文學部紀要 18 (1960), 294–317.

Miyagawa H. 宮川尚志, *Rikuchō-shih kenkyū* 六朝史研究, Tokyo, 1956.

Miyazaki, I. 宮崎市定, 清談 ('Pure Conversation'), *Shirin* 31.1 (1946), 1–15.

   Kubon kanjin-hō no kenkyū 九品官人法研究, Kyoto, 1956.

Mori M. 森三樹三郎, 六朝士大夫の精神 (The Mentality of the Elite of the Six Dynasties), *Osaka daigaku bungakubu kiyō* 大阪大學文學部紀要 3 (1954), 225–328.

Moriya M. 守屋美都雄, *Kandai kazaku no keitai ni kansuru kosatsu* 漢代家族の形態に關する考察, Kyoto, 1956.

   Rikuchō mombatsu no ichi kenkyū 六朝門閥の一研究, Tokyo, 1951.

Mou Jun-sun 牟潤孫, 漢初公主及外戚在帝室中之地位試釋 (The Position of the Imperial Princess and the Maternal Relatives of the Emperor in the Early Han Ruling House), *Essays and Papers in Memory of Late President Fu Ssu-nien of the National Taiwan University* 國立臺灣大學傳故校長紀念論文集 (Taiwan, 1952), 1–20.

   春秋時代之母系遺俗公羊義証 (The Residual Tradition of Matriarchy in the Spring-and-Autumn Period as seen from the *Kung-yang chuan*), *Hsin-ya hsueh-pao* 1.1 (1955), 381–421.

Mou Tsung-san 牟宗三, *Wei-Chin hsüan-hsueh* 魏晉玄學, Taichung, 1962.

   Ts'ai hsing yü hsüan-li 才性與玄理, Hong Kong, 1963.

Murakami Y. 村上嘉實, 魏晉交迭之際における老莊思想の展開について (On the Development of Lao-Chuang Taoist Thought in the Wei–Chin Transition Period), *Tōyōshi kenkyū* 12.1 (Sept. 1952), 35–50.

Naitó T. 內藤虎雄 *Shina shigaku shi* 支那史學史 Tokyo, 1955.

Nakajima R. 中嶋隆藏, 何休の思想 (Ho Hsiu's Thought), *Shukan Tōyōgaku* 集刊東洋學 19 (May 1968), 23–36.

Nishijima S. 西嶋定生, 魏の屯田 (The Military-Agricultural Colonies of the Wei Dynasty), *Tōyōbunka kenkyūjō kiyo* 東洋文化研究所紀要 10 (1956), 1–8.

Nunome C. 布目潮渢, 半錢半穀論 (On the Half-grain Half-money Official Salary), *Ritsumeikan bungaku* 文命館文學 148 (1957), 1–21.

Ōbuchi, N. 大淵忍爾, 五斗米道の教法について一老子想爾注を中心として (On the Religious Teaching of the Five-Bushel-Rice Sect of Taoism as seen from the Hsiang-erh Commentary to *Lao-tzu*), *Tōyōgakuhō* 49.3 (Dec. 1966), 40–68, 49.4 (Mar. 1967), 97–129.

Ochi S. 越智重明, 魏晋南朝の屯田 (The Military-Agricultural Colonies under the Wei, Chin, and Southern Dynasties), *Shigaku Zasshi* 史學雜誌 70.3 (1961), 1–24.

   魏西晋貴族制論 (On the Aristocracy of the Wei and the Western Chin), *Tōyōgakuhō* 45.1 (June 1962), 93–103.

   魏晋南朝の士大夫につて (The Privileged Elite in the Wei, Chin, and Southern Dynasties), *Tōyō shigaku* 東洋史學 29 (1966), 633–682.

Okamura S. 岡村繁, 郭泰許劭の人物評論 (Kuo T'ai and Hsü Shao's Comments of Personality), *Tōhōgaku* 10 (1955), 59–68.

Okazaki F. 岡崎文夫, *Gi-Shin nambokucho tsushi* 魏晋南北朝通史, Tokyo, 1932.

P'i Hsi-jui 皮錫瑞, *Ching-hsueh t'ung-lun* 經學通論, Commercial Press: *Kuo-hsueh chi-pen ts'ung-shu* edition.

   Ching-hsueh li-shih 經學歷史, Peking, 1959.

Sa Meng-wu 薩孟武, 魏晋南北朝 貴族政治 (Aristocracy in the Wei, Chin, Northern and Southern Dynasties), *She-hui k'o-hsueh lun-ts'ung* (Taiwan) 1 (1950), 1–28.

Shiba R. 斯波六郎, 後漢末期の談論について (On Later Han Conversationalism, *t'an-lun*), *Hirojima daigaku bungakubu kiyo* 8 (1955), 213–242.

Shigezawa T. 重澤重郎, 文獻目録を通して見た六朝の歴史意識 (On the Idea of History in the Six Dynasties as revealed in Bibliographical Works), *Tōyōshi kenkyū* 18.1 (1959), 1–16.

Sogabe S. 曾我部靜雄 市廛而不征 (On 'No Taxation on the Market-place'), *Shukan Tōyōgaku* 17 (May 1967), 81–85.

   均田法の名稱と實態について (On the Labels and the Actuality of the Land-equalization System), *Tōyōshi kenkyū* 26.3 (Dec. 1967), 1–35.

Ssu Chih-mien 施之勉, 清談 (On 'Pure Conversation'), *Ta-lu tsa-chih* 37.6 (Sept. 1968), 179.

Suzuki K. 鈴木啓造, 後漢における就官の拒絕と棄官について一徵辟召を中心として (Acceptance and Refusal of Official Appointments in the Later Han times—A study of the Special *Cheng-chao* and *P'i-chao* Systems), *Chūkoku kōdaishi kenkyū* 中國古代史研究 II, (1964), 253–83.

Tada K. 多田狷介, 黃巾の亂前史 (On the Historical Events Preceding the Yellow Turban Rebellion), *Tōyōshi kenkyū* 26.4 (Mar. 1968), 160–83.

Takeda R. 竹田龍兒, 門閥としての弘農楊氏について一考察 (A Study of the Yang Family of Hung-nung as an Aristocratic Lineage), *Shigaku* 史學 31.1–4 (1958), 613–43.

Takehashi T. 高橋徹, 六朝時代の貨幣 (The Monetary System of the Six Dynasties), *Shichō* 史潮 90 (1965), 1–23.

T'ang Chang-ju 唐長孺, *Wei-Chin nan-pei-ch'ao shih lun-ts'ung* 魏晉南北朝史論叢, Peking, 1955.

均田制度的產生及其破壞 (The Rise and Decline of the Land-equalization System), *Li-shih yen-chiu* 56.2 (1956), 1–30.

Wei-Chin nan-pei-ch'ao shih lun-ts'ung hsü-pien 續編, Peking, 1959.

T'ang Yung-t'ung 湯用彤, *Wei-Chin hsüan-hsüeh lun-kao* 魏晉玄學論稿, Peking, 1957.

Han-Wei liang-Chin nan-pei-ch'ao fo-chiao shih 漢魏兩史南北朝佛教史 Peking, second reprint, 1963.

and Jen Chi-yü 任繼愈 *Wei-Chin hsüan-hsüeh chung ti she-hui cheng-chih ssu-hsiang lüeh-lun* 魏晉玄學中的社會政治思想畧論 Shanghai, 1956.

Tseng Ch'ien 曾謇, 三國時代的社會 (Society in the Three Kingdoms Period), *Shih-huo* 食貨 5.10 (1937), 8–18.

Tseng Chih-sheng 曾資生, *Chung-kuo cheng-chih chih-tu shih* 中國政治制度, I–IV, Hong Kong: Lung-men shu-tien reprint, 1969.

Ueda S. 上田早苗, 巴蜀の豪族と國家權力 (The Powerful Families in the Pa and Shu Provinces and the Structure of the State), *Tōyōshi-kenkyū* 25.4 (Mar. 1967), 1–22.

Utsunomiya K. 宇都宮清吉, *Kandai shakai keizai shi kenkyū* 漢代社會經濟史研究, Tokyo, 1955.

漢代豪族論 (On the Powerful Families and Big Clans of the Han Dynasty), *Tōhōgaku* 23 (Mar. 1962), 6–23.

Wang Ming 王明, *T'ai-p'ing ching ho-chiao* 太平經合校, Peking, 1960.

Wang P'i-chiang 汪辟畺, *Mu-lu hsüeh yen-chiu* 目錄學研究, Shanghai, 1955.

Wang Yün-wu 王雲五 *Liang-Han San-kuo cheng-chih ssu-hsiang* 兩漢三國政治思想, Taiwan: Commercial Press, 1968.

Wu Shih-ch'ang 吳世昌, 魏晉風流與私家園林 (Romanticism and Private Estates in Wei and Chin Times), *Hsueh-wen* 學文 1.2 (1934), 80–114.

Yang Lien-sheng 楊聯陞, 老君晉誦誡經校釋 (Collation and Annotation of the Taoist Text Entitled *Lao-chün yin-sung chieh-ching*), *Bulletin of the Institute of History and Philology* (Academia Sinca) 28 (1956), 17–54.

Yang Shu-fan 楊樹藩, *Liang-Han chung-yang cheng-chih chih-tu yü fa-ju ssu-hsiang* 兩漢中央政治制度與法儒思想 Taipei, 1967.

Yano C. 矢野主稅, 鄭氏研究 (A Study of the Cheng Family), *Nagazaki daigaku shakai kagaku ronsō* 長崎大學社會科學論叢 8 (1958), 21–36; 9 (1959), 1–8; 10 (1960), 1–10.

門閥貴族の系譜試論 (A Genealogical Study of the Pedigreed Aristocracy in Ancient China), *Kōdaigaku* 7.1 (1958), 23–47.

魏晉百官世系表 (A Genealogical Table of the Wei and Chin Officials), *Special Publication of the Nagazaki daigaku shigaku-kai* 2 (1960).

六朝門閥の社會的政治的考察 (A Socio-political Study of the Aristocratic Lineages in the Six Dynasties), *Chōdai shigaku* 長大史學 6 (1961), 1–80.

Yao Ming-ta 姚名達, *Chung-kuo mu-lu-hsüeh shih* 中國目錄學史, Shanghai, 1957.

Yen Keng-wang 嚴耕望, *Liang-Han t'ai-shou tz'u-shih piao* 兩漢太守刺史表, Commercial Press, 1948.

Ch'in-Han ti-fang hsing-cheng chih-tu 秦漢地方行政制度 Taipei: The Institute of History and Philology, Academia Sinica, 1961.

Wei-Chin nan-pei-ch'ao ti-fang hsing-cheng chih-tu 魏晉南北朝地方行政制度 Taipei: The Institute of History and Philology, Academia Sinica, 1963.

Yoshikawa T. 吉川忠夫, 范曄と後漢末期 (Fan Yeh and the Last period of the Later Han), *Kōdaigaku* 13.3–4 (Mar. 1967), 158–63.

Yoshinami T. 好並隆司, 荀悦の社會背景とその政策について (The Social Background of Hsün Yüeh and His Political Counsels), *Okayama shigaku* 2 (1956), 68–86.

曹操の時代 (The Ts'ao Ts'ao Period), *Rekishigaku kenkyū* 207 (1957), 29–32.

前漢後半期における皇帝支配と官僚層の動向 (The Imperial Rule and Bureaucratic Attitudes in the Later Half of the Former Han Dynasty), *Tōyōshi kenkyū* 26.4 (Mar. 1968), 138–59).

Yü Ying-shih 余英時, 東漢政權之建立與士族大姓之關係 (The Establishment of the Eastern Han Regime and its Relationship with the Distinguished Clans and Notable Families), *Hsin-ya hsueh-pao* 1.2 (1956), 209–80.

IV. *Works in western languages*

Balazs, Etienne, *Le traite juridique du 'Souei-Chou'*, Leiden, 1954.

Chinese Civilization and Bureaucracy, tr. by H. M. Wright, Yale University Press, 1967.

Beaseley, W. G., and Pulleyblank, E. G., eds., *Historians of China and Japan*, Oxford University Press, 1961.

Bielenstein, Hans, 'The Census of China during the Period 2–742 A.D. ', *Bulletin of the Museum of Far Eastern Antiquity* (Stockholm), 19 (1947), 125–63.

'An Interpretation of the Portents in the *Ts'ien-Han-shu* ', *Bulletin of the Museum of Far Eastern Antiquity* (Stockholm), 22 (1950), 127–430.

'The Restoration of the Han Dynasty ', I–III, *Bulletin of the Museum of Far Eastern Antiquity* (Stockholm), 26 (1954), 1–209; 31 (1959), 1–287; 39 (1967), 1–198.

Bodde, Derk, *China's First Unifier*, Leiden, 1938.

'Types of Chinese Categorical Thinking ', *Journal of the American Oriental Society* 59 (1939), 200–19.

'Harmony and Conflict in Chinese Philosophy ', in Arthur Wright, ed., *Studies in Chinese Thought*, University of Chicago Press, 1953, 19–80.

'Authority and Law in Ancient China ', *Journal of American Oriental Society*, Supplement 17 (1954), 46–55.

'Evidence for Laws of Nature in Chinese Thought ', *Harvard Journal of Asiatic Studies* 20 (1957), 709–29.

Boorman, Howard, *et al.*, eds., 'The Biographical Approach to Chinese History: A Symposium ', *Journal of Asian Studies* 21.4 (August 1962), 453–89.

Brewitt-Taylor, C. H., tr., *Romance of the Three Kingdoms*, Rutland, Vt: C.E. Tuttle reprint, 1959.

Busch, Heinrich, 'Hsün Yüeh, Ein Denker am Hofe Des Letzten Han-Kaisers ', *Monumenta Serica* 10 (1945), 58–90.

Cairns, Grace E., *Philosophies of History: Meeting of East and West in Cycles-Pattern Theories of History*, New York, 1962.

Chan, Wing-tsit, ' The Evolution of the Confucian Concept *Jen* ', *Philosophy East and West* 4 (1955), 295–319.

A Source Book in Chinese Philosophy, Princeton University Press, 1963.

Chang, Carsun, *The Development of Neo-Confucian Philosophy*, New York, 1957.

Chang, Chung-li, *The Chinese Gentry*, University of Washington Press, 1955.

Chavannes, Edouard, tr., *Les Memoires Historiques de Se-ma Ts'ien*, 5 vols., Paris, 1895–1905.

Chen, Chi-yun, ' A Confucian Magnate's Idea of Political Violence: Hsün Shuang's (A.D. 128–190) Interpretation of the Book of Changes ', *T'oung-pao* 54.1–3 (1968), 73–115.

' Textual Problems of Hsün Yüeh's (A.D. 148–209) Writings: The *Han-chi* and the *Shen-chien* ', *Monumenta Serica* 27 (1968), 208–32.

Ch'ü, T'ung-tsu, *Law and Society in Traditional China*, Paris, 1961.

Local Government in China Under the Ch'ing, Harvard University Press, 1962.

Coulborn, R., ed., *Feudalism in History*, Princeton University Press, 1956.

Creel, H. G., *Chinese Thought From Confucius to Mao Tse-tung*, New York: Mentor Books, 1953.

' On Two Aspects in Early Taoism ', *Silver Jubilee Volume of the Zimbun Kagabu Kenkyuso*, Kyoto, 1954, 43–53.

' What is Taoism? ', *Journal of the American Oriental Society* 76.3 (1956), 139–52.

' The Meaning of *Hsing-ming* ', *Studia Serica Bernhard Karlgren Dedicata* (Copenhagen, 1959), 199–211.

Confucius and The Chinese Way, New York, 1960.

' The *Fa-chia*: Legalists or Administrators? ', *Bulletin of the Institute of History and Philology*, Academia Sinica, extra vol. 4 (1961), 607–36.

' The Beginnings of Bureaucracy in China: The Origin of the *Hsien* ', *Journal of Asian Studies* 23 (1964), 155–84.

Crump, J. I., *Intrigues: Studies of the Chan-kuo ts'e*, University of Michigan Press, 1964.

Dawson, Raymond, *The Legacy of China*, Oxford, 1964.

de Bary, Wm. Theodore, *et al.*, eds., *Sources of Chinese Tradition*, Columbia University Press, 1964.

de Crespigny, Rafe, ' The Military Geography of the Yangtse and the Early History of the Three Kingdoms State of Wu ', *Journal of the Oriental Society of Australia* 4.1 (June 1966), 61–76.

' The Recruitment System of the Imperial Bureaucracy of Later Han ', *Chung-chi Journal* 6 (Nov. 1966), 67–78.

' An Outline of the Local Administration of the Later Han Empire ', *Chung-chi Journal* 7 (Nov. 1967), 57–71.

' Civil War In Early China: Ts'ao Ts'ao at the Battle of Kuan-tu ', *Journal of the Oriental Society of Australia* 5.1–2 (Dec. 1967), 51–64.

The Last of the Han, Canberra, 1969.

The Record of the Three Kingdoms, Canberra, 1970.

Dubs, H. H., *Hsuntze, The Moulder of Ancient Confucianism*, London, 1927.
The Works of Hsün-tze, London, 1928.
' " Nature " in the Teaching of Confucius ', *Journal of the American Oriental Society* 50 (1930), 233–7.
The History of the Former Han Dynasty, I, Baltimore, 1938; II, Baltimore, 1944; III, Baltimore, 1955.
' The Reliability of Chinese Histories ', *Far Eastern Quarterly* 6.1 (Nov. 1946), 23–43.

Duyvendak, J. J. L., *Tao-te ching*, London, 1954.

Eberhard, W., ' The Political Function of Astronomy and Astronomers in Han China ', in J. K. Fairbank, ed., *Chinese Thought and Institutions*, University of Chicago Press, 1957, 33–70.
Conquerors and Rulers: Social Forces in Medieval China, Leiden, 1965.
tr. by Alide Eberhard, *The Local Cultures of South and East China*, Leiden, 1968.
A History of China, University of California Press, 1969.

Eisenstadt, S. N., *The Political Systems of Empires*, New York, 1963.

Fairbank, John K., ed., *Chinese Thought and Institutions*, University of Chicago Press, 1957.

Feuerwerker, Albert, ed., *History in Communist China*, The M.I.T. Press, 1968.

Forke, Alfred, *Geschichte de mittelalterlichen Chinesischen Philosophie*, Hamburg, 1934.
Lun-heng, second edition, New York, 1962.

Franke, Otto, *Studien zur Geschichte des konfuzianischen Dogmas*, Hamburg, 1920.
tr. by Ulrich Mammitzsch, ' The Meaning of Chinese Historiography ', *East and West Center Review* 2.1 (June 1965), 6–22.

Freeman, Mansfield, ' The Ch'ing Dynasty Criticisms of Sung Politico-Philosophy ', *Journal of the North China Branch of the Royal Asiatic Society* 59 (1928), 78–100.

Fung Yu-lan, tr. by Derk Bodde, *A History of Chinese Philosophy*, Princeton, 2 vols., 1952–3.
A Short History of Chinese Philosophy, Macmillan paperback, 1960.

Gale, Esson M., tr., *Discourses on Salt and Iron*, Taipei, 1967 reprint.

Gardner, Charles S., *Chinese Traditional Historiography*, Harvard University Press, 1961.

Garraty, John, ' Chinese and Western Biography: A Comparison ', *Journal of Asian Studies* 21.4 (August 1962), 487–9.

Gernet, Jacques, tr. by Raymond Rudorff, *Ancient China*, University of California Press, 1968.

Goodrich, Chauncey S., ' Two chapters in the Life of an Empress of the Later Han ', *Harvard Journal of Asiatic Studies* 25 (1964–5), 165–77; 26 (1966), 187–210.

Graham, A. C., tr., *The Book of Lieh-tzu*, London, 1960.

Han, Yü-shan, *Elements of Chinese Historiography*, Hollywood, California, 1955.

Hightower, James, tr., *Han Shih Wai Chuan*, Harvard University Press, 1952.

Ho, Ping-ti, 'Records of China's Grand Historian: Some Problems of Translation', *Pacific Affairs* 36.2 (1963), 171–82.

and Tang Chou, eds., *China in Crisis*, University of Chicago Press, 1968.

Holzman, Donald, 'Les sept sages de la foret des bambous et la societé de leur temps', *T'oung-pao* 44 (1956), 317–465.

La Vie et la pencée de Hi K'ang (223–261), Leiden, 1957.

Houn, Franklin H., 'The Civil Service Recruitment System of the Han Dynasty', *Tsing-hua Journal of Chinese Studies*, N.S. 1 (1956), 138–64.

Chinese Political Traditions, Washington, D.C., 1965.

Hsiao, Kung-chuan, 'Legalism and Aristocracy in Traditional China', *Tsing-hua Journal of Chinese Studies*, N.S. 4.2 (Feb. 1964), 108–21.

Hucker, Charles O., *The Traditional Chinese State in Ming Times (1368–1644)*, University of Arizona Press, 1961.

ed., *Chinese Government in Ming Times*, Columbia University Press, 1969.

Hulsewé, A. F. P., *Remnants of Han Law*, Leiden, 1955.

Izutsu, Toshihiko, 'The Absolute and the Perfect Man in Taoism', *Eranos Jahrbuch* 36 (1967), 37–441.

Kaltenmark, Max, tr., *Le Lie-sien tchouan*, Peking, 1953.

Kennedy, George A., 'Interpretation of the Ch'un-ch'iu', *Journal of the American Oriental Society* 62.1 (1942), 40–8.

Künstler, Mieczyslaw Jerzy, 'Activité culturelle et politique des differentes regions de la Chine sous les Han Orientaux', *Rocznik Orientalistyczny* 30 (1966), 7–29.

Kupperman, Joel J., 'Confucius and the Problem of Naturalness', *Philosophy East and West* 18.3 (July 1968), 175–85.

Lattimore, Owen, *Inner Asian Frontiers of China*, New York, 1951.

Studies in Frontier History, Oxford University Press, 1962.

Le Centre Franco-Chinois d'Etudes Sinologues, compiled, *Index du Chen Kien*, Peking, 1947.

Legge, James, 'The *Yi-king*', in F. Max Muller, ed., *The Sacred Books of the East*, XVI, Oxford, 1899.

'The Texts of Taoism', in *The Sacred Books of the East*, XXXIX–XL.

tr., *The Chinese Classics*, Hong Kong University Press, 1960.

    I   *Confucian Analects, The Great Learning, The Doctrine of the Mean*

    II *The Works of Mencius*

    III *The Shoo King, or the Book of Historical Documents*

    IV *The She King, or The Book of Poetry*

    V *The Ch'un Ts'ew with the Tso Chuen*

tr., ed. by Ch'u Chai and Winberg Chai, *Li-chi*, University Books, 1967.

Levenson, Joseph R., 'The Abortiveness of Empiricism in Early Ch'ing Thought', *Far Eastern Quarterly* 13 (1954), 155–65.

'Redefinition of Ideas in Time: the Chinese Classics and History', *Far Eastern Quarterly* 15 (May 1956), 399–404.

Levy, Howard S., 'Yellow Turban Religion and Rebellion at the End of Han', *Journal of the American Oriental Society* 74 (1956), 214–24.
'The Bifurcation of the Yellow Turbans in Later Han', *Oriens* 13–14 (1960–1), 251–5.

Liang, Ch'i-ch'ao, tr. by Immanuel C. Y. Hsü, *Intellectual Trends in The Ch'ing Period*, Harvard University Press, 1959.

Liebenthal, Walter, tr., 'T'ang Yung-t'ung: Wang P'i's New Interpretation of *I-ching* and *Lun-yü*', *Harvard Journal of Asiatic Studies* 10 (1947), 124–61.

Liu, James J. Y., *The Chinese Knight-errant*, University of Chicago Press, 1967.

Liu, James T. C., *Reform in Sung China*, Harvard University Press, 1959.

McEvilly, Wayne, 'Synchronicity and the *I-ching*', *Philosophy East and West* 18.3 (July 1968), 137–49.

Marcus, John T., 'Time and the Sense of History: West and East', *Comparative Studies in Society and History* 3.2 (1961), 123–39.

Maspero, Henri, *Melanges posthumes sur les religions et l'histoire de la Chine*, 3 vols., Presses Universitaires de France, 1967.

Masubuchi, Tatsuo, 'Wittfogel's Theory of Oriental Society and The Development of Studies of Chinese Social and Economic History in Japan', *Developing Economics* 4 (June 1966), 316–33.

Mather, Richard, 'Some Examples of "Pure Conversation" in the *Shih-shuo hsin-yü*', *Transactions of the International Conference of Orientalists in Japan* 9 (1956), 58–70.
'Chinese Letters and Scholarship in the Third and Fourth Centuries; the *Wen-hsüeh p'ien* of the *Shih-shuo hsin-yü*', *Journal of the American Oriental Society* 84 (1964), 348–91.

Mei, Y. P., 'Man and Nature in Chinese Philosophy', in Horst Frenz and G. L. Anderson, eds., *Indiana University Conference on Oriental-Western Literary Relations*, University of North Carolina Press, 1955, 151–60.

Michaud, Paul, 'The Yellow Turbans', *Monumenta Serica* 17 (1958), 47–127.

Moore, Charles A., ed., *Philosophy and Culture: East and West*, University of Hawaii Press, 1962.
ed., *The Chinese Mind*, University of Hawaii Press, 1967.

Morgan, Evan, tr., *Tao the Great Luminant*, London, 1935.

Nakamura, Hajime, 'Comparative Study of the Notion of History in China, India and Japan', *Diogenes* 42 (1963), 44–59.

Needham, Joseph, *Science and Civilization in China*, II, Cambridge, 1956; III, Cambridge, 1959.

Nivison, D. S., *The Life and Thought of Chang Hsüeh-ch'eng*, Stanford University Press, 1966.
and Wright, Arthur F., eds., *Confucianism in Action*, Stanford University Press, 1959.

Nolde, John J., 'A Plea for A Regional Approach to Chinese History: The Case of the South China Coast', *Journal of the Hong Kong Branch of Royal Asiatic Society* 6 (1966), 9–24.

O'Hara, Albert R., *The Position of Women in Early China*, The Catholic University of America Press, 1945.

Payne, Robert, ed., *The White Pony*, Mentor Book, 1947.

Pokora, Timoteus, ' An Important Crossroad of the Chinese Thought ', *Archiv Orientalni* 29 (1961), 64–79.

' On the Origin of the Notions *T'ai-p'ing* and *Ta-t'ung* in Chinese Philosophy ', *Archiv Orientalni* 29 (1961), 448–54.

Pulleyblank, E. G., *The Background of the Rebellion of An Lu-shan*, Oxford University Press, 1955.

Radhakrishnan, S. and Raju, P. T., eds., *The Concept of Man, A Study in Comparative Philosophy*, London, 1960.

Reischauer, Edwin O. and Fairbank, John K., *East Asia : The Great Tradition*, Boston, 1960.

Rickett, W. Allyn, tr., *Kuan-tzu*, Hong Kong University Press, 1965.

Rogers, Michael C., ' The Myth of the Battle of the Fei River (A.D. 383) ', *To'ung-pao* LIV.1–3 (1968), 50–72.

The Chronicle of Fu-chien : A Case of Exemplary History, University of California Press, 1968.

Sargent, Clyde B., ' Subsidized History: Pan Ku and the Historical Records of the Former Han Dynasty ', *Far Eastern Quarterly* 3.2 (Feb. 1944), 119–43.

Schafer, Edward H., ' Ritual Exposure in Ancient China ', *Harvard Journal of Asiatic Studies* 14 (1951), 130–84.

Shih, Vincent, ' Some Chinese Rebel Ideologies ', *T'oung-pao* 44 (1956), 150–226.

The Taiping Ideology, University of Washington Press, 1967.

Shryock, John K., *The Study of Human Ability : The Jen-wu Chih of Liu Shao*, New Haven, 1937.

Sivin, Nathan, ' Chinese Conceptions of Time ', *Earlham Review* 1 (1966), 82–92.

Stein, R. A., ' Remarques sur les Mouvements du Taoisme Politico-religieux au IIe Siecle AP J.-C. ', *T'oung-pao* 50. 1–3 (1963), 1–78.

Sun, Etu Zen, ed., *Chinese Social History*, Washington, D.C., 1956.

Swann, Nancy Lee, *Food and Money in Ancient China*, Princeton University Press, 1950.

Pan Chao, Foremost Woman Scholar of China, 1st Century A.D., New York, 1932.

Teng, Ssu-yü and Biggerstaff, Knight, *An Annotated Bibliography of Selected Chinese Reference Work*, Revised edition, Harvard University Press, 1950.

Tjan Tjoe Som, *Po-hu t'ung*, Leiden, 1949.

Treistman, Judith M., ' China at 1000 B.C.: A Cultural Mosaic ', *Science* 160 (24 May 1968), 853–6.

Waley, Arthur, *Three Ways of Thought in Ancient China*, New York, 1939.

The Way and Its Power, London, 1949.

Wang, Yü-ch'üan, ' An Outline of the Central Government of the Former Han Dynasty ', *Havard Journal of Asian Studies* 12 (1949), 134–87.

Ware, James, ' History of the *Wei-shu* ', *Journal of the American Oriental Society* 52 (1932), 35–45.

Watson, Burton, *Ssu-ma Ch'ien, Grand Historian of China*, Columbia University Press, 1958.

tr., *Records of the Grand Historian of China*, 2 vols., Columbia University Press, 1961.

Weber, Max, tr. and ed. by Hans H. Gerth, *The Religions of China*, Glenoise, Illinois, 1951.

Welch, Holmes, *Taoism : The Parting of the Way*, Beacon Press, 1965.

Widgery, Alban G., *Interpretations of History: From Confucius to Toynbee*, London, 1961.

Wilhelm, Hellmut, ' The Concept of Time in the Book of Changes ', in *Man and Times*, New York, 1957.

tr. by Cary F. Baynes, *Change : Eight Lectures on the I-ching*, New York, 1960.

' The Interplay of Image and Concept in the Book of Changes ', *Eranos Jahrbuch* 36 (1967), 31–57.

Wittfogel, Karl A., *Oriental Despotism : A Comparative Study of Total Power*, Yale University Press, 1957.

Wright, Arthur F., ' Review of A. A. Petrov, *Wang Pi (226–249): His Place in the History of Chinese Philosophy* ', *Harvard Journal of Asiatic Studies* 10 (1947), 75–88.

ed., *Studies in Chinese Thought*, University of Chicago Press, 1953.

Buddhism in Chinese History, Stanford University Press, 1959.

ed., *The Confucian Persuasion*, Stanford University Press, 1960.

and Twitchett, Denis, eds., *Confucian Personalities*, Stanford University Press, 1962.

Yang, L. S., *Studies in Chinese Institutional History*, Harvard University Press, 1963.

' Notes sur le régime foncier en Chine ancienne (environ 1300 av. J.-C. à 200 av. J.-C.) ', *Mélanges des sinologie afferts à Paul Demieville*, Paris, 1966.

Excursions in Sinology, Harvard University Press, 1969.

Yoshikawa, Kōjirō, tr. by Glen W. Baxter, ' The *Shih-shuo hsin-yü* and Six Dynasties Prose Style ', *Harvard Journal of Asiatic Studies* 18 (June 1955), 124–41.

' Man and the Concept of History in the East ', *Diogenes* 42 (1963), 14–19.

Yü, Ying-shih, ' Life and Immortality in the Mind of Han China ', *Harvard Journal of Asiatic Studies* 25 (1965), 80–122.

Trade and Expansion in Han China, University of California Press, 1967.

Zürcher, Erik, *The Buddhist Conquest of China*, Leiden, 1959.

Index

Five Classics, *see ching*
Five Elements *see Yin-yang* and Five Elements cosmology
'foil history' *see* historiography
Former Han dynasty, 2, 11–12, 14–15, 23, 25, 32–4, 42, 46, 50–1, 61, 71, 77, 98, 104, 105, 109, 154, 158; Hsün Yüeh's treatment of, 85ff., 112ff., 120ff. 129ff.
'free market' and free trade, 158; *see also* commerce
frontier generals, 4, 40, 41, 44, 48; *see also* Tung Cho
Fu Family, 63
Fu Hsüan, 146, 170
Fu Ku, 167, 170–1
Fu-tzu, 146
Fu Yen, 125–6

Gentleman-at-Court (*lang*), *see lang*
Golden Antiquity, 94, 108, 131, 143, 159
Golden Mean (*chung*), 6, 9; (*chung-ho*), 31
government functionaries, *see* regional and local sub-bureaucracy
Governor-general (*chou-mu*), 39, 64, 101, 102
gradualism: in law enforcement, 104–5; in moral education, 79, 104–5; in regulating landholding, 159–60; *see also* expediency
Grand Administrator (*T'ai-shou*), 12, 21, 22, 27, 33, 34, 69, 109
Grand Unity (*ta-i-t'ung, ta-t'ung*), 13, 18, 31, 164; *see also t'ai-p'ing*
'Great Peace' (*t'ai-p'ing*), 31; *see also* Taoism, *T'ai-ping tao* of
Guards as Rapid as a Tiger, *see Hu-pen*

Han-chi (Chronicles of [the Former] Han), 1, 2, 3, 4, 9, 56, 60, 69ff., 81ff., 84ff., 127ff., 133, 135, 136, 150, 153, 155, 158, 162, 169ff.; Epilogue, 90–1, 96, 112, 128, 131; form and substance, 112; *hsü* (Foreword, Preface), 84–6, 112–3, 130, 131; *lun* (Discourse), 87, 93–114, 128
Han Fu, 48, 74
Han Hao, 160
Han Hsin, 88
Han-hsüeh see Han Learning
Han Learning (*Han-hsüeh*), 176
Han loyalist, 1, 3, 4, 38, 48, 51, 88, 91, 127, 129, 132, 150, 154, 157, 163; the cause of, 52, 63, 64, 127; *see also* Hsün Yü; restoration

Han rule: glorification of, 85–6; mystique of, 80; *see also* court apologia; imperial court
Han-shu (History of the Former Han Dynasty), 2, 3, 84, 86, 87, 88, 90ff., 97, 112ff., 120ff., 129, 172, 176
Han-Ts'ao (Wei) composite regime, 60, 63, 77, 80, 146, 158; *see also* Chien-an
Han-yang Commandery, 51
Han-yü (Remarks on Han Affairs), 28, 73, 94, 125; *see also* Hsün Shuang
hao-wu (likes and dislikes), 142
Heaven, 59, 130, 141; and Earth, 104; and Earth and Men, 107, 137; Fundamental Principles of, 108; *see also* cosmology; Mandate of Heaven; Son of Heaven; Way, the
historical cycles, 90, 112, 134–5; *see also* cosmology
historical lesson, *see chien*
historical praise-and-blame (*pao-pien*), 96–7
historical situation (*shih*), Hsün Yüeh's analysis of, 99, 100, 104, 105, 110–11
historiography, 2, 3; in the Age of Disunity, 172–4; 'foul history' (*hui-shih*), 173; of the *Han-chi*, 85, 86–7, 89–93, 96–7, 112–26, 128–9, 171–2, 176
History of the Former Han Dynasty see *Han-shu*
History of the Later Han Dynasty see *Hou-Han shu*
Ho Chin, 40, 41
Ho Yen, 171
Ho Yung, 28, 29, 42, 44, 68
Ho-pei province, 35, 37
Honan province, 4, 43
Hou-chi, 98
Hou-Han chi (Chronicles of the Later Han), 127, 133, 171
Hou-Han shu (History of the Later Han Dynasty), 3, 21ff., 28, 29, 33, 35, 37, 66, 73ff., 82, 113, 170, 171
Hou Lan, 25
household soldiers (*chia-ping*), 38
Hsi Chih-ts'ai, 80
Hsi-hao ('Western Magnate', the Hsün's original residence), 24, 66
Hsi K'ang, 154, 171
Hsi Lü, 80
Hsia dynasty, 98, 131
Hsia-hou Hsüan, 169
Hsia-hou Ying, 123
Hsiang K'ai, 34–5
Hsiang Yü, 111